FINANCIAL ACCOUNTING

2nd Edition

Rick Antle
Yale University

Stanley J. Garstka
Yale University

THOMSON

SOUTH-WESTERN

Australia · Canada · Mexico · Singapore · Spain · United Kingdom · United States

Financial Accounting, 2e
Rick Antle & Stanley J. Garstka

Editor-in-Chief:
Jack Calhoun

Team Leader:
Melissa Acuña

Acquisitions Editor:
Julie Lindsay

Sr. Developmental Editor:
Ken Martin

Marketing Manager:
Mignon Tucker

Production Editor:
Amy McGuire

Manufacturing Coordinator:
Doug Wilke

Compositor:
GGS Information Services

Printer:
Transcontinental Printing, Inc.
Beauceville, QC

Sr. Design Project Manager:
Michelle Kunkler

Cover and Internal Designer:
Pagliaro Design, Cincinnati

Cover Image:
© Scott Tysick/Masterfile

Photography Manager:
Deanna Ettinger

Photo Researcher:
Terri Miller
e-visual communications

PCN: 2002113505

Package ISBN: 0-324-18075-6
Masters Package
ISBN: 0-324-27044-5
Text ISBN: 0-324-19210-X
QEPC Booklet ISBN: 0-324-19209-6
Masters QEPC Booklet
ISBN: 0-324-27045-3
Thomson Analytics Access
Card ISBN: 0-324-20156-7

Brief contents

contents

Part 3: Topics in Financial Reporting   151

Dedicated to
Nancy, Elizabeth, and Benjamin
Janet, Jennifer, Stan, and Andrew

Preface

A Framework for Analysis and Valuation

Why write another introductory financial accounting textbook? It is a question we are often asked. We wrote this text because we wanted to do things differently. In particular, we wanted to present three things in a way that we had not found them presented in other textbooks. First, we wanted to give a thorough, yet concise, introduction to the basic financial statements and the techniques of accounting. Second, we wanted to include a rich variety of real financial reports. Third, and most importantly, we wanted to develop and apply a coherent structure that would establish a solid framework for analysis and valuation.

Organization of the Text

We have organized the content of the text into three parts: fundamentals of accounting, valuation basics and accounting measures, and topics in financial reporting.

Part 1: Fundamentals of Accounting

The five chapters that make up Part 1 provide a comprehensive introduction to the basic accounting statements and techniques. Our experience in teaching financial statement analysis has taught us that this material should not be given short shrift. Cash flow statements and the articulation of financial statements are especially important, particularly for students interested in valuation. Many valuation methods begin with cash flow projections. Income statements and balance sheets are projected and analyzed to find the implied cash flows. Detailed knowledge of complex financial reporting alternatives is not required to do this kind of analysis, but understanding the articulation of balance sheets, income statements, and cash flow statements is vital. Part 1 lays this foundation.

Part 2: Valuation Basics and Accounting Measures

Part 2 develops a conceptual framework for the traditional financial accounting topics. Two main factors are identified as being at the heart of accounting problems: time and uncertainty. The first chapter in Part 2 develops the economic concepts of present value and expected value that are used to attack problems involving time and uncertainty. The second chapter of Part 2 ties these economic concepts to accounting through an exploration of market-to-book ratios and returns on equity. The advantages of taking the time to develop both present value and expected value become apparent: They allow us to develop the important benchmark of normal earnings and to explain why the generation of abnormal earnings is the key to creating value.

Part 3: Topics in Financial Reporting

In many ways, Part 3 is the payoff for the investment in techniques and concepts that we made in Parts 1 and 2. The chapters in Part 3 address traditional and important areas in

"With its continuing focus on the relation between economic and accounting principles, Antle and Garstka's book is the ideal accounting preparation for a beginning . . . student."
Stephen A. Ross, Massachusetts Institute of Technology

financial accounting, such as receivables, inventories, long-term assets, liabilities, and income taxes. We use a set structure within each of these chapters, beginning with a discussion of what the item is and what its place is in an organization. Next, the economic concepts of present value and expected value are used to explore its economic value. We then present the major accounting conventions for the item and its financial statement presentation. This allows a comparison of accounting values and economic values. Finally, we conclude each chapter in Part 3 by presenting the major financial ratios involving that item.

The organization of these chapters is intended to accomplish several things. It gives the students a sense of the commonality of the issues involved in accounting problems. It enables you, the instructor, to cut preparation time by making the book's coverage more memorable and predictable. It consistently reinforces the application of the valuation framework developed in Part 2. Finally, it allows for flexible use of the book. You may, for example, assign selected sections of each chapter if you desire to cover only the accounting conventions.

Features that Help Students Learn

We have included many features, such as a variety of tables and illustrations, which we believe will help students master the text's concepts as well as stimulate and maintain their interest in accounting. The accrual accounting table shown below is an example of how the text helps students visualize and synthesize concepts.

Figure 3.4
Accrual Accounting (Revenues and expenses need not coincide with cash flows.)

Cash Flow Before Revenue or Expense Recognition	**Income Statement**	**Cash Flow After Revenue or Expense Recognition**
Some revenues are prepayments before good is given up or service provided. For example, Company receives prepaid magazine subscriptions, Company is given a retainer to provide future services.	**Revenues** • • • • • **Expenses** • • • • • • • • • **Net Income**	Payment received after good given up or service provided. For example, normal sales on credit.
Many expenses are "prepaid." For example, the cost of inventory, plant, and equipment, the prepayment of rent or insurance.		Many expenses are paid after the expense is recognized. For example, the value of wages or interest already consumed, but not yet paid for.

Questions, Exercises, Problems, and Cases

The student activities that accompany the text are provided in a separate booklet. We believe that this arrangement will permit much greater flexibility in their use. These activities, many of which are based on real company data, have been widely praised by instructors for their variety and appropriateness to test students' understanding of the chapter content.

Use of Real Financial Reports

Real financial reports are used throughout the text as illustrations and as the basis for problem material. Our extensive use of these reports is intended to provide an accurate impression of the ultimate tasks that await students in their accounting, finance, or other business careers. We use the most recent examples that suit our purposes. For example, Chapter 1 focuses on Union Plaza Hotel and Casino, Inc.'s, financial reports for 2001.

Exhibit 1.2

Union Plaza Income Statement

Revenues equal the dollar value of all the products and services Union Plaza sold during the period (the inflow of resources from sales).

Operating expenses are the dollar value of the costs incurred by Union Plaza in running its business.

Food and beverage expense is the cost of all the food and beverage items recorded as sold under Revenues.

General administrative expense includes the resources consumed for general administrative functions during the period.

Depreciation and amortization expense is the allocation of part of the cost of property and equipment to the period.

Union Plaza Hotel and Casino, Inc. and Subsidiaries
Income Statement for the Year Ended December 31, 2001
(dollars in thousands)

REVENUES	
Casino	$37,807
Food and beverage	10,351
Rooms	11,110
Other	2,524
GROSS REVENUES	61,792
Less promotional allowances	(6,922)
NET REVENUES	54,870
OPERATING EXPENSES	
Casino	$22,865
Food and beverage	8,997
Rooms	4,294
General and administrative	5,155
Entertainment	591
Advertising and promotion	1,329
Utilities and maintenance	6,712
Depreciation and amortization	4,130
Provision for doubtful accounts	44
Other costs and expenses	1,246
TOTAL OPERATING EXPENSES	$55,363
OPERATING INCOME (LOSS)	$ (493)
OTHER INCOME (EXPENSE)	
Interest income	3
Loss on sale of assets	(159)
Interest expense	(2,265)
TOTAL OTHER INCOME (EXPENSE)	(2,421)
NET LOSS	$(2,914)

Our goal of providing students with an accurate impression of real reports means that we edit them less than is typical in an introductory text. We leave in any item that we would be willing to discuss in class within the context of the material covered to that point. If we would have answered a question about an item with, "We will get to that later," we have edited that item. For example, in the early chapters, we do not present financial statements that include the equity account, Unrealized Gains (Losses) from Available-for-Sale Securities. We do not, however, shield students from the variety of assets and liabilities that we find in real financial statements.

Debits and Credits

Although we did not write this text in order to train students as bookkeepers, we believe that students need to be exposed to the techniques that underlie financial reports. Thus, we do not shy away from presenting debits, credits, T-accounts, and journal entries.

7. On January 1, 2004, Websell paid $2,000 for an unlimited-service cellular phone contract for one year.

Prepaid Telephone (asset)   2,000
    Cash   2,000

8. On January 1, 2004, Websell acquired the rights to various software programs. The software consists of word processors and accounting programs in support of basic office functions, as well as technical packages to be used in developing its own products. Websell paid $50,000 cash for these rights that are expected to last for two years.

Software (asset)   50,000
    Cash   50,000

In-Text Study Notes and Definitions of Terms

To assist students in their study of what is sometimes complex material, we provide study notes and definitions in the margin. Students may use these notes to review the exhibits in the text and to help them recall the concepts learned by reading the material and participating in class.

Revenues equal the dollar value of all the products and services Union Plaza Hotel sold during the period (the inflow of resources from sales).

Operating expenses are the dollar value of the costs incurred by Union Plaza in running its business.

From AOL's 10K: "Cost of revenues includes network-related costs, consisting primarily of data network costs, costs associated with operating the data centers and providing customer support, royalties paid to information and service providers, the costs of merchandise sold, and product development amortization expense."

Review Questions

At appropriate points, we provide thought-provoking questions that test students' ability to apply the concepts that have just been discussed.

Review Questions

1. Define assets, liabilities, and equities. Give an example of each. How are assets valued? How are liabilities valued?

2. Explain what is meant by the entity concept.

3. A company signs a ten-year employee contract with a vice president. The salary is $500,000 per year, guaranteed. Is this contract an asset? Would it appear on the balance sheet? Explain.

4. A company purchased a parcel of land 10 years ago at a cost of $300,000. The land has recently been appraised at $900,000. At what value is the land carried in the balance sheet? How does the appraisal affect the carrying value in the balance sheet?

Unsurpassed Technology for Teaching and Learning

WebTutor Advantage

Available in either WebCT™ or Blackboard® platforms, this rich course management product is a specially designed extension of the classroom experience that enlivens the course by leveraging the power of the Internet with comprehensive educational content. This powerful, turnkey solution provides the following content customized for this edition:

- **E-Lectures**—PowerPoint™ slides of the key topical coverage with accompanying audio explanations to provide additional learning support.
- **Interactive Quizzes**—Multiple-choice, true/false, and sentence completion questions, which test the students' knowledge of the chapter content and provide immediate feedback on the accuracy of their responses. These quizzes help students pinpoint areas needing additional study.
- **Problem Demonstrations**—An example problem similar to the end-of-chapter material of the text, with an audio explanation of the concepts outlined in that problem.
- **Videos**—Short, high-interest segments focusing on chapter-related topics.
- **Flashcards**—A terminology quiz so that students have a complete understanding of the language that makes up the chapter content.
- **Reviews of Key Concepts**—Tied to each learning objective, these chapter reviews reinforce important concepts from each chapter.
- **Crossword Puzzles**—Test students' knowledge of the glossary.
- **Quiz Bowl Game**—Review of the chapter content in a Jeopardy®-type game.

Xtreme!

Providing the same content as WebTutor™ Advantage, but without the platform, this hybrid CD-ROM and Internet-based product provides your students with the most media-rich content of any financial accounting text on the market! Features include:

- Learning objectives summarize key concepts from each chapter.
- Quizzing reinforces concepts and helps students better focus their study efforts.
- Quiz Bowl is an innovative and fun way for students to review concepts.
- Crossword puzzles test students' knowledge of the glossary and make learning "the language of business" more fun.
- E-Lectures provide a PowerPoint lecture-style with audio voiceovers to help students review chapter content or work on difficult topics.
- Problem demonstrations walk through an example homework assignment.
- Video clips provide real-world examples of applications so that students can make the connection between the accounting concept and its use in the business world.

Xtra! for Financial Accounting

This CD-ROM provides lecture replacement resources and access to games and interactive quizzes so that students can test their understanding of the content of the text. Free when bundled with a new text, students receive an access code so that they can receive Xtra! reinforcement in financial accounting.

Thomson Analytics—Business School Edition

Thomson Analytics—*Business School Edition* is a Web-based portal product that provides integrated access to Thomson Financial content for the purpose of financial analysis. This is an educational version of the same financial resources used by Wall Street analysts on a daily basis! The access card will provide you with 180 days or 365 days of access to Thomson Analytics—*Business School Edition!*

For 500 companies, this online resource provides:

- **Current and Past Company Data:** Worldscope®, which includes company profiles, financials and accounting results, market per-share data, annual information, and monthly prices going back to 1980.
- **Financial Analyst Data and Forecasts:** 1/B/E/S Consensus Estimates, which provides consensus estimates, analyst-by-analyst earnings coverage, and analysts' forecasts.
- **SEC Disclosure Statements:** Disclosure SEC Database, which includes company profiles, annual and quarterly company financials, pricing information, and earnings.

Text Web Site (http://antle.swlearning.com)

The Web site for the second edition has expanded to offer you and your students even more resources for teaching and learning. Among the many elements available to ***students*** are:

- *Quizzes with feedback*
- *Hotlinks* to many resources on the Web, including all of the Web sites listed in the text, providing a quick connection to key information
- *PowerPoint™ presentation slides* for review of chapter coverage
- *Crossword puzzles* provide fun testing of vocabulary knowledge
- *Learning objectives* from the chapter are repeated as a study aid to keep clear focus on the core goals
- *Updates* for the latest information about changes in GAAP and any new, important information related to the text

Supplements for the Instructor

The supplements described below are available on a single CD-ROM as well as in print form. In addition, except for the Test Bank, these supplements can be downloaded from the text's Web site. Visit the Antle home page (**http://antle.swlearning.com**) to see the power of the Internet in accounting education for both you and your students. You may download instructor resources, including sample syllabi and author notes. Your students have links to EdgarScan for current company information, to cases for which they can e-mail their solutions, and to interactive quizzes.

- **The Current World of Accounting.** These PowerPoint slides, prepared by Rick Antle, are an excellent tool for generating classroom discussion on companies in the news, such as Enron, Worldcom, and Tyco.
- **Instructor's Manual.** Each chapter contains a list of key terms, a lecture outline, a selected bibliography of current readings, transparency masters, class participation ideas, supplemental examples and illustrations, and selected group learning activities.
- **Solutions Manual.** The Solutions Manual contains answers to all questions, exercises, problems, and cases in the text.
- **Test Bank.** The Test Bank contains a wealth of short-answer questions, problems, and discussion questions, with complete solutions.
- **Computerized Test Bank.** A computerized version of the Test Bank allows instructors to quickly and easily customize tests for their students. This supplement is located on the Instructor's CD-Rom, with ExamView®.
- **PowerPoint™ Lecture Presentations.** These presentations enhance lecture quality and shorten preparation time. Each chapter's slides outline the chapter content and feature key exhibits from the text.
- **Instructor's Resource CD-ROM with ExamView®.** Key instructor ancillaries (Solutions Manual, Instructor's Manual, Test Bank, ExamView, and PowerPoint™

presentation slides) are provided on a CD-ROM—giving instructors the ultimate tool for customizing lectures and presentations. The Test Bank files on the CD-Rom are provided in ExamView® format. This program is an easy-to-use test-creation software compatible with Microsoft® Windows. Instructors can add or edit questions, instructions, and answers and select questions (randomly or numerically) by previewing them on the screen. Instructors can also create and administer quizzes online, whether over the Internet, a local area network (LAN), or a wide area network (WAN).

· **Solutions Transparencies.** Acetate transparencies contain the numerical solutions to the exercises, problems, and cases.

Supplements for Students

Several study aids for students are available free of charge at the text's Web site (**http://antle. swlearning.com**). These include self-quizzes, PowerPoint slides, an EdgarScan Demo that facilitates the retrieval of current financial reports, and hot links to related sites and materials.

The following supplement is available for student purchase through the college bookstore or at the Antle Web site:

· **Study Guide.** The Study Guide, written by David L. Marcinko of SUNY-Albany, includes lecture outlines, extra problems, mastery problems, and study tips for additional study and review of chapter content.

Additional Financial Accounting Resources

INSIDE LOOK: Analysis from All Angles

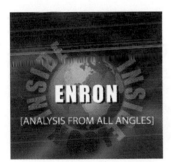

Accounting is in the news *and* in the classroom with access to this new Web site from Thomson/South-Western. The Inside Look *Access Card* allows the instructor and the student to utilize information related to Enron, Andersen, and other "names in the news" that involve accounting-related concerns. Well-known, popular news sources provide the background for the selected current events. Teaching tools are available to the instructor to implement class discussions, while analysis and questions are available to the student to utilize in many accounting discipline areas. This site is intended to help instructors teach and students to learn about critical current issues and understand them in the context of their accounting studies. For a Demo, go to **http://www.insidelook.swcollege.com.**

InfoTrac® College Edition

With this resource, students can receive anytime, anywhere online access to a database of full-text articles from hundreds of popular and scholarly periodicals, such as *Newsweek, Fortune, Entrepreneur, Journal of Accountancy,* and *Nation's Business,* among others. Students can use its fast and easy search tools to find relevant news and analytical information among the tens of thousands of articles in the database—updated daily and going back as far as four years—all at a single Web site. InfoTrac is a great way to expose students to online research techniques, with the security that the content is academically based and reliable. An InfoTrac College Edition subscription card can be packaged free with new copies of Antle/Garstka's text. For more information, visit **http://www.swcollege.com/infotrac/infotrac.html.**

NewsEdge®

NewsEdge offers flexible delivery of news and information that meets the individual needs of your classroom. The content is derived from the world's premier news and information sources. Editorial experts sift through the clutter, delivering only the stories and updates students really need.

INTACCT Financial Accounting

This Internet-based tutorial at **http://rama.swcollege.com** was designed for use in a financial accounting course or in any course where a review of key financial concepts and terminology is needed. The program offers a visual, user-friendly way to reinforce accounting principles and includes tutorials, demonstration problems, exercises, and an interactive glossary. Users will receive an access certificate that will allow them to do the online tutorial over the full term of a course.

Accounting Career Consultant: Financial Accounting
(by Charles Davis and Eric Sandburg)

This resource is an online, interactive, tutored simulation. It is designed to complement both classroom instruction and text presentations. Each module includes links to review questions with customized feedback (approximately 20 questions), links to resources to further augment learning, and company profiles for the businesses discussed.

An Introduction to Accounting, Business Processes, and ERP (by Phil Reckers, Julie Smith David, and Harriet Maccracken, all of Arizona State University)

Utilizing JD Edwards software demos, an industry-leading ERP company, students will experience an overview of the use of ERP software for accounting and business processes. They will not only learn the advantages of technology in accessing business information but will also learn to apply it in three different business models. After each module, student learning is reinforced by quizzing. Equip your students with this class-tested and easy-to-use experience to help them meet the ever-changing challenges of business and technology!

The Financial Reporting Project and Readings, 3e (by Bruce A. Baldwin of Arizona State University—West and Clayton A. Hock of Miami University)

This project book requires students to obtain and analyze "live" financial statements from publicly traded firms. Also included in the book are several high-interest articles from popular publications, such as *The Wall Street Journal* and *Business Week*. The project has a flexible format and accommodates individual or team-based learning. Students are encouraged to compose short, written responses to explain their analysis and to express their ideas based on the readings.

The Monopoly Game Practice Set (by Robert Knechel of University of Florida)

This fun practice set, based on Monopoly, helps students understand accounting transactions as triggered by real business events. Each student's solution is unique but easily graded.

Ethics in the Post-Enron Age (by Iris and Bruce Stuart of California State Unversity—Fullerton)

This ethics supplement includes problems that are appropriate for a financial accounting course.

Business & Professional Ethics for Accountants, 3e
(by Leonard J. Brooks of University of Toronto)

In this supplement, interesting, real-world situations provide students with a practical understanding of appropriate values, ethical pitfalls, applicable codes of conduct, and sound ethical reasons where codes do not apply.

Acknowledgments

Many, many people contributed to this book. Joel Demski, Frank Heflin, and Stephen Ryan contributed extensively to our thinking about this material, which has its roots in our efforts to teach the "right" first course in accounting at the Yale School of Management. Stephen and Joel helped us realize the opportunity for building some economic concepts into the book. Frank contributed greatly to our ability to incorporate actual financial statement material throughout.

Bill Beaver made a very brief but important contribution. We were discussing with him the idea of writing a text that connected economics and accounting and Bill said, "You'll never do it until you incorporate uncertainty." It took a while, but we eventually decided he was correct, and the structure of Chapter 6 is part of the result.

Three people deserve acknowledgment for different sorts of contributions. Steve Ross provided insight and experience on how to write a textbook, as well as a lot of encouragement. Oscar Hills knows what he did, and we are thankful for it. Georgia Thompson's proofing skills were invaluable.

Many of our students tolerated our various approaches during our search for the right path through this material. Some, like Jason Silvers, provided valuable, detailed editorial comments.

Several reviewers provided valuable comments on the text.

Anwer Ahmed
Syracuse University

Matt Anderson
Michigan State University

Hollis Ashbaugh
University of Wisconsin—Madison

Russell Briner
University of Texas   San Antonio

Lanny Chasteen
Oklahoma State University

E. A. Devine
Eastern Michigan University

J. Richard Dietrich
Ohio State University

Martha Doran
San Diego State University

Kenneth French
Dartmouth

Arthur Haut
Yale University

Zafar Khan
Eastern Michigan University

Janet Kimbrell
Oklahoma State University

S. P. Kothari
Massachusetts Institute of Technology

Terri Kroshus
Inver Hills Community College

Donald Leonard
Nichols College

Robin McClintock
North Carolina State University

Kevin Misiewicz
University of Notre Dame

Donald Raux
Siena College

Stephen A. Ross
Massachusetts Institute of Technology

Robert Rouse
College of Charleston

Larry Schiffres
Yale University

Leonard Stokes
Siena College

John Surdick
Xavier University

W. T. Wrege
Ball State University

Richard Young
Ohio State University

We are very thankful for the efforts of the supplements authors. Dave Marcinko produced the student Study Guide, Kathy Sevigny and Carleton Donchess wrote the Test Bank, and Scott Colvin wrote the Instructors' Manual.

About the Authors

Rick Antle

Rick Antle is Professor of Accounting and Senior Associate Dean at the Yale School of Management. Professor Antle received his Ph.D. from Stanford University and his B.S. in accounting from Oklahoma State University. He was formerly a member of the faculty at the University of Chicago. Professor Antle is an expert in areas involving the interface of accounting and economics. He has published widely on topics such as auditor independence, auditors' incentives, the economics of accounting firms, managerial compensation and performance evaluation, capital investment decisions, and transfer pricing. His consulting engagements have involved valuation, evaluation of cost accounting systems, auditing and accounting standards, auditor independence, and capital budgeting. Professor Antle served on the editorial boards of *The Accounting Review, The Journal of Accounting Research, The Journal of Business, Finance & Accounting, Review of Accounting Studies, and The British Accounting Review.*

Stanley J. Garstka

Stan Garstka is Professor in the Practice of Management and Deputy Dean at the Yale School of Management. He is also Faculty Director of the Partnership on Nonprofit Ventures. He received his Ph.D. from Carnegie Mellon University and was a member of the faculty at the University of Chicago before coming to Yale. Professor Garstka is a financial accountant with interests in the bankruptcy process, the restructuring of troubled companies, and contemporary issues in accounting. He has served on several for-profit and nonprofit boards and is a consultant in the general area of accounting methods and valuation.

PART  1

Fundamentals of Accounting

1. Introduction to Financial Accounting

2. Balance Sheet Concepts: Assets, Liabilities, and Equities

3. Income Statement Concepts: Income, Revenues, and Expenses

4. Statement of Cash Flows: Operating, Investing, and Financing Activities

5. Using the Fundamental Accounting Framework: America Online, Inc.

chapter 1

© GETTY IMAGES/PHOTO DISC

Introduction to Financial Accounting

Conversations with managers quickly reveal contradictory views of accounting. To some, accounting is a dry exercise in "bean counting." To others, accounting seems hopelessly subjective. There is an old joke about a company president interviewing accountants. The accountant who got the job had the following interview:

> President: "What's two plus two?"
>
> Accountant: "I don't know. What number did you have in mind?"

While there may not be a consensus as to whether accounting is more "bean counting" or more shady dealing, most will agree that accounting is extremely important to the operations of an organization.

This chapter begins our study of accounting. It has three goals:

1. To describe what accounting is

2. To explore why it is useful

3. To introduce three dimensions critical to understanding and using accounting:

   - economic concepts

   - accounting conventions

   - institutional context

We begin by defining accounting. We then introduce basic accounting products, or financial statements. A real company's financial statements serve as a focal point for much of this introduction. Examples present and discuss several decisions that can be improved by considering accounting information. Finally, we present the framework of economic concepts, accounting conventions, and institutional context on which we base future chapters.

What Is Accounting?

OBJECTIVE:
Learn what financial accounting is.

Accounting is the gathering and reporting of a financial history of an organization.

Union Plaza
Background

Accounting is the gathering and reporting of a financial history of an organization. This financial history requires a continual process of capturing financial data, organizing it into a useful set of accounting records, and issuing periodic financial reports to users. Accurate, up-to-date financial reports contain a great deal of valuable information for their users. The major goal of this book is to provide a clear understanding of how accounting works so you can make the most of this information.

Consider the case of the Union Plaza Hotel and Casino (hereafter, Union Plaza), a company that operates the Plaza Casino and a hotel with 1,037 guest rooms on Main Street in Las Vegas, Nevada. Formed in 1962, Union Plaza experienced phenomenal changes along with the Las Vegas area and within the gaming industry. New hotels and casinos opening up on the Las Vegas "Strip" included the massive Bellagio, a $1.6 billion development. Relative to when it began in 1962, the Union Plaza faces competition from a much wider range of sources, including Atlantic City, gaming on riverboat casinos in places such as St. Louis, Missouri, and Bay St. Louis, Mississippi, and casinos on Native American reservations across the United States.

According to its management, 2001 was a particularly difficult year for Union Plaza. Increased competition for the middle class customer necessitated lower prices, at the same time costs of goods and services went up. On top of everything else, the terrorist attacks of September 11 and their aftermath severely dampened tourism, costing Union Plaza nearly one-half of its wholesale room bookings in the following three months.

Plenty of events challenged Union Plaza in 2001, and we might expect them to significantly affect the company. Shortly, we will show you actual Union Plaza financial statements that attempt to capture the company's financial history and accurately convey it to users. However, getting the most from the information in accounting reports requires that we recognize three important factors that shape the construction of the financial statements.

Framework for Understanding Accounting Information

Economic concepts are the ideas that guide the construction of accounting reports.

Accounting conventions are the rules and customs of accounting for applying economic concepts to practical situations.

Institutional context consists of the environment that shapes the consequences of adopting specific accounting conventions.

Three aspects determine the information in accounting reports: economic concepts, accounting conventions, and institutional context. **Economic concepts** are the ideas that guide the construction of accounting reports. **Accounting conventions** are the rules and customs of accounting for applying those economic concepts to practical situations. **Institutional context** consists of the environment that shapes the consequences of adopting specific accounting conventions.

Even though estimates and predictions play a role, the "wiggle room" in an accounting history is limited by the economic concepts that guide it, the accounting conventions that govern its implementation, and the institutional context that disciplines its writers and users. Extracting the most information in accounting reports requires understanding these economic concepts (your other business classes should help here) and accounting conventions and appreciating the institutional context in which the concepts and conventions are applied.

Figure 1.1 illustrates the relationship between financial reports and the economic status of the organization. Users of financial statements must understand the "filtering" process in order to make correct assessments of the true economic status of the organization. Accounting numbers supply only approximations to economic reality; forgetting about the filtering process jeopardizes the quality of decisions. It is not so important what the accounting numbers are. Their importance lies in what they mean.

Figure 1.1

Financial Statement Construction Process

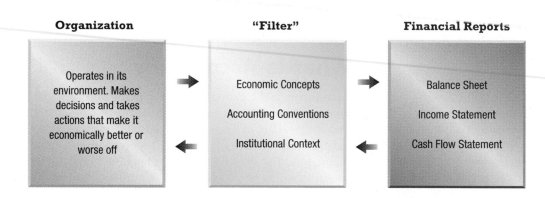

The short answer to the question, What is accounting?, might read as follows:

Accounting is the process of gathering, compiling, and reporting the financial history of an organization. Accounting's financial history is distinguished by the use of economic concepts, accounting conventions, and institutional pressures that guide its construction.

The fact that both concepts and conventions play roles in the accounting process tells us that accounting has both logical and social dimensions. To a student, this duality can be frustrating. Accounting lies somewhere between a perfectly logical science in which every assertion can either be proven correct or demonstrated to be false, and a totally subjective discipline where the validity of any statement can never be proven or disproven with certainty. Although the presence of both logical and social dimensions strains our ability to maintain a smooth flow of material, we believe it is essential to keep both dimensions in view, because denying either seriously impairs our understanding of accounting. Complete knowledge of the concepts and conventions available can be brought to bear only when the institutional context within which the reports are prepared and used is understood.

Financial Histories: The Financial Statements

OBJECTIVE:
Learn what economic information is conveyed in financial statements.

A **balance sheet** is a list of resources available, resources committed, and the difference between the two.

An **account** is a record of a specific category of asset, liability, equity, revenue, or expense.

An organization's financial history concentrates on its economic resources. Accounting periodically provides a **balance sheet,** which lists the economic resources available to an organization at a point in time. A balance sheet also describes an organization's commitments to give up economic resources to other organizations and individuals. Finally, a balance sheet shows the excess (or deficit) of resources available over those committed.

Exhibit 1.1 shows a balance sheet for Union Plaza as of December 31, 2001. The balance sheet always contains the name of the organization (entity) and the exact date of the report because the balance sheet provides a snapshot of the organization's financial condition at a particular point in time. Union Plaza's balance sheet describes its economic resources (assets) and economic commitments (liabilities) through a set of categories, or accounts.[1] Union Plaza's assets include **Cash and Cash Equivalents; Accounts Receivable; Inventories of Food, Beverage, etc.; Prepaid Expenses; Property and Equipment;** and **Other Assets.** Its liabilities include **Accounts Payable, Accrued Liabilities, Other Current Liabilities, Long-Term Debt, and Obligations under Capital Leases.** The difference between its assets and liabilities is called Stockholders' Equity. Union Plaza's Stockholders' Equity consists of **Common Stock, Additional Paid-In Capital,** and **Retained Earnings,** less the value of its own shares it has repurchased as **Treasury Stock.**

Exhibit 1.1

Union Plaza Balance Sheet

Cash equivalents are items such as bank accounts, Treasury bills, and money market funds that can readily be turned into cash.

Receivables are money owed to Union Plaza for goods sold or services provided.

Accounts payable are money owed to suppliers for items purchased from them.

Accrued liabilities are money owed to providers of goods or services.

Retained earnings are past earnings not distributed to stockholders.

Note the balance:
Total assets = Total liabilities and Stockholders' equity

Union Plaza Hotel and Casino, Inc. and Subsidiaries
Consolidated Balance Sheet as of December 31, 2001
(dollars in thousands)

ASSETS		LIABILITIES	
Cash and cash equivalents	$ 3,552	Accounts payable	$ 2,441
Accounts receivable, net	786	Accrued liabilities	2,353
Inventories of food, beverage, etc.	123	Other current liabilities	609
Prepaid expenses	793	Total current liabilities	$ 5,403
Total current assets	$ 5,554		
		Long-term debt	32,900
Property and equipment:			
Land	$ 7,012	Obligations under capital leases	1,582
Buildings	48,040	TOTAL LIABILITIES	$39,885
Leasehold improvements	3,564		
Furniture and equipment	31,659	STOCKHOLDERS' EQUITY	
	$90,275		
Less accumulated depreciation		Common stock	$ 750
and amortization	(55,903)	Additional paid-in capital	$ 5,462
Net property and equipment	$34,372	Retained earnings	$14,525
Other assets	587	Less treasury stock	(13,897)
		TOTAL STOCKHOLDERS' EQUITY	$ 628
		TOTAL LIABILITIES AND	
TOTAL ASSETS	$40,513	STOCKHOLDERS' EQUITY	$40,513

Numbers are attached to these lists of resources (assets) and commitments (liabilities). One of the major challenges of accounting is to understand the meaning of these numbers, which attempt to measure the effects of actions and decisions taken by Union Plaza's management but are subjected to the accounting filtering process. The numbers

[1] We give more rigorous definitions of assets and liabilities in Chapter 2.

actually have a variety of meanings. For example, we will see that the $786 thousand assigned to Accounts Receivable is an estimate of the actual amount Union Plaza expects to collect from the amounts owed to it by its customers. The $34,372 thousand assigned to Property and Equipment is another matter. The $7,012 thousand for land is simply the amount Union Plaza paid for the land. The amount Union Plaza paid is not necessarily a good approximation of what the land would bring if sold. The Buildings, Leasehold Improvements, and Furniture and Equipment amounts are also what Union Plaza paid. A deduction applies, however, for Accumulated Depreciation and Amortization. Cost less Accumulated Depreciation is usually not a good approximation of what the equipment would bring if sold.

The numbers on the balance sheet, whatever their origin, do add up; that is, the total of all of the assets, $40,513 thousand, is the same as the total of all liabilities and stockholder equity. For that reason it is called a balance sheet. The resources (assets) are equal to (balance) the liabilities (commitments) and stockholder equity (the excess of resources over commitments).

Accounting's financial history also describes the flows of economic resources into and out of an organization during a period of time. An **income statement** lists the economic resources acquired by an organization through its operations during a period of time. It subtracts the economic resources consumed through operations during a period of time.

Exhibit 1.2 shows an income statement for Union Plaza. The income statement is for the year ended December 31, 2001. It describes the flows of Union Plaza's economic

---

An **income statement** lists the resources acquired and consumed through an organization's operations over a period of time.

Exhibit 1.2

Union Plaza Income Statement

Revenues equal the dollar value of all the products and services Union Plaza sold during the period (the inflow of resources from sales).

Operating expenses are the dollar value of the costs incurred by Union Plaza in running its business.

Food and beverage expense is the cost of all the food and beverage items recorded as sold under Revenues.

General administrative expense includes the resources consumed for general administrative functions during the period.

Depreciation and amortization expense is the allocation of part of the cost of property and equipment to the period.

Union Plaza Hotel and Casino, Inc. and Subsidiaries Income Statement for the Year Ended December 31, 2001 (dollars in thousands)	
REVENUES	
Casino	$37,807
Food and beverage	10,351
Rooms	11,110
Other	2,524
GROSS REVENUES	61,792
Less promotional allowances	(6,922)
NET REVENUES	54,870
OPERATING EXPENSES	
Casino	$22,865
Food and beverage	8,997
Rooms	4,294
General and administrative	5,155
Entertainment	591
Advertising and promotion	1,329
Utilities and maintenance	6,712
Depreciation and amortization	4,130
Provision for doubtful accounts	44
Other costs and expenses	1,246
TOTAL OPERATING EXPENSES	$55,363
OPERATING INCOME (LOSS)	$ (493)
OTHER INCOME (EXPENSE)	
Interest income	3
Loss on sale of assets	(159)
Interest expense	(2,265)
TOTAL OTHER INCOME (EXPENSE)	(2,421)
NET LOSS	$(2,914)

resources. Increases in resources from operations are called revenues. Decreases in resources due to operations are called expenses.[2]

Union Plaza's revenues are classified as Casino, Food and Beverage, Rooms, and Other. Near the bottom of the income statement, we can see that Union Plaza also had some Interest Income. Union Plaza's expenses during that same time period are Casino, Food and Beverage, Rooms, General and Administrative, Entertainment, Advertising and Promotion, Utilities and Maintenance, Depreciation and Amortization, Provision for Doubtful Accounts, Interest Expense, and Other. Union Plaza took a Loss on Sale of Assets. All told, Union Plaza recorded a net loss for the year of $2,914 thousand.

Numbers are attached to each type of revenue and expense. For example, the revenue raised by sales of Food and Beverage was $10,351 thousand. These receipts come from restaurant and bar sales. The expense of $8,997 thousand for Food and Beverage is the cost of the food and beverage sold in the restaurant and bar. In fact, if the Union Plaza was only a restaurant and bar and had revenues only from those sources, the expense for food and beverage would probably be called Cost of Goods Sold or Cost of Sales.

As with the balance sheet, the revenue and expense numbers on income statements result from numerous calculations, and we will learn to understand them.

The difference between revenues and expenses is Net Income if positive and Net Loss if negative. Net income represents an increase in Stockholders' Equity on the balance sheet because net income is a net increase in resources over a period. Net loss represents a decrease in Stockholders' Equity, because it is a net decrease in resources over a period. Thus, an income statement helps explain why one of the numbers in the balance sheet, Retained Earnings, changes as a result of an organization's activities.

Cash is such an important economic resource, it deserves special attention. A third financial statement, the **cash flow statement,** describes the flows of cash into and out of an organization during an accounting period. The cash flows are classified as one of three types of activities that generated them: operating, financing, or investing activities. The accounting choices behind these classifications will be discussed in greater detail later.

A **cash flow statement** describes the flows of cash into and out of an organization over a period of time.

Exhibit 1.3 shows the statement of cash flow for Union Plaza. Like Union Plaza's income statement, the cash flow statement is for a period of time, the year ended December 31, 2001. Union Plaza's operating cash flows contributed $1,066 thousand in cash, while its investing activities consumed $1,131 thousand and its financing activities generated $282 thousand. Together, the three amounts tell us that Union Plaza's cash increased by $217 (in thousands) over the year.

Net cash flow from operating activities	$ 1,066
Net cash flow from investing activities	(1,131)
Net cash flow from financing activities	282
Net cash flow from all three sources	$ 217

Also like income statements, cash flow statements relate to a change in a balance sheet number. The cash flow statement always provides a reconciliation of how the cash balance changed from the beginning to the end of the period.

We will see many examples of balance sheets, income statements, and cash flow statements. Knowing how these statements are constructed and how they relate to each other will enable you to get the most information out of a set of financial statements. But why go through all the trouble? What are financial statements used for anyway? The next section describes several main categories of decisions that can be improved by using the information contained in financial statements.

---

[2]We give more formal definitions of revenues and expenses in Chapter 3.

Exhibit 1.3

Union Plaza
Cash Flow Statement

Operating activities relate to actions intended to generate net income for Union Plaza.

Investing activities are actions taken to acquire or dispose of productive assets of the company.

Financing activities relate to actions that generate receipts from or payments to suppliers of money to the firm. Typically these suppliers are investors in Union Plaza's common stock or entities that loaned it money (debt holders).

Union Plaza Hotel and Casino, Inc. and Subsidiaries
Consolidated Statements of Cash Flows for the Year Ended December 31, 2001
(dollars in thousands)

CASH FLOWS FROM OPERATING ACTIVITIES	
Cash received from customers	$54,761
Cash paid to suppliers and employees	(51,314)
Interest received	3
Interest paid	(2,384)
NET CASH PROVIDED BY (USED IN) OPERATING ACTIVITIES	$ 1,066
CASH FLOWS FROM INVESTING ACTIVITIES	
Proceeds from sale of property and equipment	$ 42
Purchase of property and equipment	(1,173)
NET CASH USED IN INVESTING ACTIVITIES	$(1,131)
CASH FLOWS FROM FINANCING ACTIVITIES	
Principal payments on short-term contracts	$ (158)
Proceeds from long-term debt	2,000
Principal payments on long-term debt	(641)
Principal payments on capital leases	(919)
NET CASH PROVIDED BY FINANCING ACTIVITIES	$ 282
NET INCREASE (DECREASE) IN CASH AND CASH EQUIVALENTS	$ 217
CASH AND CASH EQUIVALENTS, at beginning of the year	3,335
CASH AND CASH EQUIVALENTS, at end of the year	$ 3,552

Review Questions

1. Classify each of the following items as either an expense (E), a revenue (R), an asset (A), or a liability (L): Cash, Buildings, Salaries of the sales force, $5 owed to a company for work performed, Mortgage due to a bank, Sales.

2. Classify each of the following as either operating (O), investing (I), or financing (F) in a statement of cash flows: Wages paid to production workers, Cash received from a bank in the form of a mortgage, Cash dividends paid to shareholders, Cash paid to a supplier of inventory, Cash paid to purchase a new machine.

Why Study Accounting?

OBJECTIVE:
Learn how accounting information is used and why it is important.

Managers and others making financial decisions tend to be pragmatic people interested in the problems of here and now. They are interested in history only to the extent that it informs present or future decisions. The financial history summarized in an organization's financial statements is intended to do just that: inform present and future decisions. A well-designed set of statements will contain useful information about:

- The economic consequences of past decisions
- The current economic performance of the organization
- The economic performance of the organization's management
- The current economic status of the organization

Decision Making

Many decisions can be improved with accounting information. For example, a manager might make a better decision as to whether to extend credit to a customer by knowing the customer's current indebtedness and past payment history. Information about current debt might best be found in the customer's accounting records. Information about past payment history might be found in the accounting records of the manager's firm.

An investor considering whether to buy a share of stock in IBM for $125 will improve her chances of making a wise decision by inspecting IBM's financial reports. These reports help investors identify and assess a company's business strategies, its risks, its financial resources, its financial obligations, and whether it has been able to operate at a profit in the past.

If the management of Union Plaza wants to borrow money from a bank to finance the purchase of new equipment, it improves its chances of getting the loan by providing information that shows that the loan and interest are likely to be repaid. This type of evidence can be obtained from accounting records and reports.

A regulator of a public utility improves the chances of making a wise decision about the rates it allows the utility to charge its customers by looking at the utility's accounting reports. The regulator assesses whether past prices were sufficient to maintain quality service and adequate financial returns, or too generous given the services received by customers.

A potential donor informs his decision about whether to donate to the Guggenheim Museum by examining the museum's accounting statements. These statements help in evaluating the resources available to the organization and whether donated resources are likely to be used for the intended purposes.

A member of the compensation committee of the board of directors of the General Motors Company trying to determine how the president of GM is to be compensated likely uses accounting numbers to measure the president's performance. These measures might well include comparisons with the reported results of other companies in the automobile industry.

A potential competitor of Union Plaza improves its chances of making wise strategic decisions by becoming thoroughly familiar with Union Plaza's accounting reports.

A judge, determining the damages to be paid by a defendant who engaged in unfair business practices, improves the chances of making a wise decision by examining accounting records of the profits obtained by those practices.

These examples illustrate the many uses of accounting information. They indicate the high value of accounting information.

Accounting Is More Than Just Numbers

All the users in the examples benefit by being aware of more than just the numbers and descriptions in the accounting reports. The economic concepts and accounting conventions underlying the reported numbers are important to understand. Without economic concepts to provide some meaning, accounting numbers are gibberish. Economic concepts help determine what it is we are trying to measure. Often the underlying focus of measurement is not exactly clear, however, and accounting measurements are not pure. Different accounting methods may reasonably be aimed at describing the same underlying economic attribute. Knowledge of accounting conventions helps us to understand which particular method generated the numbers at hand and enables us to better place these numbers in context. It frequently also helps us to see what items of economic importance are left out of the statements altogether.

In addition to economic concepts and accounting conventions, the information in financial statements depends on a human element. Accounts (records of specific categories of assets, liabilities, stockholder equity, revenues, and expenses) are kept and reports are made by people whose character and circumstances affect their reliability. For example, it is not unusual for record keeping to be low on the priority list of managers running a rapidly growing new enterprise. The day-to-day pressure of keeping up with growing demand, late suppliers, new employees, and so on, overwhelms their ability to properly record what is happening. And it goes without saying that large-scale financial fraud in established organizations invariably involves coverups in the accounting records.

Many aspects of the accounting environment attempt to compensate for this human side of accounting. The public accounting reports of major corporations must be audited by independent, certified public accountants (CPAs) who face considerable liability when misleading accounting reports are issued. Managers of companies are also liable for issuing misleading reports. In addition, managers and companies develop reputations for honesty (or dishonesty) among shareholders, the business press, and their peers. These forces on managers and auditors, along with economic concepts and accounting conventions, help discipline the financial reporting process.

8/98 Investor lawsuit against Daou claims Daou used inappropriate accounting principles to show profit of 1 cent per share when it lost 46 cents per share.

3/99 Oxford Health Plans shareholders sue company for securities fraud and accuse auditors of propping up share value with misleading reports.

3/99 Cendant Corp. files a lawsuit against its auditors, alleging failure to detect fraudulent funds when auditing one of the companies that merged to form Cendant.

12/99 Ernst & Young agrees to pay $335 million to settle shareholders' accusations that its audits of Cendant Corp. were faulty.

1/01 SEC Chairman Pitt recommends new governing body to oversee accountants.

3/02 Andersen loses clients after Enron debacle.

It all adds up to a pretty complex situation for users of accounting reports. This complexity is what makes accounting worth studying. After all, it is important to know how to measure lengths and weights. The numbers produced by these measurements are useful in a variety of circumstances, but intense study of such measurements is worthwhile only for a few people. For most people, a basic knowledge of length and weight measurement is more than sufficient for their purposes.

This is not true of accounting. Unlike measurements of length and weight, which produce concise, well-understood numbers, accounting produces scores of numbers with vague, often misunderstood implications. The measurement of economic resources is considerably more complicated and subjective than the measurement of length or weight. Accounting produces far more than numbers. An accounting report contains labels for the numbers (i.e., account titles), summaries of the accounting procedures applied, multiple measurements of the same items, and warnings about potential obligations not yet included in the numbers presented.

Exhibit 1.4 contains excerpts from footnote 1 in Union Plaza's 2001 annual report. It presents a summary of the accounting methods used to compile its financial statements. For example, Union Plaza explains what it considers to be cash equivalents. The note talks about how Union Plaza determines the revenue from its casino, and a bit about Union Plaza's accounts receivable. The note explains that the number associated with Property and Equipment on its balance sheet represents the acquisition cost of the property and equipment. Systematic adjustments are made to record the downward movement of value (depreciation) associated with the passage of time. The note reveals that Union Plaza includes complementary items given to customers in gross revenues, then deducts them as promotion allowances to calculate net revenue.

Exhibit 1.4

Union Plaza Summary of
Accounting Policies

> **Union Plaza Hotel and Casino**
> **(Excerpts from footnote 1: A Summary of Significant Accounting Policies)**
>
> The following summarizes the significant accounting policies of the Company: For purposes of the statement of cash flows, the Company considers all highly liquid investments purchased with a maturity of three months or less to be cash equivalents.
>
> In accordance with common industry practice, the Company recognizes as casino revenue the net win (which is the difference between amounts wagered and amounts paid to winning patrons) from gaming activities. Credit is extended to certain casino customers and the Company records all unpaid advances as casino receivables on the date credit was granted. Allowances for estimated uncollectible casino receivables are provided to reduce these receivables to amounts anticipated to be collected.
>
> Property and equipment are stated at cost. Depreciation is computed using the straight-line method.
>
> The retail value of admissions, food and beverage and other complimentary items furnished to customers without charge is included in gross revenue and then deducted as promotional allowances.

Although this information may seem a bit overwhelming, understanding what it means is within reach. As we go through the way accounting works, you will learn what is meant by these and other accounting methods.

For other examples of accounting disclosures, consider the case of Kmart. Exhibit 1.5 contains part of footnote 1 found in the 1998 Kmart Corporation annual report. Kmart, one of the largest retailers in the United States, tells in this note what certain accounting numbers—the values associated with inventory on its balance sheet—would be if they had used the FIFO method instead of the LIFO method of accounting for inventories. In inventory accounting, accountants disclose multiple measures. This explanation is important because not all corporations use the same method to compute the inventory number on their balance sheet. In order to compare the inventory values of two different companies, we would need to know the basis for those numbers.

Exhibit 1.5

Kmart Summary of
Accounting Policies

> **Kmart Corporation**
> **(Excerpt from footnote 1: A Summary of Significant Accounting Policies)**
>
> INVENTORIES: Inventories are stated at the lower of cost or market, primarily using the retail method. The last-in, first-out (LIFO) method, utilizing internal inflation indices, was used to determine the cost for $6,148, $5,990, and $5,883 of inventory as of year end 1998, 1997, and 1996, respectively. Inventories valued on LIFO were $407, $457, and $440 lower than amounts that would have been reported using the first-in, first-out (FIFO) method at year end 1998, 1997, and 1996, respectively.

Exhibit 1.6 presents part of a Kmart Corporation footnote explaining future commitments and contingencies. In 1998, the Sports Authority (TSA) chain, owned by Kmart, experienced operating and financial difficulties. The footnote indicates that under certain conditions, Kmart guaranteed to pay for TSA leases. In light of its financial troubles, Kmart attempted to change the terms of the guarantees.

The purpose of going through these footnotes is to firmly establish that although accounting statements contain a great deal of information, financial disclosure is a complex business. Accounting is important and complex enough to be worth studying, and it requires an organized approach. We begin this organized approach by discussing economic concepts, accounting conventions, and the institutional environment.

Exhibit 1.6

Kmart Footnote Explaining Commitments and Contingencies

Kmart Corporation
(Excerpt from commitment and contingency footnote)

THE SPORTS AUTHORITY

On October 6, 1998, TSA announced that it would take a $55 after-tax charge, as a result of store closings, inventory writedowns and other charges and costs, and that operating results for the third quarter of 1998 would be weaker than expected. In October 1998, TSA announced that it amended certain aspects of its bank credit agreement, including modifying certain financial covenants in light of the restructuring charge. Pursuant to that amendment, TSA also granted its bank lenders a security interest in its inventory and certain accounts receivable. On December 9, 1998, in its third quarter 10-Q filing, TSA noted that its ability to satisfy ongoing working capital and capital expenditure requirements depends on successfully negotiating a new credit facility prior to the expiration of its bank credit agreement in April 1999.

Kmart's rights and obligations with respect to its guarantee of TSA leases are governed by a Lease Guaranty, Indemnification and Reimbursement Agreement dated as of November 23, 1994 (the "LGIRA"). Kmart and TSA are presently in discussions to amend and restate the LGIRA, the terms of which have not been finalized, in connection with TSA's refinancing activities related to the procurement of a new three-year credit facility prior to April 1999.

Review Questions

1. List several economic decisions that rely on accounting information.

2. Why do financial statements have footnotes, and what kinds of information might you find in them?

Economic Concepts

OBJECTIVE:

Learn a framework for understanding accounting information.

Three main economic concepts are at the heart of accounting: financial value, wealth, and economic income. Financial value is the foundation upon which wealth and income measurement rest. A financial value is an amount of money. As we saw in Union Plaza's financial statements, accounting reports contain many monetary amounts. To understand what accounting reports tell us about an organization's economic resources, we must understand what financial values are and how accounting's monetary amounts relate to them. We must appreciate the ideal measurement of wealth and income and how accounting's measurements stack up against it.

Financial Value

The **financial value** of an item is the amount of money it would bring if sold.

The **financial value** of an item is the amount of money it would bring if sold. For instance, your house might have an assessed value of $200,000 for property tax purposes, but if you wish to sell it and the best offer is $220,000, then its financial value is $220,000. In theory, financial value is a straightforward and useful concept, but in practice it becomes more difficult. How can we know how much an item would fetch if we don't actually sell it?

One way to assess the financial value of an item without selling it is to look at the sale prices of the same, or nearly the same, thing. This method tends to work best if the item is traded in a well-functioning market. For example, bushels of corn and ounces of gold are constantly traded under conditions that give us a lot of confidence in the amount a bushel of corn or an ounce of gold would bring if sold.

An example of the traditional way by which financial value is established—trading on the floor of a stock exchange. How will technology innovations such as internationally-linked computers that enable round-the-clock trading affect the way financial value is determined in the future?

© CARL/JOAN VANDERSCHUIT/INDEX STOCK

Characteristics of well-functioning markets:
• *competitive*
• *low transaction costs*
• *organized and regulated*

Well-functioning markets exhibit three characteristics: they are competitive, they have low transaction costs, and they are organized and regulated. For example, the markets for gold and corn are highly competitive. Corn and gold are commodities. One ounce of gold or one bushel of corn is as good as any other. Many people produce corn and gold, and many people have uses for them. Other people specialize in trading corn and gold. A market value that gets out of line with financial values provides incentive to speculators to buy or sell until the aggregate effect leads the prices to adjust to proper financial values.

The markets for gold and corn use up relatively few resources in their operation, which is reflected in the low transaction charges that the markets impose on traders (usually a fraction of one percent of the value of the trade). Low transaction costs are important because they lead the prices in the markets to reflect the financial values of the items being traded, without being unduly influenced by the costs to the traders of implementing their trades. Low transaction costs enable markets to closely track small changes in financial values. With high transaction costs, a change in financial value might not be reflected in the trading price because the cost of the trade exceeds the change in financial value. Low transaction costs in the gold and corn markets help their prices stay in line with financial values.

Corn and gold trade in organized, regulated exchanges. These exchanges use standard definitions of tradable items, rules and conventions for making trades, and procedures for policing traders. If better, less costly ways for an exchange to organize its activity are discovered, competition from other exchanges will pressure it to adopt them. The prices on gold and corn markets then reflect value as closely as humanly possible.

Wealth

An organization's **wealth** *is the sum of the financial values of all the things it owns.*

An organization's **wealth** is the sum of the financial values of all the things it owns. Economists and accountants break the wealth calculation down into parts. Some of the things an organization owns—for example, its delivery trucks—are useful to others who would give an organization money to acquire them. These things are expected to generate future benefits (which is why the organization owns them in the first place) and are called *assets*. In contrast, other things an organization owns involve future sacrifices. For example, in order to sell a piece of machinery the organization may have to give a warranty to the purchaser. This warranty likely creates an obligation to expend resources in the future. The things that involve future sacrifices of resources are called *liabilities*.

Separating assets and liabilities lets us think of an organization's wealth as the difference between the financial value of its assets and the financial value of its liabilities. This difference is called *equity*:

$$\text{ASSETS} - \text{LIABILITIES} = \text{EQUITY}$$

This identity is just a rewriting of the balance sheet description:

$$\text{ASSETS} = \text{LIABILITES} + \text{EQUITY}$$

The most important identity in accounting:
Assets = Liabilities + Equity

An *identity* is more than an equation, it is a *definition*. Once we determine assets and liabilities, we must know equity. So really, the balance defines equity by giving us the totals for assets and liabilities. This identity holds at every point in time. Accounting's financial history uses this identity to organize its portrayal of economic resources so much that it is often called the fundamental accounting identity. *It is the most important identity in this book!*

Union Plaza's balance sheet reflects this way of describing an organization's resources. As shown in Exhibit 1.1, at December 31, 2001, Union Plaza had assets of $40,513 thousand and liabilities of $39,885 thousand. The difference between the two is the stockholders' equity of $628 (in thousands):

Assets	$40,513
Liabilities	39,885
Equity	$ 628

Economic Income

An organization's **economic income** *over a period is the change in its wealth, excluding capital transactions with its owners.*

Wealth captures economic resources at a point in time, but we are also interested in describing resource flows. An organization's **economic income** over a period is the change in its wealth, excluding capital transactions with its owners. The idea behind economic income is to describe an organization's success in using its economic resources in a period. Although contributions from owners increase the wealth available to an organization, the increase is not generated by use of that organization's resources. Similarly, payments to owners are not resources consumed by an organization; they are distributions of its resources.

Union Plaza's accounting income statement reflects this thinking. The income statement describes the changes in wealth stemming from resources brought into the company by its operations (revenues), less the resources consumed during the period (expenses). Resources distributed to owners of corporations are called dividends and are reported in the statement of cash flows. The financing section of Union Plaza's cash flow statement in Exhibit 1.3 contains no amounts for dividends, so we can infer that Union Plaza did not distribute any cash to its owners in 2001.

Importance of Financial Value, Wealth, and Economic Income in Accounting

Accounting's use of monetary amounts, its descriptions of resources, obligations, and equities as of a given date in balance sheets, and its descriptions of resource flows arising from revenues and expenses in income statements parallel the economic concepts of financial value, wealth, and economic income. The financial value of an item is clearest within a well-functioning market for it. Measures of wealth are most directly meaningful when each asset and liability component of wealth has a clear financial value.

Economic income is the clearest when changes in wealth can be comprehensively identified and classified as being or not being a contribution from or distribution to an owner.

Measurement of financial values, wealth, and economic income under ideal conditions is useful for learning about accounting; but to put accounting in proper perspective, we must address problems of applying these concepts in practice. Practical problems arise with each of these economic concepts. Consider the issue of financial value. All organizations own many resources whose financial values are not readily determinable at all points in time.

Economic reality:
• Timing
• Uncertainty
affect the financial value of a resource or obligation.

Two main features of ***economic reality*** cause particular problems with assessing the financial value of a resource or obligation: the ***timing*** and ***uncertainty*** of its ultimate benefit or cost. For example, Union Plaza's hotel, built several years ago, occupies a unique location. Potential buyers for it are probably few. Further, a potential buyer might be uncertain about its future profitability. Things might turn around and the hotel might start producing profits immediately. On the other hand, competitors might intensify their efforts to lure away Union Plaza's customers, the "hassle factor" involved in air travel might get worse and further depress tourism, and costs might continue to rise.

Assuming that the hotel is put up for sale, finding the right buyer and negotiating the terms of the sale are time-consuming, expensive processes. Transaction costs are high.

Assessing the financial value of Union Plaza's hotel is, therefore, a challenging task—challenging, but not impossible. The financial values for some items are not available at all. For example, Union Plaza's management possesses a great deal of valuable knowledge about how to run a hotel and casino business. This type of knowledge cannot be directly bought and sold, at least partly because we are uncertain about how to even define it.

Because financial values for all items are not available, wealth measurements are incomplete. As a result, income measurements fall short of capturing all changes in wealth. We should not give up on the concepts of economic value, wealth, and economic income, however, just because we cannot make the ideal measurements. By adopting conventions of accounting measurement and disclosure, we construct accounting counterparts to these ideals and provide information about how they are related. Figure 1.2 shows the relationship between the financial statements and economic concepts.

Figure 1.2

Relationship between Financial Statements and Economic Concepts

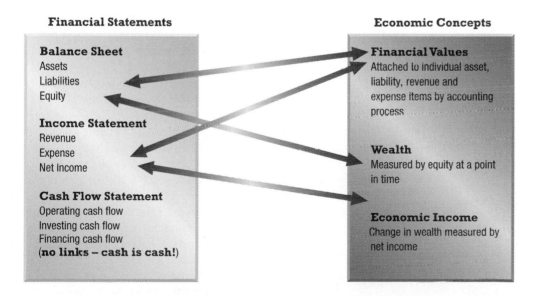

In the example of the hotel, we can make several observations. First, at the time it was built, the cost was probably a good indication of the value because the land, steel, glass, labor, and other materials and services used in constructing the hotel were purchased in markets. Their financial value at the time was likely to be closely tied to their cost to Union Plaza, who purchased them for construction of the hotel. Another useful observation is that the hotel cannot last forever. It will either be sold, in which case another well-determined market value will be established for Union Plaza, or it will continue to be used, in which case its financial value will likely diminish to zero. In any case, we expect its financial value to fall as it is used, as it depreciates. Union Plaza can decide on a reasonable schedule on which to depreciate the recorded value of the hotel in its accounting records, and be assured that errors in valuation will either be corrected by a market transaction (sale of the hotel) or go to zero in the long run if it is continually held.

Union Plaza:
Plant and equipment valuation

> Plant and equipment are carried at cost less accumulated depreciation and amortization.

Communicating to users of the accounting reports what is being done in the accounts will likely be easier if a fairly standard set of approaches to measurement problems is established. These standard ways of handling practical measurement problems are accounting conventions.

Accounting Conventions

Accounting conventions arise from practical matters and inevitably encompass human judgments, human interactions, and compromises. These conventions will be more easily understood and carry more credibility if they are commonplace. **Generally accepted accounting principles (GAAP)** are commonly understood and accepted conventions for gathering, organizing, and reporting accounting's financial history of an organization.

Generally accepted accounting principles (GAAP) are commonly understood and accepted conventions for gathering, organizing, and reporting accounting's financial history of an organization.

GAAP conventions guide accounting valuation, recognition, and disclosure.

Accounting valuation is the act of assigning an item a monetary value to be reported in the balance sheet.

Recognition is the act of recording an item in the accounting records.

Disclosure is the act of providing information about the organization and the construction of its accounting reports.

Nature of Accounting Conventions

GAAP apply to one or more of three broad areas. One is **accounting valuation:** GAAP help specify what values are placed on the items reported. If a solid financial value exists, it is likely that GAAP use that value. If a solid financial value does not exist, GAAP provide guidance and restrictions on what accounting values are placed in the accounting records. For example, in Exhibit 1.4 we saw how Union Plaza values property and equipment.

Recognition is the second area. **Recognition** is the act of recording formally some item in the accounting records. Consider an advertising campaign. The future benefits it creates, if any, do not have a readily determinable financial value. Should any amount related to the future benefits of the advertising campaign be recognized as an asset? Consider a sale on credit. When should an increase in assets be acknowledged and revenue recognized? If financial values were clear and wealth measurement all-encompassing, the issue of recognition would not arise. But in practice, many changes in wealth are not automatically known. GAAP guide their recognition.

The third area is disclosure. **Disclosure** is the act of providing information about the organization and the construction of its accounting reports. Calculating and attaching accounting values, constructing balance sheets, and compiling income statements are inexact sciences. GAAP dictate disclosures of measurement methods, assumptions, and the results of adopting alternative sets of assumptions that add to the information content of the accounting reports.

Factors Affecting Accounting Conventions

Accounting conventions tend to arise somewhat randomly as practical problems present themselves. GAAP are not logically constructed from a few underlying ideas, and getting

Factors affecting GAAP:
• *market richness*
• *complexity of transactions*
• *form of organizaiton*

all their details requires some memorization. The process of remembering GAAP for an item can be made somewhat easier by assessing three factors. The first is the **richness of the market** in which the item of interest is being traded (is it corn or gold, or a specialized building?). A rich market is a well-functioning one in which many buyers and sellers compete for relatively uniform goods in a setting with low transaction costs. Examples include the corn and gold markets we spoke of earlier. When markets are rich, GAAP tend to use market valuations to drive the accounting.

The second assessment is the **complexity of the transactions** used to trade the item. A straightforward exchange of cash for a Big Mac™ is a simple transaction. The exchange of the services of a chief executive officer of a corporation for a salary, possible bonus, generous pension plan, stock options, and other perquisites is a complex transaction. It becomes more difficult to come up with accounting values for what is given and what is received by both parties to this transaction. When transactions are simple, GAAP tend to be simple. When transactions are complex, GAAP tend to be complex.

The third assessment is the **form of the organization** for which the accounting history is being written. Different organizations engage in different activities, produce accounting reports for different constituencies with different uses for reports, and face different underlying economic circumstances. GAAP take into account the form of the organization. GAAP for sole proprietorships (single-owner companies) and partnerships differ from GAAP for corporations, which differ from GAAP for not-for-profits, which differ from GAAP for governments. For example, proprietors continually make contributions of many different types of resources to their businesses. When they withdraw resources, it is unclear whether it is a return for their financial resources contributed (a dividend) or for their time (wages). Proprietorship accounts do not distinguish the nature of a proprietor's withdrawals.

Similarly, in contrast to public corporations, not-for-profit organizations do not earn income for a set of owners, nor do they typically produce income statements. Yale University attempts to cover all research and education costs from grant, endowment, and tuition income and is content to break even—not have any dollars left over and not owe anyone money at the end of the year. Governments do not have equity. Their balance sheets do not follow the same sorts of rules for recording and valuing assets as public corporations. The objective of New York City is to make sure that various departments do not exceed their allotted budgets for the year, and their accounting reports are set up to gather that sort of information.

These three factors—market richness, complexity of transactions, and organizational form—provide a starting point for learning and understanding GAAP. They indicate the likely issues that GAAP apply to and their range of resolutions. The three factors do not and cannot provide definitive answers, but they do allow us to structure our study of accounting conventions. Your understanding of accounting conventions can be increased if you keep these three factors in mind.

Institutional Context

OBJECTIVE:
Learn to read actual financial statements by looking at excerpts from the reports of real companies.

GAAP do not dictate exact accounting treatments for all situations. They cannot. New transactions are constantly required for the exchange of novel items such as financial contracts, which are continually adapting to changing economic circumstances, advances in information technologies, and, most important for our purposes, changes in accounting conventions.

Even if GAAP did dictate exact treatments, we need to consider the human element in accounting. Were GAAP followed? What incentives were faced by the issuers of the accounting reports? Did these incentives influence their judgment at a conscious or unconscious level? For example, the total compensation of the chairman of the Chrysler Corporation depends on Chrysler's net income.[3]

[3]We do not intend to imply that Chrysler's financial statements were unduly influenced by Eaton because of his incentives. Executive bonuses tied to net income are commonplace, and any of literally thousands of other companies could be used as an illustration.

Chrysler:
Executive compensation

Robert J. Eaton received an annual bonus, as reported in the Summary Compensation Table, based on Chrysler's performance with respect to consolidated net earnings.

These questions point to the importance of considering the institutional context within which accounting takes place. The institutional context shapes the consequences associated with accounting choices. For example, for a company's stock to be traded on the New York Stock Exchange (NYSE), the company must issue regular financial reports constructed in accordance with GAAP and audited by an independent, certified public accountant. Failure to comply with this requirement can cause a company's stock to be delisted (declared ineligible for trading on the exchange). Such stock exchange rules provide a powerful incentive for publicly traded corporations to adhere to GAAP. Exhibit 1.7 contains the independent auditor's report on Union Plaza's financial statements.

Exhibit 1.7

Union Plaza: Auditor's report

Independent Auditor's Report

The Stockholders and Board of Directors—Union Plaza Hotel and Casino, Inc.

We have audited the accompanying consolidated balance sheet of Union Plaza Hotel and Casino, Inc., and subsidiaries (a Nevada Corporation) as of December 31, 2001, and 2000, the related consolidated statements of loss, stockholders' equity and cash flows for the year then ended December 31, 2001, 2000, and 1999. These consolidated financial statements are the responsibility of the Company's management. Our responsibility is to express an opinion on these consolidated financial statements based on our audit.

We conducted our audit in accordance with generally accepted auditing standards. Those standards require that we plan and perform the audit to obtain reasonable assurance about whether the financial statements are free of material misstatement. An audit includes examining, on a test basis, evidence supporting the amounts and disclosures in the consolidated financial statements. An audit also includes assessing the accounting principles used and significant estimates made by management, as well as evaluating the overall financial statement presentation. We believe that our audit provides a reasonable basis for our opinion.

In our opinion, the financial statements referred to above present fairly, in all material respects, the financial position of Union Plaza Hotel and Casino, Inc. and subsidiaries as of December 31, 2001 and 2000, and the results of their operations and their cash flows for the year then ended December 31, 2001, 2000, and 1999 in conformity with accounting principles generally accepted in the United States of America.

Conway, Stuart & Woodbury CPAs
Las Vegas, Nevada.

The **Securities and Exchange Commission (SEC)** is the agency of the U.S. federal government that regulates the trading of public companies.

The **Financial Accounting Standards Board (FASB)** is the private-sector, not-for-profit organization that sets GAAP in the United States.

Who determines GAAP? The **Securities and Exchange Commission (SEC)** is an agency of the United States federal government that has authority to determine GAAP for public companies whose stock is traded across state lines. The SEC was established by Congress under the Securities Exchange Act of 1934. The SEC publishes Accounting Series Releases that contain its views of GAAP and the principles that must be followed in reports filed with the commission.

Although it has the formal authority to establish GAAP, the SEC prefers to allow private organizations to do so. Currently, the **Financial Accounting Standards Board (FASB),** a private, not-for-profit organization, sets GAAP in the United States. The FASB follows extensive due process rules. This process involves publicly declaring its agenda, seeking input from any interested parties at various points, promulgating "Exposure

Drafts" of proposed standards, and holding all its meetings in public view. Thus, the setting of accounting conventions is a decidedly social, as opposed to a logical or scientific, process.

The institutions affecting accounting go beyond the rule-making bodies. Independent auditors face civil liability when their certifications of financial reports contribute to losses by users of those reports. Substantial damages awarded in civil suits against auditors provide powerful incentives for auditors to insist that their clients follow GAAP.

Managers responsible for the accounting reports of public corporations often care about their reputations. The business press, financial analysts, and bond-rating agencies follow public companies' accounting reports and are constantly evaluating their disclosures. Public officials responsible for government finances are also scrutinized by the press and bond-rating agencies. Investors can divest themselves of ownership in companies whose public reports they do not trust, and citizens can vote at the ballot box and "with their feet" by abandoning jurisdictions that lose credibility. Not-for-profit organizations involved in financial scandals often find that contributions decline as a result. In 1991, the president of United Way of America resigned in light of alleged extravagant spending abuses. In 1992, many local chapters withheld payments to the parent organization and saw their own contributions plummet. Contributions to the United Way in Connecticut and New Jersey were $50.8 million in 1991–1992 but dropped to $41.6 million the following year, with many pledges being cancelled and some companies refusing to run fund drives.

Institutional context combines with economic concepts and accounting conventions to affect the information content of accounting reports. Context is especially important to keep in mind in a global economy, where accounting reports are generated using a variety of conventions and under a variety of circumstances. We will further develop economic concepts and provide greater detail about accounting conventions as we proceed through the remainder of this book. We also take many opportunities to discuss institutional arrangements. Our examples are drawn primarily from the United States, but it is important to underscore that wise use of accounting reports involves knowledge of the setting in which the reports were compiled. We offer the following guidelines for assessing institutional context:

- Determine how accounting conventions are set. Are there formal rule-making bodies like the FASB? Are the rules of another jurisdiction followed?
- Assess the auditing environment. Are audits by independent auditors required? What bodies police auditor behavior? Is there a strong accounting profession with incentives for self-policing?
- Assess the legal environment. Are there criminal penalties for white-collar crimes? Are the laws enforced? Are civil remedies available?
- Is the culture within which the reports were produced characterized by a preference for openness or secrecy? What are the traditions with respect to financial disclosure?
- For what purposes are the accounting reports compiled? Are there legal requirements or exchange regulations that mandate the accounting? Are the reports issued with the hope of raising resources through contributions, loans, or sale of the organization or some of its resources?

This list of factors, while not exhaustive, indicates the incentives and the opportunities for generating and taking advantage of "wiggle room" in the accounts.

Review Questions

1. Describe the process of setting accounting standards. What are the roles of all the parties you mention?

2. Think of an example, like the executive compensation example in the chapter, where incentives might exist to bias accounting numbers one way or another.

Conclusion

The remainder of this book is aimed at helping you grasp the fundamentals of economic concepts, accounting conventions, and institutional context required for a solid understanding of accounting. The economic concepts of financial value, wealth, and economic income are so basic to accounting that they deserve careful development. The effects of timing and uncertainty on assessments of financial value and techniques for handling them also merit our attention. Many accounting conventions must be introduced and explored, and some structure for organizing them should be offered. Too many specialized rules in various countries, across different industries, and for particular items make it impossible to memorize them all. We will continually refer to the dimensions of market richness, complexity of transactions, and organizational form to try to provide a reasonably coherent structure for a wide-ranging set of accounting conventions. Finally, delving into more specifics will give us the opportunity to present a richer picture of the institutional context of accounting.

The next chapter begins our look deeper into accounting by exploring the accounting balance sheet. We focus on the accounts of a for-profit corporation, which offers the most straightforward setting. The activities of organizations, the composition and nature of their assets, and the role of assets in the wealth creation process are examined. We also explore liabilities and the implementation of the identity

$$ASSETS = LIABILITES + EQUITY$$

in the construction of the balance sheet.

Key Terms

account 5

accounting 3

accounting conventions 4

accounting valuation 16

accounts payable 5

accounts receivable 5

accrued liabilities 5

assets 5

balance sheet 5

cash equivalents 5

cash flow statement 7

contributed capital 5

cost of sales 6

depreciation and amortization expense 6

disclosure 16

economic concepts 4

economic income 14

expenses 7

Financial Accounting Standards Board (FASB) 18

financial value 12

financing activities 8

food and beverage expense 6

general administrative expense 6

generally accepted accounting principles (GAAP) 16

income statement 6

institutional context 4

inventory 5

investing activities 8

net income 7

operating activities 8

operating expenses 6

product development expense 6

property and equipment 5

receivables 5

recognition 16

retained earnings 5

revenues 6

sales and marketing expense 6

sales revenue 6

Securities and Exchange Commission (SEC) 18

shareholder equity 6

wealth 13

chapter 2

© GETTY IMAGES/PHOTO DISC

Balance Sheet Concepts: Assets, Liabilities, and Equities

In one country, as a result of a coup, career military officers with no business experience were placed on the boards of directors of several important corporations. After inspecting the financial statements of several companies, one general became very suspicious.

> General: "What are you guys trying to put over on me?"

> Executives: "What do you mean?"

> General: "Do you expect me to believe that for every one of these companies, the total assets are exactly equal to the liabilities plus equities?"

We imagine that a short lesson in accounting began immediately.

Like the General, this chapter is focused on the balance sheet. It has two goals:

1. To explore the economic concepts of assets, liabilities, and equities that underlie the balance sheet

2. To introduce the accounting techniques of debits and credits that are used to keep track of and to analyze balance sheet items

In Chapter 1 we discussed the importance of economic concepts. They guide the construction of accounting reports. In this chapter we further explain these concepts.

Basic debit/credit bookkeeping techniques are important in their own right, but it is not our main purpose for introducing them. Learning these techniques helps in understanding how financial statements work and, especially, how they are related. They help in discovering and understanding the economic events that underlie financial statements, and they help in forecasting the impact of future economic events and proposed transactions. In combination with an understanding of economic concepts, the mastery of debit and credit techniques provides a powerful tool for financial analysis.

This chapter begins by discussing the entity concept. Both the economic concepts and accounting techniques must have a point of reference, which is defined by the entity for which the accounting is done. We then move on to study assets, liabilities, and equities in detail. Then we formally introduce debits and credits. Finally, we work through a comprehensive example to illustrate the connection of debits and credits with the balance sheet.

Basic Definitions, Theories, and Examples

As we have already seen, an asset is a future benefit. But whose benefit is it? A liability is an obligation to give up resources in the future. But whose obligation is it? Think about getting a loan from a bank. You incur an obligation to repay the loan. The bank will likely insist on a regular schedule of payments. The loan is clearly a liability from your point of view because *you* must give up your resources in the future.

How does the bank view the loan? Your payments in the future will be cash receipts to the bank. From the bank's perspective the loan generates future benefits. Thus, the loan is an asset from the bank's point of view.

The Entity Concept

An **entity** is the person or organization about which accounting's financial history is written.

The first thing to realize about accounting is that it must take a point of view. Accountants refer to this point of view as the **entity** concept. Accounts are compiled for a specified entity, and benefits and obligations are assessed from that entity's point of view.

A specific entity identified in a set of financial statements might be a city, a regulated public utility, a partnership, a taxpayer, a corporation, or any set of activities for which it would be useful to generate an economic history. Once we define an entity, we establish a point of view for the accounts and can begin to know how a transaction affects the composition of the entity's assets and liabilities; that is, does the transaction generate future benefits for the entity, or obligate the entity to give up resources in the future?

Assets: Definition

An **asset** is "a probable future economic benefit obtained or controlled by an entity as a result of a past transaction or event."[1] To an accountant, an asset's economic benefits manifest themselves, one way or another, in future cash flows. Some assets, such as a customer's obligation to pay for merchandise bought on credit, turn directly into cash when the customer pays what is owed. Other assets take a more indirect route to producing a future cash flow. For example, a farmer's tractor is an asset because it is used in the process of growing a crop, which is then sold for cash. A computer may allow clerical work to be done more efficiently, reducing the need for a second secretary. This saving of future wages is a future cash benefit generated by the computer.

Assets: Examples

It is impossible to list every conceivable asset. Entities own or control too many different kinds of items that generate future economic benefits to provide an exhaustive list. Some types of assets are held by almost all entities. For example, consider the assets listed in the OshKosh B'Gosh, Inc. balance sheets in Exhibit 2.1. OshKosh B'Gosh, Inc. is a retailer of children's clothing. Its common stock trades on the New York Stock Exchange under the symbol OSK.

Let's begin our examination of OshKosh B'Gosh's assets with some overall observations. The two lists provide values for assets, one at December 30, 2000, and the other at December 29, 2001. (This slight asymmetry of dates is probably because of where weekends and holidays fell in 2001.) OshKosh B'Gosh's total assets at December 29, 2001, were $161,340 thousand. OshKosh B'Gosh breaks this total down into subcategories. **Current assets** is a major subcategory of assets whose economic benefits are expected to be realized within one year of the balance sheet date. We see that OshKosh B'Gosh's current assets totaled $125,055 thousand at December 29, 2001. Let's look at the details of the current assets.

As for virtually every entity, cash is also one of OshKosh B'Gosh's current assets. OshKosh B'Gosh holds cash and cash equivalents of $29,322 thousand at December 29, 2001.

Cash is money in the form of currency or deposits in banks. In today's global marketplace, most large companies hold currencies issued by many different countries. Cash is a future economic benefit because it can be exchanged for goods and services. Therefore, it is an asset. Because its benefits can be used immediately, it is a current asset.

OshKosh B'Gosh lists Investments at zero. These short-term investments, often called *marketable securities*, are investments in financial assets, such as shares of stock and bonds. Entities make these investments to earn the dividends or interest they generate or because the price of the stock or bond is expected to rise.

Investments in stocks or bonds might generate a higher return than putting money in a bank, but they may also carry more risk. Some bonds become worthless because the issuer defaults. In labeling a marketable security an asset, we assert that it can be converted into cash. A market price generated in a rich market would be the best evidence of the possibility of conversion into cash, and marketable securities are often carried on balance sheets at their market values. Because the existence of a rich market enables quick conversion into cash, marketable securities are current assets.

[1] *FASB Concepts Statement No. 3.*

Exhibit 2.1

OshKosh B'Gosh Balance Sheets

OshKosh B'Gosh, Inc. and Subsidiaries
Consolidated Balance Sheets
(dollars in thousands, except per share amounts)

ASSETS	December 29, 2001	December 30, 2000
Current assets		
Cash and cash equivalents	$ 29,322	$ 19,839
Investments	—	511
Accounts receivable, less allowances of $7,075 in 2001 and $5,510 in 2000	25,697	30,166
Inventories	55,429	53,185
Prepaid expenses and other current assets	1,607	1,882
Deferred income taxes	13,000	13,800
Total current assets	$125,055	$119,383
Property, plant, and equipment, net	30,001	32,285
Deferred income taxes	4,300	4,950
Other assets	1,984	1,638
Total assets	$161,340	$158,256
LIABILITIES AND SHAREHOLDERS' EQUITY		
Current liabilities		
Current portion of long-term debt	$ —	$ 10,000
Accounts payable	11,229	14,840
Accrued liabilities	38,403	39,942
Total current liabilities	$ 49,632	$ 64,782
Long-term debt	24,000	34,000
Employee benefit plan liabilities	14,008	15,001
Total liabilities	$ 87,640	$113,783
Shareholders' equity		
Preferred stock, par value $.01 per share: Authorized—1,000,000 shares; Issued and outstanding—None	$ —	$ —
Common stock, par value $.01 per share:		
Class A, authorized—30,000,000 shares; Issued and outstanding—10,020,226 shares in 2001, 9,943,762 shares in 2000	100	99
Class B, authorized—3,750,000 shares; Issued and outstanding—2,207,394 shares in 2001, 2,228,707 shares in 2000	22	22
Additional paid-in capital	5,339	—
Other	(312)	(702)
Retained earnings	68,551	112,960
Total shareholders' equity	$ 73,700	$ 44,473
Total liabilities and shareholders' equity	$161,340	$158,256

OshKosh B'Gosh shows Accounts Receivable at December 29, 2001, of $25,697 thousand. *Accounts receivable* are the amounts due from customers in payment for goods delivered or services performed by the entity. Because accounts receivable are claims to future cash payments, they are assets. One complication is that not everyone pays their bills. Some have bad luck, while others just refuse to pay. Accounts receivable are assets to the extent that it is probable they will be collected.

OshKosh B'Gosh lists accounts receivable at $25,697 thousand as of December 29, 2001. This figure is net of an "allowance" of $7,075 thousand. The term *allowance* refers to the amount OshKosh B'Gosh expects to be uncollectible. Therefore, we can deduce that customers owe OshKosh B'Gosh $32,772 thousand ($25,697 + $7,075), OshKosh B'Gosh expects to collect $25,697 thousand, and it expects to be unable to collect the remaining $7,075 thousand.

In the United States, most accounts receivable are due in 90 days. Therefore, accounts receivable is a current asset.

Inventories are stockpiles of goods to be used in the entity's operations. OshKosh B'Gosh lists Inventories of $55,429 thousand at December 29, 2001. There are many different types of inventories. Retailers like OshKosh B'Gosh typically have inventories of merchandise available for sale to customers. The Red Cross maintains an inventory of blood for use in emergencies. Manufacturers have inventories of raw materials used in making products. Products that are in various stages of manufacture are called work-in-process. Finished goods inventory is goods awaiting sale and delivery to customers. Inventories are assets to the extent that it is likely that they will be sold, thus generating a benefit. Inventories that contain damaged goods or items that are or may become obsolete are less likely to generate future economic benefits.

OshKosh B'Gosh lists Prepaid Expenses and Other Current Assets of $1,607 thousand at December 29, 2001. **Prepaid expenses** are amounts already paid for services or goods to be delivered in the future. For example, a retailer may pay four months' rent in advance. A manufacturer may pay all the money up front for a fire insurance policy that lasts for many periods. A new business may have to give an attorney a retainer from which future fees will be paid. The acid test of whether any of these prepayments is an asset is whether it entitles the entity to a probable future economic benefit. Prepaid rent entitles the retailer to use the store space in the future, an economic benefit. Prepaid insurance gives the manufacturer insurance coverage in future periods an economic benefit. Prepaid attorney's fees give the new business access to legal services in the future, a probable economic benefit. When the prepayment is for a good or service that is to be used within the next year, the prepayment is a current asset.

OshKosh B'Gosh's sales create assets in the form of cash and accounts receivable.

Deferred Income Taxes is the last asset that OshKosh B'Gosh lists in the current assets subcategory—$13,000 thousand at December 29, 2001. Because it is listed under assets, we know that this $13,000 thousand represents future benefits for OshKosh B'Gosh. In fact, OshKosh B'Gosh expects to reap these tax benefits over the next year. These benefits could come in one of two forms. The first is a refund of taxes paid in the past. The second is a reduction in future tax payments. We explore deferred income taxes in detail in Chapter 14.

Three more assets appear on OshKosh B'Gosh's balance sheet: Property, Plant, and Equipment, Deferred Income Taxes, and Other Assets. The fact that these assets are not classified as current assets tells us that OshKosh B'Gosh expects to realize their benefits over a period longer than one year. Sometimes a company will use the label "Noncurrent" or "Long-Term" to separate more clearly its current and **noncurrent assets.** But many companies, like OshKosh B'Gosh, let us infer the category from the presentation.

The first noncurrent asset that OshKosh B'Gosh lists is Property, Plant, and Equipment for $30,001 thousand. **Property, Plant, and Equipment** represents the land,

Noncurrent assets have benefits that are expected to be realized over periods beyond one year from the balance sheet date.

buildings, manufacturing machines, delivery vehicles, and so on, that entities hold for use in the business over several periods. They are assets to the extent they will be used to an entity's economic advantage. Land may be developed or sold. Buildings may provide office space for administrators, room to display goods, or space to manufacture products. Manufacturing machines make goods to be sold. Delivery vehicles convey goods to customers. However, space provided by buildings can become useless, land polluted, and manufacturing machines outdated. To be considered an asset, Property, Plant, and Equipment must generate a probable economic benefit for the entity. An outdated machine may not be an asset; it may just be junk.

OshKosh B'Gosh next lists Deferred Income Taxes of $4,300 thousand. This asset originates in the same manner as the deferred taxes already discussed. However, the benefits represented by this amount of $4,300 thousand are expected to be realized more than one year from December 29, 2001. Therefore, these deferred taxes are not current assets and must be listed separately from the $13,000 thousand in deferred income taxes listed in the current assets.

Like many firms, OshKosh B'Gosh's balance sheet includes the account *Other Assets*. In practice, most firms carry far too many accounts to list each account separately. Actual individual accounts are added together to form the balance sheet accounts we see. For example, OshKosh B'Gosh likely keeps several different inventory accounts (such as, perhaps, Children's Clothing, Adult Casual Clothing, Work Wear, etc.). For reporting purposes, OshKosh B'Gosh groups these different inventory accounts together and displays the total as Inventories on the balance sheet. The balance sheet item labeled Other Assets is a combination of all the remaining accounts OshKosh B'Gosh management deemed not important enough to disclose separately on the balance sheet. Not surprisingly, compared to many of OshKosh B'Gosh's other displayed assets, Other Assets is a small $1,984 thousand as of December 29, 2001.

OshKosh B'Gosh's other assets might include patents, copyrights, and trademarks. *Patents* give holders the right to exclude others from using the patented products or processes. *Copyrights* give holders rights to publish original works of artistic or literary expression. *Trademarks* are legal rights to names or symbols. *Licenses* are legal rights to market products, service specified territories, or use patented products or processes, copyrighted material, or trademarked names or symbols. Patents, copyrights, trademarks, and licenses are assets when it is probable that the rights they convey will be used to the entity's economic advantage.

Rights can be extremely valuable. For example, the U.S. government auctioned the rights to use certain frequencies for wireless telecommunications. The rights are represented by licenses granted by the Federal Communications Commission (FCC). The winning bids in the FCC's auction of licenses totaled $10.2 billion. One company alone, Nextwave Personal Communications, submitted winning bids totaling $4.2 billion.[2]

Asset test:
- *economic benefit*
- *owned or controlled*
- *result of past transaction or event*

To determine whether a given item is an asset, you must ask whether it generates a probable economic benefit for the entity. You must ask whether it is owned or controlled. And you must ask whether it arose from a past transaction or event. One job of accounting is to identify the major types of an entity's assets. Given the many different types of entities, the widely different activities in which they engage, and the variety of items they hold, a useful categorization of the major assets must be found on a case-by-case basis.

Assets: Valuation

A **valuation** is an assignment of a monetary amount.

Market valuation methods are the ways markets assign values.

After identifying an entity's assets, the accountant must decide what monetary amounts to assign them. Assigning a monetary amount is called a **valuation**. It is important to distinguish carefully among the different forms of valuation. **Market valuation methods** refers to the ways markets assign value. For example, auction markets assign values

[2]Edmund L. Andrews, "Big Bidders Win Auction for the Small," *The New York Times*, May 7, 1996, pp. D1 and D10.

Accounting, or **balance sheet, valuation methods** are the ways accountants assign values.

Market value is the value assigned to an item by a market.

Book value is the value assigned to an item by an accountant.

through their rules about who wins an item and how much the winner must pay for it. **Accounting,** or **balance sheet, valuation** refers to the collection of methods that accountants use to assign the values reported in balance sheets.

A value is the result of a valuation. For example, the price of an auctioned item is its **market value** as determined by the auction market. The **book value** of an item is the result of a balance sheet valuation. Sometimes market values and book values are the same, but most often they are not. One of the keys to really understanding accounting information is to understand the relation between market and book values, and we devote significant attention to that in Part III of this text. There we will learn many of the different accounting valuation methods for particular assets.

Several accounting valuation methods are reflected on OshKosh B'Gosh's balance sheet. Cash equivalents, such as amounts held in foreign currencies and short-term investments, are carried at market value. Market value is the amount of cash that would be raised by selling an asset at the available market price. Accounts receivable are valued at expected net realizable value. Expected net realizable value is the amount OshKosh B'Gosh expects to collect from the total it is due. Inventories are valued at the lower of cost or market (the cost to replace them). Some long-term investments are valued at the estimated present value of their future cash flows.[3] Property and equipment are valued at historical cost, less accumulated depreciation. Historical cost is the market price paid for an item when purchased. Accumulated depreciation is the total deduction from the historical cost that takes approximate account of the use of the plant and equipment over time (more about this topic in Chapter 3).

No one answer can be given to the question of what is represented by the values reported on a balance sheet. The accounting process of recording values, however, always starts from the same place. Assets are recorded at cost at the time the assets are acquired. Subsequent deviations from historical cost are adjustments to the recorded values.

Liabilities: Definition

OBJECTIVE:
Learn basic definitions of assets, liabilities, and equities.

A **liability** is "a probable future sacrifice of economic benefits arising from present obligations of an entity to transfer assets or provide services as a result of a past transaction or event."

OBJECTIVE:
Learn to read real company reports.

A **liability** is "a probable future sacrifice of economic benefits arising from present obligations of an entity to transfer assets or provide services as a result of a past transaction or event."[4] Like the case of assets, to an accountant, a liability's economic sacrifices ultimately manifest themselves in future cash flows. Liabilities reduce future cash flows, either directly or indirectly. For example, a bank loan taken out by a business directly reduces future cash flows because it must be repaid with cash. An obligation to fulfill a subscriber's prepaid magazine subscription implicitly reduces future cash flows, because it requires cash outflows to produce and deliver the magazines.

Liabilities: Examples

Current liabilities are liabilities whose expected sacrifice will occur within one year.

Just as we could not list all conceivable assets, it is impossible to list every conceivable liability. Entities enter into too many different kinds of obligations that require the probable future sacrifice of economic benefits to give an exhaustive list. However, some types of liabilities are common to almost all entities. For example, consider the liabilities listed on OshKosh B'Gosh, Inc.'s balance sheet given in Exhibit 2.1. As we did with assets, let's begin with some overall observations. OshKosh B'Gosh's total liabilities at December 29, 2001, were $87,640 thousand. Current liabilities is a major subcategory of liabilities. **Current liabilities** are those liabilities whose economic sacrifice is expected to be made within one year of the balance sheet date. OshKosh B'Gosh has $49,632 thousand of current liabilities at December 29, 2001.

---

[3]A present value calculation weighs interest factors to acknowledge the time value of money (a dollar today has a different economic value than a dollar received sometime in the future). We discuss present values further in Chapter 6.

[4]*FASB Concepts Statement No. 3.*

OshKosh B'Gosh has three kinds of current liabilities: Current Portion of Long-Term Debt, Accounts Payable, and Accrued Liabilities. **Current Portion of Long-Term Debt** is the amount of long-term debt that must be repaid within one year of the balance sheet date. Oshkosh had no such amounts at December 29, 2001, but at December 30, 2000, it had $10,000 thousand of long-term debt it had to repay within one year.

Accounts Payable (sometimes called Trade Payables or Trade Accounts Payable) represents amounts owed to suppliers of goods previously delivered. Accounts Payable are usually due within a fairly short period of time (generally between 30 and 90 days) and carry no explicit interest charges. Discounts for prompt payment are often offered. Accounts Payable are liabilities because they obligate the entity to give up cash and because they arise from the transaction of buying goods from suppliers. OshKosh B'Gosh owed $11,229 thousand to suppliers of goods at December 29, 2001.

Accrued Liabilities, sometimes called Accrued Expenses, are amounts due for taxes, rent, wages, and so forth, that OshKosh B'Gosh owes. Looking at OshKosh B'Gosh's balance sheet, we see that it owes a total of $38,403 thousand for these various items. Looking at OshKosh B'Gosh's various other liabilities, we notice that Accrued Liabilities is the largest liability OshKosh B'Gosh lists on its balance sheet. As such, we might be at least curious as to what sorts of items OshKosh B'Gosh groups together under this name. A skill you will want to become adept at is connecting information you see presented in financial statements with information presented in the **notes to financial statements.** As described in Chapter 1, every set of corporate financial statements is accompanied by a set of explanatory notes. If we seek additional information about something we see in a balance sheet, income statement, or statement of cash flows, a good place to start looking is in the notes.

Looking through OshKosh B'Gosh's notes, we find Note 5 (Exhibit 2.2) is about Accrued Liabilities. It provides a more detailed decomposition of the items that comprise the $38,403 thousand in that account. We see that $7,181 thousand of the $38,403 thousand is Compensation. This categorization means that, at December 29, 2001, OshKosh B'Gosh owes employees $7,181 thousand for work they performed but for which they had not been paid. Workers' Compensation amounts to $8,900 thousand, which is actually payments due to cover insurance for employees injured on the job. (You would only know what *workers' compensation* means if you have some experience with payroll terms.) The last component of the $38,403 thousand is $17,140 thousand, labeled simply "Other" in Note 5.

Notes to financial statements contain vital information.

Exhibit 2.2

OshKosh B'Gosh, Note 5 to Consolidated Financial Statements

OshKosh B'Gosh, Inc. and Subsidiaries
Note 5 to Consolidated Financial Statements
(dollars in thousands)

Note 5. Accrued liabilities

A summary of accrued liabilities follows:

	December 29, 2001	December 30, 2000
Compensation	$ 7,181	$ 6,648
Workers' compensation	8,900	9,000
Income taxes	5,182	8,375
Other	17,140	15,919
Total	$38,403	$39,942

Unfortunately, OshKosh B'Gosh's annual report provides no further information that leads to our understanding the components of OshKosh B'Gosh's accrued liabilities. This lack of information illustrates the discretion firms have in disclosing information in annual reports. No specific GAAP or SEC rules require that OshKosh B'Gosh provide a specific level of detail in its disclosures. Some firms provide more detail about the components of accrued liabilities, while other firms provide less. As financial statement readers, we must live with whatever level of detail OshKosh B'Gosh decides to provide.

Although OshKosh B'Gosh does not list them, we can define some other commonly found current liabilities. ***Short-term borrowings*** are monetary amounts due for the repayment of bank loans, notes payable, and other commercial paper that must be paid within one year. They are liabilities because they obligate the entity to give up cash and because they arise as part of the transaction of accepting cash from the lender. Bank loans, notes payable (written promises to pay), and commercial paper (notes issued by corporate borrowers) carry interest charges; that is, the total amount that must be repaid exceeds the amount borrowed.

Unearned revenues are the monetary amounts received by an entity that accepts up-front payments of cash in exchange for future delivery of its products. For example, you buy a three-year subscription to *Sports Illustrated*. Acceptance of your subscription obligates *Sports Illustrated* to either deliver magazines to you for the term of the subscription or to refund a portion of the amount you paid. Delivery of magazines requires the sacrifice of economic resources to compile, print, and transport the magazine. Your subscription is a liability to *Sports Illustrated* because it requires a probable future sacrifice of resources and because it arises from the transaction of taking your cash in exchange for promising to deliver a magazine. It is called unearned revenue because it carries an obligation—delivery of the magazine discharges the obligation and converts the liability into recognized revenue. The amount of your subscription becomes earned revenue to *Sports Illustrated* as it fulfills its obligations under the terms of your subscription.[5]

Dividends are payments that corporations make to their shareholders. Corporations are not legally obligated to pay dividends. Most do pay dividends, but some do not. The shareholders of a corporation that pays dividends usually expect the corporation to continue to do so. Dividends are one way that shareholders receive a return on their investments. It involves a past transaction, the purchase of shares in a corporation, and the probable sacrifice of future economic benefits, the payment of cash by the corporation. Dividends do not become a liability, however, until an obligation to pay arises, which occurs when the corporation's directors vote to pay the dividend. Therefore, ***dividends payable*** is the amount owed by the corporation to shareholders when dividends declared by the board of directors are yet to be paid. The total future stream of dividends, although expected by shareholders and a probable sacrifice of economic benefits, is not a liability because it is not yet an obligation. It will be one in the future when and if the board of directors formally declares that dividends will be paid.

Returning to OshKosh B'Gosh's balance sheet, we see that it lists two **noncurrent or long-term liabilities**: *Long-Term Debt* and **Employee Benefit Plan Liabilities**. The $24 thousand for long-term debt represents amounts borrowed by Oshkosh that will be repaid over a period of years. The $14,008 thousand obligation for employee benefit plans represents sacrifices that OshKosh B'Gosh must make more than one year from December 29, 2001, for pensions, health care benefits in retirement, and other benefits that its employees earned. For example, OshKosh B'Gosh, like most companies in the United States, offers its employees a pension plan that provides for cash payments during retirement. Depending on the terms of the plan, obligations to make probable future economic sacrifices can arise and must be reported on the balance sheet.[6]

OshKosh B'Gosh lists only two noncurrent liabilities, but many firms have more. For example, many firms accrue liabilities associated with warranties and bonds. ***Warranties*** are rights held by purchasers of a company's products to get damaged or malfunctioning

Noncurrent or **long-term liabilities** are liabilities whose expected sacrifice will occur after one year.

---

[5]We take up the concept of revenue and the process of measuring it in Chapter 3.

[6]Pensions and postretirement benefits other than pensions (e.g., health care benefits received in retirement) are complicated areas of accounting. Some of the complication stems from the complexity of pension and benefit plans. However, much of the complexity stems from the accounting process itself. GAAP in these areas contain many special features that affect the recording of assets and liabilities. We examine these in greater detail in a later chapter.

products repaired or replaced. Entities usually offer warranties to provide assurance about the quality of their products. Some individual units of product break during the warranty period. Some warranty repairs are more expensive than others. Because warranties arise from the terms of a sales transaction, warranties payable are liabilities to the extent that they will result in the probable future sacrifice of economic resources to fulfill their terms.

Bonds are financial instruments an entity uses to raise money. They promise payment of cash in the future from the issuer. Bonds payable are the amounts due to purchasers of bonds, issued by the entity, under the terms of the bonds. They represent obligations to give up cash (an economic benefit) arising from the past transaction of selling the bonds (a form of borrowing). Bonds payable are liabilities.

To determine whether a given item is a liability, you must ask whether it requires a probable future sacrifice of an economic benefit. You must ask whether it is an obligation. And you must ask whether it arises out of a past transaction or event. As with assets, one job of accounting is to identify the major types of an entity's liabilities. Given the many different types of entities, the widely different activities in which they engage, and the variety of obligations they have, a useful categorization of the major liabilities must be found on a case-by-case basis.

Liability test:
• probable sacrifice
• obligation
• result of past transaction or event

Liabilities: Valuation

As with assets, assigning monetary amounts to identified liabilities is called *valuation*. Markets are available for some liabilities, such as the bonds issued by large corporations. The market values of such liabilities are the prices at which they trade. Fewer accounting, or balance sheet, valuation processes are required for liabilities than for assets. For example, the book value of OshKosh B'Gosh's accounts payable, $11,229 thousand on December 29, 2001, is the amount that OshKosh B'Gosh expects to pay to settle these obligations. A more complicated process leads to the $14,008 thousand listed for employee benefit plan liabilities. Because these sacrifices will occur far in the future, consideration of the time value of money is part of the accounting valuation process for these items. We explore the time value of money in Chapter 6.

Equities: Definition

OBJECTIVE:
Learn basic definitions of assets, liabilities, and equities.

Total equity is the difference between total assets and total liabilities.

Total equity is the difference between total assets and total liabilities. To the extent that assets are valued at the present value of future economic benefits and liabilities are valued at the present value of obligations to sacrifice economic benefits in the future, equity is the net benefit left over for the owners of the entity. No owners are involved if the entity is a not-for-profit organization, and the difference between total assets and total liabilities is the net amount of resources available for use in accomplishing the entity's mission. In practice, equity arises from a number of sources. One source is the contributions of owners. Recall the accounting identity:

$$\text{ASSETS} = \text{LIABILITIES} + \text{EQUITY}$$

OBJECTIVE:
Learn to read real company reports.

When owners provide assets to the entity, no obligations are created. To preserve the identity, equity must increase. For instance, if the owners contribute $100 thousand in the form of stock, then cash (asset) would increase by $100 thousand and common stock (equity) would increase by $100 thousand. If the entity's operations generate economic benefits (assets) in excess of the economic obligations incurred (liabilities), equity increases. As we will see in Chapter 3, the income statement is aimed at explaining increases in equity that result from the entity's operation.

Equities: Examples

Classifying different types of equity is a major emphasis of the equity section of the balance sheet. One objective is to separate the equity that arose from contributions from owners from the equity that arose from net assets generated through the entity's operations.

Owners contribute assets using many different types of equity. For example, ***common stock*** is the primary financial instrument that corporations use for signifying ownership in the corporation. The owner of common stock is entitled to vote on major corporate decisions, such as whether to sell the firm in a takeover attempt, whether to retain or replace existing management, how to structure executive compensation, and who should serve on the board of directors. The owners of common stock also have a residual claim on the assets of the firm; that is, if the firm is liquidated, the common shareholders receive what is left after all the entity's other obligations are settled.

Some firms, such as OshKosh B'Gosh, establish different classes of common stock, where the different classes can exercise different voting rights and/or different rights regarding the receipt of dividends. OshKosh B'Gosh's $100 thousand of Class A common stock and $22 thousand of Class B common stock as of December 29, 2001, indicates that, at some point(s) in the past, OshKosh B'Gosh issued stock with a total par, or stated, value of $122 thousand ($100 + $22). We could look at the notes to the financial statements to learn more about the features that differentiate OshKosh B'Gosh's two classes of common stock.

OshKosh B'Gosh issued common stock for more than its par value. The excess of the amount raised over par value is the $5,339 thousand in ***Additional Paid-In Capital (APIC)***. The par value, and therefore the additional paid in capital, presents no real significance in the United States. In some countries, such as Norway, the par value plays a role in determining whether dividends to common shareholders can be legally paid.

Preferred stock is another instrument that corporations use to raise contributions from owners. The owner of preferred stock typically is not entitled to vote on corporate decisions. If the firm is liquidated, preferred shareholders receive the stated value of their shares. In addition, the preferred stock may contain a variety of dividend provisions. OshKosh B'Gosh's balance sheets tell us that OshKosh B'Gosh completed the legal and regulatory requirements necessary to issue preferred stock, but had not actually issued any as of December 29, 2001.

The preferred stock, common stock, and additional paid-in-capital accounts reflect the contributions of owners. The final account on OshKosh B'Gosh's balance sheet is **Retained Earnings**, which reflects equity generated from operations. The qualifier *Retained* tells us that Retained Earnings represents net assets generated from operations but not yet distributed to owners. The balance in OshKosh B'Gosh's Retained Earnings was $68,551 thousand at December 29, 2001.

Examples: Concluding Remarks

We presented several examples of assets, liabilities, and equities. Be aware that the discussion so far by no means provides a complete list of the assets, liabilities, and equities you will encounter on balance sheets. Firms in other industries, by the nature of their business, generate assets and liabilities that don't exist for OshKosh B'Gosh. Also, not all firms refer to the same assets, liabilities, and equities by exactly the same name. For example, *short-term investments* might be labeled *securities held* by another firm. However, the structure of the balance sheet provides a thread of reporting commonality. All balance sheets are structured with an asset section. We can rest assured that someone decided, be it management or the FASB, that the items we see listed as assets generate future cash inflows, either by themselves or in combination with other assets. Similarly, all balance sheets, provided the firm has liabilities, contain a liability section, which includes items expected to generate future cash outflows. It is left to financial statement readers to make their own assessments about the magnitude and probability of these future cash inflows and outflows. We take up this subject in considerable detail in later chapters, but for now offer Figure 2.1 as a general overview of the structure of a balance sheet.

Figure 2.1

Balance Sheet Classifications

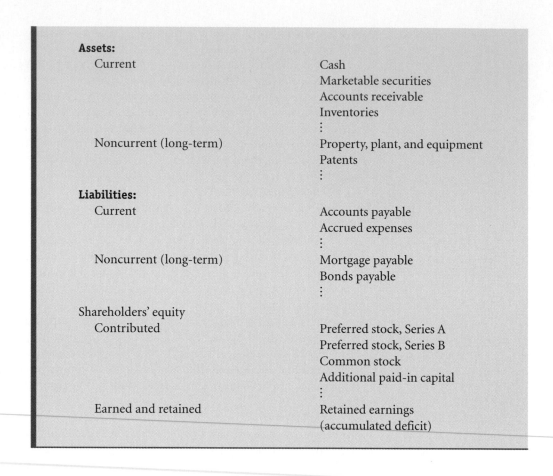

Assets:	
Current	Cash
	Marketable securities
	Accounts receivable
	Inventories
	⋮
Noncurrent (long-term)	Property, plant, and equipment
	Patents
	⋮
Liabilities:	
Current	Accounts payable
	Accrued expenses
	⋮
Noncurrent (long-term)	Mortgage payable
	Bonds payable
	⋮
Shareholders' equity	
Contributed	Preferred stock, Series A
	Preferred stock, Series B
	Common stock
	Additional paid-in capital
	⋮
Earned and retained	Retained earnings
	(accumulated deficit)

Balance Sheet Construction: Using the Accounting Identity

OBJECTIVE:

Learn to analyze transactions in terms of their effects on balance sheet accounts.

The basic structure of balance sheets and the examples of assets, liabilities, and equities we saw in the previous section give us the foundation we need to go deeper into the construction of balance sheets. Our primary aim is to enable you to better understand and analyze financial statements. Understanding and analyzing financial statements involves making inferences—basically working backward from financial statements into what economic events led to them. Experience indicates that it is best to begin learning this process by working through some examples "front to back," which means starting from some transactions and events and constructing the resultant financial statements. In this section, we illustrate the basics of the construction and interpretation of balance sheets through a series of hypothetical transactions and events. It also serves to identify more commonly used balance sheet accounts and terms.

An Example: Websell

Bob and his cousin, Betsy, form Websell Corporation to develop and market software over the Internet and supply Internet consulting services. Bob and Betsy realize they must have office space, some computers, and other miscellaneous items before operations can begin. At this point, however, the *entity*, Websell, has no cash. In fact, we can prepare a simple initial balance sheet for Websell relying on the accounting identity.

$$\text{ASSETS} = \text{LIABILITIES} + \text{EQUITY}$$
$$0 \quad = \quad 0 \quad + \quad 0$$

As an entity, Websell has nothing yet. Even though Bob and Betsy, as individuals, may have bank accounts, cars, car loans, and other assets, the entity Websell does not.

The legal and tax systems may not make a distinction between Websell and Bob and Betsy, but for financial reporting purposes, they are to be distinguished. We will prepare the balance sheet, and other financial statements, from the perspective of the separate entity, Websell, which will be *owned* by Bob and Betsy.

Bob and Betsy decide to **incorporate** Websell. This move establishes Websell as a separate entity recognized by the U.S. legal system. Incorporation comes with a number of implications. Among the most important is that, as a separate legal entity, Websell's owners cannot be held legally liable for its debts. In other words, Bob and Betsy cannot be held financially responsible for money borrowed by the entity Websell. They decide to split ownership of Websell equally. On January 1, 2004, they each contribute $500,000 cash to the business.

In the United States, ownership rights to business entities are referred to as **stock.** Bob and Betsy now each own half of the stock of Websell. When no special ownership rights (such as special voting privileges) are attached to stock, it is referred to as common stock. As already discussed, owners of common stock hold residual claims on the assets of the firm; that is, if the firm is liquidated, the common shareholders receive what is left after all the entity's other obligations are settled. In this example, Bob and Betsy own this residual claim.

Now the entity, Websell, has $1,000,000 cash at its disposal. That $1,000,000 came from somewhere, specifically, from Bob and Betsy, the owners. They are Websell's **equity holders (shareholders, stockholders, residual owners, residual claimants, stakeholders).** It simply means they own the rights to whatever Websell has. The accounting identity reflects both Websell's $1,000,000 in cash and that owners contributed it.

> **Equity holders, shareholders, stakeholders, stockholders, residual owners,** and **residual claimants** all refer to the holders of the common stock of a corporation.

$$\text{ASSETS} \quad = \text{LIABILITIES} + \quad \text{EQUITY}$$
$$\$1{,}000{,}000 = \qquad 0 \qquad + \$1{,}000{,}000$$

At this point, we can construct a simple balance sheet (shown in Exhibit 2.3).

Exhibit 2.3

Websell, Inc. Balance Sheet

Websell, Inc. Statement of Financial Position as of January 1, 2004 (amounts in thousands)			
ASSETS		**LIABILITIES**	
Cash	$1,000		
		Total liabilities	$ 0
		EQUITY	
		Common stock	$1,000
		Total equity	$1,000
Total assets	$1,000	Total liabilities & equity	$1,000

It is important to note two things at this point. First, "Cash" and "Common Stock" are both referred to as **accounts.** The term *account* is not synonymous with a bank account. For accounting purposes, an account is simply a dollar amount that represents something. For example, Websell's account Common Stock represents the dollar amount contributed to Websell by the owners. Websell's account Cash represents the $1,000,000 cash owned by Websell. That $1,000,000 might be distributed across several different bank accounts at several different banks. It might also be one thousand $1,000 bills stuffed in a drawer. The point is, balance sheet accounts are essentially mental constructs used to organize an entity's resources and obligations.

Second, notice that the heading on Websell's statement of financial position, or balance sheet, includes the phrase, "as of January 1, 2004," because Websell has $1,000,000 cash on January 1, 2004. Other transactions and events can cause Websell to have a different amount of cash at a different date. Balance sheets are essentially lists of an entity's resources and obligations. By their nature, resources and obligations exist at a point in time. Thus, accountants carefully identify at what point in time the entity's resources and obligations were measured.

Continuing, Bob and Betsy decide Websell will borrow some money. As we explained earlier, borrowing, or obtaining **credit financing,** takes on many forms. In this particular instance, on January 2, 2004, Websell opts to issue bonds, receiving $2,000,000 cash. The bonds pay 6% interest annually (on January 2 of each year). They fall due on January 2, 2010.

Let us reexamine the accounting equation and construct a balance sheet as of January 2, 2004.

$$\text{ASSETS} = \text{LIABILITIES} + \text{EQUITY}$$
$$\$3,000,000 = \$2,000,000 + \$1,000,000$$

The new balance sheet is shown in Exhibit 2.4.

Exhibit 2.4

Websell, Inc. Balance Sheet

Websell, Inc.
Statement of Financial Position as of January 2, 2004
(amounts in thousands)

ASSETS		LIABILITIES	
Cash	$3,000	Bonds payable	$2,000
		Total liabilities	$2,000
		EQUITY	
		Common stock	$1,000
		Total equity	$1,000
Total assets	$3,000	Total liabilities & equity	$3,000

Notice that the $2,000,000 borrowed affected Websell's balance sheet in two ways. First, the cash account increased by $2,000,000. Second, because the $2,000,000 must be repaid in the future, liabilities (Bonds Payable) increased by $2,000,000. Websell now has $3,000,000 cash, as indicated by the left side of the accounting identity. The right side tells us where that $3,000,000 came from. Creditors contributed $2,000,000. Owners contributed $1,000,000.

The notion of the owners as residual claimants is more apparent now. The owners claim Websell's residual assets. In other words, if Websell were **liquidated** (i.e., broken up and appropriate amounts distributed to creditors and owners) on January 2, 2004, bondholders would receive $2,000,000. Anything left (in this case, $1,000,000) would go to the equity holders, Bob and Betsy.

Liquidation is the selling of all of an entity's assets and distributing them to debtors and residual claimants.

Websell begins acquiring productive assets. We place each event in the context of the accounting identity. Consistent with common accounting practice, we show negative numbers in parentheses. We also show the incremental effect of each transaction on the balance sheet identity; that is, we indicate which assets, liabilities, and equities change as a result of the particular transaction. (Change will be denoted by delta, Δ.)

On January 3, Websell buys computers and office equipment for $300,000. Computers and office equipment are considered assets (property, plant, and equipment) because they will be used to generate cash flows in future periods.

On January 3, 2004, Websell purchases computers and equipment for $300,000 cash.

ΔAssets		=	ΔLiabilities	+	ΔEquities
Cash	$(300,000)				
Property, Plant, and Equipment	300,000				
	0	=	0	+	0

On January 3, Websell prepays $75,000 for one year's rent on office space. Prepaid items are considered assets. Essentially, Websell is buying the right to use the office space for one year. Again, the office space will be used to generate cash flows during that year. Thus, prepaid rent is an asset to Websell.

On January 3, 2004, Websell prepays $75,000 rent for one year.

ΔAssets		=	ΔLiabilities	+	ΔEquities
Cash	$(75,000)				
Prepaid Rent	75,000				
	0	=	0	+	0

On January 4, 2004, Websell establishes a business account at OfficeMax™. The account allows Websell to buy up to $10,000 of merchandise on credit. Websell has 90 days to pay any purchases on account. Websell buys $2,000 of office supplies on account on January 5, 2004.

On January 5, 2004, Websell purchases $2,000 of merchandise on credit.

ΔAssets		=	ΔLiabilities		+	ΔEquities
Supplies	$2,000		Accounts Payable	$2,000		
	$2,000	=		$2,000	+	0

Notice that we made no balance sheet recognition of the $10,000 credit line, because gaining approval for $10,000 of credit does not closely enough match our definition of a liability. Recall that our definition of a liability is a future cash outflow resulting from a past event. As of January 4, Websell has no obligation to surrender cash in the future. The agreement simply allows Websell to purchase up to $10,000 worth of supplies without paying cash immediately. Thus, it incurs no liability as of January 4, 2004. On the fifth, however, Websell gets some supplies under the agreement. Now Websell has an obligation to surrender cash in the future, $2,000 within 90 days to be exact. Assets increase by $2,000 because Websell hopes to use those supplies to generate cash (i.e., the supplies are an asset).

On January 7, 2004, Websell pays $1,000 on its account at OfficeMax. This payment satisfies part of Websell's obligation to OfficeMax. Thus, the liability for Accounts Payable declines. The transaction also reduces Cash.

On January 7, 2004, Websell pays $1,000 of the account payable.

ΔAssets		=	ΔLiabilities		+	ΔEquities
Cash	$(1,000)		Accounts Payable	$(1,000)		
	$(1,000)	=		$(1,000)	+	0

At this point, it is useful to construct a new balance sheet (Exhibit 2.5). We add new asset and liability accounts since the last balance sheet, but the accounting identity remains intact.

The balance sheet captures the cumulative effect of all transactions up to the date of the balance sheet. For instance, the cash balance of $2,624,000 can be explained as follows: $1,000,000 from common stock investment of owners + $2,000,000 from sale of bonds −

Exhibit 2.5

Websell, Inc. Balance Sheet

Websell, Inc.
Statement of Financial Position as of January 7, 2004
(amounts in thousands)

ASSETS		LIABILITIES	
Cash	$2,624	Accounts payable	$ 1
Supplies	2	Total current liabilities	$ 1
Prepaid rent	75		
Total current assets	$2,701	Bond payable	2,000
		Total liabilities	$2,001
Property, plant, and equipment	300		
		EQUITY	
		Common stock	$1,000
		Total equity	$1,000
Total assets	$3,001	Total liabilities & equity	$3,001

$300,000 used to purchase equipment − $75,000 to pay for prepaid rent − $1,000 paid to supplier. Similarly, the Accounts Payable total of $1,000 is the $2,000 original obligation reduced by the $1,000 payment. All other accounts include only the effect of one transaction. As expected, the balance sheet is still in balance (assets of $3,001,000 equal liabilities of $2,001,000 plus equity of $1,000,000).

Websell now has several assets. They total $3,001,000. Websell obtained $2,001,000 of financing for these assets from creditors (which means Websell owes $2,001,000). The remaining $1,000,000 of financing was obtained from owners. Put another way, if Websell were liquidated on January 7, 2004, $2,001,000 of its assets would be distributed to creditors, and the remaining $1,000,000 would be distributed to Bob and Betsy.

The format clearly separates probable future economic benefits (assets) from probable future economic sacrifices (liabilities). Short-term (current) and long-term assets and liabilities are clearly distinguished. These distinctions should help the reader see important facts about the economic status of Websell.[7]

In this section, we looked at how balance sheets reflect basic transactions. To this point, we only considered transactions where the entity either obtains financing or acquires productive resources. In the next chapter, we consider how balance sheets are affected by transactions and/or events that use productive resources. In the next section of this chapter, we discuss some techniques accountants use to aid in the preparation of balance sheets and other financial statements. However, you will also likely find these techniques invaluable in analyzing and interpreting financial statement information.

Review Questions

1. Define assets, liabilities, and equities. Give an example of each. How are assets valued? How are liabilities valued?

[7]For example, it is readily apparent that Websell has a lot of cash, few long-term assets, and generated most of its assets through borrowing and issuing common stock. Websell is liquid, meaning it can quickly generate cash in excess of that required to pay its debts, but has not established that it will be profitable. Profitability depends on the ability to generate assets in excess of resources consumed through operations.

2. Explain what is meant by the entity concept.

3. A company signs a 10-year employee contract with a vice president. The salary is $500,000 per year, guaranteed. Is this contract an asset? Would it appear on the balance sheet? Explain.

4. A company purchased a parcel of land 10 years ago at a cost of $300,000. The land was recently appraised at $900,000. At what value is the land carried in the balance sheet? How does the appraisal affect the carrying value in the balance sheet?

T-Accounts, Debits, and Credits

OBJECTIVE:

Learn to use debits, credits, and T-accounts to analyze transactions and construct balance sheets.

The operations of an entity that required only a few transactions would probably present no reason to look beyond the basic accounting identity to keep track of the transactions and balances in various accounts. Even moderate-sized entities, however, engage in millions of transactions per year involving hundreds of accounts.[8]

For purposes of recording the effects of a transaction on the balance sheet accounts, accountants derived a system of *T-accounts* and rules to make entries to the accounts so that the basic accounting identity is preserved. For example, consider the asset cash. Graphically, the cash account can be represented as a large T with the name Cash written on the top. When analyzing transactions, the convention we will adopt is to always show increases in Cash on the left-hand side of the T-account, and to show decreases in Cash on the right-hand side of the T-account. That way we don't have to worry about minus signs or brackets to show decreases.

Cash	
Increases	Decreases

Accountants call entries on the left side *debits* and entries on the right side *credits*. In the recording of accounting transactions there is no meaning for debit (abbreviated Dr), other than left, or for credit (abbreviated Cr), other than right. If we use the following rules to record changes in T-accounts, we will get a handy result:

Assets		**Liabilities/Equities**	
Increases	Decreases	Decreases	Increases
(Dr.)	(Cr.)	(Dr.)	(Cr.)

That is

Debits (left-side entries) increase assets and decrease liabilities and equities.

Credits (right-side entries) increase liabilities and equities and decrease assets.

These rules imply that any entry with debits equal to credits preserves the balance sheet identity. Also, in any entry that preserves the balance sheet identity debits equal credits. This redundancy gives us an easy way to preserve the accounting identity. For every transaction, we make sure the debits (entries to left-side columns) equal the credits (entries to right-side columns). Total debits must equal total credits for every transaction and for every period. This rule of accounting provides a check on our accuracy.[9]

$$\text{DEBITS} = \text{CREDITS}$$

and

$$\text{ASSETS} = \text{LIABILITIES} + \text{EQUITY}$$

[8]Almost all of these accounts are aggregated into larger groups for purposes of presenting balance sheets, income statements, and statements of cash flows. Good management of the entity's resources and good accounting usually require keeping far more detailed records than are ultimately conveyed in public financial reports.

[9]Unfortunately, these techniques do not catch all possible errors. For example, if we erroneously credit a liability instead of an asset, we preserve the accounting identity and have debits equal credits, but we misstate assets and liabilities. In this case, both assets and liabilities are too high, which means that accountants can never make one mistake, but they can make two!

Both must hold.

You might think, "This method provides a reasonable way to compile accounting information, but I just want to read and analyze financial statements." Do not underestimate the power of these simple techniques. Many times you may wish to determine how a firm's financial statements will change if the firm engages in a particular transaction. Many people find the easiest way to solve this problem is to write down T-accounts for the affected accounts and then enter the appropriate dollar amounts to determine the new balances in those accounts. Many times you may wish to use financial statements to determine the dollar amount of a particular transaction. Many people find that using T-accounts offers the easiest way to solve this problem. Many financial analysts, investment managers, consultants, project directors, budget analysts, and others find T-account analysis to be an important skill.

To illustrate how debits and credits are entered into T-accounts, let's go back and record Websell's previous transactions.

(1) The owners invest $1,000,000 in Websell by purchasing 1,000,000 shares of $1 par common stock. (If the owners paid more than $1,000,000, we would create an account called Paid-In Capital in Excess of Par.)

On January 1, 2004, Bob and Betsy invest $1,000,000 in Websell.

Cash					Common Stock		
Dr.	Cr.				Dr.	Cr.	
(1) 1,000,000						1,000,000	(1)

(2) Websell sells $2,000,000 in bonds.

On January 2, 2004, Websell sells $2,000,000 of bonds.

Cash					Bonds Payable		
Dr.	Cr.				Dr.	Cr.	
(1) 1,000,000						2,000,000	(2)
(2) 2,000,000							

(3) Websell purchases computer and office equipment for $300,000 cash.

On January 3, 2004, Websell purchases computers and equipment for $300,000 cash.

Cash					Equipment		
Dr.	Cr.				Dr.	Cr.	
(1) 1,000,000	300,000 (3)		(3)		300,000		
(2) 2,000,000							

(4) Websell prepays rent in the amount of $75,000.

On January 3, 2004, Websell prepays $75,000 rent for one year.

Cash					Prepaid Rent		
Dr.	Cr.				Dr.	Cr.	
(1) 1,000,000	300,000 (3)		(4)		75,000		
(2) 2,000,000	75,000 (4)						

(5) Websell purchases $2,000 of supplies on credit.

On January 3, 2004, Websell purchases $2,000 of merchandise on credit.

Supplies					Accounts Payable		
Dr.	Cr.				Dr.	Cr.	
(5) 2,000						2,000	(5)

(6) Websell pays $1,000 of the account payable.

On January 7, 2004, Websell pays $1,000 of the account payable.

Cash					Accounts Payable		
Dr.	Cr.				Dr.	Cr.	
(1) 1,000,000	300,000 (3)		(6)		1,000	2,000	(5)
(2) 2,000,000	75,000 (4)						
	1,000 (6)						

Websell T-Accounts (amounts in thousands)

	Cash			Supplies			Prepaid Rent			Equipment	
	Dr.	Cr.		Dr.	Cr.		Dr.	Cr.		Dr.	Cr.
(1)	1,000	300	(3)(5)	2		(4)	75		(3)	300	
(2)	2,000	75	(4)								
		1	(6)	2			75			300	
	2,624										

	Accounts Payable			Bonds Payable			Common Stock	
	Dr.	Cr.		Dr.	Cr.		Dr.	Cr.
(6)	1	2	(5)		2,000	(2)		1,000	(1)
		1			2,000			1,000

Exhibit 2.6

Websell T-Accounts

After all transactions are entered into the T-accounts, the balances in the accounts are totaled and a balance sheet is constructed. Exhibit 2.6 summarizes all of the entries in the T-accounts. The ending balance in individual accounts appears below the double line. In each instance the debits and credits are netted against each other.

The final step, listing and adding the total debits and credits in all of the T-accounts, is called making a ***trial balance*** (Exhibit 2.7).

Exhibit 2.7

Websell Trial Balance

Websell, Inc.
Trial Balance as of January 7, 2004
(amounts in thousands)

ACCOUNT	DR.	CR.
Cash	$2,624	
Supplies	2	
Prepaid rent	75	
Equipment	300	
Accounts payable		$ 1
Bonds payable		2,000
Common stock		1,000
Totals	$3,001	$3,001

Notice that total debits equal the total credits in the trial balance. The account balances can then be copied, in proper format, to generate the balance sheet in Exhibit 2.5. By using debits and credits, we are assured we will end up satisfying the fundamental accounting identity. *This result is true no matter how we define assets and liabilities;* that is, the system of debits and credits can be used with any set of economic definitions and accounting conventions. This accounting identity makes it handy to all users of accounting reports, not just to accountants. For example, we will see that U.S. GAAP typically do not recognize expenditures on research and development as assets, which holds true even though the managers who authorized these expenditures are likely to believe they create future economic benefits. An analyst may use debits and credits to recast U.S. financial statements, assuming expenditures on research and development create assets.

Analyses Using Balance Sheet Information

We can learn some commonly used financial indicators based on what we know about balance sheets at this point. Consider, again, OshKosh B'Gosh's balance sheet (Exhibit 2.1). We know that OshKosh B'Gosh has $161,340 thousand in total assets at December 29, 2001. Because total shareholders' equity is $73,700 thousand, the financing for $73,700 thousand of those assets came from equity holders. The remaining $87,640 thousand ($161,340 − $73,700) came from creditors; it was borrowed, which immediately tells us that OshKosh B'Gosh relies on creditors for most of its financing. In fact, of the total of $161,340 thousand of financing needed, 54.3% comes from borrowing. Using a slightly different take on the same inference, analysts often speak of the ratio of debt financing to equity financing as the **debt-to-equity ratio**. For OshKosh B'Gosh, this ratio is 1.19 (87,640/73,700), meaning that for every dollar of financing supplied by owners, an additional $1.19 is supplied by creditors.

Debt-to-equity ratio = Total liabilities/Total equities

Another question we might ask is, what is OshKosh B'Gosh's ability to meet its short-term credit obligations? History provides many examples of firms that, because of insufficient attention to cash management, found they were unable to pay their immediate bills, even though their long-term prospects were quite positive. The current versus noncurrent balance sheet classifications are useful in this regard. Recall that current liabilities are ones that (generally) will be due within one year of the balance sheet date. OshKosh B'Gosh has $49,632 thousand of such obligations. Current assets are those expected to be converted to cash or some other asset within one year. So a rough guide to OshKosh B'Gosh's ability to pay the $49,632 thousand it owes in the next year is whether it has an equal or greater amount of current assets. OshKosh B'Gosh has $125,055 thousand in current assets.

Working capital = Current assets − Current liabilities

Current ratio = Current assets/Current liabilities

Analysts use at least two ways to combine current assets and current liabilities into indicators of the ability to meet commitments in the near term. The first is to determine their difference: current assets − current liabilities. This difference is called **working capital**. The second is to determine their ratio: current assets/current liabilities. This ratio is called the **current ratio**.

OshKosh B'Gosh has working capital of $75,423 thousand ($125,055 − $49,632) at December 29, 2001. Its current ratio at that date is 2.52 ($125,055/$49,632). The working capital of $75,423 thousand gives us a dollar measure of OshKosh B'Gosh's ability to meet its current liabilities. The current ratio of 2.52 tells us that OshKosh B'Gosh has $2.52 of current assets for every dollar of current liabilities.

These examples show what kinds of information the balance sheet provides us. More information can be gleaned by comparing balance sheet information across time and across companies. We will conduct such exercises later.

Conclusion

This chapter introduced basic economic concepts, used them in creating a balance sheet, and showed how a system of debits and credits can be used to implement them on a transaction-by-transaction basis. We purposely focused our attention on a few simple transactions. The real power of linking the economic concepts with debits and credits comes in other ways. For the accountant, the power comes when a great many transactions must be recorded. For the analyst, the power comes when the transactions become complex. When faced with a complex transaction, you can ask, "What accounting entry should be made to record this transaction?" The accounting entry calls for a set of debits and credits to a specified set of accounts, which in turn requires you to think about the whole of the transaction. If resources were acquired, what was the source? Were obligations also acquired, or was equity increased? If a resource was given up, what was gained? Was another resource increased? Was an obligation lessened? Was equity decreased?

Every transaction always has two sides: what is given and what is received. The accounting identity and the technique of debits and credits always prompt us to think about both sides. To the manager or the analyst, this discipline is important.

In the next chapter, we extend our economic definitions and the system of debits and credits to the income statement. Aside from the concepts we must develop, you will see how the system developed thus far is helpful in keeping the additional records needed to go beyond the balance sheet. The balance sheet is a snapshot. It is a picture of the economic resources and obligations of an entity at a point in time. To get the balance sheet, we look only at the ending balance in each account. The income statement tells us something about how we get from one balance sheet to the next. It is concerned with the trip, not just the destination. Therefore, it is not enough for us just to know the ending balance in our accounts. We must know something about the process of getting from the beginning to the end. Fortunately, the system of debits and credits can help us accomplish this job, too.

Key Terms

accounting valuation methods 27

accounts 33

accounts payable 28

accounts receivable 24

accrued liabilities 28

additional paid-in capital (APIC) 31

asset 23

balance sheet valuation methods 27

bonds 30

book value 27

cash 23

common stock 31

copyrights 26

credit financing 34

credits (right-side entries) 37

current assets 23

current liabilities 27

current ratio 40

debits (left-side entries) 37

debt-to-equity ratio 40

deferred income taxes 25

dividends 29

dividends payable 29

employee benefit plan liabilities 29

entity 22

equity holders (shareholders, stakeholders, stockholders, residual owners, residual claimants) 33

incorporate 33

inventories 25

liability 27

licenses 26

liquidation 34

market valuation methods 26

market value 27

marketable securities 23

noncurrent or long-term liabilities 29

patents 26

preferred stock 31

prepaid expenses 25

property, plant, and equipment 25

retained earnings 31

short-term borrowings 29

stock 33

T-accounts 37

total equity 30

trademarks 26

trial balance 39

unearned revenues 29

valuation 26

warranties 29

working capital 40

chapter 3

© GETTY IMAGES/PHOTO DISC

In this chapter you will learn:

1 Basic definitions of income, revenue, and expense

2 To analyze transactions and their effects on income statement accounts

3 To use debits, credits, and T-accounts to analyze transactions and construct income statements

4 To continue to read actual company reports

Income Statement Concepts: Income, Revenues, and Expenses

Did you ever receive a chain letter asking you to send, say $10, to the person who sent it to you? It also tells you to send the letter on to 10 friends.

After telling you about the awful things that happened to people who break these chains, the letter will try to convince you to go along by pointing out how much money you could make. Just think: After each of your 10 friends sends you $10, you are $90 ahead! What easy money!

Would you really be $90 ahead though? Nothing of value is produced. Money is only shuffled around. The $100 your friends sent you is really a contribution of equity. The same is true for the $10 you sent up the chain. No one really earns any income. In accounting terms, the people who subscribe to these chains are confusing income and capital.

Many financial calamities are disguised forms of chain letters, and they rely on confusing capital contributions with income. One of the latest occurred in Albania in 1997. Fresh from abandoning a Communist regime and inhabiting one of Europe's poorest nations, Albanians sold their apartments and borrowed money from relatives abroad to invest in schemes promising interest rates as high as 25% per month. (That's equivalent to an interest rate of 1,355% per year!) About the lowest rate promised by these schemes was 8% per month, which is equivalent to 152% per year. Early on, these rates appeared real to investors because some were actually paid—from the capital contributions of other investors! Because wealth was not being created, the schemes collapsed. When many Albanians lost all their wealth, the country plunged into turmoil. Widespread arson, looting, and violence caused the Albanian government to impose a nationwide state of emergency in its attempt to restore order.

This chapter focuses on the income statement, and it has two main goals:

1. To explore the economic concepts that underlie the income statement: income, revenues, and expenses

2. To extend the accounting techniques of debits and credits to the measurement of income

The economic concept of income is one of the most powerful and important ideas accountants use in writing the financial histories of organizations. An entity's income for a period is almost always the primary measure of its financial performance. Income plays a major role in the decisions of investors and financial analysts who assign value to the entity's stock, assess its creditworthiness, and evaluate the performance of its management. Income is important, and we will study it in depth in this chapter and throughout the book.

As we did in Chapter 2, we show how debits and credits are used to record transactions as they occur. Because the income statement relates to economic events over a period of time, tracking things as they occur is more important for the income statement than for the balance sheet. It is so important that we will see a whole new set of accounts invented just to record revenues and expenses, which are the components of income. These accounts, called temporary accounts, are used only to measure income and appear only on the income statement. They never appear on the balance sheet.

We begin by defining income, revenue, and expense. We give many examples of revenues and expenses, but as with assets and liabilities, it is impossible to list them all. The activities of the entity affect the exact titles of the revenue and expense accounts that appear on its income statement. We demonstrate how to use debits and credits to record revenues and expenses. We work through a comprehensive example to illustrate how debits and credits are used in measuring income. Along the way, we look at an actual corporate income statement.

Income (Loss)

OBJECTIVE:
Learn basic definitions of income, revenue, and expense.

Income (loss) is the increase (decrease) in net assets resulting from operations over a period of time.

Income is an increase in an entity's net assets resulting from its operations over a period of time. If an entity's operations over a period of time result in a decrease in its net assets, it has a **loss**. Three important pieces make up the definition of income and loss:

- Increase (or decrease) in net assets
- Resulting from an entity's operations
- Over a period of time

We now discuss each of these three parts in detail. First, let us define net assets. We start from the fundamental identity for the balance sheet:

$$\text{ASSETS} = \text{LIABILITIES} + \text{EQUITIES}$$

Net assets are the excess of economic resources over obligations.

Net assets are the excess of the entity's economic resources (assets) over its obligations (liabilities). Rewriting the accounting identity, we see:

$$\text{NET ASSETS} = \text{ASSETS} - \text{LIABILITIES} = \text{EQUITIES}$$

That is, net assets is another name for stockholders' equity.

Now with a definition of net assets in hand, we can explore how net assets increase or decrease over a period. For example, consider an increase in net assets. Net assets increase over a period when the entity increases the gap between its economic resources and its obligations, which can happen in many ways. Obligations could remain fixed and resources could increase; or resources could remain constant and obligations decrease. Both obligations and resources could increase, but resources more than obligations. We will see this scenario is usually the case for growing companies. Finally, both obligations and resources could decrease, with resources decreasing less than obligations.

To see whether net assets increased or decreased over a period, all we need is two balance sheets: one as of the beginning of the period and another as of the end of the period. If the total shareholders' equity increased, we know that net assets increased. We can then look at the assets and liabilities on the two balance sheets to figure out which combination of increases and decreases in the assets and liabilities generated the increase in shareholders' equity.

An increase in net assets over a period is only one of the requirements for income, however. To be income, the increase in net assets must be the result of the entity's operations. "Operations" is a difficult concept to explain. It is easier to see what is *not* operations and define operations as everything else than it is to define operations directly. Here are the things that are not operations: capital transactions with owners. For example, exchanging shares of the entity's common stock for cash is a capital transaction, not operations. It increases net assets by getting the shareholders to put up more money, not by using resources to create value.

Another good example of a capital transaction with owners is the payment of cash dividends. The payment of a cash dividend to shareholders is a capital transaction with owners, not operations. Net assets decrease because cash has been distributed to owners, not used up in operations. Intuitively, the payment of a cash dividend to shareholders is a way of returning to them part of their investment in the entity. It is not the consumption of resources by the entity in carrying out its functions.

The final important factor in the definition of net income is that the increase in net assets occurs over a particular period of time. *Income statements are always presented for an interval of time, be it a month, a quarter, or a year.* In assessing an increase in net assets, we should specify an increase from a beginning point to an end point. Any chopping up of time is artificial, and an accountant or manager must pay careful attention to dates. An income statement is always presented for the period between the dates of two balance sheets; that is, a beginning balance sheet describes the state of net assets at the start of the period, an income statement describes the changes in net assets from operations over the period, and an ending balance sheet describes the state of net assets at the end of the period. The time covered by the accounting history should be free from any "gaps." Figure 3.1 illustrates the time aspects of income statements and balance sheets.

Figure 3.1

Time Aspects of Income Statements and Balance Sheets

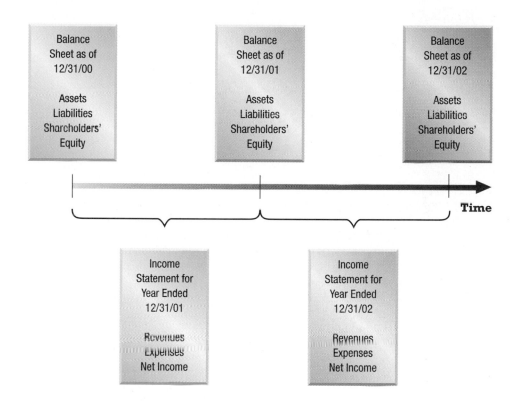

OBJECTIVE:

Learn to read actual company reports.

These points can be seen in CACI International's balance sheets and income statements in Exhibits 3.1 and 3.2 shown on pages 46 and 47, respectively. CACI is an information systems and technology services company. It provides custom software, communications, and network services, imaging, and document management to a variety of governmental and private sector organizations.

CACI's total shareholders' equity (net assets) went from $141,968 thousand on June 30, 2000, to $160,204 thousand on June 30, 2001, an increase in net assets of $18,236 thousand. CACI's income statement reveals the part of this change in net assets that resulted from operations (in fact, CACI titles its income statement a statement of operations). Revenues, direct costs, indirect and selling expenses, depreciation, and amortization all arise from operations. CACI does not pay dividends, but if it did, the dividends would not appear as part of the net income calculation in the income statement. Remember that common stock cash dividends are distributions to owners, not an expense of the company. CACI's income statement shows that operations over the year ended June 30, 2001, increased net assets by $22,301 thousand. Other items decreased net assets to a final total of $18,236 thousand.

Note how the 2001 income statement is "boxed" by the June 30, 2001, and June 30, 2000, balance sheets. To see the link between the income statement for the year ended June 30, 2001, and the June 30, 2000, and June 30, 2001, balance sheets, begin with the observation that net asset increases from operations (net income) are reflected in the

Exhibit 3.1 CACI International Balance Sheet

CACI International, Inc.
Consolidated Balance Sheets
(dollars in thousands, except share data)

ASSETS			LIABILITIES AND SHAREHOLDERS' EQUITY		
	June 30,			**June 30,**	
	2001	**2000**		**2001**	**2000**
Current assets			Current liabilities		
Cash and equivalents	$ 14,842	$ 4,931	Accounts payable	$ 7,532	$ 7,087
Accounts receivable			Other accrued expenses	28,322	23,843
Billed	114,953	98,178	Accrued compensation		
Unbilled	11,038	12,404	and benefits	26,866	24,458
Total accounts receivable	$125,991	$110,582	Income taxes payable	156	1,707
Deferred income taxes	407	235	Deferred income taxes	6,421	5,021
Deferred contract costs	1,456	1,488	Total current liabilities	$ 69,297	$ 62,116
Prepaid expenses and other	8,562	7,372			
Total current assets	$151,258	$124,608	Note payable, long-term	48,888	28,263
			Deferred rent expenses	1,286	1,025
Property and equipment, net	$ 15,685	$ 15,039	Deferred income taxes	116	125
Accounts receivable, long-term	13,686	11,136	Other long-term obligations	4,940	2,500
Goodwill	88,895	75,402	Total liabilities	$ 45,230	$ 31,913
Other assets	12,898	7,024			
Deferred income taxes	2,309	2,788	Shareholders' equity		
Total assets	$284,731	$235,997	Common stock		
			$0.10 par value, 40,000,000		
			shares authorized,		
			15,286,000 and 15,007,000		
			shares issued	$ 1,529	$ 1,501
			Capital in excess of par	24,797	19,716
			Retained earnings	159,298	136,997
			Other equity items	(25,420)	(16,246)
			Total shareholders' equity	$160,204	$141,968
			Total liabilities and		
			shareholders' equity	$284,731	$235,997

retained earnings accounts in the balance sheet. With a few unusual exceptions, the following is true:

> Beginning Retained Earnings
> + Net Income
> − Cash Dividends
> ──────────────
> = Ending Retained Earnings

This point is important to remember because one of the essential skills in reading financial statements is to understand how a number or item in one statement is likely to affect a number or item in another. Figure 3.2 provides a graphical illustration of this point. Please be absolutely certain that you understand it.

Exhibit 3.2

CACI International
Income Statement

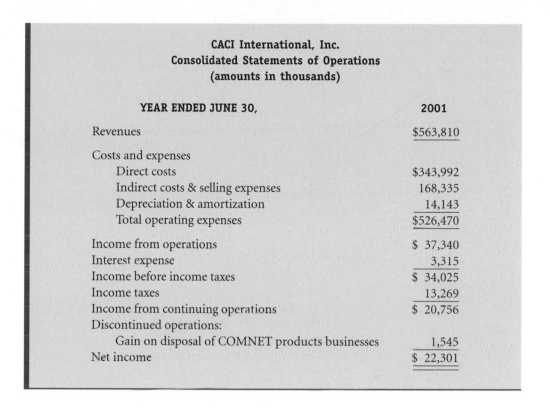

CACI International, Inc.
Consolidated Statements of Operations
(amounts in thousands)

YEAR ENDED JUNE 30,	2001
Revenues	$563,810
Costs and expenses	
Direct costs	$343,992
Indirect costs & selling expenses	168,335
Depreciation & amortization	14,143
Total operating expenses	$526,470
Income from operations	$ 37,340
Interest expense	3,315
Income before income taxes	$ 34,025
Income taxes	13,269
Income from continuing operations	$ 20,756
Discontinued operations:	
Gain on disposal of COMNET products businesses	1,545
Net income	$ 22,301

Figure 3.2 Relationship of Income Statement to Beginning and Ending Balance Sheets

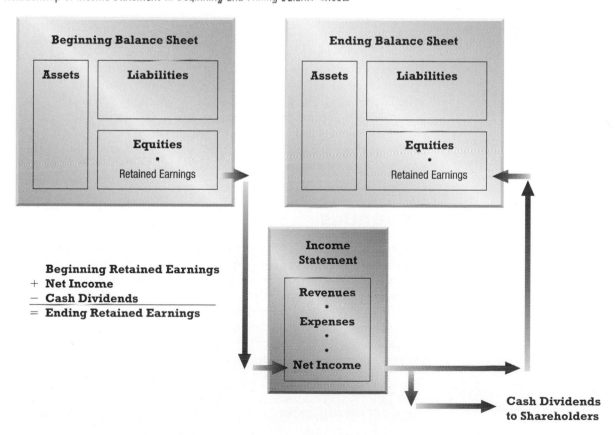

Beginning Retained Earnings
+ Net Income
− Cash Dividends
= Ending Retained Earnings

CACI International (Net Income Explains Change in Retained Earnings)

In the case of CACI International, we see from the income statement and balance sheets in Exhibits 3.1 and 3.2 that the following is true:

Retained Earnings (6/30/00)	$136,997
+ Income (6/30/00–6/30/01)	22,301
= Retained Earnings (6/30/01)	$159,298

The change in retained earnings over the year is exactly explained by net income, which enables us to make the correct inference that CACI did not pay cash dividends to shareholders during the year.

CACI's net income of $22,301 thousand is more than enough to explain the $18,236 thousand increase in its net assets between June 30, 2000, and June 30, 2001. Therefore some reductions must occur somewhere. The remaining amount to be explained is:

$ 18,236	Increase in net assets
(22,301)	Net income
$ (3,065)	Decrease in net assets from sources other than net income

The decrease in net assets to be explained is actually larger than $3,065 thousand. The common stock and capital in excess of par accounts also increased. The increase in these accounts is caused by a capital transaction with shareholders: the issuance of common stock at a value above par. The common stock account increased by $28 thousand:

$ 1,529	Balance on June 30, 2001
(1,501)	Balance on June 30, 2000
$ 28	Increase in Common Stock between June 30, 2000, and June 30, 2001

The capital in excess of par account increased by $5,081 thousand:

$ 24,797	Balance on June 30, 2001
(19,716)	Balance on June 30, 2000
$ 5,081	Increase in Capital in Excess of Par between June 30, 2000, and June 30, 2001

The net income and the changes in Capital in Excess of Par and in Common Stock went up by a total of $27,410 ($22,301 + $28 + $5,081) thousand. Net Assets went up by $18,236 thousand. The difference, $9,174 thousand, is explained by changes in the shareholders' equity account for Other Equity Items. This account is a little tricky for two reasons. First, we see that it is negative, which means it has a debit balance. Second, the entries that give rise to this account are beyond our reach at this point in the book. For now, let's explore further the income statement.

Revenues

CACI's income statement shows the typical breakdown of income into revenues and expenses. Net income is the net result of subtracting the expenses from the revenues.

Revenues are gross increases in net assets resulting from operations over a period of time.

Revenues are increases in assets or decreases in liabilities resulting from operations. Revenues increase income through some combination of increasing assets and decreasing liabilities. A good intuitive definition would be that revenue is the dollar value (monetary measure) received in exchange for the good given up or service provided.

In the Websell example of Chapter 2, suppose that the company billed clients $3,000 for programming services performed.

On March 10, 2004, Websell bills clients for $3,000 of work performed.

ΔAssets		=	ΔLiabilities	+	ΔEquities	
Accounts Receivable	$3,000				Retained Earnings	$3,000
	$3,000	=	0	+		$3,000

In this case an asset, Accounts Receivable, is created when recording the $3,000 of revenue by increasing retained earnings.

On the other hand, suppose Websell initially received a $3,000 retainer from a client prior to the performance of any service. That transaction affects the balance sheet as follows:

On March 10, 2004, cash advance of $3,000 from client.

ΔAssets		=	ΔLiabilities		+	ΔEquities	
Cash	$3,000		Obligation for Service to Client	$3,000			
	$3,000	=		$3,000	+	0	

When the services are finally provided to the client, Websell would record the revenue (increase Retained Earnings) and decrease its obligation to provide service to the client by $3,000.

On April 20, 2004, all of the service is provided and revenue is now recorded.

ΔAssets	=	ΔLiabilities		+	ΔEquities	
		Obligation for Service to Client	$(3,000)		Retained Earnings	$3,000
0	=		$(3,000)	+		$3,000

Recognition is the act of making an entry into the accounts.

The major issue in accounting for revenues is when to recognize them in the accounts. **Recognition** is the act of formally entering an item into the accounting records. An item is recognized when an accountant makes the debits and credits required to account for it. In the first example, Websell recognized the revenue from the consulting assignment when the work was completed and the client was billed. At that point, an accounting entry was made debiting Accounts Receivable and crediting Retained Earnings.

Why did we recognize revenue upon Websell's billing of the client? If Websell is like most organizations, the process of earning revenues is continual and many types of revenue-generating activities are occurring simultaneously. When Websell gets its business into full swing, it is likely to be training programmers and consultants to provide services to future clients, searching for new clients, submitting bids for new work, performing work in various stages for existing clients, and awaiting collection of accounts for jobs completed. These activities will all be happening at the same time, although for any one client they occur in sequence.

Even if we focus on one client, no purely logical time specifies when in the earnings process the revenue should be recognized. Recognizing revenue at the time consultants complete their training would seem premature. Who will be the clients? Will the projects be completed on time? How much will clients pay? How many clients will not pay up?

At the other extreme, recognizing revenue only when clients settle their accounts seems too severe. Most clients can be expected to pay for jobs that Websell completes. Websell probably won't work for clients it believes won't pay for its services.

Revenue Recognition Criteria:
* *Earnings process complete*
* *Exchange taken place*
* *Reasonably certain collection*

This thinking leads us to look somewhere between the training of consultants and the collection of cash from clients. It is a broad territory, and we are unlikely to be able to settle the matter with logic. What we need is a convention. The basic idea of a revenue is that it is an increase in income from operations. Operations are the entity's activities that are aimed at earning a profit. The ***convention for revenue recognition*** is when the earnings process is complete or substantially complete, when an exchange has taken place, and when the amount of the revenue can be measured with some accuracy and the entity is reasonably sure of collection. In the case of Websell's consulting activities, the revenue recognition criteria would be met when the work is completed and the client is billed. At that point, Websell fulfills its end of the bargain. It is simply awaiting the client's fulfillment of its end.

© TERRI MILLER/E-VISUAL COMMUNICATIONS, INC.

Wal-Mart is one of the for-profit firms in the United States that calls its main source of revenue "Sales."

Substantial completion of the earnings process is a practical, but rough, guide as to when to recognize revenue. It is too rough for some specialized circumstances, and accountants use specially tailored rules as the need arises. For example, specialized revenue recognition rules are used for long-term construction projects and mining. However, in most cases substantial completion means when the good or service is delivered to the customer.

An exchange taking place requires an identified buyer. Just because a vacuum cleaner manufacturer produces a cleaner that is packaged and waiting to be sold does not mean that manufacturer has the right to recognize revenue. A buyer of the machine must be found.

Finally, if the good or service is produced and a buyer is found, in order to recognize revenue we must also be reasonably certain of the amount the buyer is to pay us and the date of receipt of the payment.

A great many for-profit firms in the United States call their main revenue "Sales." Merchandising firms, such as Wal-Mart and J.C. Penney, buy goods from suppliers and sell them to retail customers. Manufacturing firms, like the steel producer USX, make products to sell to other firms. In their case, Sales is a good description of the major source of the revenues.

Service firms, such as Accenture and some divisions of General Electric, might list revenues from performance of services as "Sales of Services" or "Total Billings," or simply "Revenues." Financial institutions such as the Harrington Financial Group earn revenues by lending money and charging interest. Their income statements have a line for "Interest Income," which is another name for "Interest Revenue."

Merrill Lynch has revenues from "Commissions," "Asset Management and Portfolio Service Fees," and "Investment Banking." The company charges these fees for the various financial services it performs for customers.

Insurance companies use "Premium Revenue." A company that holds the copyright for a popular novel might use "Royalties." Yale University lists "Tuition Revenue" and revenue from "Grants and Contracts." A landlord collects "Rent." A city collects revenues from "Property Taxes," "Licenses and Permits," and "Fines."

As with assets, liabilities, and equities, too many different sources of revenues and too many differences in account names prevent providing a comprehensive list of all types of revenues.[1] If you read many financial statements, you will often infer what an item is from the way it is treated. For example, interest may be received or paid. If "interest" is listed among other revenues or ends up increasing income, you may be reasonably sure that the amounts represent interest revenue, not interest expense.

Expenses

Economists usually take credit for saying, "There is no such thing as a free lunch." But no one takes this saying more seriously than an accountant. An accountant who recognizes revenues, which are increases in net economic resources, immediately asks what resources were consumed in the process of earning those revenues.

[1]Differences in account names cause major annoyances in international accounting. Even within English-speaking countries, it is often challenging to simply recast a financial report using familiar names. For example, in the United Kingdom, sales revenue is sometimes called "turnover."

Expenses are gross decreases in net assets resulting from operations over a period of time.

Expenses are the assets used or liabilities incurred in the process of carrying out operations. Expenses are the things that decrease income, the costs incurred in the generation of revenues. This amount usually involves some combination of decreasing assets and increasing liabilities. For example, when Websell serves its consulting clients, it is likely to incur several different kinds of expenses. Websell almost surely uses someone's time and skill, for which compensation must be paid. If Websell pays workers in cash, then the asset Cash would be decreased. If Websell has not yet paid workers, it has an obligation to them in the form of Wages Payable. An accountant's instinct would be to make sure obligations to workers were recorded whenever the revenue from the client is recognized.

Matching is the process of making sure all the costs incurred in generating the revenues recognized in a period are taken as expenses in that period.

The process of looking for the expenses corresponding to recognized revenue is called **matching.** Matching involves looking for assets consumed or liabilities incurred in the generation of revenues. If some of Websell's rent was prepaid and then expires during the term of a consulting assignment, it should record Rent Expense associated with the use of these rental rights. Figure 3.3 illustrates the accounting logic that underlies construction of the income statement.

Figure 3.3

Construction of an Income Statement

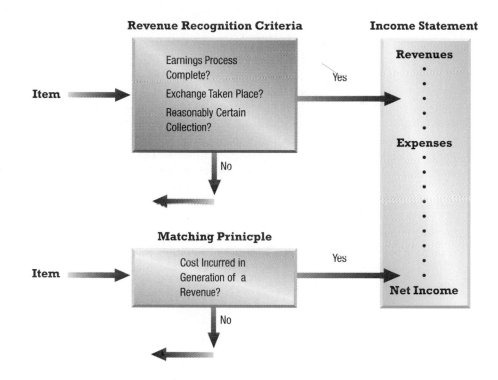

We can find as many different types of expenses as there are assets and payables. Examples of some of the most common types of expenses follow.

For Wal-Mart and J.C. Penney the "Cost of Sales" is the expense associated with the cost of merchandise sold to customers. "Interest Expense" is the cost of using money for a period of time. "Salaries and Wages" is the cost of labor. "Rent Expense" is the cost of renting assets, usually land or buildings such as offices or warehouses. "Depreciation" is the cost of using long-term assets such as Property, Plant, and Equipment.

Recognizing expenses means making the formal accounting entry to record the expiration of an asset or the incurrence of a liability. As with revenue recognition, recognizing expenses rapidly gets into the use of conventions, and for much the same reasons. Firms continually acquire and consume assets, and it may be unclear how the consumption of an asset relates to a particular revenue. For example, many lumberyards sell sand at retail. The sand is purchased by the truckload and dumped into an open area with three walls. Customer orders are filled by shoveling sand out of the area. No accountant can really tell what particular truckload a particular customer's order was filled from. In fact, the customer may purchase sand that was a mixture of several truckloads.

Because it is not possible and not essential to settle the issue of exactly what sand the customer bought, we rely on conventions to match the cost of sales with sales. It is not important in such a situation to match revenues with consumed assets so precisely. What will determine the success of the lumberyard in selling sand is the total revenue it generates from sand sales relative to the total cost of purchasing and stocking sand.[2]

We see many different conventions for recording expenses, and they are somewhat harder to capture in a summary intuitive concept such as "substantial completion of the earnings process." The conventions for expenses vary a lot depending on the type of the expense. Some costs are directly related to an amount of revenue. For example, in many service industries, such as law, consulting, and auditing, clients are directly billed for the professional time spent serving them. The amount the professional is paid for his or her time is therefore directly related to the revenue generated from that client. Matching such costs to revenues is easy. Other costs, however, are only indirectly related to revenue. These costs are usually matched to revenue by using some systematic, yet somewhat arbitrary, method. For example, $1,000 of rent paid in advance for the next two months' use of a facility would be recognized as expense at the rate of $500 per month. Depreciation of the cost of plant and equipment is often straight-line, which is simply a fixed amount each year.

Rent, insurance, and building costs are examples of what accountants call *period expenses.* They are indirectly linked to specific products produced, but are generally necessary to carry on operations during an accounting period.

Some costs are not related to any revenue. For example, Ben and Jerry's might have the freezer break on one of their trucks, and two tons of ice cream might melt. No revenue will be generated by the melted ice cream. Such costs are included in the expenses of the period in which they occur. That is, they are deemed to be period expenses for accounting purposes.

The recognition of revenues and expenses as defined in the preceding sections is at the heart of what is called **accrual accounting.** The definitions of revenue and expense contain no mention of cash flows. The idea is to define terms that truly measure the results of operating performance in dollar terms, but are independent of when the dollars actually flow in and out of the entity. As Figure 3.4 illustrates, the recognition of a

Accrual accounting is any method of accounting that separates the measurement of revenues and expenses from the receipt and expenditure of cash.

Figure 3.4
Accrual Accounting (Revenues and expenses need not coincide with cash flows.)

Cash Flow Before Revenue or Expense Recognition	Income Statement	Cash Flow After Revenue or Expense Recognition
Some revenues are prepayments before good is given up or service provided. For example, Company receives prepaid magazine subscriptions, Company is given a retainer to provide future services.	**Revenues** · · · · · **Expenses** · ·	Payment received after good given up or service provided. For example, normal sales on credit.
Many expenses are "prepaid." For example, the cost of inventory, plant, and equipment, the prepayment of rent or insurance.	· · · · **Net Income**	Many expenses are paid after the expense is recognized. For example, the value of wages or interest already consumed, but not yet paid for.

[2]This point is not always true. In some cases, the measures of the profitability of individual customers are an important concern for management. For example, banks now pay much more attention to the profits they earn from each customer, because they recognize that a relatively small number of customers generates most of their profits.

revenue does not exactly coincide with the timing of the associated cash flow. The same is true for expenses.

Gains and Losses

Usually, the increases and decreases in net assets generated by a transaction are reflected separately on the income statement. For example, suppose that Wal-Mart sells, for $6 each, 50 towels from inventory at a cost of $4 each. Wal-Mart would record revenue of $300 (50 towels × $6 per towel). It would also record an expense, *cost of goods sold,* of $200 (50 towels × $4 per towel). The difference of $100 ($300 − $200) is Wal-Mart's *gross profit* on the sale. Although the net income is ultimately affected by the $100 gross profit, Wal-Mart would show the revenues and expenses separately in its income statement.

Some items on income statements are shown net. Suppose that Wal-Mart sold for $15,000 a delivery truck that had a value in the accounts of $10,000. The effects of this transaction would be shown on the income statement as a net amount, *gain on sale of equipment,* of $5,000 ($15,000 − $10,000). If Wal-Mart had sold the truck for only $7,000, it would have shown a *loss on sale of equipment* of $3,000 ($7,000 − $10,000).

The difference between the sale of towels and the sale of the truck is that Wal-Mart is in the business of selling inventory items such as towels. The sale of the delivery truck is only an incidental transaction in its main business of retailing. The difference between the value of what was received and the book value of what was given up in transactions only incidentally related to an entity's main business are reported net as *gains and losses.* Examples are gains and losses on the sale of fixed assets and the retirement of debt. This convention of reporting gains and losses separately from revenues and expenses lets us distinguish increases and decreases in assets from the main thrust of operations from those caused by transactions only indirectly related to operations.

Review Questions

1. Define revenue and expense. How does one decide to list an item as revenue in an income statement? What is matching?

2. Give an example, not found in the text, of an expense that is paid for in cash in a prior accounting period. In a subsequent accounting period.

3. Give an example, not found in the text, of a revenue that is received in cash in a prior accounting period. In a subsequent accounting period.

4. Explain why it is right to think of an asset as a cost and an expense as an expired cost.

Debits and Credits

OBJECTIVE:
Learn to use debits and credits to construct income statements.

We want to extend the method of debits and credits to recording revenues and expenses. Because revenues and expenses relate to what happens to assets and liabilities over a period of time, the debits and credits we use to record revenues and expenses are related to those used to record assets, liabilities, and equities. Two things are very important to recognize about revenues and expenses and the accounts used to record them. First, unlike balance sheet accounts, revenues and expenses relate to what happens over a period of time. Balance sheet accounts reflect the accounting identity at a given point in time. Revenue and expense accounts are used to accumulate amounts over a period, and then are *closed.* **Closing an account** is the act of making an entry to bring the account's balance to zero. Revenue and expense accounts are closed at the date of each balance sheet.

Closing an account is the act of bringing an account's balance to zero.

Revenue and expense accounts are like simple rain gauges. A simple rain gauge is a container with marks up the side. To measure the rainfall over a day, you would make sure the gauge was empty and set it outside. You would come back 24 hours later and read the amount of rainfall on the side of the gauge. You would then empty the gauge to prepare it for the next day's measurement. Rain gauges start the day empty and they end the day empty.

The same is true of revenue and expense accounts. They begin the period with a zero balance. They accumulate revenues and expenses over the period. Their totals are used to prepare an income statement, and they are closed to ready them to capture the next period's revenues and expenses. Closing the accounts takes their balances to zero. Because revenue and expense accounts are closed and always have zero balances at each balance sheet date, they are called **temporary accounts.** We will go through the process of closing revenue and expense accounts in detail in the Websell example later in the chapter.

Temporary accounts are accounts that are always closed before the preparation of a balance sheet.

The second thing to know about debits and credits for revenues and expenses is how they work. Recall, before we knew anything about revenues and expenses, if an asset was used up by operations in a period, the asset's value in the account would decrease. In order to keep the accounting equation in balance we would decrease retained earnings in the equities. Now expenses are reflecting expirations of assets, and therefore *increases in expenses are debits to* **Retained Earnings.**

Retained Earnings are past earnings not distributed to stockholders.

The easiest way to visualize the rules for making debit and credit entries to revenue and expense accounts is to think of these accounts as sitting right on top of the retained earnings account. (Remember, the change in Retained Earnings is revenues minus expenses for the period, less cash dividends.) As assets are used up they become expenses and create debit entries to Retained Earnings. Temporarily, instead of putting them directly into Retained Earnings, we will debit an expense account instead. It's just the opposite for revenues, which increase assets, and therefore have offsetting credit entries to Retained Earnings. We will temporarily credit a revenue account instead of making an entry directly to Retained Earnings. Figure 3.5 illustrates the rules for the use of debits and credits when making entries to revenue and expense accounts. It should help you visualize that revenue and expense accounts collect information for the construction of the income statement, which along with cash dividend information for the period explains the change in Retained Earnings for the period.

Figure 3.5

Relationship of Revenue and Expense Accounts to the Retained Earnings Account

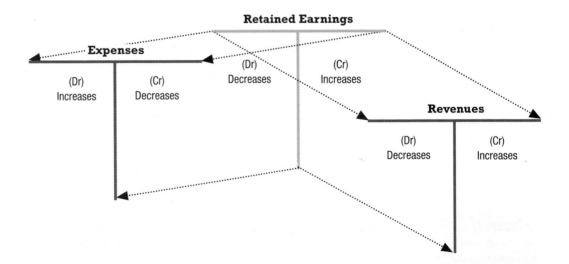

Once we come to the end of the period and have constructed the income statement, we drive the balances in the revenue and expense accounts to zero. Suppose at the end of an accounting period an expense account shows a debit balance of $1,000. After listing the expense on the income statement, the temporary expense account has served its purpose and the balance in it must be driven to zero to prepare it for the start of the next accounting period. We can make the balance in the expense account zero by crediting the account for $1,000. If we then debit the permanent retained earnings account for $1,000, we will have transferred the $1,000 from the expense account to the retained earnings account.

Expense			Expense			Retained Earnings	
Dr.	Cr.		Dr.	Cr.		Dr.	Cr.
1,000			1,000	1,000		1,000	Beginning
				0			Balance

Of course, even though the expense account balance is now zero, the balance in the retained earnings account will be the beginning balance (we've assumed it's a credit balance) reduced by the newly entered $1,000 debit.

In general, through the closing process, revenues end up increasing Retained Earnings, and expenses end up decreasing Retained Earnings. Stated in terms of equity instead of retained earnings, revenues end up increasing equity, and expenses end up decreasing equity.

It will take a bit of practice to completely understand how the debit and credit entries really work. In the next section, we extend the Websell illustration begun in Chapter 2 to include revenue and expense accounts. We will close the revenue and expense accounts and prepare an income statement and a balance sheet.

A Word About Ledgers and Journals

Before continuing the Websell example, we describe the mechanics of the bookkeeping process in more detail. As we have already seen, an account is a place to keep totals of each of the different categories of assets, liabilities, equities, revenues, and expenses. Individual accounts are kept on separate sheets (or in separate computer files) in a book (master file) called a *general ledger.*

In order to maintain a chronological history of the transactions the entity is involved in, each transaction is first recorded in one book of original entries, called a *journal.* A single journal, called a general journal, may be used to record all transactions, or multiple journals to record transactions of specific types. For example, a cash receipts journal (to record all transactions involving a receipt of cash) or a cash disbursements journal (to record all transactions involving an outflow of cash) might be used.

The format to be followed in making an entry to the general journal (*journal entry*) is to first list the exact title of the account to be debited and then the amount of the debit. The account to be credited and the amount of the credit follows on the second line and is indented to the right. Usually a simple explanation of the journal entry is written under the accounts debited and credited. Once the transaction is recorded it is posted to the accounts.

An Example: Continuing Websell

Before we describe and record additional transactions for Websell, we will post to the journal the original six transactions described in Chapter 2. These journal entries are presented in Exhibit 3.3.

Additionally, Websell entered into the following transactions:

7. On January 1, 2004, Websell paid $2,000 for an unlimited-service cellular phone contract for one year.

   Prepaid Telephone (asset) 2,000
       Cash 2,000

8. On January 1, 2004, Websell acquired the rights to various software programs. The software consists of word processors and accounting programs in support of basic office functions, as well as technical packages to be used in developing its own

Exhibit 3.3

Websell Journal (Original
Six Transactions)

DATE	ACCOUNTS	DR	CR
1/1/2004	Cash	1,000,000	
	Common Stock		1,000,000
	(Owners invest $1,000,000 in the business.)		
1/2/2004	Cash	2,000,000	
	Bonds Payable		2,000,000
	(Websell sells $2,000,000 of bonds.)		
1/3/2004	Equipment	300,000	
	Cash		300,000
	(Websell purchases computers and equipment for $300,000 cash.)		
1/3/2004	Prepaid Rent	75,000	
	Cash		75,000
	(Websell prepays rent for one year for $75,000 cash.)		
1/5/2004	Supplies	2,000	
	Accounts Payable		2,000
	(Websell purchases $2,000 of merchandise on credit.)		
1/7/2004	Accounts Payable	1,000	
	Cash		1,000
	(Websell pays $1,000 cash to suppliers of merchandise.)		

products. Websell paid $50,000 cash for these rights that are expected to last for two years.

Software (asset)	50,000	
Cash		50,000

9. On January 1, 2004, Websell pays an Internet access supplier $40,000 cash for rights and services to be received over the next four years.

Internet Access Rights (asset)	40,000	
Cash		40,000

10. On January 1, 2004, Websell pays $100,000 for the rights to copyrighted materials. They are expected to be useful for the next five years.

Copyright Permissions (asset)	100,000	
Cash		100,000

11. On January 1, 2004, Websell purchases, for $15,000, a liability insurance policy providing coverage for 12 months.

Prepaid Insurance (asset)	15,000	
Cash		15,000

12. On February 2, 2004, Websell enters into agreements with various software retailers to distribute Websell products in their stores.

No entry. While the contracts may be legally binding, no exchange has taken place and it is not an accounting transaction. This is an example of an executory contract, an agreement that won't require a payment until the retailers actually do something for Websell. Another example of such a contract would be a labor contract between an employee and a company.

OBJECTIVE:
Learn to analyze transactions and their effects on income statement accounts.

13. On February 5, 2004, Websell completes a consulting engagement for a client and bills the client for $3,000.

Accounts Receivable (asset) 3,000
    Consulting Revenue 3,000

14. On March 31, 2004, Websell pays developers of its Web site $1,200,000 for programming and design services. The Web site becomes operational on April 1, 2004.

Web Site (asset) 1,200,000
    Cash 1,200,000

15. On April 1, 2004, Websell enters into an agreement to provide Internet consulting services to a major corporation. The agreement calls for Websell to receive immediately $65,000 as a prepayment for future consulting services.

Cash 65,000
    Revenue Received in Advance 65,000

16. On May 15, 2004, Websell completes the consulting job. In addition to earning the entire $65,000 it received in advance, Websell bills the client an additional $55,000 for the job.

Revenue Received in Advance 65,000
Accounts Receivable 55,000
    Consulting Revenue 120,000

17. During the 6-month period to June 30, 2004, Websell paid wages of $377,000.

Wages Expense 377,000
    Cash 377,000
    (The above is a summary transaction for perhaps identical weekly transactions of smaller amounts, aggregating to $377,000.)

18. During the 6-month period to June 30, 2004, Websell paid $38,000 for various marketing and distribution expenses.

Marketing & Distribution Expense 38,000
    Cash 38,000

19. During the 6-month period to June 30, 2004, Websell sold software through its Web site and collected the entire sales price of $762,000 in cash. Because Websell wants to track the success of sales from its Web site separately from those in retail outlets, management decides to use separate revenue accounts for sales from these two sources.

Cash 762,000
    Software Sales—Web Site 762,000

20. Websell sells software through its retail distributors and collects the entire sales price of $620,000 in cash.

Cash 620,000
    Software Sales—Retail 620,000

21. Per the distribution agreement, Websell pays its retail distributors a commission of 10% on retail sales.

Commissions Expense 62,000
    Cash 62,000

22. Websell collected $48,000 of its accounts receivable during the 6-month period to June 30, 2004.

Cash 48,000
    Accounts Receivable 48,000

Let's suppose these transactions cover all of Websell's transactions for the first six months of its operations. And, as the boxes indicate, we have made all the necessary entries to the general journal. Now, to gauge the company's progress, management wants to prepare an income statement and a balance sheet as of June 30, 2004.

Preparing financial statements from Websell's records is more complicated than simply adding up the accounts and putting them in good format. Think about the rent that Websell prepaid, its prepaid telephone expenses, and its payment for Internet rights. As of June 30, Websell has used some of the services it bought with these prepayments. That is, some of the assets expired. We need to analyze the accounts to try to find any assets whose expiration we should recognize.

Similarly, Websell may have incurred liabilities that are not yet recorded. For example, its workers might have put in some time for which they have not yet been paid. We should analyze Websell's activities to try to find liabilities whose incurrence we should recognize.

The Process of Adjusting

Adjusting is the process of updating the amounts in the accounts in the absence of a specific transaction.

The process of making entries to record expiration of assets and incurrence of liabilities before making up the financial statements is called **adjusting.** Adjusting is required to make accurate periodic estimates. Not all relevant financial information comes in the form of a transaction. The passage of time itself, as with the expiration of prepaid rent, can cause a change in the economic condition of the entity. Adjusting is the accountant's process of reflecting these changes in the accounts.

Adjusting is a difficult process because we have to search out what needs to be done. In an organization of any size, even one with so few accounts as Websell, we must take a systematic approach to the adjustment process so as to minimize the possibility of omitting something. A good first step in a systematic adjusting process is to compile a trial balance. Remember that a trial balance is just a systematic list of all the accounts along with their balances. We can then go down the trial balance, account by account, and ask ourselves if any adjustments for that account need to be made. An added bonus is that we might catch some accounting errors, either arithmetical mistakes or improperly analyzed transactions. If we label the balance of each account as a debit or a credit, we can check to make sure the total debits we record equal the total credits. This cross-checking ensures at least the possibility that the balance sheet will balance! Exhibit 3.4 contains a preclosing trial balance for Websell as of June 30, 2004. Exhibit 3.5 on pages 60–61 presents all of the T-accounts that result from posting all of the journal entries to the proper accounts. The trial balance is a systematic listing of all these accounts.

We now go through Websell's accounts and record adjustments. For clarity, we use letters instead of numbers to label adjusting entries.

a. Cash and Accounts Receivable require no adjustment.
b. Some of the Prepaid Insurance has expired. Checking the policy we find that it took effect January 1, and the premium covered one year. Therefore one-half of the prepaid insurance has been used. We recognize the use of this economic benefit by decreasing the asset account and increasing an expense.

Insurance Expense 7,500
    Prepaid Insurance 7,500

c. Similarly, the Prepaid Telephone covered one year of service. Instead of using a separate account for telephone expenses, we will record them in Miscellaneous Expenses.

Miscellaneous Expenses 1,000
    Prepaid Telephone 1,000

Exhibit 3.4

Websell Trial Balance
(Unadjusted)

Websell, Inc. Unadjusted Trial Balance as of June 30, 2004		
ACCOUNT	**DR.**	**CR.**
Cash	$2,235,000	
Accounts Receivable	10,000	
Supplies	2,000	
Prepaid Insurance	15,000	
Prepaid Rent	75,000	
Prepaid Telephone	2,000	
Copyright Permissions	100,000	
Software	50,000	
Equipment	300,000	
Internet Access Rights	40,000	
Web Site	1,200,000	
Accounts Payable		$ 1,000
Revenue Received in Advance		0
Bonds Payable		2,000,000
Common Stock		1,000,000
Retained Earnings		0
Software Sales—Web Site		762,000
Software Sales—Retail		620,000
Consulting Revenue		123,000
Wages Expense	377,000	
Commissions Expense	62,000	
Marketing & Distribution Expense	38,000	
Totals	$4,506,000	$4,506,000

d. Prepaid rent was for 12 months.

Rent Expense 37,500
   Prepaid Rent 37,500

e. Some of the supplies have been used. A check of the stockroom reveals that $500 of supplies remain. Instead of using a separate account for supplies expenses, we will record them in Miscellaneous Expenses.

Miscellaneous Expenses 1,500
   Supplies 1,500

f. One-tenth of the Copyright Permissions has lapsed. The expense for this item is recorded as amortization, a fancy name for the expiration of assets that are intangible.

Amortization Expense 10,000
   Copyright Permissions 10,000

g. The software is expected to be obsolete two years after its purchase. Again, we record this as an amortization expense.

Amortization Expense 12,500
   Software 12,500

h. The equipment has a useful economic life of five years. Websell uses straight-line depreciation. Straight-line depreciation allocates a fixed fraction of the asset's cost to expense in each period. Instead of decreasing the balance in the equipment account

Exhibit 3.5 Websell T-Accounts

Websell T-Accounts (amounts in thousands) (June 30, 2004) Preadjustment

ASSETS

	Cash				Accounts Receivable				Supplies				Prepaid Insurance	
	Dr.	Cr.			Dr.	Cr.			Dr.	Cr.			Dr.	Cr.
(1)	1,000	300	(3)	(13)	3	48	(22)	(5)	2			(11)	15	
(2)	2,000	75	(4)	(16)	55									
(15)	65	1	(6)										15	
(19)	762	2	(7)		10				2					
(20)	620	50	(8)											
(22)	48	40	(9)											
		100	(10)											
		15	(11)											
		1,200	(14)											
		377	(17)											
		38	(18)											
		62	(21)											
	2,235													

	Prepaid Rent				Prepaid Telephone				Copyright Permissions				Software	
	Dr.	Cr.			Dr.	Cr.			Dr.	Cr.			Dr.	Cr.
(4)	75			(7)	2			(10)	100			(8)	50	
	75				2				100				50	

	Equipment				Internet Access Rights				Web Site	
	Dr.	Cr.			Dr.	Cr.			Dr.	Cr.
(3)	300			(9)	40			(14)	1,200	
	300				40				1,200	

LIABILITIES

	Accounts Payable				Revenue Rec'd in Advance				Bonds Payable	
	Dr.	Cr.			Dr.	Cr.			Dr.	Cr.
(6)	1	2	(5)	(16)	65	65	(15)			2,000	(2)
		1								2,000
						0				

Websell T-Accounts (amounts in thousands) (June 30, 2004) Preadjustment

EQUITY

Common Stock				Retained Earnings	
Dr.	Cr.			Dr.	Cr.
	1,000	(1)			
	1,000				
					0

REVENUES

Software Sales—Web Site			Software Sales—Retail			Consulting Revenue		
Dr.	Cr.		Dr.	Cr.		Dr.	Cr.	
	762	(19)		620	(20)		3	(13)
							120	(16)
				620				
	762						123	

EXPENSES

Wages Expense			Commission Expense			Mktg. & Distribut. Exp.		
	Dr.	Cr.		Dr.	Cr.		Dr.	Cr.
(17)	377		(21)	62		(18)	38	
	377			62			38	

we will create another account, Accumulated Depreciation, which will keep track of total depreciation to date and will be subtracted from the original value of the equipment account. That way, the original cost of the equipment will always be apparent on the balance sheet.

Depreciation Expense	30,000	
Accumulated Depreciation		30,000

i. The Internet Access Rights were acquired for a four-year period. Six months have elapsed since their acquisition.

Amortization Expense	5,000	
Internet Access Rights		5,000

j. The Web site presents a special problem. To be effective it must be continually updated. These costs will likely be counted as expenses as they occur. The thinking is that they generate the current benefit, not the future benefit, of maintaining viability of the Web site. The $1,200,000 recorded in Web Site, however, represents an initial investment in the site's basic structure and the one-time cost of transforming printed material into electronic form. Websell management expects the basic Web structure to last three years.

Amortization Expense	100,000	
Web Site		100,000

k. An examination of Wages Expense shows that employees earned $33,000 in wages not yet represented in the accounts. These wages will be paid at the next regularly scheduled pay day. We must recognize the value of the work performed in this 6-month period and set up a liability account for its payment.

Wages Expense	33,000	
Wages Payable		33,000

l. Commissions Expense, Marketing and Distribution Expense, Accounts Payable, and Revenue Received in Advance all require no adjustment.

m. We should record the interest on the Bonds Payable, because we used the money for six months. The bonds pay 6% annual interest. For the six months elapsed since their issuance, the bonds accumulated 1/2 of 6% of $2,000,000, or $60,000 in interest. We must set up a liability account and recognize the interest as an expense.

Interest Expense	60,000	
Interest Payable		60,000

n. Consulting Revenue, Common Stock, Software Sales—Web Site, and Software Sales—Retail require no adjustment.

o. Retained Earnings, however, is another matter. The temporary accounts held income statement items out of Retained Earnings. We must adjust the retained earnings account by closing all the temporary revenue and expense accounts. We begin with the revenue accounts.

Consulting Revenue	123,000	
Software Sales—Web Site	762,000	
Software Sales—Retail	620,000	
Retained Earnings		1,505,000

p. Now we close the expense accounts.

Retained Earnings	775,000	
Wages Expense		410,000
Rent Expense		37,500
Insurance Expense		7,500
Depreciation Expense		30,000

Amortization Expense	127,500
Interest Expense	60,000
Commissions Expense	62,000
Miscellaneous Expenses	2,500
Marketing & Distribution Expense	38,000

Having adjusted and closed the accounts, we are ready to prepare an income statement and a balance sheet. The income statement is prepared by analyzing the retained earnings account for revenue and expense entries. The balance sheet is a properly formatted listing of all accounts with nonzero balances. Being a stickler for always including on your balance sheets any account with a nonzero balance will help you catch any revenue and expense accounts that you may have forgotten to close. Also, another reason for the name balance sheet is that it lists the balances in the accounts.

Websell's income statement for the 6-month period ending June 30, 2004, is presented in Exhibit 3.6. Websell's balance sheet as of June 30, 2004, is shown in Exhibit 3.7 on page 64.

The Websell example takes us through the mechanics of the bookkeeping process. Transactions occur, they are analyzed to determine how they affect individual accounts, and they are recorded in the journal and posted to the accounts. At the end of an accounting period adjusting entries are made, the financial statements are constructed, and temporary accounts are closed to ready them for the next period.

Conclusion

This chapter introduced the economic concepts and accounting techniques behind the income statement. In particular, we defined revenues, expenses, and net income. We showed how temporary accounts are used in compiling an income statement. Compiling

Exhibit 3.6

Websell, Inc. Income Statement

Websell, Inc.
Income Statement for the Six Months Ended June 30, 2004
(amounts in thousands)

REVENUES

Software sales—Web	$ 762.0
Software sales—retail	620.0
Consulting revenues	123.0
Total revenues	$1,505.0

EXPENSES

Wages	$ 410.0
Amortization	127.5
Commissions	62.0
Interest	60.0
Marketing & distribution	38.0
Rent	37.5
Depreciation	30.0
Insurance	7.5
Miscellaneous	2.5
Total expenses	$ 775.0
Net Income	$ 730.0

Exhibit 3.7

Websell, Inc. Balance Sheet

Websell, Inc.
Statement of Financial Position as of June 30, 2004
(amounts in thousands)

ASSETS			LIABILITIES		
Current assets:			Current liabilities:		
Cash		$2,235.0	Accounts payable	$	1.0
Accounts receivable		10.0	Wages payable		33.0
Supplies		500.0	Interest payable		60.0
Prepaid insurance		7.5	Total current liabilities	$	94.0
Prepaid rent		37.5			
Prepaid telephone		1.0	Noncurrent liabilities:		
Total current assets		$2,291.5	Bond payable		2,000.0
			Total liabilities		$2,094.0
Noncurrent assets:					
Software		$ 37.5	**EQUITY**		
Copyright permissions		90.0	Common stock		$1,000.0
Equipment	$300.0		Retained earnings		730.0
Less accum. dep.	30.0	270.0	Total equity		$1,730.0
Internet access rights		35.0			
Web site		1,100.0			
Total noncurrent assets		$1,532.5			
Total assets		$3,824.0	Total liabilities & equity		$3,824.0

the income statement prompts us to adjust the accounts to bring them up-to-date and to close the revenue and expense accounts.

The concepts and techniques introduced in Chapters 2 and 3 are remarkably general and robust. They can be used with any set of conventions that specify rules for defining assets and liabilities, for recognizing revenue, and for recognizing expenses and matching them to revenues. These concepts and techniques are useful across a variety of contexts, including the international setting in which the conventions of accounting vary greatly. Regardless of the conventions, the concepts and techniques introduced here can be applied.

The next chapter reverses our trend of introducing more and more examples of assets and liabilities to concentrate on just one type of asset: cash. We introduce the statement of cash flows for many reasons, not the least of which is the information it contains for the users of financial statements. As we will see, cash flow statements are also useful devices for cementing your knowledge of basic accounting skills.

Key Terms

accrual accounting *52*	**income** *44*	**period expenses** *52*
adjusting *58*	**journal** *55*	**recognition** *49*
closing an account *53*	**loss** *44*	**retained earnings** *54*
expenses *51*	**matching** *51*	**revenues** *48*
general ledger *55*	**net assets** *44*	**temporary accounts** *54*

chapter 4

© GETTY IMAGES/PHOTO DISC

Statement of Cash Flows: Operating, Investing, and Financing Activities

Throughout recorded history, people used many unusual items as money, but perhaps the oddest is the special stones used by the Yapese. The Yapese inhabit the island of Yap in Federated States of Micronesia. They used stones from a distant island for money. The larger the stone, the greater its value. Some of the most valuable weighed several tons. This certainly hindered theft, but we understand it was very hard on parking meters!

Money is important to every society, and accounting pays special attention to cash. Cash is so important a resource that a special accounting report is devoted exclusively to cash: the statement of cash flows. As seen in Chapter 1, the statement of cash flows stands with the income statement and the balance sheet as one of the major outputs of GAAP accounting. In fact, these three statements are interlinked as shown in Figure 4.1. In the language of accounting, the three statements articulate. In addition to going through the details of cash flow statements, we will also see the articulation of the three primary accounting statements.

Cash is also the key to the financial value of any for-profit business. People own for-profit businesses to enjoy the financial returns they generate. Financial returns are generated by actual or prospective distributions of cash to owners. Financial analysts and investment advisers are concerned about an organization's ability to generate cash flows, not just profits. As we will see, the timing of cash flows is a crucial determinant of financial values.

This chapter focuses on the statement of cash flows, and it has four main goals:

1. To explore the definition of cash

2. To examine the operating, investing, and financing activities used to structure the statement of cash flows

3. To show the relation between cash flows from operations and net income

4. To provide two ways of constructing and presenting cash flow statements

This chapter is organized as follows. In an electronic age, cash is coming in more and more forms, so we begin by discussing the defining characteristics of cash. We present an example of a cash flow statement, and explore its main sections: operations, investment, and financing. We construct a short example that shows why cash flow information is useful to have in addition to the net income figure. The next section explains the direct and indirect methods of presenting cash flow statements. We use a worksheet for compiling the cash flow statement using the indirect method. We show the logic of the worksheet and the indirect method in a way that reveals the inner workings of the accrual method of accounting. We conclude by presenting some financial analysis techniques that use the information in cash flow statements.

Basic Definitions, Theories, and Examples

Although it may be obvious in most day-to-day situations, defining just what is and is not cash can get tricky.

OBJECTIVE:
Learn the basic definition of cash.

Cash is readily transferable value.

Definition of Cash

Cash is readily transferable value. It is the most common way organizations acquire the goods and services they use to carry out their activities. It is also a common way they accept payment from customers.

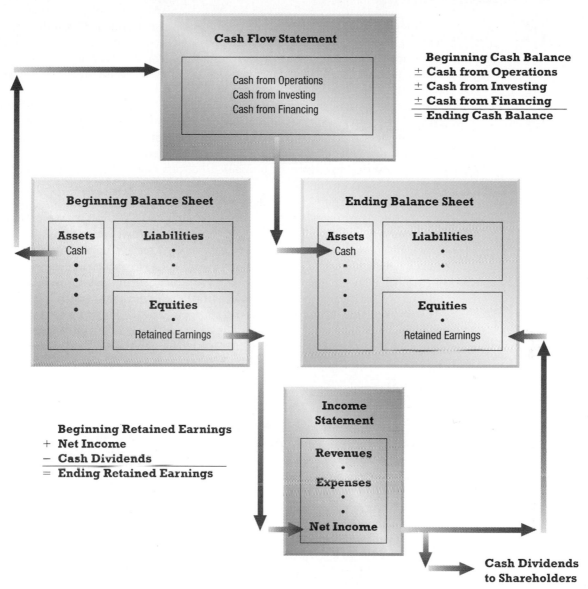

Figure 4.1

Articulation of Income Statement, Balance Sheets, and Cash Flow Statement

It is easy to steal or waste. Therefore keeping track of cash is crucial, both to safeguard it and to make careful plans for ensuring enough of it is available when it is needed.

Cash comes in many forms. *Currency* is one form of cash. Currencies are the coins and pieces of paper that governments issue for use in making economic exchanges. Multinational organizations usually hold the currencies of several governments in order to engage easily in transactions in many geographic regions. Currency is the most familiar form of cash.

Amounts on deposit in *checking accounts* are also cash. For example, Yale University uses a checking account to pay its faculty and staff. Yale issues checks, which employees either cash (i.e. change into currency) or deposit into their own bank accounts. Many employees prefer a shortcut method of receiving payment: their checks are directly deposited in their own accounts. Yale simply instructs the bank to reduce its account and increase the employees' accounts by the amounts earned. The amount held by the bank that is available to Yale for the payment of its employees and suppliers is part of Yale's cash.

It is reasonable to wonder where to draw the line about what is and is not cash. For example, some organizations collect the frequent-flier miles earned by their employees. These miles can be used to purchase air travel, rent cars, and acquire hotel accommodations. Are frequent-flier miles cash?

Although they share some of the attributes of cash, frequent-flier miles are not considered cash. The primary reason is that their use is restricted to the acquisition of goods and services from particular suppliers. Only suppliers that are affiliated with a specific frequent-flier program will accept the miles from that program. In contrast, U.S. dollars are almost universally accepted.

We bring up the issue of frequent-flier miles as a form of cash for two reasons. First, increased ability to keep track of and process large amounts of information may lead a great many organizations to issue their own very limited forms of currency. Automobile companies now issue credit cards that, when used, generate dollars that can be used by the credit card user to reduce the purchase price of a new car from that company. We expect this trend to continue.

The second reason we raise the issue is to highlight the importance of considering restrictions in assessing whether we count something as cash. For example, banks sometimes require as part of a loan agreement that the borrower keep a minimum amount on deposit. This amount is called a *compensating balance*. Compensating balances are restricted in their use and are not considered part of an organization's cash.

Another example is restricted currency. At times, various governments enforce prohibitions against taking their currencies out of their countries, which limits the ability of the organization to use that currency in transactions. If the limitations are severe enough, we would not think of that asset as cash. Cash is readily transferable value. Currencies that cannot be taken out of a specific geographic region are not readily transferable.

Cash Flows

However we define cash, a **cash flow** is simply a change in cash. A change in cash can be an increase (inflows to the entity) or decrease (outflows from the entity). The cash flow statement describes the changes in an entity's cash over a period of time by grouping the increases and decreases into a set of categories that describe the activities that caused them.

Recall the cash flow statement of the Union Plaza Hotel and Casino that was presented in Chapter 1. It is reproduced in Exhibit 4.1. Notice that its main categories are cash flow from operating activities, cash flow from investing activities, and cash flow from financing activities. This classification of cash flows reflects a pragmatic view of the major economic activities of any organization. It is perhaps best explained by reference to the income statement and the balance sheet. Financing activities are those that relate to the acquisition and disposition of funds by issuing and retiring long-term debt and equities. These activities help raise the cash required for investing, which is the acquisition (and disposition) of long-term assets. Operations are reflected in the income statement. Operating activities involve using current assets and current liabilities in the ongoing, day-to-day operation of the organization in accomplishing its purposes. Roughly speaking, then, cash flows from operations represent cash raised through, or required by, the day-to-day operating activities of the firm. Cash flows for investing represent cash flows used to make long-term investments in fixed assets required over the long run. Cash flows from financing represent cash raised from activities whose objective is to provide funds for the longer term. We now discuss each of these three sections of the cash flow statement in more detail.

Even though cash flows from operations are often the most important, we first discuss cash flows from investing and financing activities because cash flows from operations are defined as a residual. They are what remain after cash flows from investing and financing. Investing and financing are better-defined activities than "operations." It is easier to spell out exactly what they mean and let "operations" be a catchall for everything else. This distinction reflects the practical requirement that these conventions must cover all cases. As we will see, this technique of compiling things into some well-defined categories and one "other" category is used quite often in accounting conventions.

Exhibit 4.1
Union Plaza Cash
Flow Statement

Union Plaza Hotel and Casino, Inc. and Subsidiaries
Consolidated Statements of Cash Flows
For the Year Ended December 31, 2001
(dollars in thousands)

CASH FLOWS FROM OPERATING ACTIVITIES

Cash received from customers	$ 54,761
Cash paid to suppliers and employees	(51,314)
Interest received	3
Interest paid	(2,384)
NET CASH PROVIDED BY (USED IN) OPERATING ACTIVITIES	$ 1,066

CASH FLOWS FROM INVESTING ACTIVITIES

Proceeds from sale of property and equipment	$ 42
Purchase of property and equipment	(1,173)
NET CASH USED IN INVESTING ACTIVITIES	$ (1,131)

CASH FLOWS FROM FINANCING ACTIVITIES

Principal payments on short-term contracts	$ (158)
Proceeds from long-term debt	2,000
Principal payments on long-term debt	(641)
Principal payments on capital leases	(919)
NET CASH PROVIDED BY FINANCING ACTIVITIES	$ 282

NET INCREASE (DECREASE) IN CASH AND CASH EQUIVALENTS	$ 217
CASH AND CASH EQUIVALENTS, at beginning of the year	3,335
CASH AND CASH EQUIVALENTS, at end of the year	$ 3,552

Investing Activities

OBJECTIVE:
Learn to distinguish cash flows from investing, financing, and operating activities.

Investing activities are actions aimed at acquiring and disposing of assets that generate a financial return over a long period of time.

Organizations engage in many types of investing activities. For example, in 1994 Quaker Oats spent $1.7 billion to acquire all of the common stock of Snapple. As of June 30, 1999, Microsoft had accumulated about $22 billion in assets. The Boeing Corporation made $420 million in loans to its customers in 1996.

Investing activities are aimed at acquiring assets that will generate a financial return over a long period of time. This definition fits our casual notion of investing activities. We commonly think of an investment as a cash payment for an item that will produce a dividend over the long haul. In the official language of the FASB:

Investing activities include making and collecting loans and acquiring and dis-posing of debt or equity instruments and property, plant and equipment and other productive assets, that is, assets held for or used in the production of goods or services by the enterprise (other than materials that are part of the enterprise inventory).

The investing section of Union Plaza's 2001 cash flow statement (Exhibit 4.1) is sim-ple. Union Plaza's purchase and sale of property and equipment are the only items. Union Plaza received $42 thousand in cash from the sale of property and equipment, and it spent $1,173 thousand to purchase property and equipment. The total is an outflow of cash of $1,131 thousand for investing activities.

The Boeing Corporation generates operating cash flows from the sale of the aircraft it produces in its manufacturing facilities. The corporation also makes loans, which will generate cash flows over a much longer period of time.

© MICK ROESSLER/INDEX STOCK

Financing Activities

Financing activities are actions aimed at acquiring and repaying funds to be used over a long period of time.

Organizations typically must engage in activities that raise funds used over the long term, called **financing activities.** In the "old days," acquiring financing usually meant incurring long-term debt or issuing common equity. The increasing development and sophistication of financial markets, however, led to the development of a great variety of financial instruments. Many of these financial instruments are not simply debt or equity. Regardless of the specific financial instrument used, however, financing activities are aimed at raising cash.

For example, IBM raised $7.67 billion by the issuance of new debt in 1996, and in that same year, used $4.99 billion to pay off debt. Microsoft raised $504 million by issuing common stock in 1996 and used $1.26 billion of cash to repurchase its own common stock.

These activities are aimed at acquiring and paying back funds that will be used and repaid over a long period of time. This definition fits our casual notion of financing activities. For example, we finance the purchase of a car or a house by getting a loan. The loan provides the cash used for the purchase, and we repay the loan over an extended period of time. In the official language of the FASB:

> *Financing activities include obtaining resources from owners and providing them with a return on, and a return of, their investment; receiving resources that by donor stipulation must be used for long-term purposes; borrowing money and repaying amounts borrowed, or otherwise settling the obligation; and obtaining and paying for other resources obtained from creditors or long-term creditors.*

Union Plaza's financing activities included paying down its indebtness from short-term contracts (outflow of $158 thousand), issuing long-term debt (inflow of $2,000 thousand), repaying long-term debt (outflow of $641 thousand), and paying obligations under capital leases (outflow of $919 thousand). The net of these financing activities in 2001 generated a total of $282 thousand.

Operating Activities

Operating activities are actions that are neither investing nor financing activities.

All cash flows that are not investing or financing are classified as arising from **operating activities.** Operating activities include selling to customers, compensating debt-holders for the use of their money, acquiring and selling inventory, and acquiring and using labor. For example, Union Plaza received $54,761 thousand from customers and $3 thousand in interest in 2001. It paid $51,314 thousand to suppliers and employees and $2,384 thousand in interest. The net of these operating activities generated a total of $1,066 thousand.

Operating activities are at the core of the organization's purpose. Public corporations are formed to generate a financial return to owners through operating activities. Not-for-profit organizations, such as the Red Cross and private universities, exist to supply services through their operations. In this sense, understanding the cash flows from operations is a key to understanding the financial performance of an organization. The FASB states:

> Operating activities include all transactions and other events that are not defined as investing or financing activities. . . . Operating activities generally involve producing and delivering goods and providing services. Cash flows from operating activities are generally the cash effects of transactions and other events that enter into the determination of net income.

Cash flow statements use these categories of activities to describe cash flows, but cash flow statements do not stand alone. They are intimately related to balance sheets and income statements. We next begin to discuss the ties between operating, investing, and financing activities and balance sheets by exploring the relation between types of cash flows and types of balance sheet accounts. Then we explore the relation between cash flow from operations and income statements.

Types of Cash Flows and Types of Balance Sheet Accounts

The sections of the cash flow statement and various types of balance sheet accounts roughly correspond. Cash flows from investing are usually, but not exclusively, related to the noncurrent asset accounts. Cash flows from financing are usually, but not exclusively, related to the noncurrent liability and equity accounts. Cash flows from operations are usually, but not exclusively, related to the current asset and current liability accounts, retained earnings, and the income statement accounts. These relationships will be clearer after we introduce the worksheet many accountants use to prepare the statement of cash flows.

Some cash flows may relate to more than one type of activity. For example, buying from a supplier on credit is usually considered to be the result of operating activities, even though it is a form of borrowing money. A formalized loan from a supplier might be considered a financing activity. In such cases, the classification of the cash flow item into investing, financing, or operating must be done according to the accountant's judgment. The guiding principle is to classify the item according to the predominant source of cash flows.

Dividends and interest are two cash flow items that underscore the importance of knowing how accountants classify cash flows. Although both are costs of using someone else's money, the statement of cash flows treats them differently. Dividends are classified as a financing cash flow. Interest payments are classified as an operating cash flow, even though both are payments for the use of invested capital. The treatment of these items in the statement of cash flows is related to their treatment for income statement purposes. Recall that interest expense is considered when determining net income, whereas dividends are not. This differentiation brings into play the FASB's statement that "Cash flows from operating activities are generally the cash effects of transactions and other events that enter into the determination of net income."

One last issue deserves mention here. Sometimes an organization will engage in investing, financing, or operating activities that do not involve cash. For example, an organization may trade common stock for land. These noncash transactions are not part of the cash flows of an organization, but they must be reported. For example, the Rouse Company, a large developer of commercial real estate, had several noncash transactions in 1993, 1994, and 1995. In 1994, Rouse issued $23 million in convertible preferred stock to satisfy a mortgage debt. Although noncash transactions are typically of much less importance than cash flows, it is important to consider them in assessing the financial performance and condition of an organization. Sometimes good reasons motivate non-cash transactions, most often related to taxes. A comprehensive financial analysis will incorporate these noncash items.

Cash Flow from Operations versus Net Income

OBJECTIVE:
Learn to understand the relation between net income and cash flow from operations.

The accrual income statement discussed in Chapter 3 is based on the notions of revenue and expense. Revenue and expense attempt to measure economic performance—how well a company is doing at creating value—over a period. We introduced income in conceptual terms without reference to the activities of the entity, but the relation between the kinds of activities portrayed in the cash flow statement and income is important. In particular, income results from operating activities, not from investing and financing activities. Therefore, it is natural and useful to compare income with cash flows from operations.

Actually, it is more than useful to understand the relation between cash flow from operations and net income—it is vital. We will see in Part 3 that numerous estimates and accounting choices go into the calculation of net income. Comparing net income to cash flow from operations provides vital information about how "real" the net income actually is.

So it is important to understand the relation between net income and cash flow from operations. We begin the process of gaining this understanding by working through a simple example that shows how an intelligent reader of a financial statement can use both accrual and cash flow information to better assess what is happening in a company. Brian Carsberg, an FASB expert on cash flow, once said, "Asking which one is better, cash flow or earnings, is like asking which you should cut out, your heart or your lungs." Hopefully, you will come to appreciate the importance of that observation!

An Example: Total Toy Company

The economics of
**Total Toy Company are
shown in the following
graph:**

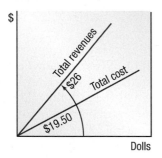

The Total Toy Company was incorporated on January 1, 2004, and authorized the issue of 100 shares of no par common stock. It promptly sold these 100 shares to investors for $7,800. Its balance sheet immediately after selling its shares is shown in Exhibit 4.2. The company purchases dolls at wholesale for $19.50 and sells them to customers in its retail outlet for $26 each. Let us assume, for ease of illustration, that the $19.50 cost per doll is Total Toy's only cost.

The company operates under the following policies: It always maintains an inventory of dolls equal to 50 more than the number of dolls sold during the previous 30 days. Because Total Toy was a new company, the manufacturer of the dolls required Total Toy

Exhibit 4.2

Total Toy Balance Sheet as of
January 1, 2004

Total Toy Company Balance Sheet January 1, 2004			
ASSETS		**LIABILITIES**	
Cash	$7,800	Total liabilities	$ 0
Total assets	$7,800	**EQUITY**	
		Retained earnings	0
		Common stock	7,800
		Total liabilities & equity	$7,800

to pay cash upon receipt of the dolls. Total Toy's customers paid the company at the end of the month after they bought the dolls.

On January 31, after the first month of operations, the company's balance sheet appeared as in Exhibit 4.3. The president was pleased that Total Toy made a profit of $650 on January sales of 100 dolls. He predicted that sales would increase at a rate of 50 dolls per month for the next six months. His predictions came true through the end of April, and the company adhered to all of its policies for immediate payments to suppliers of inventory and delayed collections of receivables from customers. The number of dolls purchased for inventory and the number of units sold during each month are shown in Exhibit 4.4.

Exhibit 4.3

Total Toy Balance Sheet as of January 31, 2004

Total Toy Company
Balance Sheet
January 31, 2004

ASSETS		LIABILITIES	
Cash	$2,925	Total liabilities	$ 0
Accounts receivable	2,600		
Inventory	2,925	**EQUITY**	
		Retained earnings	650
Total assets	$8,450	Common stock	7,800
		Total liabilities & equity	$8,450

Exhibit 4.4

Total Toy Inventory Purchases and Sales (Chart in units)

	JANUARY	FEBRUARY	MARCH	APRIL
Beginning inventory	0	150	200	250
Units sold in month	100	150	200	250
Units purchased in month	250	200	250	300
Ending inventory	150	200	250	300

At the end of April, the president of the company was discussing with friends the profits for the first four months, when the controller told him that the company's bank balance was zero and the company needed to borrow funds in order to continue operating in May. This announcement came as quite a shock to the president. He could not understand how he could be making a profit, yet run out of cash. He decided to rethink the company's economics and pay particular attention to the connection between its profits and its cash flows.

Total Toy makes a profit of $6.50 on each doll sold:

$26.00	Sales price
19.50	Cost
$ 6.50	Profit

The company sold 700 dolls during the first four months: 100 (January) + 150 (February) + 200 (March) + 250 (April). The president therefore figured the company's profit as:

$ 6.50	Profit per doll
× 700	Number sold
$4,550	Profit

He was sure that this figure for profits was correct because the revenues from the sales were:

700	Number of dolls
× $26	Revenue per doll
$18,200	Total revenue

The expenses from the sales were:

700	Number of dolls
×$19.50	Cost per doll
$13,650	Total expenses

So again, the profit on these 700 dolls was $4,550:

$ 18,200	Revenues
(13,650)	Expenses
$ 4,550	Profit

After redoing these calculations, the president realized that they did not at all refer to cash flows! In particular, the $19.50 cost per doll had to be paid immediately upon the company's purchase of the doll. Each doll then sat in inventory for 30 days before being sold. Even after it was sold, it was another month before the company collected cash from its customers. A 2-month gap separated Total Toy's payment of $19.50 from its collection of $26 for each doll. The president decided he needed to analyze cash flows separately from profits.

The company paid for 1,000 dolls from January to the end of April: 250 (January) + 200 (February) + 250 (March) + 300 (April). Therefore, the company paid its supplier $19,500:

1,000	Number of dolls bought and paid for
×$19.50	Cost per doll
$19,500	Total expenditures

Total Toy's *expenditures* of $19,500 from January 1 to April 30 were more than its *expenses* of $13,650 over the same period.

Another problem was that the company only collected on 450 dolls: 0 (January) + 100 (February) + 150 (March) + 200 (April). Therefore, the company only received $11,700 from its customers:

450	Number of dolls customers bought and paid for
× $26	Cost per doll
$11,700	Total receipts

Total Toy's *receipts* of $11,700 from January 1 to April 30 were less than its *revenues* of $18,200 over the same period.

Total Toy's cash flow from January 1 to April 30 is its receipts less expenditures:

$ 11,700	Receipts
(19,500)	Expenditures
$ (7,800)	Cash flow

The president realized that this calculation confirmed what the controller told him: the company was out of cash. The president knew that the company started with $7,800 in cash, and a negative cash flow of $7,800 from January 1 to April 30 would take the bank balance exactly to zero.

The president was shocked by the difference between the net income and the cash flow figures:

$ 4,550	Net income
− (7,800)	Cash flow
$12,350	Difference

He decided to break this $12,350 difference down into pieces. First, revenues exceed receipts by $6,500:

$18,200	Revenues
11,700	Receipts
$ 6,500	Difference

Second, expenditures exceed expenses by $5,850:

$19,500	Expenditures
13,650	Expenses
$ 5,850	Difference

The two together explain the $12,350 difference:

$ 6,500	Revenues − Receipts
5,850	Expenditures − Expenses
$12,350	Total difference

Although he was feeling better because he was beginning to understand what happened, the president felt he needed to examine the company's accounts to cement this understanding. He asked the controller to show him the company's accounts and any financial statements that the controller might have prepared.

The company's accounts are kept in a simple journal, shown in Exhibit 4.5. All of the company's operating transactions for the first four months are entered in this journal and are posted to T-accounts in Exhibit 4.6. The company's financial statements prepared at the end of April are shown in Exhibits 4.7, 4.8, and 4.9. The president was

Exhibit 4.5 Total Toy Journal

January			March		
Inventory	4,875		Inventory	4,875	
Cash		4,875	Cash		4,875
Accounts Receivable	2,600		Accounts Receivable	5,200	
Sales		2,600	Sales		5,200
Cost of Goods Sold	1,950		Cost of Goods Sold	3,900	
Inventory		1,950	Inventory		3,900
(To record purchase of 250 units and sales of 100 units.)			Cash	3,900	
			Accounts Receivable		3,900
February			(To record purchase of 250 units, sales of 200 units,		
Inventory	3,900		and collection of accounts receivable for 150 units sold		
Cash		3,900	in February.)		
Accounts Receivable	3,900				
Sales		3,900	**April**		
Cost of Goods Sold	2,925		Inventory	5,850	
Inventory		2,925	Cash		5,850
Cash	2,600		Accounts Receivable	6,500	
Accounts Receivable		2,600	Sales		6,500
(To record purchase of 200 units, sales of 150 units,			Cost of Goods Sold	4,875	
and collection of accounts receivable for 100 units sold			Inventory		4,875
in January.)			Cash	5,200	
			Accounts Receivable		5,200
			(To record purchase of 300 units, sales of 250 units,		
			and collection of accounts receivable for 200 units sold		
			in March.)		

Exhibit 4.6   Total Toy T-Accounts

	Cash				Accounts Receivable				Inventory		
Dr.		**Cr.**		**Dr.**		**Cr.**		**Dr.**		**Cr.**	
Jan.	7,800	1,950	Jan.	Jan.	2,600	2,600	Feb.	Jan.	1,950	1,950	Jan.
Feb.	2,600	2,925	Jan.	Feb.	3,900	3,900	Mar.	Jan.	2,925	2,925	Feb.
Mar.	3,900	3,900	Feb.	Mar.	5,200	5,200	Apr.	Feb.	3,900	3,900	Mar.
Apr.	5,200	4,875	Mar.	Apr.	6,500			Mar.	4,875	4,875	Apr.
		5,850	Apr.					Apr.	5,850		

	Equity Common Stock				Revenues Sales				Expenses Cost of Goods Sold		
Dr.		**Cr.**		**Dr.**		**Cr.**		**Dr.**		**Cr.**	
		7,800	Jan.			2,600	Jan.	Jan.	1,950		
						3,900	Feb.	Feb.	2,925		
						5,200	Mar.	Mar.	3,900		
						6,500	Apr.	Apr.	4,875		

Exhibit 4.7

Total Toy Balance Sheet as of April 30, 2004

Total Toy Company
Balance Sheet on
April 30, 2004

ASSETS		LIABILITIES	
Cash	$ 0	Total liabilities	$ 0
Accounts receivable	6,500		
Inventory	5,850	**EQUITY**	
		Retained earnings	4,550
		Common stock	7,800
Total assets	$12,350	Total liabilities & equity	$12,350

Exhibit 4.8

Total Toy Income Statement for 1/1/2004 to 4/30/2004

Total Toy Company
Income Statement
1/1/2004 to 4/30/2004

Sales (700 @ $26)	$18,200
Cost of goods sold	
(700 @ $19.50)	13,650
Net income	$ 4,550

indeed correct; profits for the first four months of operations totaled $4,550. Unfortunately, the controller was also correct; the cash balance shown on the balance sheet was now zero.

The president can use the January 1, 2004, balance sheet in Exhibit 4.2 and April 30, 2004, balance sheet in Exhibit 4.7 with the income statement for the period January 1 to April 30, 2004, to understand the cash flows. Accounts Receivable were 0 on January 1 and grew to $6,500 as of April 30, 2004. This is equal, and not by accident, to the excess

Exhibit 4.9

Cash Flow Statement 1/1/2004
to 4/30/2004

Total Toy Company
Statement of Cash Flows
1/1/2004 to 4/30/2004

Cash flow from operations:	
Collections from customers	$ 11,700
Payments to suppliers	(19,500)
Net cash flow from operations	$ (7,800)
Cash flow from financing:	
Sale of common stock	$ 7,800
Net cash flow	$ 0
Cash balance, April 30, 2004	$ 0
Cash balance, January 1, 2004	0
Increase (decrease) in cash	$ 0

of revenues over collections. For Total Toy, any revenues that are not turned into cash by April 30 are present on the April 30 balance sheet in the form of accounts receivable. Accounts receivable on the balance sheet represents amounts recognized as earned by the company but not yet collected in cash. It restates the fact that accounts receivable is an asset: it is a *future* cash inflow.

Similarly, inventory was 0 on January 1, 2004, and grew to $5,850 as of April 30, 2004. This increase in inventory is equal to the excess of expenditures over expenses associated with the cost of the dolls. For Total Toy, all amounts spent on dolls not yet sold are present on the April 30 balance sheet in the form of inventory. It restates the fact that inventory is an asset: it is a *future* economic benefit. It will be recognized as an expense in the period that it is matched against the revenue earned by selling the dolls.

The only differences between cash flows and net income for Total Toy, or the shortfall of Total Toy's cash flow relative to its net income, are equal to the increase in accounts receivable plus the increase in inventory:

$ 6,500	Increase in accounts receivable
5,850	Increase in inventory
$12,350	Difference between net income and cash flow

Although not happy about having run out of cash, the president of Total Toy was much more satisfied with his understanding of the situation. In terms of the company's balance sheets, the profit it earned between January 1 and April 30, 2004, is reflected in the increase in the company's net assets not derived from capital transactions with owners:

$12,350	Net assets on 4/30/2004
0	Net assets on 1/1/2004
$12,350	Increase
(7,800)	Less: Amount contributed by owners
$ 4,550	Net income from 1/1 to 4/30/2004

An increase in net assets does not necessarily imply an increase in cash. The company's net assets increased, but the composition of its assets also changed. By April 30, all the company's assets were in the form of accounts receivable and inventory.

The Total Toy Company example illustrates many important points. First, accrual accounting income statements and balance sheets reflect economic performance. Total Toy's economic foundations are solid: it buys dolls for $19.50 and sells them for

$26, and demand is expected to grow. These economics are reflected in the company's earning of income. Second, a statement explicitly tracking cash flows is useful. You can't spend accrual accounting income at the grocery store, only cash! The statement of cash flows is an important addition to the income statement and balance sheet. Third, the company's net income, balance sheets, and cash flows are all related. Solid understanding of their relationship is necessary in completely understanding the company's financial performance and future prospects.

The remainder of this chapter builds on these points. Total Toy is a simple example with only one product, three kinds of assets, and no liabilities. We now lay out more completely how cash flow statements are constructed for more realistic situations. In doing so, we will see even more clearly how income statements, balance sheets, and cash flow statements are related.

Construction of Cash Flow Statements

OBJECTIVE:

Learn two methods for constructing cash flow statements (the direct and indirect methods).

The cash flow statement is one of the major accounting statements, but it differs from the income statement and the balance sheet in many important ways. Unlike other accounting statements, the cash flow statement focuses on only one resource, cash. Also, a cash flow statement is organized around pragmatic classifications of an entity's activities, not economic concepts.

Another difference between cash flow statements and the other accounting statements is that no new accounts are used to accumulate the information presented in a cash flow statement. Deriving a cash flow statement requires analyzing the accounts already compiled for the balance sheet and income statement. Performing this analysis can be done in essentially two ways. The cash flow statement itself reflects the way this analysis was done. The two kinds of cash flow statements are *direct method* and *indirect method* statements.

Direct Method

The **direct method** of presenting cash flow statements presents cash flows from operations in terms of their uses and sources.

One way to produce a cash flow statement is simply to analyze the cash account through the **direct method.** After all, if an item is a cash flow, it must be reflected in entries to Cash. Collections from customers result in debits to Cash, as does receipt of proceeds from a loan or a sale of common stock. Payments to suppliers of merchandise inventory generate credits to Cash. The detail of the cash account contains all these amounts, plus the beginning and ending balances.

Analyzing the cash account involves going through each entry in the account and determining its source. We identify amounts from operating, investing, and financing sources, aggregate these by some appropriate set of categories, and compile the cash flow statement. Let's apply this technique to Websell's cash account. Recall the cash T-account as of June 30, 2004.

Entries 1 and 2 result from financing activities. Entry 1 reflects the issuance of common stock. Entry 2 reflects the issuance of bonds payable. These activities are the only cash flows related to financing. Therefore, a total of $3,000 thousand was provided by Websell's financing activities.

The investing activities are harder to track down. Websell bought computers and office equipment (Entry 3), software (Entry 8), Internet access rights (Entry 9), and copyright permissions (Entry 10) and paid for the development of a Web site (Entry 14). Each of these expenditures represents the purchase of a long-term asset. No long-term assets were sold. Adding up the amounts of each of these purchases of long-term assets, we find that Websell's investment activities used a total of $1,690 thousand.

The remaining entries to cash must represent cash flows from operations. Entries 15, 19, 20, and 22 are collections from customers. These total $1,495 thousand. Entries 4, 6, 7, 11, 17, 18, and 21 are expenditures for operating items ranging from rent to supplies to labor to commissions. These total $570 thousand. The net cash flows from operations

Cash (000s)

	Dr.	Cr.	
(1)	1,000	300	(3)
(2)	2,000	75	(4)
(15)	65	1	(6)
(19)	762	2	(7)
(20)	620	50	(8)
(22)	48	40	(9)
		100	(10)
		15	(11)
		1,200	(14)
		377	(17)
		38	(18)
		62	(21)
	2,235		

is $925 thousand ($1,495 thousand − $570 thousand). The sum of cash flows from financing, investing, and operating activities is $2,235 thousand ($3,000 + $1,690 + $925 thousand), the change in cash over the period.

Websell's cash flow statement for the first six months of operations in 2004, prepared using this direct approach, is presented in Exhibit 4.10. Despite the specific encouragement of the FASB in FAS 95, few companies portray their cash flows using the direct method.[1] Most use the indirect method. For example, CACI and Oshkosh both use the indirect method, and their cash flow statements are given in Exhibits 4.11 and 4.12.

The indirect method usually seems mysterious to those who first confront it. One of the primary causes of confusion is the way the derivation of cash flow from operations starts with net income, as shown in Exhibits 4.11 and 4.12. We already laid the groundwork for understanding the indirect method. As we will see, the indirect method

Exhibit 4.10 Direct Method Cash Flow Statement

Websell, Inc.
Statement of Cash Flows
For the six months ended June 30, 2004
(amounts in thousands)

OPERATIONS

Collections from customers	$ 1,495
Labor	(377)
Rent	(75)
Commissions	(62)
Marketing and distribution	(38)
Insurance	(15)
Other	(3)
CASH FLOWS FROM OPERATIONS	$ 925

INVESTING

Web site	$(1,200)
Equipment	(300)
Copyright permissions	(100)
Software	(50)
Internet access rights	(40)
CASH FLOWS FROM INVESTING	$(1,690)

FINANCING

Common stock	$ 1,000
Bonds	2,000
CASH FLOWS FROM FINANCING	$ 3,000

NET CASH FLOW — $ 2,235

Beginning cash	$ 0
Ending cash	2,235
CHANGE IN CASH	$ 2,235

[1]It is difficult to find a company that uses the direct method. Compaq used the direct method until 1997. MCI used the direct method until 1998. Both now use the indirect method.

Exhibit 4.11

CACI Cash Flow Statement

CACI International Inc.
Consolidated Statements of Cash Flows
For the Year Ended June 30, 2001
(amounts in thousands)

CASH FLOWS FROM OPERATING ACTIVITIES

Net income	$ 22,301
Reconciliation of net income to net cash provided by operating activities	
Depreciation and amortization	14,143
Gain on sale of property and equipment	(15)
Provision for deferred income taxes	1,837
Gain from sale of COMNET product business	(1,545)
Changes in operating assets and liabilities	
Accounts receivable	(9,870)
Prepaid expenses and other assets	(1,415)
Accounts payable and accrued expenses	2,820
Accrued compensation and benefits	1,986
Deferred rent expenses	153
Income taxes payable (receivable)	(1,604)
Deferred contract costs	31
Other long-term obligations	2,498
NET CASH PROVIDED BY OPERATING ACTIVITIES	$ 31,320

CASH FLOWS FROM INVESTING ACTIVITIES

Acquisitions of property and equipment	$ (8,717)
Purchase of businesses	(29,404)
Proceeds from sale of business	1,481
Proceeds from sale of property and equipment	19
Capitalized software costs and other	(2,547)
NET CASH USED IN INVESTING ACTIVITIES	$(39,168)

CASH FLOWS FROM FINANCING ACTIVITIES

Proceeds under line of credit	$208,763
Payments under line of credit	(188,138)
Proceeds from stock options	5,109
Purchase of common stock for treasury	(7,272)
NET CASH PROVIDED BY FINANCING ACTIVITIES	$ 18,462

Effect of exchange rates on cash and equivalents	$ (703)

Net increase in cash and equivalents	$ 9,911
Cash and equivalents, beginning of year	4,931
Cash and equivalents, end of year	$ 14,842

SUPPLEMENTAL DISCLOSURES OF CASH FLOW INFORMATION

Cash paid during the year of income taxes, net of refunds	$ 8,768
Cash paid during the year for interest	$ 3,304

Exhibit 4.12

OshKosh Cash Flow Statement

OshKosh B'Gosh, Inc. and Subsidiaries
Consolidated Statements of Cash Flows
For the Year Ended December 29, 2001
(amounts in thousands)

CASH FLOWS FROM OPERATING ACTIVITIES

Net income	$ 32,808
Adjustments to reconcile net income to net cash provided by operating activities:	
Depreciation	7,210
Amortization	806
Loss on disposal of assets	76
Deferred income taxes	1,450
Compensation earned under restricted stock plan	390
Income tax benefit from stock option exercises	3,754
Benefit plan expense, net of contributions	(993)
Changes in operating assets and liabilities:	
Accounts receivable	4,469
Inventories	(2,244)
Prepaid expenses and other current assets	275
Accounts payable	(3,611)
Accrued liabilities	(1,539)
NET CASH PROVIDED BY OPERATING ACTIVITIES	$ 42,851

CASH FLOWS FROM INVESTING ACTIVITIES

Additions to property, plant and equipment	$ (5,106)
Proceeds from disposal of assets	104
Sale of investments, net	511
Changes in other assets	(1,152)
NET CASH USED IN INVESTING ACTIVITIES	$ (5,643)

CASH FLOWS FROM FINANCING ACTIVITIES

Payments on long-term debt	$(20,000)
Dividends paid	(2,620)
Net proceeds from issuance of common shares	5,239
Repurchase of common shares	(10,344)
NET CASH USED IN FINANCING ACTIVITIES	$(27,725)

Net increase (decrease) in cash and cash equivalents	$ 9,483
Cash and cash equivalents at beginning of year	19,839
Cash and cash equivalents at end of year	$ 29,322

SUPPLEMENTARY DISCLOSURES

Cash paid for interest	$ 2,467
Cash paid for income taxes	$ 18,658

is essentially the same kind of reconciliation of cash flows from operations with net income that the president of Total Toy performed in analyzing his company's cash flow. One likely reason most companies use the indirect method is that GAAP require a reconciliaiton of net income and cash flow from operations. Exhibit 4.13 presents the reconciliation of net income and cash flow from operations presented by the Union Plaza,

Exhibit 4.13

Union Plaza Hotel and Casino
Reconciliation of Net Loss to
Cash Flow from Operations

> **Union Plaza Hotel and Casino**
> **Reconciliation of Net Loss to Cash Flow from Operations**
> **For the Year Ended December 31, 2001**
>
> | | |
> |---|---:|
> | Net loss | $(2,914) |
> | ADJUSTMENTS TO RECONCILE NET LOSS TO NET CASH PROVIDED BY (USED IN) OPERATING ACTIVITIES: | |
> | Depreciation and amortization | $ 4,130 |
> | (Gain)loss on sale of property and equipment | 159 |
> | Provision for doubtful accounts | 44 |
> | (Increase) decrease in assets: | |
> | Accounts receivable | (109) |
> | Inventories | 29 |
> | Prepaid expenses | (76) |
> | Other assets | 17 |
> | Increase (decrease) in liabilities: | |
> | Accounts payable | (51) |
> | Accrued liabilities | (163) |
> | TOTAL ADJUSTMENTS | $ 3,980 |
> | NET CASH PROVIDED BY OPERATING ACTIVITIES | $ 1,066 |

whose direct method cash flow statement appears in Exhibit 4.1. Notice the similarities between Union Plaza's reconciliation and the indirect method cash flow statements for CACI and Oshkosh.

Indirect Method

The **indirect method** of presenting cash flows from operations shows how net income must be adjusted to get back to cash flows.

The **indirect method** of computing cash flows uses the fundamental accounting identity to help derive cash flows. We begin by writing out the accounting identity in greater detail than previously. In particular, we separate current from noncurrent accounts, and we separate cash from the other current assets:

$$\left\{ \begin{array}{c} \text{CASH} \\ + \\ \text{OTHER CURRENT ASSETS} \\ + \\ \text{NONCURRENT ASSETS} \end{array} \right\} = \left\{ \begin{array}{c} \text{CURRENT LIABILITIES} \\ + \\ \text{NONCURRENT LIABILITIES} \\ + \\ \text{EQUITIES} \end{array} \right\}$$

We can solve the preceding fundamental identity for the amount of cash:

$$\text{CASH} = \left\{ \begin{array}{c} \text{CURRENT LIABILITIES} \\ + \\ \text{NONCURRENT LIABILITIES} \\ + \\ \text{EQUITIES} \\ - \\ \text{OTHER CURRENT ASSETS} \\ - \\ \text{NONCURRENT ASSETS} \end{array} \right\}$$

Now, cash flow is the change in cash. Let C_{EB} denote the ending balance of cash and C_{BB} denote the beginning balance. Use similar subscripts to denote the ending and beginning balances of other current assets (OCA_{EB} and OCA_{BB}), noncurrent assets (NCA_{EB} and NCA_{BB}), current liabilities (CL_{EB} and CL_{BB}), noncurrent liabilities (NCL_{EB} and NCL_{BB}), and equities (EQ_{EB} and EQ_{BB}). The change in cash is:

$$C_{EB} - C_{BB} = (CL_{EB} - CL_{BB}) + (NCL_{EB} - NCL_{BB}) + (EQ_{EB} - EQ_{BB})$$
$$- (OCA_{EB} - OCA_{BB}) - (NCA_{EB} - NCA_{BB})$$

Convince yourself that this equation works by inserting the beginning and ending balances for Websell (see Exhibit 3.7).

We call this equation the cash flow equation. You might recall that earlier we mentioned a rough correspondence exists between the categories of cash flows and the types of accounts. The cash flow equation expresses the cash flow of an organization in terms of the other accounts on the balance sheet. Operations relate most directly to current assets, current liabilities, and equity accounts. Investing relates most directly to long-term asset accounts. Financing relates most directly to long-term liability and equity accounts. We can regroup the cash flow equation to reflect this correspondence:

$$C_{EB} - C_{BB} = (CL_{EB} - CL_{BB}) - (OCA_{EB} - OCA_{BB}) - (NCA_{EB} - NCA_{BB})$$
$$+ (NCL_{EB} - NCL_{BB}) + (EQ_{EB} - EQ_{BB})$$

In words:

Cash flow
= Change in current liabilities and current assets (roughly, operating items)
− Change in noncurrent assets (roughly, investing items)
+ Change in noncurrent liabilites (roughly, financing items)
+ Change in equities (roughly, financing and operating items)

This form of the accounting identity may seem imposing and unwieldy. We develop a worksheet that guides our application of the indirect method, but the equation form is useful for understanding what the worksheet does. For example, the change in equity is related to both operating and financing cash flows. Some equity accounts, such as Common Stock and Additional Paid-In Capital, relate only to financing. Retained Earnings, however, relates to both operating and financing. Retained Earnings is increased by net income and decreased by net losses, which are related to cash flow from operations. Retained Earnings is decreased by the payment of cash dividends. Dividend payments are financing items.

Except by chance, revenues, expenses, and dividends will not directly correspond to cash flows. For example, most organizations sell to customers on account. Revenues are not the same as cash receipts. To relate revenues to operating cash flows, we must consider how Accounts Receivable absorbs the impact of Sales. You saw a specific example of this issue in Total Toy Company earlier in this chapter.

Accounts Receivable is increased by Sales and decreased by Cash Collections. A T-account picture is provided in Figure 4.2.

Notice that what is in the income statement, sales revenue, appears on the left-hand side of the T-account. The cash inflow from sales, the collections, is shown on the right-hand side of the account. This amount should appear on the cash flow statement. The difference between these two numbers can be exactly explained by the change in the Accounts Receivable balance. If the balance in receivables did not change from the beginning to the end of the period, then sales revenue would be exactly equal to cash collections from sales. (Think of this situation as one where all sales are cash sales and no accounts receivable is kept—the balance always stays at zero and never changes.) Now, when the balance in receivables increases from the beginning to the end of the period, it means more sales (in the income statement) occurred than cash collections from customers (the cash flow statement). In the case of Websell, the balance in Accounts Receivable went from $0 to $10 thousand. Therefore, the cash collections from customers was $10 thousand less than the amount of sales revenue in the income statement. Exhibit 4.10 shows that Websell's collections from customers are $1,495 thousand. Exhibit 3.6 shows that Websell's revenues amount to $1,505 thousand, exactly $10 thousand more than cash collections.

Why go to so much effort? Because we arrive at the cash receipts that are part of operating cash flows without having to analyze the cash account; that is, we found one of

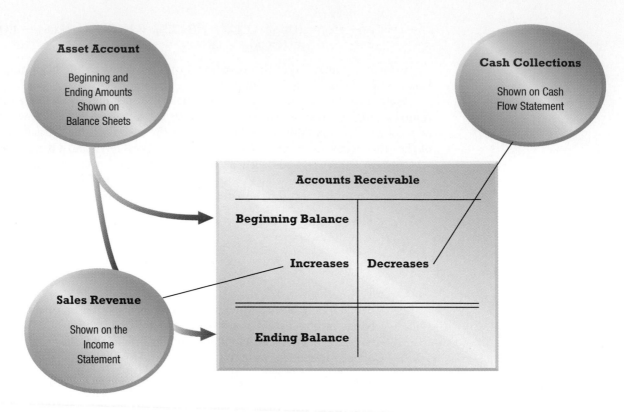

Figure 4.2

Example of Articulation of
Accounts Receivable T-Accounts

the ingredients of the cash flow statement "indirectly." The indirect method of finding the cash flow statement applies this technique to produce the entire statement. It requires adjusting for all the other current asset accounts, the noncurrent asset accounts, the current liability accounts, and the noncurrent liability accounts. Therefore, the indirect method of deriving the cash flow statement works through the cash flow equation item by item.

The cash flow statement could be compiled by working through equations as we did previously, but it would be a complicated task. It is better to use a worksheet to organize all the required calculations. A worksheet is a place for making calculations. It can be a sheet of paper, or it can take electronic form, such as a page of a spreadsheet program. Although a worksheet may contain information from an organization's accounts, the worksheet itself is not a set of accounts. A worksheet is used for structuring calculations, not for keeping records.

The usefulness of the system of debits and credits comes in its structuring and organizing of calculations. The cash flow worksheet uses debits and credits to calculate its answers. Even so, the debits and credits on the cash flow worksheet are used only there. They are not entered into the organization's accounting system.

The cash flow worksheet begins by laying out the beginning and ending balances of cash in a T-account form that has divisions for operating, investing, and financing cash flows. Conceptually, the cash flow equation can be viewed in T-account format as follows:

$(C_{EB} - C_{BB})$		$=$	$(CL_{EB} - CL_{BB})$		$+$	$(NCL_{EB} - NCL_{BB})$		$+$	$(E_{EB} - E_{BB})$		$-$	$(OCA_{EB} - OCA_{BB})$		$-$	$(NCA_{EB} - NCA_{BB})$	
Cash		$=$	Current Liabilities		$+$	Noncurrent Liabilities		$+$	Equities		$-$	Other Current Assets		$-$	Noncurrent Assets	
Dr.	Cr.		Dr.	Cr.		Dr.	Cr.		Dr.	Cr.		Dr.	Cr.		Dr.	Cr.
BB				BB			BB			BB		BB			BB	
Operations																
				EB			EB			EB		EB			EB	
Investing																
Financing																
EB																

The basic worksheet as laid out here is a bit unwieldy, but it gives us some idea of what we need in order to construct the cash flow statement indirectly. We need the beginning and ending balances in all the accounts and, as we shall see, any supplemental information that will help us to explain why the account balances changed.

A more user-friendly, compact worksheet similar to the preceding T-account graphic is given in Exhibit 4.14. The upper portion of the worksheet contains the beginning and ending balances in all of the accounts except Cash, which is singled out at the bottom of the worksheet. The idea is to write "explanations" in the form of journal entries that explain why the account balances changed. These entries can be posted to the worksheet, which guides and summarizes our efforts. Information in the income statement, as well as other supplemental information, will be useful.

Exhibit 4.14 Websell Cash Flow Worksheet (Beginning)

Websell Cash Flow Worksheet
For the Six Months Ended June 30, 2004

	JANUARY 1, 2004		EXPLANATIONS		JUNE 30, 2004	
	DEBIT	CREDIT	DEBIT	CREDIT	DEBIT	CREDIT
Accounts Receivable	$0				$ 10,000	
Supplies	0				500	
Prepaid Insurance	0				7,500	
Prepaid Rent	0				37,500	
Prepaid Telephone	0				1,000	
Software	0				37,500	
Copyright Permissions	0				90,000	
Equipment	0				300,000	
Accumulated Depreciation		$0				$ 30,000
Internet Access Rights	0				35,000	
Web Site	0				1,100,000	
Accounts Payable		0				1,000
Wages Payable		0				33,000
Interest Payable		0				60,000
Bond Payable		0				2,000,000
Common Stock		0				1,000,000
Retained Earnings		0				730,000
	$0	$0			$1,619,000	$3,854,000

CASH FLOW SUMMARY		
	INCREASES	DECREASES
Beginning balance	$ 0	
Operations		
Investing		
Financing		
Ending balance	$2,235,000	

The best way to learn this process is to walk through an example. We entered Websell's beginning and ending balance sheet balances, and we now construct Websell's statement indirectly. Let's begin by entering what we know about net income into the accounts.

(1) Cash (Operations) 730,000
     Retained Earnings 730,000

Net income, as we know, is closed to Retained Earnings. Because most of the items of revenue and expense "almost" correspond to cash flows, you can think of this entry as "guessing" that cash flow from operations is equal to net income. The approach will be to look for adjustments to this initial estimate. For instance, we already talked about how to adjust sales revenue to cash inflows from customers.

One thing we know about the income statement is that it contains depreciation expense. Depreciation expense doesn't involve a cash flow; it increases accumulated depreciation (decreases the carrying value of a fixed asset). In this sense, net income underestimates cash from operations, and depreciation should be added back to net income to make the estimate better. The following entry does just that:

(2) Cash (Operations) 30,000
     Accumulated Depreciation 30,000

Now, other items in the income statement, such as amortization of various long-term assets, are conceptually similar to depreciation and for which net income must be adjusted. Remember, expenditures for noncurrent assets are to be included in the investing section of the cash flow statement when the assets are acquired. As with depreciation, the using up of these other long-term assets is not an operational cash flow. Thus, we must add back to net income the amortization of the web, copyright, software, and Internet access in order to get the net income figure closer to measuring cash flow from operations.

(3) Cash (Operations) 127,500
     Web Site 100,000
     Copyright Permissions 10,000
     Software 12,500
     Internet Access Rights 5,000

We already explained the adjustment for Accounts Receivable in order to convert sales revenue to cash flow from customers.

(4) Accounts Receivable 10,000
     Cash (Operations) 10,000

Inventories are operating assets. If inventory levels increase over the period, it means that purchases were larger than the amount of inventory shown to be "used up" (cost of good sold, cost of supplies) in the income statement.

(5) Supplies 500
     Cash (Operations) 500

Similarly, the increase in Prepaid Insurance during the 6-month period was paid for with cash, is an operating expenditure, and is not reflected in the income statement.

(6) Prepaid Insurance 7,500
     Cash (Operations) 7,500

The same argument holds for Prepaid Rent and Prepaid Telephone.

(7) Prepaid Rent 37,500
     Cash (Operations) 37,500

(8) Prepaid Telephone 1,000
     Cash (Operations) 1,000

So far, everything we did accurately measures cash flow from operations. We see a few other items (short-term liabilities) later on that further refine our estimate of cash flow from operations. Now let's consider the changes in account values of some of the long-term assets. In Exhibit 4.14, we see that the software balance went from $0 to $37,500.

But in Entry 3, to account for amortization, we credited the software account for $12,500, the amount of amortization for the period. Thus, the only way to justify the ending balance is to debit the software account for $50,000. In fact, it indicates the cash outflow to acquire the software during the period and represents an investing activity.

(9) Software 50,000
       Cash (Investing) 50,000

Similar logic applies to equipment, the Web site, and the Internet access rights.

(11) Equipment 300,000
       Cash (Investing) 300,000

(12) Web Site 1,200,000
       Cash (Investing) 1,200,000

(13) Internet Access Rights 40,000
       Cash (Investing) 40,000

Now consider Wages Expense and Wages Payable. Wages Expense needs to be adjusted by the change in Wages Payable in order to get the operational cash outflow for wages during the period. This logic is exactly the same as with receivables, except it is on the other side of the balance sheet. If Wages Payable increased over the period, then Wages Expense overestimates the expenditure of cash on wages.

(14) Cash (Operations) 33,000
       Wages Payable 33,000

The other two short-term payable accounts for interest and accounts payable are analyzed in the same fashion. The following two explaining journal entries result:

(15) Cash (Operations) 60,000
       Interest Payable 60,000

(16) Cash (Operations) 1,000
       Accounts Payable 1,000

The only two accounts with "unexplained" changes at this point are Common Stock and Bond Payable. These changes are easy to explain, however. They are the two financing sources of capital for the period.

(17) Cash (Financing) 1,000,000
       Common Stock 1,000,000

(18) Cash (Financing) 2,000,000
       Bond Payable 2,000,000

All eighteen of the preceding explanations are entered into the worksheet. The completed worksheet is shown in Exhibit 4.15.

Preparing the statement of cash flows from the completed worksheet is a straightforward task. The worksheet helps us account for the change in cash and classify the items into operating, investing, and financing sections. The presentation of a statement of cash flows that uses the indirect method follows the logic discussed earlier. As shown in Exhibit 4.16 for Websell, the presentation starts with net income and uses adjustments to arrive at cash flow from operations. We get the same results regardless of whether we use the direct or the indirect method, a fact that is underscored by the alternative explanation of the indirect method given next.

Alternative Explanation of the Indirect Method

You perhaps noticed that the presentations of direct and indirect method cash flow statements differ only in how they show cash flow from operations. In fact, another way to think of the indirect method is that it calculates cash flows from operations by

Exhibit 4.15 Websell Cash Flow Worksheet (Completed)

Websell Cash Flow Worksheet
For the Six Months Ended June 30, 2004

	JANUARY 1, 2004		EXPLANATIONS		JUNE 30, 2004	
	DEBIT	CREDIT	DEBIT	CREDIT	DEBIT	CREDIT
Accounts Receivable	$0		(4) $ 10,000		$ 10,000	
Supplies	0		(5) 500		500	
Prepaid Insurance	0		(6) 7,500		7,500	
Prepaid Rent	0		(7) 37,500		37,500	
Prepaid Telephone	0		(8) 1,000		1,000	
Software	0		(9) 50,000	(3) $ 12,500	37,500	
Copyright Permissions	0		(10) 100,000	(3) 10,000	90,000	
Equipment	0		(11) 300,000		300,000	
Accumulated Depreciation		$0		(2) 30,000		$ 30,000
Internet Access Rights	0		(13) 40,000	(3) 5,000	35,000	
Web Site	0		(12) 1,200,000	(3) 100,000	1,100,000	
Accounts Payable		0		(16) 1,000		1,000
Wages Payable		0		(14) 33,000		33,000
Interest Payable		0		(15) 60,000		60,000
Bond Payable		0		(18) 2,000,000		2,000,000
Common Stock		0		(17) 1,000,000		1,000,000
Retained Earnings		0		(1) 730,000		730,000
	$0	$0			$1,619,000	$3,854,000

		CASH FLOW SUMMARY	
		INCREASES	DECREASES
Beginning balance		$ 0	
Operations		(1) 730,000	(4) $ 10,000
		(2) 30,000	(5) 500
		(3) 127,500	(6) 7,500
		(14) 33,000	(7) 37,500
		(15) 60,000	(8) 1,000
		(16) 1,000	
			(9) 50,000
			(10) 100,000
Investing			(11) 300,000
			(12) 1,200,000
			(13) 40,000
Financing		(17) 1,000,000	
		(18) 2,000,000	
Ending balance		$2,235,000	

Exhibit 4.16

Indirect Method Cash Flow
Statement

Websell, Inc.
Statement of Cash Flows
For the Six Months Ended June 30, 2004
(amounts in thousands)

OPERATIONS:

Net income	$ 730.0
Add: Expenses not requiring cash	
Amortization expense	127.5
Depreciation expense	30.0
Add: Increases in current liabilities	
Wages payable	33.0
Interest payable	60.0
Accounts payable	1.0
Deduct: Increases in current assets	
Accounts receivable	(10.0)
Inventory	(0.5)
Prepaid insurance, rent, telephone, supplies	(46.0)
CASH FLOWS FROM OPERATIONS	$ 925.0

INVESTING:

Web site	$(1,200.0)
Equipment	(300.0)
Copyright permissions	(100.0)
Software	(50.0)
Internet access rights	(40.0)
CASH FLOWS FROM INVESTING	$(1,690.0)

FINANCING:

Common stock	$ 1,000.0
Bonds	2,000.0
CASH FLOWS FROM FINANCING	$ 3,000.0
Net cash flow	$ 2,235.0

"guessing" that it equals net income, then making adjustments to bring that "guess" to cash flow from operations.

The "guess" that cash flow from operations equals net income is reflected in the first entry in the worksheet that enters net income into the cash flow from operations section. For Websell, this entry puts the net income of $730 thousand as the starting point for the derivation of cash flows from operations. It is important to note that putting in the net income of $730 thousand is really just a short way of putting in all the various items that comprise net income: revenues, wage expenses, commissions, depreciation, and so on. The adjustments on the cash flow worksheet take these components of net income to their cash flow counterparts.

Exhibit 4.17 lays out this process for Websell. It gives an explanation of how the amounts on the income statement are modified by the adjustments to yield the proper cash flow amount for cash flow from operations. In total, the net income of $730 thousand is adjusted to the cash flow from operations of $925 thousand. We already discussed how the adjustment for changes in accounts receivable gets revenues to collections from customers. It is well worth your time to go through each line of Exhibit 4.17 and see how each adjustment helps bring the income statement item (either

INCOME STATEMENT		ADJUSTMENTS		CASH FLOW STATEMENT	
Item	Amount	Amount	Ref.	Amount	Item
Total revenues	$1,505.0	$ (10.0)	(4)	$1,495.0	Collections
Wages	410.0	33.0	(14)	377.0	Labor
Amortization	127.5	127.5	(3)		Noncash item
Commissions	62.0			62.0	Commissions
Marketing and distribution	38.0			38.0	Marketing and distribution
Rent	37.5	(37.5)	(7)	75.0	Rent
Depreciation	30.0	30.0	(2)		Noncash items
Insurance	7.5	(7.5)	(6)	15.0	Insurance
Miscellaneous and interest	62.5	59.5	(5), (8), (15), (16)	3.0	Other
Net income	$ 730.0	$ 195.0		$ 925.0	Cash flow from operations

revenue or expense) into the cash flow from operations item (either an inflow or out-flow of cash).

By understanding these basics of the construction of cash flow statements, you will be able to better use the information in cash flow statements in financial analyses. The next section introduces some of the ways that cash flow statement information is used.

Analyses Using Cash Flow Statements

Some common questions posed in financial analysis can be answered using the information in cash flow statements. These questions include:

- Is cash flow from operations positive or negative?
- How much of the company's earnings is cash, and how much is accruals?
- Is the company growing?

As long as operations produce cash, it is unlikely that the entity will go bankrupt. However, the Total Toy example demonstrated how an entity can show positive net income, yet run into a liquidity problem. We did not examine a situation in which cash flow from operations is positive and net income is negative, but this situation can happen as well. For example, we see from Exhibit 4.1 that Union Plaza's cash flow from operations is a positive $1,066 thousand, which is true even though its net income is negative.

Union Plaza's negative cash flow from investing shows that it acquired property and equipment, which is consistent with growth. Given that it only spent $1,173 thousand on property and equipment, it is unlikely that Union Plaza acquired another hotel or casino. More likely, it purchased new gaming equipment or furniture.

From the reconciliation of cash flows from operations and net income in Exhibit 4.13, we see that Union Plaza recorded depreciation and amortization in 2001 of $4,130 thousand. The fact that depreciation and amortization exceeds the amount of cash spent investing in property and equipment suggests that Union Plaza may not have spent enough in 2001 to compensate for its usage of those assets. As we will see in Chapter 11, however, the calculation of depreciation is not tied exactly to usage of assets; therefore, we should be careful in drawing firm conclusions from the fact that depreciation and amortization expenses exceed investing cash outflows.

Conclusion

The statement of cash flows introduced in this chapter helps us track a vital resource of any organization—cash. Cash is readily transferable value, and all organizations need cash to carry out their basic functions. The separation of cash flows from operating, investing, and financing activities helps us understand the sources and uses of cash, and should help us better understand the financial position and performance of an organization.

We also showed two ways of compiling cash flow statements. The more straightforward method is to analyze the cash account and is called the direct method. The indirect method uses the balance sheet equation to derive the cash flows. The balance sheet identity itself guarantees that we can express the change in cash as the sum of the changes in the noncash, permanent accounts. The rough correspondence between current accounts and operations, long-term assets and investing, and long-term liabilities and equities and financing provides a good starting point for using the balance sheet accounts to derive the three sections of the cash flow statement.

The indirect method of deriving cash flows is useful for more than just deriving a cash flow statement. It is also a useful method of analysis for a potential lender to assess the probability of repayment of a proposed loan, or for an investment banker to estimate a value of a company. In either of these two applications, the problem is to predict the future cash flows of an organization. It is often useful to break up this problem into smaller steps. First, future sales are forecast. Then, expenses are forecast, and forecasts of income result. The assets required to generate this income are estimated, as is any current operating borrowing, such as purchasing on account; that is, forecasts are made of future balance sheets. Given these forecasts of future income and future balance sheets, the indirect method is applied to derive the implied forecasts of cash flows. For this reason, we devoted much attention to the indirect method in this chapter—it is a commonly used analytical device in its own right.

We have now completed our introduction of the basic financial statements. You should now know quite a bit more about balance sheets, income statements, and cash flow statements than you did when you started reading this book. Sophisticated financial analysis often calls for more than just knowledge of these statements in isolation, however. Knowing how balance sheets, income statements, and cash flow statements fit together, that is, how they articulate, you can often use the information in the three statements together to powerful effect. In the next chapter, we demonstrate this technique by analyzing America Online, Inc.'s financial reports for a particularly interesting year–1997. For the first time, our focus shifts from working backward from the information presented in financial statements to discover what happened during the period in question. We hope you will find it enlightening and perhaps even interesting.

Key Terms

cash *66*	currency *67*	indirect method *82*
cash flows *68*	direct method *78*	investing activities *69*
checking accounts *67*	financial activities *70*	operating activities *70*

chapter 5

© AFP/CORBIS

Using the Accounting Framework: America Online, Inc.

In the olden days, a Caribbean traveler came across an elderly pirate. The pirate had a peg leg, a hook for a hand, and a patch over one eye. The traveler asked the pirate what caused him to require these aids.

The pirate explained: "Lost the hand in a cutlass battle with a royal marine. The smithy made this useful hook."

"Lost the leg to a musket ball while boarding the St. Marie," the pirate said. "Ship's carpenter made this excellent peg leg."

"What about the eye?" asked the traveler.

"Oh, right after I got the hook, a bit of sand flew in my eye. I forgot I had the hook, and poked out my own eye rubbing at the sand!" replied the pirate.

The first four chapters of this book introduced many useful concepts and techniques. Like the pirate's peg leg and hook, these concepts and techniques can be useful aids. They can also lead to self-inflicted wounds. This chapter has two purposes:

1. To demonstrate the value of understanding balance sheets, income statements, and cash flow statements

2. To help you learn to apply your knowledge properly to the analysis of a real company's financial reports

We examine America Online, Inc.'s (AOL) financial reports in the periods around 1997. The balance sheets, income statement, and statement of cash flows all provide important information about AOL's operations and performance.

Any good analysis of financial reports begins with an understanding of the entity's business and the context within which it operates. Our analysis of AOL is no exception. We begin by examining AOL's strategy and economic environment in 1997, which provides the background for our first look at AOL's financial statements. We then focus the analysis on some specific areas of the reported results.

AOL: Business and Environment

AOL was incorporated in 1985. With 8.6 million subscribers worldwide by June 30, 1997, AOL was the global leader in providing connections to the Internet. From its 1997 Form 10K report to the Securities and Exchange Commission, AOL described its mission to become:

> . . . the recognized brand leader in the development of an interactive medium that transcends traditional boundaries between people and places to create an interactive global community that holds the potential to change the way people communicate, stay informed, learn, shop, and do business.

Of the many aspects of developing this "interactive medium," one part involved the installation and maintenance of the technology required to connect subscribers. Another was the development and acquisition of programming and content that would draw subscribers.

Then, as now, Internet businesses were in an extremely uncertain and rapidly changing environment. One of the biggest uncertainties at the time was the revenue model—a description of the way the company's activities generate revenues. AOL's revenue model was in a state of flux in 1997. From the 10K:

> The Company generates two types of revenues, online service revenues and other revenues. Online service revenues are generated by customers subscribing to the Company's online services. . . . Other revenues include electronic commerce and advertising revenues. . . .

As we discuss in greater detail later, rapid changes occurred in the manner in which subscription revenue was generated. Therefore, a key part of AOL's strategy was to increase the nonsubscription revenues, such as advertising and fees, from electronic commerce. The subscriber base was still considered the most important ultimate source of value. However, it was unclear exactly how much revenue AOL could generate through advertising and transaction fees.

AOL also had many competitors:

> *Online services and Internet service providers, including CompuServe Corporation, the Microsoft Network and Prodigy Services Company . . . currently compete with the Company for both subscribers and for advertising and electronic commerce revenues. The Company also competes for advertising and electronic commerce revenues with major Web sites operated by search services and other companies such as Yahoo! Inc., Netscape Communications Corporation, Infoseek Corporation, CNET, Inc., Lycos, Inc., and Excite, Inc., and media companies such as The Walt Disney Company and Time Warner Inc.*

Even with this competition and uncertainty, AOL was a rapidly growing business. Total revenues went from $39 million in 1992 to $1.6 billion in 1997, approximately a 40-fold increase in five years!

This setting of growth and uncertainty in attempting to develop (and profit from!) an interactive medium provides the backdrop to our exploration of AOL's financial reports. The technological component of AOL's strategy would lead us to expect to see some property and equipment assets on its balance sheets. It might also show assets reflecting AOL's development and purchase of programming and content. The early stages of AOL's efforts, the intense competition, and the uncertainty about the revenue model might lead us to expect AOL to be unprofitable. Further, its early stage of growth might mean that operating cash flows are negative.

Before we look at the financial statements, we want to give one word of caution. We used AOL's *actual* financial statements. We did not shorten them to make you more comfortable with their length and terminology.

AOL's Balance Sheets

OBJECTIVE:
Learn to read real company financial reports: balance sheets.

Exhibit 5.1 contains balance sheets for 1996 and 1997. They contain a great deal of detail, so let's get the big picture first. Look at the total assets line: Total assets at June 30, 1996, were about $959 million ($958,754 million, to be exact), and total assets at June 30, 1997, were about $847 million. AOL's total assets declined over the year by about $112 million, which would seem to be a pretty bad situation for a company that was trying to establish a new interactive medium. What happened? Here are some possibilities:

• AOL might have gotten trounced by its competition and incurred heavy losses.
• AOL might have distributed assets to its shareholders.
• AOL might have used assets to pay off some debt.

We can see quickly that AOL did not pay off debt: Total liabilities went up about $273 million, from $446 million to $719 million. Even without looking, our knowledge of the balance sheet identity tells us that shareholders' equity must have gone down:

$$\text{ASSETS} \downarrow = \text{LIABILITIES} \uparrow + \text{SHAREHOLDERS' EQUITY} \downarrow$$

Shareholders' equity did decrease from about $513 million at June 30, 1996, to about $128 million at June 30, 1997, a decrease of about $385 million.

A closer inspection of the shareholders' equity section can tell us more about what happened. We see some accounts encountered before: Preferred Stock, Common Stock, and Additional Paid-In Capital. Preferred Stock did not change. Both Common Stock and Additional Paid-In Capital increased during fiscal 1997. This change means AOL

America Online, Inc.
Consolidated Balance Sheets
(amounts in thousands, except share data)

ASSETS	JUNE 30, 1997	1996	LIABILITIES AND STOCKHOLDERS' EQUITY	JUNE 30, 1997	1996
Current assets:			Current liabilities:		
Cash and cash equivalents	$124,340	$118,421	Trade accounts payable	$ 69,703	$105,904
Short-term investments	268	10,712	Other accrued expenses and		
Trade accounts receivable	65,306	49,342	liabilities	297,298	127,876
Other receivables	26,093	23,271	Deferred revenue	166,007	37,950
Prepaid expenses and other			Accrued personnel costs	20,008	15,719
current assets	107,466	65,290	Current portion of long-term		
Total current assets	$323,473	$267,036	debt	1,454	2,435
Property and equipment at			Total current liabilities	$ 554,470	$289,884
cost, net	$233,129	$111,090	Long-term liabilities:		
Other assets:			Notes payable	$ 50,000	$ 19,306
Restricted cash	$ 50,000	$ —	Deferred income taxes	24,410	135,872
Product development costs, net	72,498	44,330	Deferred revenue	86,040	—
Deferred subscriber acquisition			Minority interests	2,674	22
costs, net	—	314,181	Other liabilities	1,060	1,168
License rights, net	16,777	4,947	Total liabilities	$ 718,654	$446,252
Other assets	84,618	29,607	Stockholders' equity:		
Deferred income taxes	24,410	135,872	Preferred stock, $0.01 par value;		
Goodwill, net	41,783	51,691	5,000,000 shares authorized,		
Total assets	$846,688	$958,754	1,000 shares issued and		
			outstanding at June 30, 1997,		
			and 1996, respectively	1	1
			Common stock, $0.01 par value;		
			300,000,000 shares authorized,		
			100,188,971 and 92,626,000		
			shares issued and outstanding		
			at June 30, 1997, and 1996,		
			respectively	1,002	926
			Unrealized gain on available-		
			for-sale securities	16,924	—
			Additional paid-in capital	617,221	519,342
			Accumulated deficit	(507,114)	(7,767)
			Total stockholders' equity	$ 128,034	$512,502
			Total liabilities and stockholders'		
See accompanying notes.			equity	$ 846,688	$958,754

Exhibit 5.1

America Online, Inc. Consolidated Balance Sheets

actually issued shares in 1997 and certainly did not return any of the shareholders' investment.

Shareholders' equity accounts include Unrealized Gain on Available-for-Sale Securities. We will go into exactly what this account is when we study marketable securities in detail later in the book. All we need to know now are two things, both of which we already covered. First, this account is an equity account, so we know the role it plays in maintaining the balance sheet identity. Second, the amount of the account went up by about $17 million: from $0 on June 30, 1996, to $17 million on June 30, 1997. An increase in an equity account could reflect an increase in assets, but not a decrease. Whatever the source of this equity account, it only deepens the mystery of AOL's decline in total assets.

The remaining equity account is Accumulated Deficit, which is another name for Retained Earnings when the cumulative earnings are negative. We see that AOL's accumulated deficit went from about $8 million to about $507 million, a decline of about $499 million. This change would seem to point to some large loss as the cause of the decline in total assets. To explore this issue further, we should examine AOL's income statement.

OBJECTIVE:

Learn to read real company financial reports: income statements.

AOL's Income Statement

AOL calls its income statements "Consolidated Statements of Operations." The income statement for fiscal 1997 is reproduced in Exhibit 5.2. Going straight to the bottom line, we see that AOL did, indeed, report a net loss of about $499 million for 1997.

Exhibit 5.2

America Online, Inc. Consolidated Statement of Operations

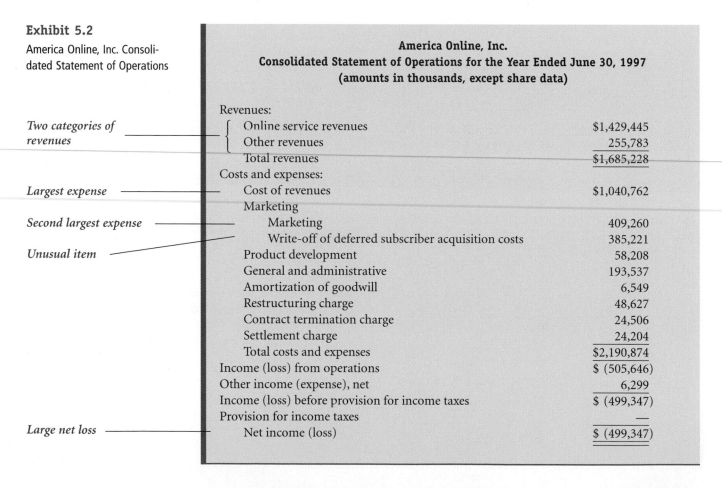

Two categories of revenues

Largest expense

Second largest expense

Unusual item

Large net loss

America Online, Inc.
Consolidated Statement of Operations for the Year Ended June 30, 1997
(amounts in thousands, except share data)

Revenues:	
Online service revenues	$1,429,445
Other revenues	255,783
Total revenues	$1,685,228
Costs and expenses:	
Cost of revenues	$1,040,762
Marketing	
Marketing	409,260
Write-off of deferred subscriber acquisition costs	385,221
Product development	58,208
General and administrative	193,537
Amortization of goodwill	6,549
Restructuring charge	48,627
Contract termination charge	24,506
Settlement charge	24,204
Total costs and expenses	$2,190,874
Income (loss) from operations	$ (505,646)
Other income (expense), net	6,299
Income (loss) before provision for income taxes	$ (499,347)
Provision for income taxes	—
Net income (loss)	$ (499,347)

Like its balance sheets, AOL's income statements contain a lot of detail. Let's examine the big picture again to try to see what caused AOL's loss.

We know that income statements show revenues and expenses, and AOL's statement reflects that basic truth. Its revenues are broken down into Online Service Revenues and Other Revenues. These classifications fit the description in the section on its business and environment.

AOL's revenues in 1996 were $1.1 billion. Revenues increased to $1.7 billion in 1997. It does not appear then that the competition stole all of AOL's customers that year!

Because it posted a loss in 1997, we know that AOL's expenses must have exceeded its revenues. We see from the total expenses line that expenses were about $2.2 billion. We need to go into the detail of these expenses to better understand the loss.

From AOL's 10K: "Cost of revenues includes network-related costs, consisting primarily of data network costs, costs associated with operating the data centers and providing customer support, royalties paid to information and service providers, the costs of merchandise sold, and product development amortization expense."

We can start by just scanning the expenses section. After the cost of revenues, AOL's largest expense at $409 million is Marketing. It is also what we might expect from a company that is rapidly expanding its revenues.

AOL's next largest expense is something called Write-Off of Deferred Subscriber Acquisition Costs. Further, it is a large one, about $385 million. The fourth largest expense is the roughly $194 million for General and Administrative. We may not be able to assess how reasonable the amount is yet, but certainly we would expect AOL to have this type of expense.

We should probe further into the write-off of the deferred subscriber acquisition costs. We can proceed in at least three ways. First, we can look at the notes to the financial statements for explanations. Second, we can look at the cash flow statements to try to find the cash portion of the write-off. Finally, we can use what we learned in Chapters 2, 3, and 4 about the connections between income statements, balance sheets, and cash flow statements to put together all the information.

Notes to AOL's Financial Statements

OBJECTIVE:

Learn to read real company financial reports: notes to the financial statements.

Any time you encounter something unfamiliar in a financial statement, the first place you should look for an explanation is the notes. AOL's financial statements themselves give us that advice when they tell us to "See accompanying notes." All public financial statements have a similar phrase.

We will not reproduce all of the notes to AOL's financial statements; Exhibit 5.3 contains the parts of Note 2, "Summary of Significant Accounting Policies," that are relevant to subscriber acquisition costs.

This note contains a lot of information even though it is written in the technical style of accounting. The note begins by referring to *Statement of Position (SOP) 93-7,*

Exhibit 5.3

America Online, Inc.
Excerpts from Note 2 to the
1997 Financial Statements

AOL expenses all advertising as incurred.

Previous treatment of direct response advertising costs.

Description of amortization policy.

Management review of the estimates.

2. Summary of Significant Accounting Policies

. . .

Subscriber Acquisition Costs: The Company accounts for subscriber acquisition costs pursuant to Statement of Position 93-7, "Reporting on Advertising Costs" ("SOP 93-7"). As a result of the Company's change in accounting estimate (see Note 3), effective October 1, 1996, the Company began expensing all costs of advertising as incurred.

Prior to October 1, 1996, the Company accounted for the cost of direct response advertising as deferred subscriber acquisition costs to comply with the criteria of SOP 93-7. These costs consist solely of the costs of marketing programs which result in subscriber registrations without further effort required by the Company. Direct response advertising costs relate directly to subscriber solicitations and principally include the printing, production and shipping of starter kits and the costs of obtaining qualified prospects by various targeted direct marketing programs and from third parties. These subscriber acquisition costs have been incurred for the solicitation of specifically identifiable prospects. The deferred costs were amortized, beginning the month after such costs were incurred, over a period determined by calculating the ratio of current revenues related to direct response advertising versus the total expected revenues related to this advertising, or twenty-four months, whichever was shorter. All other costs related to the acquisition of subscribers, as well as general marketing costs, were expensed as incurred. . . .

On a quarterly basis, management reviewed the estimated future operating results of the Company's subscriber base in order to evaluate the recoverability of deferred subscriber acquisition costs and the related amortization period. Management's assessment of the recoverability and amortization period of deferred subscriber acquisition costs was subject to change based upon actual results and other factors.

. . .

A Statement of Position is an authoritative statement issued by the American Institute of Certified Public Accountants. It deals with matters not addressed by the FASB. It is not binding in the way FASB statements are binding. Rather it is strongly suggestive of the proper approach to an accounting matter.

OBJECTIVE:
Learn to analyze how companies' accounting choices affect their financial statements.

"Reporting on Advertising Costs." This reference is good to know, because if we really get stuck we'll go look it up. For now, let's just try to figure out what's going on without researching this SOP.

We next learn that the company began "expensing" all advertising costs on October 1, 1996. The reason given is a change in an accounting estimate, and we are referred to Note 3, which we will examine shortly.

We see that before October 1, 1996, AOL accounted for the costs of Direct Response Advertising as Deferred Subscriber Acquisition Costs. This note indicates that amounts spent for a certain kind of advertising—direct response—were set up as an asset on the balance sheet. To "defer" the cost, as used in this context, means to put off recording it as an expense. We know from Chapters 2 and 3 that asset accounts are created when a cost is incurred earlier than the related expense is recognized.

The next bit tells us that what constitutes these Direct Response Advertising costs are only the costs of certain kinds of marketing programs. These marketing programs result in subscribers signing up with AOL without any further effort from the company. The costs related directly to the solicitation of specifically identifiable prospects.

Some general knowledge of what AOL was doing is really useful at this point. One of the ways they were signing up subscribers was by mailing out diskettes with AOL software and a limited-time, free access to AOL. Exhibit 5.4 contains a picture of one such diskette.

Exhibit 5.4

The costs of identifying suitable targets to whom the disks were mailed, of printing the envelopes and sales materials that were included with the disks, and of producing and mailing the disks are all examples of the costs AOL was deferring (i.e., recording as an asset) before October 1, 1996.

How can such costs be classified as an asset? The conceptual test is simple: Are these costs generating a future benefit? Are the benefits sufficiently assured and quantifiable enough to justify recording? And if they are recorded as an asset, what method is to be employed to record their usage?

The note tells us that the deferred costs "were amortized, beginning the month after such costs were incurred, over a period" related to the revenues expected to be generated by the advertising. In no case would the amortization period exceed 24 months. (We can tell from the balance sheet that they were being amortized over a period longer than one year. They were not classified as a current asset.) The note also assures us that AOL management was monitoring the subscriber base "to evaluate the recoverability of deferred subscriber acquisition costs and the related amortization period."

To recap, before October 1, 1996, AOL set up some advertising costs as an asset and amortized them over something less than 24 months. After October 1, 1996, AOL began to expense these costs as incurred. It is now time for Note 3, part of which is reproduced in Exhibit 5.5.

Exhibit 5.5

America Online, Inc. Excerpts from Note 3 to the 1997 Financial Statements

AOL decides that deferred subscriber acquisition costs are not an asset.

3. Change in Accounting Estimate

As a result of a change in accounting estimate, the Company recorded a charge of $385,221,000 ($4.03 per share), as of September 30, 1996, representing the balance of deferred subscriber acquisition costs as of that date. . . . The Company's changing business model, which includes flat-rate pricing for its online service, increasingly is expected to reduce its reliance on online service subscriber revenues for the generation of revenues and profits. This changing business model, coupled with a lack of historical experience with flat-rate pricing, created uncertainties regarding the level of expected future economic benefits from online service subscriber revenues. As a result, the Company believed it no longer had an adequate accounting basis to support recognizing deferred subscriber acquisition costs as an asset.

. . .

Note 3 tells us that because of changes in AOL's business and environment, as of October 1, 1996, it "no longer had an adequate accounting basis" to keep these costs on the books as an asset. So it took the balance as of September 30, 1996, in the asset account, Deferred Subscriber Acquisition Costs, and "recorded a charge of $385,221,000." It means that on September 30, 1996, AOL looked at the balance in the asset account Deferred Subscriber Acquisition Costs of $385,221,000 and decided that it could no longer sustain an argument that the future benefits associated with these expenses were reasonably certain and quantifiable. Without adequate foundation for the future benefits of these costs, they can no longer be carried as an asset; they must be taken against income immediately. (People use a lot of phrases for this act—"taking a charge," "incurring a write-off," and "recording an asset impairment" are a few.) An accountant can do this write-off with a stroke of a pen or, more likely, a keyboard, by making the following entry (in thousands):

OBJECTIVE:
Learn to use debits, credits, and T-accounts to analyze real company reports.

Write-Off of Deferred Subscriber Acquisition Costs . .   385,221
    Deferred Subscriber Acquisition Costs, net   385,221

It explains how the $385,221,000 reduction in operating income came about. An amount that had been accumulating over the years in an asset account was written-off all on October 1, 1996.

We can flesh out the picture even more by looking at the cash flow statements.

AOL's Cash Flow Statement

OBJECTIVE:
Learn to read real company financial reports: cash flow statements.

AOL's cash flow statement is contained in Exhibit 5.6. AOL uses the indirect method of showing its cash flows. The big-picture look shows us three things. Despite the loss, operations actually provided cash of about $123 million. Consistent with a growing company, investing activities consumed about $197 million. Finally, in accord with our observation from the balance sheets that AOL issued equity in 1997, we see that financing activities provided about $79 million.

Exhibit 5.6

America Online, Inc.
Consolidated Statement of
Cash Flows

America Online, Inc.
Consolidated Statement of Cash Flows for the Year Ended June 30, 1997
(amounts in thousands)

CASH FLOWS FROM OPERATING ACTIVITIES

Net income (loss)	$(499,347)
Adjustments to reconcile net income to net cash provided by (used in) operating activities:	
Write-off of deferred subscriber acquisition costs	$ 385,221
Noncash restructuring charges	22,478
Depreciation and amortization	64,572
Amortization of subscriber acquisition costs	59,189
Changes in assets and liabilities:	
Trade accounts receivable	(16,418)
Other receivables	2,083
Prepaid expenses and other current assets	(44,394)
Deferred subscriber acquisition costs	(130,229)
Other assets	(38,902)
Trade accounts payable	(36,944)
Accrued personnel costs	2,979
Other accrued expenses and liabilities	139,134
Deferred revenue	214,097
Other liabilities	(470)
Total adjustments	$ 622,396
NET CASH PROVIDED BY (USED IN) OPERATING ACTIVITIES	$ 123,049

Add-back of write-off of deferred subscriber acquisitions costs

Add-back of amortization of deferred subscriber acquisitions costs

Cash spent for deferred subscriber acquisition costs

CASH FLOWS FROM INVESTING ACTIVITIES

Short-term investments	$ 10,444
Purchase of property and equipment	(149,768)
Product development costs	(56,795)
Purchase costs of acquired businesses	(475)
NET CASH USED IN INVESTING ACTIVITIES	$(196,594)

CASH FLOWS FROM FINANCING ACTIVITIES

Proceeds from issuance of preferred stock of subsidiary	$ 15,000
Proceeds from issuance of common stock, net	84,506
Principal and accrued interest payments on line of credit and long-term debt	(19,811)
Proceeds from line of credit and issuance of long-term debt	50,000
Restricted cash	(50,000)
Principal payments under capital lease obligations	(231)
NET CASH PROVIDED BY FINANCING ACTIVITIES	$ 79,464
Net increase in cash and cash equivalents	$ 5,919
Cash and cash equivalents at beginning of year	118,421
Cash and cash equivalents at end of year	$ 124,340

SUPPLEMENTAL CASH FLOW INFORMATION

Cash paid during the year for:	
Interest	$ 1,567
Income taxes	—

Now let's take a closer look, especially for information that might be relevant to the write-off. Three lines contain the phrase "subscriber acquisition costs," all under cash flows from operating activities. They all fall under "Adjustments to reconcile net income to net cash provided by (used in) operating activities."

"Write-off of deferred subscriber acquisition costs" results in an add-back to the net loss of about $385 million—$385,221,000 to be exact, and that is exactly equal to the expense reported on the income statement.

"Amortization of subscriber acquisition costs" results in another add-back of about $59 million. Recall that amortization, like depreciation, is a noncash expense. We would expect that to result in an add-back to the net loss.

Finally, "Deferred subscriber acquisition costs" results in a subtraction of about $130 million. This amount could be the cash spent on deferred subscriber acquisition costs.

Using Articulation to Complete the Picture

OBJECTIVE:

Learn more about the articulation of balance sheets, income statements, and statements of cash flows.

We will now put these pieces together. Let's begin by relating the balance sheets and the income statement. The bottom line loss in the income statement should impact the accumulated deficit. Exhibit 5.7 uses our knowledge of the articulation of balance sheets and income statements to understand completely what happened in the accumulated deficit account.

Exhibit 5.7

AOL's Accumulated Deficit Account

	Accumulated Deficit (amounts in thousands)
Balance at June 30, 1996 (from 1996 balance sheet)	$ 7,767
Loss for fiscal 1997 (from income statement)	499,347
Balance at June 30, 1997 (from 1997 balance sheet)	$507,114

Now look at AOL's assets. The three main categories are current assets, property and equipment, and other assets. The other assets contain a line titled "Deferred subscriber acquisition costs, net." Further, this asset went from about $314 million at June 30, 1996, to $0 at June 30, 1997. Although this $314 million decline is not exactly equal to the expense of $385 million, it is in the neighborhood. The wording tells us they are both related to deferred subscriber acquisition costs.

We know from the cash flow statement that amortization of about $59 million was taken before the October 1 write-off. Further, about $130 million was spent increasing the deferred subscriber costs.

A lot of pieces are swirling around. We can use our knowledge of debits and credits to organize them. Exhibit 5.8 combines what we know about the deferred subscriber acquisition costs in a T-account analysis.

The deferred subscriber acquisition costs account works out exactly; that is, when we put together everything we know, we explain all the items related to it. Information from all three major financial statements fits together in the analysis. The beginning and ending balances from the balance sheets tell us where we start and where we must end. The amortization and the write-off are decreases in the asset, which are reflected in the income statement. The cash spent for these costs are the additions to the account.

Exhibit 5.8

Deferred Subscriber Acquisition
Costs Account

Deferred Subscriber Acquisition Costs
(amounts in thousands)

Balance at June 30, 1996 (from 1996 balance sheet)	314,181		
Increases (from cash flow statement)	130,229	59,189	Amortization (from cash flow statement)
Balance at September 30, 1996	385,221		
		385,221	October 1 write-off (from income statement)
Balance at June 30, 1997 (from 1997 balance sheet)	0		

The write-off of $385 million is shown as a separate item on the income state-
ment, so we can take the amount directly from there. The amortization of $59 million
is included in the $409 million marketing expenses on the income statement. Just from
the income statement, we do not know the amount of this amortization. Fortunately,
AOL uses the indirect method for its cash flow statement. The amortization of deferred
subscriber acquisition costs is added back to the net loss as a separate line in the statement of cash flows. Otherwise, we would have to try to "plug" this amount, and we might
be less sure of our analysis.

Analysis and Discussion

Our analysis of AOL's financial statements reveals that the primary cause of its loss in
1997 was the write-off of deferred subscriber acquisition costs. Before October 1, 1996,
AOL viewed these costs of advertising campaigns as generating future benefits and
recorded them as assets. This treatment was acceptable under GAAP because of *Statement of Position 93-7*.

Between July 1, 1996, and September 30, 1996, AOL spent about $130 million on
these advertising campaigns and added that amount to the asset account. Also between
July 1, 1996, and September 30, 1996, AOL recorded amortization of the asset of $59 mil-
lion, which left a balance of about $385 million in the asset Deferred Subscriber Acqui-
sition Costs.

On October 1, 1996, AOL wrote off that asset. You might wonder whether the price
of AOL's common stock fell when this write-off was announced. The answer: no! The
stock price actually went up by $1 per share on that day.

Financial analysts already knew what this asset represented. AOL's notes to its financial statements explained its accounting for these advertising costs. The 1997 financial
statements and some press releases explained that the write-off would cause a dip in earnings. Financial analysts were well aware that AOL's revenue model was changing and did
not change their assessment of AOL's value as a result of this accounting entry.

So why are we bothering with this analysis? Consider the consequences of taking
AOL's financial reports at face value. Let's look at some numbers, including the results
for 1998 so you will more clearly see the effects on analysis of AOL's trends.

Exhibit 5.9 gives some selected financial data from AOL's 1998 10K. We see total revenues and net income (loss) for each of the five years ended June 30, 1994 through 1998.
We see total assets and shareholders' equity at June 30 for each of those years.

Exhibit 5.9

America Online, Inc.
Selected Consolidated
Financial Data

		America Online, Inc. Selected Consolidated Financial Data From 1998 Form 10K (amounts in millions)			
		YEAR ENDED JUNE 30,			
	1994	1995	1996	1997	1998
STATEMENT OF OPERATIONS DATA:					
Total revenues	$115	$394	$1,094	$1,685	$2,600
Net income (loss)	2	(36)	30	(499)	92
BALANCE SHEET DATA:					
Total assets	$155	$405	$ 959	$ 833	$2,214
Stockholders' equity	99	217	513	140	598

AOL's revenues grew explosively, from $115 million to $2.6 billion. Figure 5.1 graphs these revenues.

Figure 5.1

Total Revenues

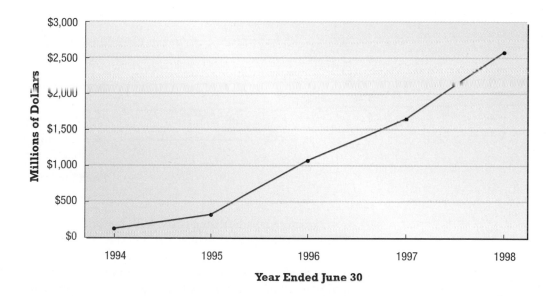

The picture for reported income is not so appealing. Figure 5.2 shows that reported income takes a huge dip in 1997. What if we ignored the reason for this dip? Might we conclude that AOL was headed for bankruptcy in 1997? The write-off does not affect just our view of 1997. The income in 1998 was $92 million, $591 million higher than the loss of $499 million in 1997. Should we conclude that AOL made a spectacular turnaround?

Figure 5.3 graphs the total assets, both as reported and adjusted for the accounting for deferred subscriber acquisitions costs. Total assets are on a nice growth path and then decline in 1997. By 1998, they are back on track. The graph of the assets as reported invites the reader to fill in the dip in 1997.

Figures 5.2 and 5.3 also show AOL's restated net income and total assets as if it had never deferred subscriber acquisition costs. Instead of looking at results measured in different ways before and after October 1, 1996, the restatements attempt to show them with a consistent accounting treatment. Both Figures 5.2 and 5.3 merit close study.

Figure 5.2

Net Income (Loss) as Reported and Restated

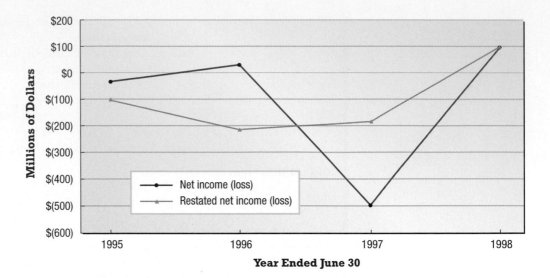

Figure 5.3

Total Assets as Reported and Restated

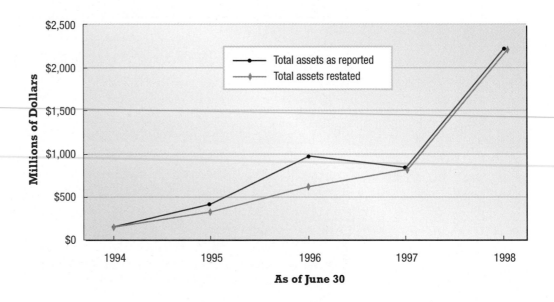

By deferring advertising costs, AOL *increased* its reported net incomes prior to 1997. Think of it this way: the difference between the costs of subscriber acquisition and the amount recorded in marketing expenses for those costs is equal to the change in the asset account, Deferred Subscriber Acquisition Costs (recall Chapter 4). Because the balance in Deferred Subscriber Acquisition Costs increased in each year before 1997, some of AOL's cost of subscriber acquisition prior to October 1, 1996, ended up on the balance sheet. It resulted in income higher than if these costs were taken immediately as expenses.

So the restated net income graph is "smoother" for two reasons: it shows no big write-off in 1997 and the restated incomes for earlier years were lower.

Finding the dollar effect of the write-off on 1997 reported income requires us to think carefully about the articulation of the financial statements. At first blush, it might seem that the effect of the write-off was its total amount, about $385 million. This assumption is incorrect. Before the write-off, AOL had already recorded amortization expense for these deferred costs of $59 million, but it had also deferred an additional $130 million in costs. The difference: $130 − $59 = $71 million is the amount by which the $385 million write-off *overstates* the effect on income. The net effect of the write-off on 1997 income is: $385 − $71 = $314 million. It is no coincidence that $314 million is the beginning balance in the deferred subscriber acquisition costs account, that is, the total that had been held off the income statement to the start of the period.

The effects on total assets are slightly different. Once AOL wrote off the deferred subscriber acquisitions costs in 1997, its balance sheet looked at that point as if it had never deferred them. The write-off eliminated the entire amount of the accumulated asset. It reduced income in 1997, which was closed to Accumulated Deficit, thus reducing shareholders' equity. The restatement affects our view of the trend in AOL's total assets because it affects the years *before* 1997. Total assets in 1996 would have been $314 million lower if AOL had not been deferring these costs. Total assets in 1995 would have been $77 million lower. The effect of lower 1996 and earlier assets is to make AOL's growth seem more smooth, and more in line with its revenue growth pattern.

Conclusion

Financial statement analysis is the art of applying knowledge of a business, its context, and the structure of accounting to better understand an organization's financial reports. We illustrated this art by analyzing America Online's financial statements for fiscal 1997, a particularly interesting year because of changes in AOL's business. More important for our purposes, however, it was interesting because its reported results were dramatically affected by a change in its accounting. By taking information from the balance sheets, income statement, cash flow statement, and notes, we were able to assess the effects of this change in accounting on AOL's reported performance. By changing 1997's reported performance, the change in accounting also affects our attempts to compare 1997 to other years.

This chapter completes our study of the basic structure of accounting. We explored in some detail how balance sheets, income statements, and statements of cash flows are structured and how they interrelate. We pushed a lot of numbers through accounts and showed how they work their way through the various financial statements.

We did not, however, detail how the numbers that we pushed around are generated. That task occupies the remainder of this book. A lot of work is required here, because a number of different techniques are used. We approach it in two steps. In Chapter 6, we present some basics of valuation; we then illustrate their importance in Chapter 7. Beginning in Chapter 8, we apply these basics to particular items such as receivables, inventories, long-term assets, liabilities, and equities.

PART 2

Valuation Basics and Accounting Measures

chapter 6

© GETTY IMAGES/EYE WIRE

Economic Concepts: Behind the Accounting Numbers

An apocryphal story is told of a wealthy but none too bright young man who purchased a fancy new van. While driving it home down the freeway at 70 miles per hour, he got a little thirsty. So he set the cruise control and got up to fix himself a drink. Needless to say, he awoke in the hospital with bigger worries than being a little thirsty!

This fellow's problem was a lack of understanding of how cruise control connected with the task of driving the car. In his mind, cruise control was an automatic pilot. This misconception led him to use his cruise control to turn his car into an unguided missile.

To avoid turning your organization or your investment portfolio into an unguided missile, you need to understand that you cannot rely on accounting "cruise control." Good use of financial statements requires judgment and an understanding of how accounting numbers are connected to underlying economics.

Of course, you can't know how accounting is connected to underlying economics without knowing something about economics. This chapter introduces some basic economic concepts and connects them to accounting. It has four main goals:

1. To show how economic reasoning is used in the process of making accounting adjustments

2. To define and show how to compute
   - Present value
   - Expected value

3. To show how to use present value and expected value to compute the economic value of a sequence of uncertain cash flows occurring in different accounting periods

4. To show how information impacts economic value

We begin achieving these goals by discussing accounting adjustments. Adjustments are the heart of accounting. Their purpose is to bring the amounts in the accounts more into line with the stocks and flows of economic resources. A **stock** of a resource is the amount of the resource an entity has at a point in time. A **flow** is the change in the amount of the resource over a period of time.

Adjustments are required because of the passage of time or the arrival of new information. The adjustments we have seen up to this point in the book reflect only the effects of the passage of time on economic value. They have been fairly straightforward, such as the expiration of prepaid rent. More complicated adjustments are required by the effects of time on economic value, and we need to lay the groundwork for them by going deeper into the effects of time.

Many of the adjustments we will see in the remaining chapters reflect the effects of new information on economic value. We have not yet seen such adjustments, and they require some expansion of our thinking. Information resolves uncertainty, so we begin by exploring economic value under uncertainty. Then we can address how information affects economic value.

Cash flows are the starting point in understanding economic value. Because money has time value, we must have a procedure to compare dollar amounts at different points in time. Is having $1.05 a year from now better than having $1.00 right now? Of course, $1.05 is larger than $1.00. But what if we could safely deposit our dollar in the bank for a year and earn 6% interest? If we deposit our dollar in the bank we will have $1.06 next year, rather than $1.05.

The timing of cash flows is handled by present value techniques. The uncertainty of cash flows

Accounting Adjustments

OBJECTIVE:

Learn the two approaches to
accounting adjustments.

Recall how the accounting process works. It begins with identification of the *transactions*
in which an organization has engaged. The concepts of assets, liabilities, equities, revenues, and expenses are used to classify and record these transactions. Before financial
statements are prepared, the accounts are analyzed and all required *adjustments* are made.
Temporary accounts are then *closed,* and financial statements are prepared.

Though each of these phases of the accounting process is important, the initial recording of a transaction and the process of adjustment are really the essence of financial accounting. Because many transactions are routine and can be captured electronically and
the preparation of financial statements from a proper set of accounts is a routine task,
the adjustment process is often where the action is.

We make adjustments because the amounts in the accounts do not automatically reflect the correct amounts of economic stocks and flows. We can approach adjusting any
given account in one of two ways. The first is to estimate the appropriate ending balance
in the account. We then plug in the required activity to the account to generate that ending balance. The second way is to estimate the activity in the account, then calculate the
implied ending balance.

Perhaps the best way to see these approaches is to review some of the example adjustments made in previous chapters.

Websell's Adjustments

*Review the Websell example
in Chapter 3.*

The adjustments to Websell's accounts are presented in Chapter 3 and are reproduced in
Exhibit 6.1. Recall that the adjustment process began after all Websell's transactions were
entered into the accounts. Before making up financial statements, we analyzed Websell's
accounts to see whether adjusting entries were required to bring account balances to
amounts that better reflect economic values.

Accounting Cycle:
Analyze Transactions
↓
Record Transactions
↓
*Make Necessary Adjustments
at the End of the Period*
↓
Close Temporary Accounts
↓
*Prepare the Financial
Statements*

Excluding the entries that close the revenue and expense accounts to Retained Earnings, eleven adjustments were made to Websell's accounts. Four adjustments (b, c, d, and
e) reduced the value of a current asset account and increased an expense account. Three
of the four (b, c, and d) reduced the value of a prepaid asset and increased an expense
account. The prepaid assets that were reduced were Prepaid Insurance, Prepaid Telephone,
and Prepaid Rent. The expenses that were increased were Insurance Expense, Miscellaneous Expenses, and Rent Expense. The fourth, (e), reduced Supplies Inventory and increased Miscellaneous Expenses.

When an asset account is reduced and an expense account is increased, two things
are accomplished. By reducing the asset account, the adjustment makes the balance sheet
reflect a more accurate picture of the value of the asset at the balance sheet date. By increasing the expense account, the adjustment makes the income statement reflect a more
accurate picture of the value of the asset used during the period in the process of generating revenues.

Exhibit 6.1

Websell's Adjustments

REF	ACCOUNT	DR	CR
b	Insurance Expense	7,500	
	Prepaid Insurance		7,500
	(Expiration of insurance.)		
c	Miscellaneous Expenses	1,000	
	Prepaid Telephone		1,000
	(Expiration of telephone rights.)		
d	Rent Expense	37,500	
	Prepaid Rent		37,500
	(Expiration of rental rights.)		
e	Miscellaneous Expenses	1,500	
	Supplies Inventory		1,500
	(Usage of supplies.)		
f	Amortization Expense	10,000	
	Copyright Permissions		10,000
	(Expiration of copyright permissions.)		
g	Amortization Expense	12,500	
	Software		12,500
	(Expiration of software licenses.)		
h	Depreciation Expense	30,000	
	Accumulated Depreciation		30,000
	(Depreciation of equipment.)		
i	Amortization Expense	5,000	
	Internet Access Rights		5,000
	(Expiration of rights to access Internet.)		
j	Amortization Expense	100,000	
	Web Site		100,000
	(Expiration of investment in creating Web site.)		
k	Wages Expense	33,000	
	Wages Payable		33,000
	(Wages owed but not paid.)		
m	Interest Expense	60,000	
	Interest Payable		60,000
	(Interest owed but not paid.)		

Adjustment Approach 1: Estimate the Remaining Asset Value

For a specific example, consider adjustment (e) that debited Miscellaneous Expenses and credited Supplies Inventory. Before the adjustment, Supplies Inventory had a balance of $2,000, which reflected the only transaction involving the account—the purchase of supplies (entry 5 in Chapter 2). A count of the inventory showed that only $500 of supplies was on hand at June 30, 2004. How did this happen? Some supplies were used (or stolen), but the balance in the account was not kept up-to-date. Instead of keeping track of what was used in real time, Websell decided to count the inventory periodically (just before it needed to construct financial statements) and adjust the supplies inventory account to reflect what still remained (was unused).

A count of the inventory revealed that $500 of supplies remained at June 30, meaning $1,500 was used. The adjustment takes $1,500 out of Supplies Inventory and increases

Miscellaneous Expenses to reflect this usage of supplies. Figure 6.1 displays these relationships visually.

Figure 6.1

Adjusting the Inventory Account

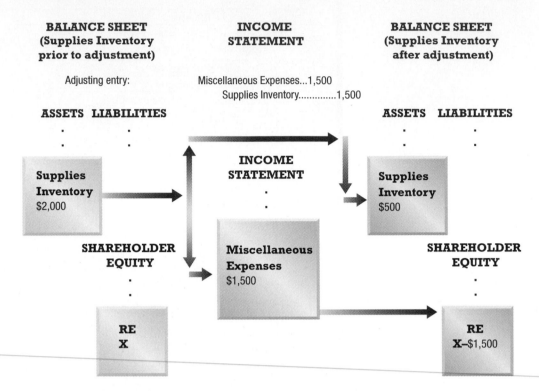

Figure 6.2 shows this adjustment process from the point of view of the supplies inventory T-account. The count of the supplies allowed us to estimate directly the ending balance in the account, which is the book value that will be shown on the balance sheet. We then plug (make an inference as to the amount taken out) the activity in the account.

Figure 6.2

Two Approaches to Accounting Adjustments

Approach 1: Estimate ending account balance and "plug" expense

Supplies Inventory

Balance prior to adjustment	2,000	1,500	"Plug" needed to balance the account
Ending balance (estimated)	500		

Approach 2: Estimate expense and "plug" ending account balance

Web Site

Balance prior to adjustment	1,200,000	100,000	Amount used up during the period (estimated)
"Plugged" ending balance	1,100,000		

Adjustment Approach 2: Estimate the Amount of Expense for the Period

Another way to approach an adjustment is to estimate the value of what was used—that is, the expense. The value of what remains would then be a plug—that is, it would be derived from the amount in the account and the expense estimate.

An **allocation process** is any procedure that assigns costs in a mechanical way.

For example, consider adjustment (j) that records Amortization Expense and reduces the asset Web Site. We made this adjustment by estimating the benefits used (Amortization Expense) through an **allocation process.** For the Web site, this reasoning was:

- Websell spent $1.2 million developing the Web site.
- Websell expects it to last three years.
- One-fourth a year has gone by between March 31 and June 30.

So we allocate:

$$[(1/4 \text{ year}) \times (\$1,200,000/3 \text{ years})] = \$100,000$$

to Amortization Expense from the asset account, Web Site. This adjustment leaves a book value of the Web site on Websell's balance sheet of $1.1 million.

Figure 6.2 shows this adjustment process from the point of view of the Web site T-account. The estimation of the amount used up during the period permits us to make an inference as to the remaining value of the asset; that is, we plug for the ending value of the Web site.

It may seem that we have gone overboard in describing these two ways to approach adjustments. After all, it seems as though we should get the same numbers on the income statement and the balance sheet regardless of the approach. Will we get the same numbers? A lot of research on decision making shows our answers often depend on how we *frame* the problem. Estimating the expense might cause us to use one type of logic and estimation method. Estimating the value of the asset or liability remaining might cause us to use a different type of logic and estimation method. In practice, the resulting financial statements might well differ depending on which framing of the problem we adopt.

The FASB currently favors a **balance sheet approach** to adjustment.

Many accountants believe that the framing in U.S. GAAP has been changing. They think that recent FASB rules force them to estimate the balance sheet number and plug the income statement number. Older approaches often focus on estimating the income statement number and plugging the balance sheet. The recent approach is often referred to as the FASB's adopting a **balance sheet approach** in making accounting policy.

For example, we might get quite different numbers for Amortization Expense and Web Site if we approached the problem as one of estimating the economic value of the Web site as of June 30. We are likely to have a difficult time even getting started on this problem. What is the economic value of Websell's Web site? Websell is not likely to be able to sell the site to anyone without selling its entire business. No doubt, the Web site is expected to deliver future benefits over the next two and three-fourths years of its life, but how do we estimate their value? Any such process is likely to be as rough as the allocation process that yielded the amortization of $100,000 and left a net book value of $1,100,000. It is unlikely, however, that the outcome of a process of valuing the Web site at June 30 would give us these same numbers. Now you might start to get an inkling of how the two approaches to adjustments might make a difference. It is one thing to say that Websell expects the Web site to last three years; Websell spent $1,200,000 developing it, so we will *allocate* $100,000 to expense for the period from April 1 to June 30. It is quite another thing to say that we are going to *estimate the remaining value* of the Web site at June 30.

OBJECTIVE:
Learn the importance of valuation processes in determining accounting adjustments.

Articulation is the fitting together of the financial statements. For example, the income statement ties in to the beginning and ending balance sheets.

Adjustments and Valuation

All 11 of Websell's adjustments share a similar purpose. Each adjusts an income statement item (in Websell's case, the adjustments all related to expenses, but often adjustments relate to revenues) and a balance sheet item (either an asset or a liability). Adjustments clearly reflect the **articulation** of the income statement and balance sheet. Assets get used up and become expenses. Satisfying the obligations associated with liabilities can cause revenues to be recognized (e.g., Revenue Received in Advance), or liabilities can be used to record unpaid expenses (e.g., Wages Payable). The process of *reporting income* in the income statement, therefore, is intimately linked to the process of *reporting value* in the balance sheet. As we mentioned, GAAP are increasingly framed as requiring value estimates first, and then deriving (plugging) the expense and revenue implications. A focus on valuation is what necessitates this chapter on the determinants of value.

Valuation is a complex and evolving combination of science, skill, and guesswork. To keep things manageable, we present the elements of value most important to accounting. Far and away, the most important thing is to realize that the value of concern to us is tied to cash flows. We discuss this first and then go into two important properties of cash flows: uncertainty about collecting or paying them and their timing. We introduce elementary techniques for dealing with uncertainty and timing and apply these techniques in later chapters in which we encounter complex adjustments.

Review Questions

1. For each of the Websell adjustments (Exhibit 6.1), indicate whether the approach taken to adjustment was to estimate the expense and plug the ending account balance or if it was to estimate the ending balance in the account and plug for the expense.

2. Pick one or two of the Websell adjustments and talk through the ease or difficulty of making the adjustment from the opposite of the perspective taken (e.g., if the ending balance sheet number was estimated and the expense plugged, how difficult or easy would it have been to estimate the expense and plug the ending balance?).

Cash Flows and Economic Value

OBJECTIVE:

Learn about the role of cash flow streams in determining economic value.

Donald Trump once said, "Cash is king." Although he was talking about what he thought were the best kinds of investments at the time, he aptly captured the importance of cash in affecting values. In fact, the economic value of an asset is determined by the cash flows the asset will generate. It is what separates the economic value of business assets from the consumption value of the things that we use in our private lives.

For example, consider buying a car. When we buy a car for our own private transportation, we weigh many factors that affect our enjoyment of the use of the car. Some prefer a sports car, others a luxury car, others a sport-utility vehicle, and others a pickup. Others do not get much enjoyment out of the car they drive and might prefer the most basic model available. The important point here is that the car's value for private transportation is de-

When the purchase of a new car is for business, not personal use, the economic opportunities the purchase brings to the buyer are a business asset.

© GETTY IMAGES/PHOTO DISC

rived from the stream of *consumption* it generates. We are not concerned in this book with value generated from consumption.

The situation is different if we are considering buying a car for business use. In a business context, the value of the car is the financial value of the stream of services it provides to the business. For example, it might enhance a saleswoman's ability to make calls on customers. This enhancement translates into dollars and cents for the business. In fact, the car is an *asset* because it generates future benefits, that is, cash. Although it may be difficult to determine the cash consequences of supplying a saleswoman a car to use in making calls, that difficulty does not alter the fact that the value of the car is determined by the stream of cash its services generate. The value of the car depends on its *cash flows*. This source of value is our concern in this book.

Two properties of cash flow streams affect their value. One is their *timing*. A dollar today is worth more than a dollar tomorrow because it allows immediate consumption or it may be invested. The second property is *uncertainty*. When cash flows extend into the future, no one can be sure if the amounts of cash will actually turn out to be what they are currently estimated to be. Websell may extend credit to a customer, but no one is sure of how much ultimately will be collected. The next sections cover these two properties.

<table>
<tr><td>

OBJECTIVE:
Learn about two important properties of cash flow streams: timing and uncertainty.

</td></tr>
</table>

Cash Flows over Time: The Time Value of Money

When cash flows occur over time, interest must be taken into account. People can do a number of things with their money: they can use it to buy goods and services for consumption; they can invest it in the stock market or put it in the bank; or they can put it in a jar under their bed. All these opportunities imply that a dollar in hand today is worth more than a dollar to be received tomorrow.

Interest is the charge levied to postpone the payment or receipt of funds. If you deposit money in a savings account, the bank pays you interest for allowing it to use your money. Similarly, if you take out a loan, the lender charges you interest for using its money until you repay the loan.

Interest can be thought of as the charge (price paid) for the ability to transfer cash across time periods.

Future Value

OBJECTIVE:
Learn how to compute compound interest.

The calculation of interest at first may seem a bit complicated, but really only one idea is involved: compound interest. To illustrate, consider what happens if you deposit $100 in a savings account that pays 4% interest per year. At the end of one year, assuming you made no withdrawals, you earn $100 \times 0.04 = $4 in interest. Your account balance will be $100 + $100 \times 0.04 = $104 (the original $100 deposit plus the $4 interest earned for the year). It is revealing to rewrite this last expression.

$$\$100 + (\$100 \times 0.04) = \$100 \times (1 + 0.04) = \$100 \times (1.04)$$

Assuming no withdrawals, this $104 becomes your beginning balance for the next year. How much would you have at the end of the second year if you left all this money in your account? Carrying the previous calculation of the ending balance onward, we have:

$$\$104 + (\$104 \times 0.04) = \$104 \times (1 + 0.04)$$
$$= \$104 \times (1.04)$$
$$= \$108.16$$

Now, let's rewrite this calculation to state everything in terms of the original $100 deposit:

$$\$108.16 = \$104 \times (1.04)$$
$$= [\$100 \times (1.04)] \times (1.04)$$
$$= \$100 \times (1.04) \times (1.04)$$
$$= \$100 \times (1.04)^2$$

In real applications, the **period** is the longest length of time over which interest is not compounded.

We can generalize this logic to an arbitrary interest rate, i, and an arbitrary number of **periods**, t. An initial deposit of $D that earns interest at the rate i per period left for t periods will accumulate to:

$$\$D \times (1 + i)^t$$

It is called the ***future value*** of D dollars at i% interest per period for t periods.

You might be wondering where the term ***compound interest*** comes from. We illustrate by rewriting the future value of $100 at 4% annual interest in two periods in a way that tracks what happens to the interest payments.

EXAMPLE: Suppose a bank pays 6% interest on deposits and agrees to compound the interest semiannually (twice each year). Then t = 2 and i = 0.03. Therefore, a $10 deposit will grow to $10 × (1.03)² at the end of the year.

$$\$108.16 = \$100 \times (1 + 0.04) \times (1 + 0.04)$$
$$= (\$100 + \$4) \times (1 + 0.04)$$
$$= \$100 + \$4 + \$4 + \$0.16$$

| *Initial deposit* | *First period's interest on initial deposit* | *Second period's interest on initial deposit* | *Second period's interest on first period interest* |

The interest on previous interest is where the ***compounding*** comes from. Although at $0.16 it looks small in this example, it can really add up over long periods of time. For example, Figure 6.3 shows how an initial deposit of $100 accumulates to $394.61 over 35 years when the interest rate is 4% per year and no money is withdrawn (i.e., interest remains in the account and earns interest):

$$\$100 \times (1.04)^{35} = \$394.61$$

Figure 6.3
Compound Growth of $100 at 4%

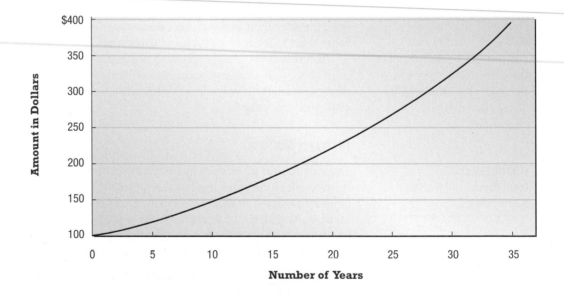

This $394.61 consists of the initial deposit of $100 and $294.61 in interest. Let's break down this $294.61 in interest into the part that is due to the effect of 4% on the initial balance (called **simple interest**) and the effect of interest on interest (compounding). There is $4 per year interest on the $100 deposit. That would give a total of $140 in simple interest over the 35 years:

Simple interest is interest on the initial amount and does not include any interest on interest.

$$(\$100 \times 0.04) \times 35 = \$140$$

That means that $154.61 of the total interest over the 35 years is due to compounding:

Total interest over 35 years	$ 294.61
Simple interest on the $100 deposit	(140.00)
Interest due to compounding	$ 154.61

To show the effect of compounding in practice, Figure 6.4 tracks the Ibbotson Associates *Index of Total Returns on Long-Term Government Bonds* sampled every fifth year from 1965 to 1995. The accelerating growth due to compounding is quite evident in the general shape of the plot of the index. The chart shows that if an investor put approximately $4 into long-term government bonds in 1965, and if all of the interest were reinvested every year when it was received, then the $4 investment would have grown to be in excess of $34 by 1995.

Figure 6.4

Index of Total Returns on Long-Term Government Bonds

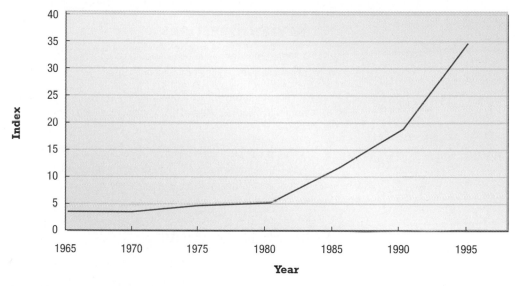

Source: Ibbotson Associates, SBBI 1999 Yearbook.

Review Questions

1. How much will $5,000 deposited today at 6% interest compounded annually be worth in 10 years?

2. How much will the $5,000 deposit grow if the 6% interest is compounded semiannually? (6% interest compounded semiannually means to apply 3% every six months.)

3. If you deposit $1,000 on January 1, 2005, another $1,000 on January 1, 2006, and a third $1,000 on January 1, 2007, how much money will you have on December 31, 2007, if the bank pays 5% interest compounded annually?

4. What would you have in (3) if the bank compounded the 5% interest five times a year (paid 1% interest every 1/5 of a year and compounded it)?

Present Value

OBJECTIVE:

Learn how to use present value techniques to calculate the economic value of cash flow streams received over time.

Future values are important in financial planning, but their reverse, present values, are more important in accounting and in decision making. The concept underlying the calculation of present values is the same as with future values: compound interest. We just need to reverse our calculations. In a future value, we seek to find the ending amount that a given starting amount will produce at the given interest rate at a specified time in the future. In a **present value**, we seek to find the *starting amount* that will produce a given ending amount at some specified date in the future at the given interest rate.

Suppose we want to know how much would have to be deposited in an account earning 4.5% to end up with $1,567.50 one year after the deposit date. We have the following equation:

$$\$1,567.50 = \$B \times (1.045)$$

so,

$$\$B = (\$1,567.50) \times (1/1.045)$$
$$= (\$1,567.50) \times (0.956938)$$
$$= \$1,500$$

We call $1,500 the present value at 4.5% of $1,567.50 to be received one year hence. We may also call $1,500 the *discounted value* of $1,567.50 to be received one year hence at an interest rate of 4.5%. We call (1/1.045 = 0.956938) a *discount factor.*

Review Questions

1. What amount has to be invested right now in order to have $3,000 at the end of three years if you can earn 7% interest compounded yearly?

2. Are you better off right now with $1,000 cash, or would you rather have $1,300 two years from now? You can earn a 10% compounded annual rate of return on your money. Explain your answer.

3. Suppose you can earn an 8% annual compounded rate of return on your investments. What is the most you would be willing to pay right now for the right to receive $1,000 cash at the end of each of the next three years?

Relation to Accounting

OBJECTIVE:

Learn the importance of valuation processes in making accounting adjustments.

We should take a moment here to tie all this work on values back to accounting. Think about what an asset is: It is something that generates *future benefits* for its owner. From an economic or financial perspective, those benefits are the future cash flows associated with the asset. The economic value of an asset is determined by its future cash flows, and those cash flows must be discounted in finding its present value at any point in time.

Several adjustments stipulated by GAAP require assessment of the economic value of the asset. For some assets, the economic value of the asset is obtained by examination of market prices. For example, as we shall see shortly, in the accounting for marketable securities GAAP require adjusting their book values to market values obtained from quoted prices in financial markets.

The more interesting cases, however, are when markets for the assets do not exist. This is the case for many of an organization's fixed assets, such as *manufacturing plants.*

Generally accepted accounting principles warrant recording the estimated future cash flows of a recently acquired business asset.

An **asset impairment adjustment** reduces the book value of an asset to its economic value when the economic value has fallen significantly.

GAAP may require calculation of a present value of the estimated future cash flows that the asset is expected to generate in order to obtain an assessment of the current economic value of the asset. For example, if a company finds that one of its plants will generate future cash flows less than the current book value of the plant, it must make an adjustment. It will write down the carrying value of the plant in the balance sheet to the present value of the future cash flows it is expected to generate. This kind of adjustment is called an **asset impairment adjustment.**

Present Values of Sequences of Cash Flows

OBJECTIVE:

Learn how to use present value techniques to calculate the economic value of cash flow streams received over time.

Most applications involving future and present values involve more complicated sequences of cash flows than the single cash flow we considered thus far. For example, a home mortgage or a car loan requires a sequence of monthly payments that results in repayment over its life. A $1,000 corporate bond might require payment of $25 every six months, plus payment of $1,000 at its maturity date. Building a new manufacturing facility might involve an initial outlay of $10 million in construction costs and generate inflows of $1 million per year over its life of 15 years. A strip mine might require an initial investment to remove the cover of an ore deposit, then generate a sequence of cash inflows as the ore is mined and sold, and then require another cash outlay to restore the site to proper environmental standards.

The fundamentals of calculating future and present values we introduced can be applied to each of these examples. The key is to apply them in a step-by-step fashion. The first task is to compile a list of all the cash inflows and outflows and the dates at which they are to be received. One useful device in compiling this list is a time diagram that provides a visual representation of the cash flow sequence. For example, suppose an asset requires an immediate cash outflow of $2,000 and will generate $1,000 at the end of each of the next three periods. The time diagram begins with a time line that lists the dates at which the cash flow is received across the top. The amount of the cash flow at each date is shown underneath the line as follows:

Date	0	1	2	3
Cash flow	$(2,000)	$1,000	$1,000	$1,000

The next step is to calculate the present value of the cash flow at each date. Suppose the periods represent one year and the annual interest rate is 4%. The $2,000 outflow at date zero has present value $2,000 at date 0. The $1,000 cash inflow at date 1 has a present value of $961.54 as of date 0:

$$\$961.54 = (\$1,000) \times (1/1.04)$$

The cash flows at dates 2 and 3 have present values of $924.56 and $889.00, respectively, as of date 0:

$$\$924.56 = (\$1,000) \times (1/1.04)^2$$

and

$$\$889.00 = (\$1,000) \times (1/1.04)^3$$

The present value of the entire sequence of cash flows is simply the sum of the present values of each of cash flow in the sequence:

Date of cash flow	Present value of cash flow as of date 0
0	$(2,000.00)
1	961.54
2	924.56
3	889.00
Total	$ 775.10

To help you visualize the entire process of computing present values, Exhibit 6.2 shows how to combine the present value calculations with the timeline diagram of cash flows.

Exhibit 6.2

Present Value Diagram

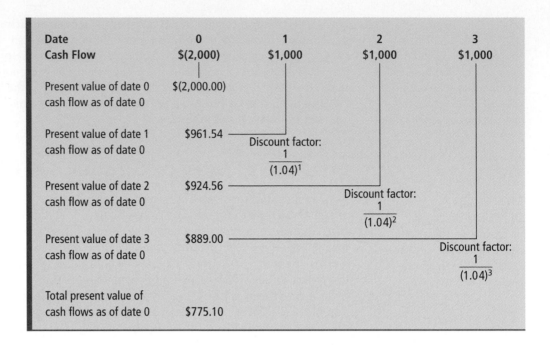

Uncertain Cash Flows: Expected Value

Another property of cash flows that affects their value is the likelihood that they will actually be received. For example, if a business extends credit to 1,000 customers, chances are that not all 1,000 of them will pay the entire amount owed. Some of the customers are likely to fall into financial difficulty and be unable to pay their bills. Others may formally declare bankruptcy. Still others may simply flee.

Uncertainty affects almost every stream of cash flows. We take an especially simple approach to economic value under uncertainty by just considering *expected values.* The expected value of a cash flow is a weighted average: the amount of the cash flow times the probability of that amount. For example, suppose there is a 40% chance that an asset will pay off $1,000 and 60% that it will pay off $1,500. Its expected value is $1,300:

$$0.4(\$1,000) + 0.6(\$1,500) = \$1,300$$

We don't need to go deeply into where probabilities come from, but it is important for us to recognize that they are a function of information. The flow of information affects probabilities, and that affects value.

ACQUISITION COST: An asset normally is initially listed in the balance sheet at its acquisition cost. This cost is no greater than the expected discounted future cash benefits of the asset, otherwise management would not have acquired it. Acquisition costs are known, verifiable, and objective. As we have seen, asset values are usually systematically adjusted to reflect the change in value with the passage of time.

For example, suppose you own an asset that is going to pay off either $1,000 or $1,500 on December 31, 2005. Ignore the effect of interest (time value of money). Let's suppose that at December 1, 2005, the available information leads you to believe that a payoff of $1,000 or $1,500 is equally likely; that is, the probability of each is 0.5. The expected cash flow from the asset is:

$$0.5(\$1,000) + 0.5(\$1,500) = \$1,250$$

At December 8, 2005, information is more favorable. It leads you to estimate that the probability of receiving $1,000 is now only 20% and the probability of receiving $1,500 is 80%. The expected cash flow from the asset is then:

$$0.2(\$1,000) + 0.8(\$1,500) = \$1,400$$

By December 15, information shifts the probabilities adversely to 70% for $1,000 and 30% for $1,500. The expected cash flow from the asset is then:

$$0.7(\$1,000) + 0.3(\$1,500) = \$1,150$$

When management believes an asset's value has been compromised and its book value exceeds its economic value, they are required to estimate its remaining future cash flows in order to find a new, more accurate book value for the asset.

By December 22, information shifts the probabilities favorably to 10% for $1,000 and 90% for $1,500. The expected cash flow from the asset is then:

$$0.1(\$1,000) + 0.9(\$1,500) = \$1,450$$

At December 29, 2005, you receive the unfortunate news that the asset will definitely pay off only $1,000. The expected cash flow is now the certain amount:

$$1.0(\$1,000) + 0.0(\$1,500) = \$1,000$$

This sequence of expected values is recorded in Exhibit 6.3 and is graphed in Figure 6.5.

Exhibit 6.3

Expected Values as Probabilities Change

Date	Expected Value
December 1, 2005	$1,250
December 8, 2005	1,400
December 15, 2005	1,150
December 22, 2005	1,450
December 29, 2005	1,000

Figure 6.5

Expected Value Changes with Information Changes

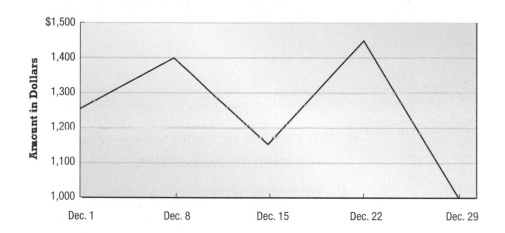

Values affected by uncertainty typically do not follow a smooth trajectory. They can jump up or down over short periods of time as information changes probabilities. For example, Figure 6.6 plots the daily closing prices (prices at the end of the day) of

Figure 6.6

GM Common Stock Closing Prices

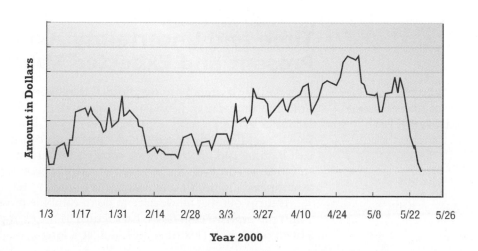

General Motors (GM) common stock from January 3, 2000, to May 26, 2000. You can see that the value of the common stock jumps around like the example in Figure 6.6. Most finance scholars believe that this behavior is the result of the flow of information about the expected cash flows from owning GM common stock.

Probability Trees and Uncertain Cash Flows

Uncertain cash flows can be visualized using probability trees. A probability tree shows the possible cash flows and their probabilities. The branches of the tree represent different possibilities. The probability and cash flow associated with each branch are attached. Figure 6.7 shows a probability tree for a situation with a 50% chance of getting $1,000 and a 50% chance of getting $1,200.

Figure 6.7

Probability Tree

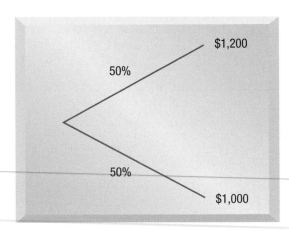

Relation to Accounting

OBJECTIVE:
Learn about the importance of valuation processes in determining accounting adjustments.

The accounting adjustments for many important items are driven by information. For example, placing a value on the liabilities for warranties issued on products calls for an estimation of the likelihood that products will break down in their warranty period. Estimating the liability associated with health care benefits to be paid to workers in retirement requires estimating the probabilities that retirees will enjoy varying lifespans, as well as the likelihood of having to supply various types of medical services and their costs, and the growth rate of assets invested to cover these costs. The valuation of accounts receivable requires estimating the likelihood that they will be collected. Information that changes these probability assessments may necessitate adjusting the accounts.

Time and Uncertainty: Combining Present and Expected Values

OBJECTIVE:
Learn how to combine present and expected values into expected net present value.

Only in the classroom are we afforded the luxury of analyzing separately the effects of time and uncertainty. In practice, cash flows are affected by both. The purpose of this section is to use the tools of present and expected values together to handle situations in which cash flows are uncertain and stretch over long periods of time. Items characterized by time and uncertainty are some of the largest on the balance sheet and often result in large effects on the income statement. These items include fixed assets, intangible assets, pensions, health care benefits to be paid to retired workers, and income taxes.

It turns out that all we have to do to combine present and expected values is to discount the *expected* cash flows. Let's return to the example of an asset that will pay either $1,000 or $1,500. This time, let's look at a long enough time horizon for interest to be an important factor. Suppose the payoff will occur on December 31, 2008, and assume the interest rate is 6%. Let's use the same probabilities that generated the expected values in Exhibit 6.3 but assume these probabilities are the result of information on more spread out dates as given in Exhibit 6.4.

Exhibit 6.4

Expected Values as Probabilities Change

Date	Expected Value
December 31, 2004	$1,250
December 31, 2005	1,400
December 31, 2006	1,150
December 31, 2007	1,450
December 31, 2008	1,000

So on December 31, 2004, the expected cash flow from the asset is $1,250. This expected cash flow would occur on December 31, 2008, so it must be discounted back to December 31, 2004:

$$\$1,250 \times (1/1.06)^4 = \$990.12$$

By December 31, 2005, two things change. First, one year has passed since December 31, 2004, so the cash flow that will occur on December 31, 2008, is one year closer. Second, information affects the probabilities so that the expected cash flow is $1,400. These factors combine to yield a discounted expected cash flow on December 31, 2005, of:

$$\$1,400 \times (1/1.06)^3 = \$1,175.47$$

The total change in value between December 31, 2004, and December 31, 2005, is $185.35. This change in value is the economic earnings on the asset.

Discounted expected value at December 31, 2005	$1,175.47
Less discounted expected value at December 31, 2004	(990.12)
Economic earnings in 2005	$ 185.35

Normal and Abnormal Earnings

OBJECTIVE:

Learn the concepts of normal and abnormal economic earnings.

We can separate the 2005 economic earnings of $185.35 into two parts. One reflects only the effects of interest. The other reflects the change in probabilities.

If the probabilities remained at 50–50, the discounted expected cash flow would be:

$$\$1,250 \times (1/1.06)^3 = \$1,049.52$$

Another way to get $1,049.52 is to reason that if the probabilities had not changed, the discounted expected value at December 31, 2005, is just $990.12, compounded up one year:

$990.12 × 1.06 = $1,049.52

The increment in value due solely to the effects of interest is then:

Discounted expected value at December 31, 2005, using the probabilities in effect at December 31, 2004	$1,049.52
Less discounted expected value at December 31, 2004	(990.12)
Value increase in 2005 due solely to interest ($990.12 × 0.06)	$ 59.40

We can use this result to find the part of the value increase due to probabilities by observing that any change in value not attributable solely to interest is attributable to changes in probabilities. We have:

Total increase in value	$185.35
Less effect of interest only	(59.40)
Value increase in 2005 due to change in probabilities	$125.95

Financial theorists use special language for these two parts of the value increase. The value increase of $59.40 due solely to the effects of interest is called the ***normal economic*** *earnings* on the $990.12 asset. The value increase of $125.95 due to the change in probabilities is called the ***abnormal economic earnings*** on the $990.12 asset. Figure 6.8 depicts the normal and abnormal economic earnings on the asset in 2005. It also shows normal economic earnings in 2006, given the information available at December 31, 2005.

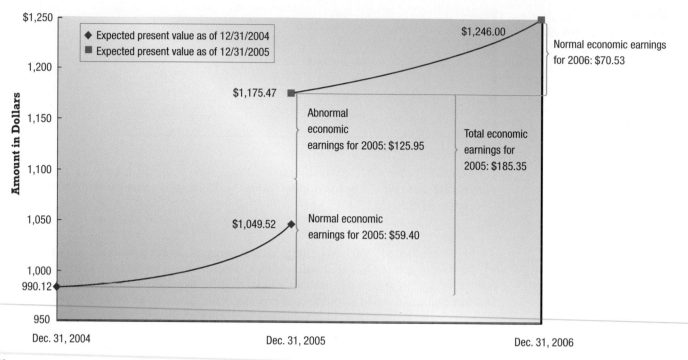

Figure 6.8
Normal and Abnormal Economic Earnings

Stock prices of publicly traded firms can rise relative to the general market only if the firm earns abnormal earnings. If a firm's investments only return the cost of obtaining capital, then no value is really added. This general principle provides the foundation of economic value added approaches to valuation using accounting numbers.

Of course good or bad news, or changes in probabilities, can be dramatically affected by good or bad management, or by forces external to the firm (markets may change and new technologies may be discovered).

This pattern of analysis could be continued for the asset's life. In each period, asset value would be affected by both interest and new information. The effects of interest can only be positive; that is, interest effects would only increase values, so normal economic earnings are always positive. New information, however, is a different story. Information can convey good news or bad news. If good news arrives, abnormal economic earnings will be positive. But if bad news arrives, abnormal economic earnings will be negative.

Review Questions

1. Verify that, given the information available at December 31, 2005, the normal earnings for 2006 as shown in Figure 6.8 are $70.53.

2. Calculate normal and abnormal earnings for the example in Exhibit 6.4 for the year 2006.

Conclusion

We began this book with the idea that accounting writes a financial history of an organization. Accounting focuses on the status of economic resources at points in time and the flows of economic resources over periods of time. Being a financial history, accounting naturally centers on the monetary values associated with economic resources and resource flows.

With all this emphasis on economic resources and financial values, it should be clear that understanding economics would really help in understanding accounting. This chapter presented two building blocks that allow us to deepen our understanding of economics: present values and expected values. Present and expected values allow us to calculate the financial value of a stream of future cash flows. Present value handles the fact that cash flows may be spread out over time, and money is worth more now than later. Expected value handles the possibility that the amounts of cash received or paid may not be known with certainty. Combining present and expected values allows us to handle both timing and uncertainty of cash flows.

Present and expected values give us tools to explore the evolution of economic values. The central question for accounting is how to portray the evolution of book values, that is, the amounts shown in the accounts. Comparing the evolution of economic values with book values allows us to:

- Better understand the information in financial reports
- Better evaluate alternative accounting methods that yield differing book values

We begin using present and expected values to deepen our understanding of accounting in the next chapter. There, we explore two important financial statistics used by analysts, managers, bankers, and others who want to extract information about the economic well-being of an organization from its accounting numbers. One statistic is the *market-to-book ratio,* which is the market value of an organization's equity divided by the book value of its equity. Market-to-book is defined only for organizations whose equity has a market value, so when we look at market-to-book, we are almost always looking at a publicly traded corporation. Market-to-book ratios provide a direct comparison of the equity market's assessment of value with the accounting system's assessment.

The other statistic is the return on equity. A *return on equity* is the income attributable to equity over a period of time divided by the amount of that equity. We distinguish economic and accounting returns on equity. By comparing the two, we gain insight into how accounting systems do and do not capture underlying economic performance. Separating normal and abnormal earnings is especially important in assessing economic performance, and our work combining expected and present values lays the foundation for this important task.

We use market-to-book and return on equity to explore alternative methods of accounting for various items such as accounts receivable, marketable securities, inventories, fixed assets, and liabilities.

Key Terms

abnormal economic earnings *124*	compound interest *116*	interest *115*
allocation process *113*	discounted value *118*	normal economic earnings *123*
articulation *113*	discount factor *118*	period *116*
asset impairment adjustment *119*	expected value *120*	present value *117*
balance sheet approach *113*	flow *109*	simple interest *116*
compounding *116*	future value *116*	stock *109*

Appendix 6.1: Calculating Present Values Using Calculators, Spreadsheets, and Tables of Discount Factors

The calculations involved in finding present values can be carried out in many ways. Many calculators and spreadsheets have built-in functions that perform the calculations, but it is often easier and more instructive to use more "brute force" approaches. The purpose of this appendix is to illustrate these approaches.

Calculators

Most calculators can easily be used to perform the simple, repetitive calculations involved in present values. For example, suppose we want to calculate the present value of $1,500 to be received three periods from now at an interest rate of 6%. We can view the job of calculating the present value as "moving" the $1,500 back one period at a time until we arrive at the present. The time diagram is given in Exhibit 6A.1.

Exhibit 6A.1

Calculating Present Values with a Hand Calculator

Date	0	1	2	3
Cash flow				$1,500
Present value of cash flow received at date 3 as of date 2			$1,415.09	Divide by 1.06
Present value of cash flow received at date 3 as of date 1		$1,334.99	Divide by 1.06	
Present value of cash flow received at date 3 as of date 0	$1,259.43	Divide by 1.06		

Spreadsheets

Spreadsheets were made for calculations such as present values. It is worth experimenting with a few of the many ways to structure the calculations so you can adapt your spreadsheet to the particular requirements of different problems. We begin by entering the cash flow diagram in the spreadsheet to arrive at something that looks like the sheet in Exhibit 6A.2.

Exhibit 6A.2

Setting up a Spreadsheet Calculation of Present Values

	A	B	C	D	E
1	Date	0	1	2	3
2	Cash flow				1,500

One way to calculate the present value of $1,500 to be received at date 3 as of date 0 is to enter into any cell:

$$=E2/1.06^\wedge 3$$

Because raising something to a power is done before multiplication and division, the spreadsheet will first raise 1.06 to the third power, then divide what is in cell E2 by the result.

Other techniques rely on the way spreadsheets typically handle cutting and pasting. For example, we could enter into cell D2 the following:

$$=E2/1.06$$

If we copy cell D2 into cell C2, the spreadsheet changes the E2 in the numerator to D2. In effect, the program divides E2 by 1.06 twice, which gives the present value of $1,500 to be received at date 3 as of date 2. When we copy into cell B2, we in effect divide E2 by 1.06 three times, which is the same as dividing it by 1.06 cubed. The answer is the present value as of date 0. The formulas in the spreadsheet would look like those contained in Exhibit 6A.3.

Exhibit 6A.3

Example: Spreadsheet Calculation of Present Values

	A	B	C	D	E
1	Date	0	1	2	3
2	Cash flow	=C2/1.06	=D2/1.06	=E2/1.06	1,500

A fancier version of this approach gives more complete control over the exponents used in the discount factors. We begin by entering the following into cell D2:

$$=E2/1.06^\wedge(\$E1-D1)$$

Note how this formula uses the date in the exponent of the denominator to calculate the discount factor.

The dollar sign fixes the reference so it is not changed when the cell is copied. Copying cell D2 into cells C2 and B2 results in the formulas in Exhibit 6A.4.

Exhibit 6A.4

Alternative Spreadsheet Calculation of Present Values

	A	B	C	D	E
1	Date	0	1	2	3
2	Cash flow	=C2/1.06^($E1−B1)	=D2/1.06^($E1−C1)	=E2/1.06^($E1−D1)	1,500

Tables of Discount Factors

The discount factors for various interest rates have been compiled in table form, as in Exhibit 6.A5. Present values are found by locating the appropriate discount factor for the interest rate and number of periods in the future in which the cash flow is to be received, then multiplying the amount of cash to be received by the discount factor. For example, we find the discount factor 0.860 in the third row under the column for an interest rate of 6%. The present value of $1,500 to be received three periods from now at an interest rate of 6% is therefore:

$$\$1,500 \times 0.840 = \$1,260$$

which, except for rounding error, is the same answer as our other methods.

Exhibit 6A.5 Discount Factors

							Interest Rate								
Period	3.0%	3.5%	4.0%	4.5%	5.0%	5.5%	6.0%	6.5%	7.0%	7.5%	8.0%	8.5%	9.0%	9.5%	10.0%
1	0.971	0.966	0.962	0.957	0.952	0.948	0.943	0.939	0.935	0.930	0.926	0.922	0.917	0.913	0.909
2	0.943	0.934	0.925	0.916	0.907	0.898	0.890	0.882	0.873	0.865	0.857	0.849	0.842	0.834	0.826
3	0.915	0.902	0.889	0.876	0.864	0.852	0.840	0.828	0.816	0.805	0.794	0.783	0.772	0.762	0.751
4	0.888	0.871	0.855	0.839	0.823	0.807	0.792	0.777	0.763	0.749	0.735	0.722	0.708	0.696	0.683
5	0.863	0.842	0.822	0.802	0.784	0.765	0.747	0.730	0.713	0.697	0.681	0.665	0.650	0.635	0.621
6	0.837	0.814	0.790	0.768	0.746	0.725	0.705	0.685	0.666	0.648	0.630	0.613	0.596	0.580	0.564
7	0.813	0.786	0.760	0.735	0.711	0.687	0.665	0.644	0.623	0.603	0.583	0.565	0.547	0.530	0.513
8	0.789	0.759	0.731	0.703	0.677	0.652	0.627	0.604	0.582	0.561	0.540	0.521	0.502	0.484	0.467
9	0.766	0.734	0.703	0.673	0.645	0.618	0.592	0.567	0.544	0.522	0.500	0.480	0.460	0.442	0.424
10	0.744	0.709	0.676	0.644	0.614	0.585	0.558	0.533	0.508	0.485	0.463	0.442	0.422	0.404	0.386
11	0.722	0.685	0.650	0.616	0.585	0.555	0.527	0.500	0.475	0.451	0.429	0.408	0.388	0.369	0.350
12	0.701	0.662	0.625	0.590	0.557	0.526	0.497	0.470	0.444	0.420	0.397	0.376	0.356	0.337	0.319
13	0.681	0.639	0.601	0.564	0.530	0.499	0.469	0.441	0.415	0.391	0.368	0.346	0.326	0.307	0.290
14	0.661	0.618	0.577	0.540	0.505	0.473	0.442	0.414	0.388	0.363	0.340	0.319	0.299	0.281	0.263
15	0.642	0.597	0.555	0.517	0.481	0.448	0.417	0.389	0.362	0.338	0.315	0.294	0.275	0.256	0.239
16	0.623	0.577	0.534	0.494	0.458	0.425	0.394	0.365	0.339	0.314	0.292	0.271	0.252	0.234	0.218
17	0.605	0.557	0.513	0.473	0.436	0.402	0.371	0.343	0.317	0.292	0.270	0.250	0.231	0.214	0.198
18	0.587	0.538	0.494	0.453	0.416	0.381	0.350	0.322	0.296	0.272	0.250	0.230	0.212	0.195	0.180
19	0.570	0.520	0.475	0.433	0.396	0.362	0.331	0.302	0.277	0.253	0.232	0.212	0.194	0.178	0.164
20	0.554	0.503	0.456	0.415	0.377	0.343	0.312	0.284	0.258	0.235	0.215	0.196	0.178	0.163	0.149
21	0.538	0.486	0.439	0.397	0.359	0.325	0.294	0.266	0.242	0.219	0.199	0.180	0.164	0.149	0.135
22	0.522	0.469	0.422	0.380	0.342	0.308	0.278	0.250	0.226	0.204	0.184	0.166	0.150	0.136	0.123
23	0.507	0.453	0.406	0.363	0.326	0.292	0.262	0.235	0.211	0.189	0.170	0.153	0.138	0.124	0.112
24	0.492	0.438	0.390	0.348	0.310	0.277	0.247	0.221	0.197	0.176	0.158	0.141	0.126	0.113	0.102
25	0.478	0.423	0.375	0.333	0.295	0.262	0.233	0.207	0.184	0.164	0.146	0.130	0.116	0.103	0.092

chapter 7

© GETTY IMAGES/PHOTO DISC

In this chapter you will learn:

1 How stock markets provide estimates of the economic values of firms

2 To understand the strengths and weaknesses of accounting valuations

3 What financial statement analysis is and begin to develop a conceptual framework for it

4 Two basic ratios useful in financial analysis

5 To apply the financial analysis conceptual framework to real companies

Financial Statement Analysis: Connecting Economic Concepts to Accounting Reports

A quite tasteless joke made the rounds during the 1996 presidential election campaign. The candidates were Bill Clinton, still young by presidential standards, and Bob Dole, who was over 70 years old at the time. In an appearance on MTV, Clinton was asked whether he wore boxers or briefs. The joke was that when Bob Dole was asked that same question, he replied, "Depends." The "humor" came from the double meaning: Either Dole chooses his underwear based on some changing preference, or he is referring to the brand name of an adult incontinence product.

Our interpretation is that he meant his preference depends on other factors. That's going to be the main thing we find out about how closely accounting is connected with economics: It depends. In Chapter 6 we explained that the accounting adjustment process attempts to bring asset and liability valuations in balance sheets more into line with their economic values. We also indicated how adjustments can make revenues and expenses in the income statement better measures of the flows of economic resources in and out of the firm during the accounting period. Economic value, as explained, is best measured by computing expected net present values of future cash flows. In future chapters we will see many applications of this present value technique in the accounting treatment of specific categories of assets and liabilities. The goal of this chapter is to illustrate, with two examples, how closely the process adjusts accounts to economic values. As we will see, it depends on the types of assets and liabilities appearing in a particular firm's balance sheet.

Asset and liability types vary widely across industries. An airline must have access to the services of airplanes, the rights to land at various airports (gate access), sophisticated reservation systems, and so on. An automobile manufacturer must have access to manufacturing equipment, inventories of the raw materials and parts required to make a car, and so on. A consulting firm must have access to the human capital required to deliver its serv-

ices, a reputation to reassure potential clients that it can perform the required tasks, and so on.

In some industries, GAAP accounting accurately captures the economic values of assets employed and liabilities created; that is, the account valuations listed closely convey their economic values. In other industries, GAAP accounting does not accurately capture the types of assets employed and liabilities created. Either the GAAP valuations are inaccurate or, in some instances, GAAP fail to record the asset or liability on the balance sheet.

In Part I of this book, we saw that balance sheets and income statements are the two types of financial statements defined in terms of economic concepts. A balance sheet shows book values at a point in time. The concepts of assets, liabilities, and equities are central to its construction. An income statement shows the flows of resources over time generated by the earnings process. Income (earnings) is measured using the concepts of revenues, expenses, and income. When the accounts of a firm closely reflect economic values, its balance sheets give clear pictures of the economic values of assets and liabilities at the balance sheet dates, and its income statements give clear pictures of the flows of economic resources in and out of the firm over periods of time. When the accounts of a firm do not closely capture the economics of the firm, its balance sheets give cloudy pictures of the economic values of assets and liabilities at the balance sheet dates. Its income statements also fail to clearly convey the flows of economic resources over periods of time. To get the most information from a set of financial statements, you need to understand whether they present clear or cloudy pictures. Obviously, with less clear statements you will have to work harder at understanding what the accounting numbers mean, and you will need to seek information not in the financial statements to complete your analysis.

This chapter compares and contrasts accounting valuation of balance sheet and income statement accounts, determined using GAAP, with their underlying economic values. It has four main goals:

1. To develop an understanding as to why GAAP and economic valuations of companies differ.

2. To show how understanding this difference provides a basic framework for the analysis of financial statements.

3. To introduce two ratios commonly used to facilitate financial statement analysis—the market-to-book ratio and the return on equity ratio.

4. To show you by looking at two particular companies in detail that financial statement analysis is as much an art as it is a science.

Alternative Measures of Value: A Framework for Financial Statement Analysis

Three different basic valuations are important to understanding the financial health of a firm. We already briefly discussed two of them in this book, accounting and economic valuations of individual assets and liabilities. The third is the overall valuation of publicly traded firms provided by the stock market. We will now spend some time discussing each of these three measures. Then we will show how these three measures provide a framework for financial statement analysis.

The Value of a Firm in the Stock Market

Buyers and sellers perform a financial statement analysis to inform their transactions.

The Boeing Corporation has about 897 million shares of common stock outstanding. On August 7, 2000, the stock sold for about $49 per share. The total economic value attributed to Boeing by the stock market was therefore in excess of $44 billion (897 million times $49).

One way to resolve the question, "What is the total economic value of a company?" is to look to the stock markets for an answer. The total economic value of a firm is the market value of the common shareholders' equity, which is also known as the firm's **market capitalization.** It is calculated by taking the number of common shares outstanding times the price per share.

Buyers and sellers determine the prices at which shares of stock sell on a stock market. Both buyers and sellers show a strong interest in getting a "good deal" for themselves. The market provides incentives for them to study the situation and carefully evaluate their options. Because buyer and seller must agree for a transaction to take place, and because neither is under any compulsion to act, both must conclude that the terms are acceptable. Thus, a market valuation offers an extremely strong indication of the aggregate economic value of a firm.

How do buyers and sellers determine what price is acceptable to them? They process information about the future cash flows of a company, and they form expectations about what these cash flows will be. GAAP financial statements are one source of information used by buyers and sellers in their assessments of market value. They continually reevaluate their assessments in light of GAAP balance sheets, income statements, and supporting disclosures.

The main point is that stock market prices are pretty good measures of the aggregate economic value of a company. They value all of the assets and liabilities as one bundle. The stock market does not provide estimates of economic values of *individual* company assets and liabilities.

GAAP Valuation

Financial statements constructed using GAAP serve multiple users. To be useful they are constructed in an objective and verifiable fashion. The numbers arrived at by accountants and auditors must be capable of replication by other accountants and auditors assigned the same task. The numbers require some evidence to substantiate them.

Objectivity and verifiability create rigidity in financial statements. GAAP statements are not always flexible enough to capture the precise economic structure and status for every firm in every industry. Furthermore, as we shall see in future chapters, GAAP take a conservative bias—they disclose the economic effects of "bad events" as soon as it is known they are likely to occur and wait to disclose the economic effects of "good events" until they actually occur. Another important point to keep in mind is that GAAP are created to report on historical events and the current status of economic resources, whereas most decision making looks to the future.

GAAP numbers differ from economic numbers in two main ways: recognition and book valuation. Relative to economic valuation, GAAP uses **restrictive recognition** of assets and liabilities. For example, the rights acquired and obligations generated by an employment contract are not recognized under GAAP because they are part of an executory contract. (Something will be reported in the financial statement numbers when the work is actually performed.) These rights and obligations might be important components in developing expectations of future cash flows used in assessing the economic value of the firm, which means a firm may have *assets and liabilities, economically speaking, that GAAP do not consider to be assets and liabilities.*

Recognition determines what gets into a set of GAAP records, and adjustment determines the **book valuation** afterward. For example, GAAP adjust the book value of a building by allocating its cost across future periods using straight-line depreciation. This process of allocation might not match a process of economic valuation; that is, the change in the book value of an asset reflects an allocation over time, but the change in its economic value reflects a change in the expected present value of its future cash flows. Only in special circumstances will the two coincide.

Recognizing that GAAP impose objectivity and verifiability, take a conservative bias, and therefore might not be as flexible in generating an accurate financial report for every firm, we should approach financial statement analysis cautiously. Recognizing problems of restrictive recognition and shortcomings of the adjustment process should also concern us. When do GAAP accurately capture what is happening in the firm? This issue has no easy answer, and, as we will learn, financial statement analysis is more of an art than a science.

Financial Statement Analysis

The information in GAAP financial statements provides input to many decisions. A banker must decide whether to grant a loan to a firm. A portfolio manager must decide whether to invest in the stock of a particular company. A board of directors might be interested in evaluating managerial performance. A manager might be assessing competition as part of a strategic analysis. Regardless of the context, the decision maker looks at the assets and liabilities of the firm and how the firm manages and utilizes these assets and liabilities. Depending on the particular decision, the emphasis might be on different assets and liabilities.

No matter what the decision context, the attempt should always be to place accounting numbers in their proper economic context. It is not what the accounting numbers *are*; rather it is what they *mean* in an economic sense. Ultimately, decisions are based on a careful analysis of cash flows, not necessarily accounting numbers. Central to good decision making is an understanding of and intuition about whether particular accounting numbers serve as good surrogates for the economic values of the assets, liabilities, revenues, and expenses.

Conceptual Framework for Financial Statement Analysis

The previous concepts and ideas can be combined as follows to form a general conceptual foundation for financial statement analysis. Refer to Figure 7.1 as you read through these steps.

Figure 7.1 Economic and Accounting Valuations—A Conceptual Basis for Financial Statement Analysis

Accounting Balance Sheet (book values)			Economic Balance Sheet (economic values)
Book Value of Assets	**BvA₁** Recognized assets with valuations close to their economic values	**A₁** Examples include cash, accounts receivable, and marketable securities	**EvA₁** Assets with economic value equal to their book value

Accounting Balance Sheet (book values)

Book Value of Assets

BvA₁
Recognized assets with valuations close to their economic values

BvA₂
Recognized assets with known economic values different from the accounting values

BvA₃
Recognized assets for which it is difficult to obtain economic values

By definition, these economic assets have zero book value.

A₁
Examples include cash, accounts receivable, and marketable securities

A₂
Examples include some inventories and automobiles

A₃
Examples include specially constructed manufacturing facilities and some plots of land

A₄
Examples include some types of intellectual property, human capital, and valuable relationships

Economic Balance Sheet (economic values)

Economic Value of Assets

EvA₁
Assets with economic value equal to their book value

EvA₂
Assets with economic value likely greater than their book value

EvA₃
Assets with economic value likely greater than their book value

EvA₄
Unrecognized assets (i.e., assets with economic value but not listed in the balance sheet)

minus

minus

Book Value of Liabilities

BvL₁
Recognized liabilities with valuations close to their economic values

BvL₂
Recognized liabilities with known economic values different from the accounting values

BvL₃
Recognized liabilities for which it is difficult to obtain economic values

By definition, these economic obligations have zero book value.

L₁
Examples include accounts payable and short-term debt

L₂
Examples include some types of long-term debt

L₃
Examples include estimated warranty liabilities

L₄
Examples include obligations under employment contracts, some leases, and some employee stock options

Economic Value of Liabilities

EvL₁
Obligations with economic value equal to their book value

EvL₂
Obligations with economic value likely greater or less than their book value

EvL₃
Obligations with economic value likely less than their book value

EvL₄
Unrecognized liabilities (i.e., economic obligations not listed in the balance sheet)

equals

equals

Book Value of Equity

BvE
The total of all the shareholders' equity accounts on the GAAP balance sheet

Economic Value of Equity

EvE
The economic value of the equity can be estimated by the stock market value of the common stock. Usually, this valuation will be more than the book value of the equity, implying that the understatement of the book value of assets is greater than any understatement of the book value of liabilities.

EvE is the price per share times the number of shares outstanding.

Under GAAP, it is easier to write asset values down than it is to write them up. Therefore, most of the time we would expect EvA_2 to exceed BvA_2.

Similar to EvA_2 and BvA_2, we would expect EvA_3 to be greater than BvA_3, even if EvA_3 is difficult to estimate.

Examples here might be internally developed patents, residual advertising, internal goodwill, and obligations under employment agreements.

OBJECTIVE:
Learn the two basic ratios useful in financial analysis.

Of course, if our total valuation of individual assets and liabilities greatly exceeds EvE and we think our list is reasonably complete, then maybe we have identified an undervalued stock!

It is not surprising that financial analysis and valuation of high-tech companies is difficult because most of their assets fall into the EvA_3 and EvA_4 categories.

In terms of Figure 7.1, the market-to-book ratio is equal to EvE divided by BvE.

1. Estimate the economic value of the firm's equity (EvE) using stock market valuation.
2. Identify individual assets and liabilities that have accounting valuations close to their economic values (A_1 and L_1). Look to the financial statements for values.
3. Identify accounting assets and liabilities for which we can find a reasonable economic value, but which are not carried at that value in the financial statements (A_2 and L_2). Look to individual asset and liability markets for values.
4. List all the remaining accounting assets and liabilities of the firm for which economic values cannot be reasonably estimated (A_3 and L_3). Use techniques such as present value of expected future cash flows to estimate values.
5. Search for assets and liabilities that are not listed on the balance sheet yet are economic assets and liabilities (A_4 and L_4). Use techniques such as present value of expected future cash flows to estimate values.

Neither of the columns in Figure 7.1 represents absolute truth, but comparing and contrasting the three approaches to value help financial readers to understand better the financial status of a particular firm. It would be nice if all the accounting assets and liabilities fell into the book value categories BvA_1 and BvL_1. Then we would know that GAAP agree with economic values. If, in addition, BvE were also close in value to EvE we would know that we are not likely missing any assets and liabilities in the accounting statements.

Conceptually, we want to understand a company economically by developing a complete list of assets and liabilities with individual economic values that have a total net economic value close to the value the stock market places on the firm, EvE. If we identify assets and liabilities with a total net economic value near EvE, then the two independent measures of value agree and we can be reasonably certain we did not omit anything. If $EvA_1 + EvA_2 + EvA_3 + EvA_4 - EvL_1 - EvL_2 - EvL_3 - EvL_4$ is much greater or less than EvE, then perhaps the stock market is telling us something. Perhaps we left out some assets or liabilities in an analysis.

Obviously, the closer $BvA_1 - BvL_1$ by itself is to EvE, the more reliance we can place on the accounting numbers in any financial analysis. More assets and liabilities in EvA_3, EvA_4, EvL_3, and EvL_4 make the financial analysis more subjective.

Future chapters look more at the specifics for different types of assets and liabilities. Here, we use three important financial statistics to gauge the closeness of the connection between GAAP book values and economic values for a given firm. The market value of a firm's common stock (number of shares outstanding times the price per share) divided by its book value indicates its **market-to-book ratio.** In general, a ratio is one number divided by another number. Accountants use ratios to measure liquidity (cash flows in and out of the firm), profitability, efficiency, and long-run financial survival (solvency). Specifically, the market-to-book ratio indicates how closely the balance sheet reflects aggregate economic values *at a point in time.* In turn, this affects how income statements reflect the flows of value. The other important statistics include forms of return on equity, which show value *flows* and how they relate to shareholders' resources employed in the business. A return on equity provides a measure of the firm's net income divided by a measure of its stockholders' equity. Return on equity can be measured in at least two ways. We could use GAAP measures of income and equity to calculate accounting return on equity, or we could use economic measures of income and equity to calculate economic return on equity. If the accounts closely capture the economics, the two returns on equity will be close. If the accounts do not closely capture the economics, the two returns on equity will not be close.

A firm whose balance sheets clearly reflect economic values will most likely have accounting returns on equity different from a firm whose balance sheets do not clearly reflect economic values. Accounting return on equity is often used as a measure of performance over a period, and we will want to compare a firm's accounting return on equity against a reasonable expectation. Also, we need to understand the connection between market-to-book ratios and accounting returns on equity in assessing trends in accounting returns on equity.

Figure 7.2 shows a subjective schematic diagram illustrating the level of reliance that GAAP numbers merit as a function of the market-to-book ratio. Regulated companies and savings and loans tend to be analyzed easily just by looking at GAAP statements, whereas an analysis of a high-tech company places less reliance on the accounting numbers. Manufacturing firms fall somewhere in the middle. With time you will develop an intuition about where a particular firm falls on this line and how much looking you will have to do outside of the financial statements.

Figure 7.2

Relative Reliance on GAAP in Financial Analysis

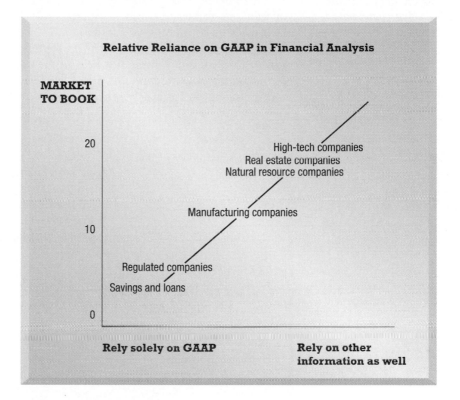

This topic is fairly complicated, so we use examples to illustrate what we mean. Harrodsburg First Financial Bancorp uses assets and creates liabilities whose economic values are captured well by GAAP. Microsoft uses assets and creates liabilities whose economic values are not captured well by GAAP. We explore the market-to-book ratios, accounting returns on equity, and economic returns on equity for these two companies. We discuss how the processes of recognition and adjustment affect these financial statistics.

Review Questions

1. Give examples of assets and liabilities that fall into categories A_1, A_2, and A_3 as defined in Figure 7.1.

2. Pick a specific company in each of two different industries and log on to EDGAR at http://www.sec.gov/edgar.shtml to find their latest financial reports. In each case compute their market-to-book ratio as of the date of the annual report. Subjectively locate the companies on the chart in Figure 7.2.

OBJECTIVE:

Learn to apply the financial analysis conceptual framework to real companies.

Harrodsburg First Financial Bancorp, Inc.

Harrodsburg First Financial Bancorp, Inc. (hereafter, Harrodsburg), is a small savings and loan in Kentucky. Its 1998 Form 10K contained the following statement:

This description of the business is typical of a savings and loan.

In the stockholders' equity section of the balance sheet, we see there are 2,182,125 shares issued and outstanding. But the company has repurchased 258,607 shares and holds them in the company. Only shares in the public domain, 2,182,125 less 258,607, or 1,923,518, have claims against the company. (We will explain more in Chapter 13.)

The Bank conducts a general banking business in central Kentucky which primarily consists of attracting deposits from the general public and applying those funds to the origination of loans for residential, consumer, and nonresidential purposes. The Bank's profitability is significantly dependent on net interest income, which is the difference between interest income generated from interest-earning assets (i.e., loans and investments) and the interest expense paid on interest-bearing liabilities (i.e., customer deposits and borrowed funds).

Harrodsburg's balance sheet as of September 30, 1998, is shown in Exhibit 7.1. As you can see, total stockholders' equity under GAAP was $28,981,600. The price of Harrodsburg's common stock closed at $15.125 per share on September 30, 1998. We see on Harrodsburg's balance sheet that on September 30, 1998, 1,923,518 shares of common stock outstanding were not held in the company. Therefore, the market value of Harrodsburg's stockholders' equity was $29,093,200 (the economic value that the stock market attaches to Harrodsburg):

$$\$15.125/\text{share} \times 1,923,518 \text{ shares} = \$29,093,200 \text{ (rounded)}$$

Exhibit 7.1

Harrodsburg First
Financial Bancorp
Balance Sheet

Harrodsburg First Financial Bancorp, Inc. and Subsidiary
Consolidated Balance Sheet
September 30, 1998
(amounts in thousands)

ASSETS

Cash and due from banks	$ 739.8
Interest-bearing deposits	7,334.3
Securities available-for-sale at fair value	3,825.5
Securities held-to-maturity, fair value of $11,226,762	11,140.8
Loans receivable, net	85,271.9
Accrued interest receivable	660.8
Premises and equipment, net	852.1
Other assets	94.1
TOTAL ASSETS	$109,919.3

LIABILITIES AND STOCKHOLDERS' EQUITY

Deposits	$ 78,995.7
Advance payments by borrowers for taxes and insurance	71.8
Deferred federal income tax	1,398.2
Dividends payable	354.5
Other liabilities	117.5
TOTAL LIABILITIES	$ 80,937.7

STOCKHOLDERS' EQUITY

Common stock, $0.10 par value, 5,000,000 shares authorized; 2,182,125 shares issued and outstanding	$ 218.2
Additional paid-in capital	21,154.1
Retained earnings, substantially restricted	11,003.2
Accumulated other comprehensive income	2,475.0
Treasury stock, 258,607 shares, at cost	(4,477.5)
Unallocated employee stock ownership plan (ESOP) shares	(1,391.4)
Total stockholders' equity	$ 28,981.6
TOTAL LIABILITIES AND STOCKHOLDERS' EQUITY	$109,919.3

The supply and demand of investors assessing the net present value of their future cash flows from Harrodsburg stock determine the market value of Harrodsburg's shares. GAAP that guide the construction of the financial statements determine the book value of Harrodsburg's stockholders' equity. With Harrodsburg, these two different measures of value (stock market and accounting) yield extremely close results; the difference is only $111,600, whereas the book and market values are about $30 million:

As we shall see, the book and market values are not this close for most companies!

Market value	$ 29,093,200
Book value	(28,981,600)
Excess of market over book	$ 111,600

A common way to look at the relation between market and book values is to form the market-to-book ratio, which for Harrodsburg at September 30, 1998, was

$$\$29{,}093{,}200/\$28{,}981{,}600 = 1.004$$

The market value of Harrodsburg's equity can be thought of as *the stock market's estimate of the economic value of its assets less the economic value of its liabilities:*

$$\text{ASSETS (economic)} - \text{LIABILITIES (economic)} = \text{EQUITY (economic)}$$

The stock market has no particular need to assess the values of the Harrodsburg's assets and liabilities separately. When you own a share of stock you own a little piece of the entire basket of assets minus liabilities. In fact, if Harrodsburg's management succeeds in creating an organization that is more than the sum of its parts, then the market value of the individual assets and liabilities will not capture the value of the whole firm. So while the market assesses the value of the equity as $29,093,200, we don't really know how the market would separately assess the values of Harrodsburg's individual assets and liabilities.

A GAAP balance sheet, however, must provide separate values for Harrodsburg's assets and liabilities. We can use the stock market's assessment of Harrodsburg's equity, some additional disclosures Harrodsburg provides, and knowledge of how accounting for individual assets and liabilities works to gain some insight into how close GAAP might come to estimating economic values of individual assets and liabilities. What we will do is certainly not foolproof, as we will discuss, but it does demonstrate a conceptual framework for thinking about financial statement analysis.

Exhibit 7.2 on page 138 presents a worksheet that will allow us to analyze systematically the economic value of individual GAAP assets and liabilities. The idea is to come up with an economic valuation, as best we can, for each of the accounting assets and liabilities. We will then see how close our explanation comes to justifying the market value of Harrodsburg's stock. If we come close, then we can be reasonably sure we truly understand what the assets and liabilities of Harrodsburg are and what its economic values are as well. If we do not come close, we must look for more assets and liabilities to move the valuations closer together, or we will conclude that the market is not correct in its assessment of the value of Harrodsburg.

The GAAP column in Exhibit 7.2 copies the GAAP balance sheet from Exhibit 7.1. The Economic column lists our best guess at the economic value of the asset or liability. Finally, the Source column indicates which chapter in the text explains the item in detail. In essence it provides a roadmap for past and future chapters. Chapter 6 is the source of the basic economic argument for all items. Each asset or liability is labeled A_i or L_i to indicate its category, i, in Figure 7.1.

Remember, the more liquid something is the more readily it can be converted to cash.

Harrodsburg is in the savings and loan business, and most of its assets and liabilities are close to being cash, or mostly *liquid.* We see that GAAP value these assets close to the economic values that would be obtained using the methods from Chapter 6.

We enter $739.8 for cash under the Economic column in Exhibit 7.2 as well as $7,334.3 for interest-bearing deposits.

The economic value of Harrodsburg's Cash and Due from Banks and Interest-Bearing Deposits is essentially the amount of cash and money they have on deposit. It appears on the GAAP balance sheet. We would expect GAAP and economic value to be identical for these items.

Exhibit 7.2   Worksheet—Harrodsburg First Financial Bancorp Balance Sheet

Worksheet—Harrodsburg First Financial Bancorp, Inc. and Subsidiary
Consolidated Balance Sheet
September 30, 1998
(amounts in thousands)

ASSETS	GAAP	ECONOMIC	DIFFERENCE	SOURCE
Cash and due from banks (A₁)	$ 739.8	$ 739.8	$ 0	Chapter 2
Interest-bearing deposits (A₁)	7,334.3	7,334.3	0	Chapter 2
Securities available-for-sale at fair value (A₁)	3,825.5	3,825.5	0	Chapter 10
Securities held-to-maturity, fair value of $11,226,762 (A₂)	11,140.8	11,226.8	85.0	Chapter 10
Loans receivable, net (A₁)	85,271.9	85,271.9	0	Chapter 8
Accrued interest receivable (A₁)	660.8	660.8	0	Chapter 3
Premises and equipment, net (A₃)	852.1	?	?	Chapter 11
Other assets (A₃)	94.1	?	?	
Assets not recognized by GAAP (A₄)	0.0	?	?	
TOTAL ASSETS	$109,919.3	?	?	

LIABILITIES AND STOCKHOLDERS' EQUITY				
Deposits (L₁)	$ 78,995.7	$78,995.7	$ 0	Chapter 2
Advance payments by borrowers for taxes and insurance (L₁)	71.8	71.8	0	Chapter 2
Deferred federal income tax (L₃)	1,398.2	?	?	Chapter 14
Dividends payable (L₁)	354.5	354.5	0	Chapter 2
Other liabilities (L₁)	117.5	117.5	0	Chapter 12
Liabilities not recognized by GAAP (L₄)	0.0	?	?	
TOTAL LIABILITIES	$ 80,937.7	?	?	Chapter 7

STOCKHOLDERS' EQUITY				
Common stock, $0.10 par value, 5,000,000 shares authorized; 2,182,125 shares issued and outstanding	$ 218.2			
Additional paid-in capital	21,154.1			
Retained earnings, substantially restricted	11,003.2			
Accumulated other comprehensive income	2,475.0			
Treasury stock, 258,607 shares, at cost	(4,477.5)			
Unallocated employee stock ownership plan (ESOP) shares	(1,391.4)			
Total stockholders' equity	$ 28,981.6	$29,093.2	$111.6	Chapters 7, 16
TOTAL LIABILITIES AND STOCKHOLDERS' EQUITY	$109,919.3			
			$ 26.6	Unexplained

$3,825.5 is entered in the Economic column for these securities.

$11,226.8 is entered in the Economic column for these securities. These securities are in category A₂.

The next asset is Securities Available-for-Sale. Chapter 10 explains that GAAP for these assets require adjustments to bring the book values in line with market values at each balance sheet date. Therefore, the economic value of these assets is listed on the GAAP balance sheet.

The next asset is Securities Held-to-Maturity. Chapter 10 also reveals that GAAP require accounting for these securities at cost, and do not require adjusting them to their market values. The value on the GAAP balance sheet, therefore, is not equal to the economic value of these securities. However, Harrodsburg's balance sheet discloses the fair value of these securities ($11,226.8 in Exhibit 7.1), which we take as a good approximation to their market value. Assessment of fair value requires examination of market prices or application of the discounted expected cash flow techniques we saw in Chapter 6. So fair value is an approximation of economic value.

$85,271.9 is entered in the Economic column.

Chapter 8 discusses how receivables are accounted for at the present value of their future cash flows, with an allowance for uncollectible amounts. This amount is in line with the value of their discounted expected cash flows. So the book value of Loans Receivable should be close to their economic value.

$660.8 is entered in the Economic column.

Accrued Interest Receivable is just interest owed to Harrodsburg and should be close to its economic value through simple accrual methods.

Chapter 11 explains how the book value of Premises and Equipment is tied to the historical costs of these assets adjusted for the passage of time. Under some circumstances, GAAP require adjustments to bring the book value into line with market value, but only if the market value is below the book value, and sometimes not even then. Therefore, we put a question mark in Exhibit 7.2 for the economic value of Premises and Equipment.

A question mark seems appropriate for Other Assets, too, because we don't even know what they are. We know that they are *not* Cash, Interest-Bearing Deposits, Securities, Loans Receivable, or Premises and Equipment, but we remain uncertain as to exactly what is in this category.

We are also uncertain about whether the list of assets on Harrodsburg's balance sheet includes all the items that the stock market counts as Harrodsburg's assets. We handle that possibility in Exhibit 7.2 by including the line for Assets Not Recognized by GAAP. Any assets not recognized by GAAP have an implicit book value of zero, even though their economic value is greater than zero. For example, if Harrodsburg conducted valuable research or developed valuable goodwill through years of operating in its area, it might hold economic assets not recognized by GAAP.

How do we assess whether significant amounts of assets (and liabilities) are not recognized by GAAP? We must combine knowledge of GAAP with knowledge of the business of the particular entity we are analyzing. Relevant factors include:

Financial analysis goes well beyond an understanding of the rules of accounting. A good financial analyst has good general business knowledge and instincts.

- The industry or industries in which the entity has operations
- The competition it faces
- The business strategies it employs
- The inputs it uses
- The history of the firm
- The outputs it produces
- The risks it faces

We usually get information about these factors from management, in its discussion and analysis; from disclosures in footnotes to the financial statements; from newspapers, magazines, and online information producers; from industry groups; and from experience with similar firms. Assessing the gaps in GAAP financial statements is part of the art of financial statement analysis. Although it can be frustrating at first, after you gain the requisite experience, it will often be the most fun and rewarding part of an analysis task.

Given the business it is in and the competition it faces, Harrodsburg is unlikely to have significant economic assets not recognized by GAAP. Harrodsburg's 1998 10K indicates that it is a traditional savings and loan operation that raises money from savings deposits, interest on loans, and profits from investment securities. It loans money out for real estate purchases, construction, and consumer purchases:

The Bank attracts deposits from the general public and uses such deposits primarily to originate loans secured by first mortgages on one- to four-family residences located in its market area. . . . The Bank originates and retains adjustable rate loans as well as, to a lesser extent, fixed-rate loans for its mortgage loan portfolio. The Bank has not sold mortgage loans into the secondary market during the past five years. In addition, the Bank originates multi-family, commercial and agricultural real estate loans. . . . These loans are primarily secured by apartment buildings, office buildings, churches, farms and other properties. The Bank also offers construction loans. . . . These loans are primarily secured by residential properties and become permanent loans of the Bank upon completion of the construction. The Bank offers consumer loans. . . . These loans consist primarily of home equity loans secured by second mortgages, loans secured by savings deposits, and personal loans which are either secured or unsecured. . . .

Principal sources of income are interest on loans, interest-earning deposits and to a lesser extent investment securities. The Bank's principal expense is interest paid on deposits.

It operates in a relatively small market area whose economy is driven by agribusiness:

The Bank's primary market area consists of Mercer and Anderson Counties, Kentucky. This area is primarily rural with a large amount of agribusiness. The primary lending concentration is in the Bank's market area, an area mainly comprised of the cities of Harrodsburg and Lawrenceburg, which have populations of approximately 8,118 and 6,655, respectively. Historically, the economy in the Bank's market area has been dependent on agriculture, agriculture related industries and manufacturing. Tourism is the second largest industry in Mercer County, next to agriculture. The largest employers in the market area are Hitachi Automotive, Trim Masters, Corning, Inc. and Bay West Paper.

Harrodsburg also faces competition:

The Bank is one of nine financial institutions serving its immediate market area. The competition for deposit products comes from six commercial banks in the Bank's market area, and two credit unions. Deposit competition also includes a number of insurance products sold by local agents and investment products such as mutual funds and other securities sold by local and regional brokers. Loan competition comes from commercial banks in the Bank's market area, credit unions, and mortgage bankers who serve the area and varies depending upon market conditions.

Given that it is a savings and loan in a small area with significant competition, it is unlikely that any of Harrodsburg's significant assets are not captured by GAAP.

What about liabilities? By the identity Assets = Liabilities + Equities, we know that if the aggregate GAAP assets are close to economic value and if the GAAP equity is close to its economic value, then aggregate GAAP liabilities must also be close to economic value.

Harrodsburg's 10K discusses items that may be economic, but not GAAP, liabilities:

Loan Commitments. The Bank issues written commitments to prospective borrowers on all approved real estate loans. Generally, the commitment requires acceptance within 20 days of the date of issuance. At September 30, 1998, the Bank had $7.0 of commitments to cover originations, undisbursed funds for loans-in-process, and unused lines of credit. The Bank believes that most of the Bank's commitments will be funded. Generally, the percentage of commitments that expire without being funded is less than 1%.

The Bank, from time to time, is a party to ordinary routine litigation, which arises in the normal course of business, such as claims to enforce liens, condemnation proceedings on properties in which the Bank holds security interests, claims involving the making and servicing of real property loans, and other issues incident to the business of the Bank. There were no material lawsuits pending or known to be contemplated against the Bank or the Company at September 30, 1998. (Emphasis added.)

From notes to the financial statements:

9. Financial Instruments with Off-Balance Sheet Risk and Concentration of Credit Risk

The Bank is party to financial instruments with off-balance sheet risk in the normal course of business to meet the financing needs of its customers. These

In fact we have just argued this point in the case of Harrodsburg. Initially we demonstrated that the market value of the stock was close to the book value, and we showed that most assets have book values close to their economic values.

*FILLING IN EXHIBIT 7.2
FOR LIABILITIES:*

The liabilities labeled Deposits, Advance Payments by Borrowers for Taxes and Insurance, Dividends Payable, and Other Liabilities, are likely items whose economic value is measured accurately by GAAP (for the most part they are cash payments to Harrodsburg). Thus, we enter the GAAP valuation of these items in the Economic column.

We will learn in Chapter 14 that the economic value of Deferred Federal Income Tax is difficult to estimate, so we enter a question mark in the Economic column for this item.

In stockholders' equity, we list the stock market valuation of $29,093.2. The Difference column shows an aggregate difference of $26.6 between the GAAP and Economic columns. If the amount were larger we might look outside the accounting system to find estimates of the items marked with a question mark to try to explain this difference.

financial instruments include mortgage commitments outstanding which amounted to approximately $1,854,000 plus unused lines of credit granted to customers totaling $2,178,848 at September 30, 1998. . . .

14. Commitments

As of September 30, 1998, the Company had entered into a contract in the amount of approximately $72,000 with their data service provider to acquire new equipment and software changes in preparing the Company for the year 2000.

These disclosures provide corroborating evidence that the amount of economic liabilities not recorded as liabilities in Harrodsburg's GAAP accounts is small.

An accurate picture of economic assets and liabilities within the GAAP accounts translates into an accurate picture of the entity's economic resources and obligations. In turn, it offers us a fairly clear view of its future GAAP earnings. Think of it this way: The economic assets of a firm are the resources it has to work with. Economic liabilities are the sources of capital *not* from owners. Net income is the return to owners, which should be what the assets earn less the returns due to the nonowner sources of funds, that is, the costs to service the liabilities. If GAAP accurately capture the economic assets and economic liabilities of a firm, the GAAP balance sheet accurately shows what resources are at work generating a return, and what nonowner sources of resources must be paid before the owners get their share.

From September 30, 1998, to September 30, 1999, interest rates in the United States were fairly low. Therefore, we might expect that the return on equity in the business of borrowing and lending also would be fairly low. As long as Harrodsburg's GAAP books recognize almost all of its economic assets and liabilities, as we have decided that they do, we would expect Harrodsburg's accounting return on equity to be close to its economic return. We expect this economic return to be fairly small.

Exhibit 7.3 on page 142 contains Harrodsburg's income statement for the period September 30, 1998, to September 30, 1999. As you can see, Harrodsburg's net income over this period was $1,508,500. Based solely on its September 30, 1998, GAAP shareholders' equity of $28,981,600, Harrodsburg's **accounting return on equity** from September 30, 1998, to September 30, 1999, was 5.2%:

$$\$1,508,500/\$28,981,600 = 0.052$$

This calculation roughly matches interest rates in the United States during this period.

We chose Harrodsburg First Financial because it works out so well. The market-to-book ratio at September 30, 1998, is virtually one, and the accounting return on equity for the following fiscal year is virtually the normal return we would expect on its shareholders' equity. Even for firms with a beginning market-to-book near one, however, unexpected events could cause its economic return on equity to be abnormally high or low. These events may not be captured in GAAP financial statements. In such cases, we would expect the ending market-to-book to be different from one, reflecting the divergence of economic values and GAAP valuation over the period.

We can see in Harrodsburg's case that its **economic return on equity** for fiscal 1999 differed somewhat from its accounting return on equity. A shareholder who purchased one share of Harrodsburg's common stock on September 30, 1998, paid $15.125 for it. The share paid dividends of $0.85 during the year, and was worth only $13.25 on September 30, 1999. Therefore, the return to holding one share of Harrodsburg common stock from September 30, 1998, to September 30, 1999, was:

$$\frac{(\text{Ending price} + \text{Dividends}) - \text{Beginning price}}{\text{Beginning price}} = -0.0678$$

$$= \frac{(\$13.25 + \$0.85) - \$15.125}{\$15.125} = -0.0678$$

This charge occurred because the market believed Harrodsburg experienced some bad news during its 1999 fiscal year, which GAAP failed to pick up. Harrodsburg's

Exhibit 7.3

Harrodsburg First
Financial Bancorp
Statement of Income

Harrodsburg is in a business with few barriers to entry. If it were to earn a return much higher than the prevailing interest rates, other savings and loans would enter the market, offering better terms to customers, driving Harrodsburg's profits and returns down.

Harrodsburg First Financial Bancorp, Inc. and Subsidiary
Consolidated Statement of Income
For the Year Ended September 30, 1999
(amounts in thousands)

Interest income:	
Interest on loans	$ 6,757.3
Interest and dividends on securities	552.2
Other interest income	435.8
Total interest income	$ 7,745.3
Interest expense:	
Interest on deposits	(3,812.6)
Net interest income	$ 3,932.7
Provision for loan losses	(35.0)
Net interest income after provision for loan losses	$ 3,897.7
Noninterest income:	
Loan and other service fees, net	$ 99.9
Other	16.4
	$ 116.3
Noninterest expense:	
Compensation and benefits	$ (934.8)
Occupancy expenses, net	(144.8)
Federal and other insurance premiums	(48.3)
Data processing expenses	(135.1)
State franchise tax	(124.0)
Other operating expenses	(341.4)
	$(1,728.4)
Income before income tax expense	$ 2,285.6
Income tax expense	(777.1)
Net income	$ 1,508.5

We obtained the share figures for Harrodsburg from its September 31, 1999, balance sheet, which is not shown here. Can you find this financial statement for yourself and check our calculations?

market-to-book ratio at September 30, 1999, should show this investor assessment. At September 30, 1999, shareholders held 1,700,875 shares.

Shares listed under common stock	2,182,125
Shares held in Treasury stock	(481,250)
Shares in the hands of shareholders	1,700,875

The market value of Harrodsburg's stockholders' equity on September 30, 1999, was $22,536,600:

$$(\$13.25/\text{share}) \times (1,700,875 \text{ shares}) = \$22,536,600$$

The book value of Harrodsburg's stockholders' equity on September 30, 1999, was $26,220,200, which exceeds the market value by $3,683,600:

Market value	$ 22,536.6
Book value	(26,220.2)
Excess of market over book	$ (3,683.6)

The market-to-book ratio for Harrodsburg at September 30, 1999, can be calculated:

$$\frac{\$22,536.6}{\$26,220.2} = 0.86$$

Perhaps the stock market, which is forward-looking, is telling us something about the future earning prospects of Harrodsburg. It may expect earnings to go down in the future.

Still, Harrodsburg remains a case in which economic valuation and GAAP are fairly close, at least at the beginning of fiscal 1999. We now turn to an example that doesn't work out well, even at the start: Microsoft.

Microsoft Corporation

OBJECTIVE:

Learn to apply the financial analysis conceptual framework to real companies.

Although most of us know something about Microsoft Corporation, let's begin with a description of its business in the words of its 10K:

> Microsoft develops, manufactures, licenses, and supports a wide range of software products for a multitude of computing devices. Microsoft software includes scalable operating systems for intelligent devices, personal computers (PCs), and servers; server applications for client/server environments; knowledge worker productivity applications; and software development tools. The Company's online efforts include the MSN network of Internet products and services; e-commerce platforms; and alliances with companies involved with broadband access and various forms of digital interactivity. Microsoft also licenses consumer software programs; sells PC input devices; trains and certifies system integrators; and researches and develops advanced technologies for future software products.
>
> . . .
>
> Microsoft has three major segments: Windows Platforms; Productivity Applications and Developer; and Consumer, Commerce, and Other.

On June 30, 1998, the closing price of Microsoft common stock was $108.375 per share. The stockholders' equity section of Microsoft's balance sheet, presented in Exhibit 7.4 on page 144, shows 2.47 billion shares of common stock outstanding on June 30, 1998. Therefore, the stock market valued Microsoft's common stock as calculated here:

$$(2.47 \text{ billion shares}) \times (\$108.375/\text{share}) = \$267.686 \text{ billion}$$

Let's compare that value to the book value that Microsoft's accounting methods assign to its common shareholders' equity. This comparison is complicated by the fact that Microsoft has more than one kind of stock. The equity section of Microsoft's balance sheet lists Convertible Preferred Stock, Common Stock and Paid-In Capital, and Retained Earnings. These accounts combine to a total book value of shareholders' equity of $16.63 billion. Of course, that figure includes the convertible preferred stock, which is not included in our market value calculation. We will see in Chapter 13 that preferred stock is a hybrid financial instrument that can be more like debt than equity. Here's what Microsoft's 1998 10K says about its preferred stock:

> Convertible Preferred Stock. During 1996, Microsoft issued 12.5 million shares of 2.75% convertible exchangeable principal-protected preferred stock. Dividends are payable quarterly in arrears. Preferred stockholders have preference over common stockholders in dividends and liquidation rights. In December 1999, each preferred share is convertible into common shares or an equivalent amount of cash. . . .

Because Microsoft's preferred shareholders are entitled to regular, quarterly dividend payments (sound like interest?) and can convert their shares into either common stock or cash (sound like a repayment of principal?), we treat the preferred stock as debt from an economic point of view. Although we go into more details later, for now we subtract the $0.98 billion book value of the convertible preferred stock out of the book value of shareholders' equity in comparing the book value of Microsoft to its market value. This calculation leaves us with (in billions):

Exhibit 7.4

Microsoft Corporation
Balance Sheet

Microsoft Corporation Balance Sheet
As of June 30, 1998
(amounts in millions)

ASSETS

Current assets:	
Cash and short-term investments	$13,927
Accounts receivable	1,460
Other	502
Total current assets	$15,889
Property and equipment	1,505
Equity and other investments	4,703
Other assets	260
TOTAL ASSETS	$22,357

LIABILITIES AND STOCKHOLDERS' EQUITY

Current liabilities:	
Accounts payable	$ 759
Accrued compensation	359
Income taxes payable	915
Unearned revenue	2,888
Other	809
Total current liabilities	$ 5,730
Stockholders' equity:	
Convertible preferred stock—shares authorized 100;	
shares issued and outstanding 13	$ 980
Common stock and paid-in capital—shares authorized 8,000;	
shares issued and outstanding 2,470	8,025
Retained earnings, including other comprehensive income of $666	7,622
Total stockholders' equity	$16,627
TOTAL LIABILITIES AND STOCKHOLDERS' EQUITY	$22,357

Book value of Microsoft's shareholders' equity including preferred stock	$16.627
Book value of preferred stock	(0.98)
Book value of common equity	$15.647

as the book value of Microsoft's *common shareholders'* equity.

Needless to say, these calculations lead to quite a difference between the market value of $267.686 billion and the book value of $15.647 billion. The difference between the supply-and-demand set market value for shares of Microsoft stock and the GAAP-calculated book value of Microsoft tops $252 billion:

Market value	$267.686
Book value	(15.647)
Excess of market over book	$252.039

Compare Microsoft's market and GAAP values using the market-to-book ratio on June 30, 1998:

$$\frac{\$267.686}{\$15.647} = 17.108$$

A market value more than 17 times its book value on June 30, 1998, clearly signals significant gaps in GAAP for Microsoft. It must be failing to capture the economics of Microsoft's business.

Even though the outcome of the process is likely to be far different, let's go through the same stages of comparing the GAAP balance sheet with economic values as we did for Harrodsburg.

The process of adjusting an item to its market value is called marking-to-market.

Exhibit 7.5 looks in greater detail at Microsoft's balance sheet. Perhaps some of the $252 billion gap between the market value and book value can be explained. On the other hand, if the economic value of liabilities exceeds their book values, the gap might grow. Let's go through the balance sheet item by item and see what happens.

Cash and Short-Term Investments consist of cash, which has a book value equal to its economic value, and short-term investments. Chapter 10 explains why the book value of short-term investments must be adjusted to market value. Therefore, book value and

Exhibit 7.5 Worksheet—Microsoft Corporation Balance Sheet

Worksheet—Microsoft Corporation
Consolidated Balance Sheet
June 30, 1998
(amounts in millions)

ASSETS	GAAP	ECONOMIC	DIFFERENCE	SOURCE
Cash and short-term investments (A₁)	$13,927	$ 13,927	$ 0	Chapter 10
Accounts receivable (A₁)	1,460	1,460	0	Chapter 8
Other current assets (A₃)	502	?	?	
Property and equipment, net (A₃)	1,505	?	?	Chapter 11
Equity and other investments (A₃)	4,703	?	?	Chapters 10, 15
Other assets (A₃)	260	?	?	
Assets not recognized by GAAP (A₄)	0	?	?	
TOTAL ASSETS	$22,357	>$312,931	>$290,574	Chapter 7

LIABILITIES AND STOCKHOLDERS' EQUITY				
Accounts payable (L₁)	$ 759	$ 759	$ 0	Chapter 2
Accrued compensation (L₁)	359	359	0	Chapter 2
Income taxes payable (L₃)	915	?	?	Chapter 14
Unearned revenue (L₁)	2,888	2,888	0	Chapter 2
Other liabilities (L₃)	809	>809	?	
Liabilities not recognized by GAAP (L₄)	0	>39,380	>39,380	Chapter 12
TOTAL LIABILITIES	$ 5,730	>$ 44,195	>$ 38,465	Chapter 7

STOCKHOLDERS' EQUITY				
Convertible preferred stock—shares authorized 100; shares issued and outstanding 13	$ 980	$ 1,050	$ 70	Chapters 7, 13
Total liabilities plus preferred stock	$ 6,710			
Common stock and paid-in-capital—shares authorized 8,000; shares issued and outstanding 2,470	$ 8,025			
Retained earnings, including other comprehensive income of $666	7,622			
Total common stockholders' equity	$15,647	$267,686	$252,039	Chapters 7, 16
TOTAL LIABILITIES AND STOCKHOLDERS' EQUITY	$22,357	>$312,931		
			>$290,574	Unexplained

economic value are equal for Cash and Short-Term Investments at $13,927 in the Economic column in Exhibit 7.5.

Chapter 8 discusses why Accounts Receivable book values are close to their economic values. So, $1,460 is entered in the Economic column for Accounts Receivable.

We cannot say much about the economic value of the Other Current Assets, because we don't even know what they are. We do know, however, that Microsoft lists them as current assets; therefore, they are expected to be recovered within the next operating year. Some of these assets are probably inventory, as described in Chapter 9, which can have an economic value that exceeds book value. However, given the business it is in, Microsoft is unlikely to have inventories with a substantially larger economic value than book value. In fact, Microsoft is unlikely to have inventories with much economic value at all. We put a question mark in the Economic column for these assets, but their economic value is unlikely to differ significantly from their book value.

Even if the market value was five times book, it would still explain only about $5 billion: Five times book value is 7.525. If we subtract the book value, 1.505, that would say the economic value was 6.020 higher than the book value—small in comparison to the $252 billion by which the stock market value exceeds the book value of the firm.

Chapter 11 explains how the economic value of Property and Equipment could be greater than its book value. Microsoft, incorporated in 1981, is still a relatively young firm. It does not require much property to conduct its operations. Most likely then, Microsoft's Property and Equipment's economic value is, relative to the market-to-book ratio of 17, only slightly higher than its book value. Nonetheless, we put a question mark in the Economic column of Exhibit 7.5.

Equity and Other Investments are difficult to give an economic value. Some of the investments included in this category are marketable securities, which are adjusted so that book value equals market value (see Chapter 10). Unfortunately, this category also includes other investments recorded at historical cost. From Microsoft's 10K:

Therefore, we insert a question mark in the Economic column for Equity and Other Investments.

> *Equity and other investments include debt and equity instruments. Debt securities and publicly traded equity securities are . . . recorded at market. . . . All other investments, excluding joint venture arrangements, are recorded at cost.*

Because we don't know what Other Assets represent we can't easily assign a market value and hence, the question mark in the Economic column.

Assets not recognized by GAAP have a book value of zero. Let's think about what the economic value of those assets might be for Microsoft. Microsoft creates substantial intellectual property. Windows, the Office suite of programs, and Internet Explorer are some of Microsoft's more visible products. The computer programs, knowledge, and organizations that develop and maintain these products will likely generate enormous future benefits for Microsoft. Microsoft also carries substantial brand name recognition and presence in the software industry. These economic assets do not appear on Microsoft's GAAP balance sheet, yet surely they are an essential part of the economic value of Microsoft's equity.

Estimating economic value of these assets not recognized by GAAP can be particularly difficult, therefore we will back into an estimate after going through Microsoft's liabilities.

Accounts Payable, Accrued Compensation, and Unearned Revenue all have economic values equal to GAAP values.

Accounts Payable, Accrued Compensation, and Unearned Revenue are straightforward obligations whose book values are close to their economic value. We don't know exactly what the Other Liabilities are, but we can safely assume in most cases that the economic value of these liabilities is at least as much as their book value (see Chapter 12). It is extremely difficult to put an economic value on Income Taxes Payable, as noted in Chapter 14, hence, the question mark in the Economic column in Exhibit 7.5.

We want to concentrate now on Microsoft's Liabilities not Recognized by GAAP, because they are likely to be substantial. One area of future sacrifices that appears only in very limited circumstances on GAAP balance sheets is potential losses in litigation. Microsoft's 1998 10K states the following:

> *Litigation Litigation regarding intellectual property rights, patents, and copyrights occurs in the PC software industry. In addition, there are government regulation and investigation risks along with other general corporate legal risks.*

Although it is difficult to place an economic value on the future sacrifices that will result from litigation, we should acknowledge that they could be substantial. In particular, Microsoft lost an antitrust case brought by the U.S. Department of Justice, and at the time of this book's publication, it remained unclear what future costs this ruling will impose on Microsoft.

Microsoft, like most high-technology companies, compensates its employees in part with stock options. These options carry the right to purchase Microsoft stock at fixed prices (called *exercise prices*), regardless of the price at which the stock is currently selling in the market. The holder of an option will exercise only if the market price exceeds the exercise price. In this case, Microsoft must deliver a share valued at the market price in exchange for receiving the exercise price. The difference between the economic value of the share and the amount of the exercise price received represents resources sacrificed by Microsoft.

From its 1998 10K, we find that at June 30, 1998, Microsoft had outstanding options on 466 million shares. The average exercise price for these options was $23.87 per share. Recall, on June 30, 1998, Microsoft stock was selling for $108.375 per share. Therefore, if Microsoft had to settle its obligations under options on June 30, 1998, it would give up a share worth $108.375 and receive $23.87 in cash for each option exercised. The amount of Microsoft's obligation is about $39 billion—$39,380 million to be more precise:

Cost of shares:	466 million shares × $108.375 per share	$ 50,503
Cash received:	466 million shares × $23.87 per share	(11,123)
	Excess of cost of shares over cash received	$ 39,380

We enter $39,380 in the Economic column in the line for liabilities not recognized by GAAP.

As discussed earlier, Convertible Preferred Stock is, economically, more like a liability than equity. There are 12.5 million shares of preferred stock that are convertible into common shares or cash. Repeating the earlier excerpt from Microsoft's 1998 10K:

> . . . each preferred share is convertible into common shares or an equivalent amount of cash determined by a formula that provides a floor price of $79.875 and a cap of $102.24 per preferred share . . .

You will be able to do this analysis when you learn about equity in Chapter 13. For now, enter $1,050 in the Economic column preferred stock line.

Similar to management stock options, when Microsoft stock rises in price, the line listing preferred stock at face value in the balance sheet underestimates the amount of the obligation. In an economic sense, it now includes the amount of dollars that would be forgone by giving preferred stockholders common stock in excess of the face value of their preferred stock. By analyzing the terms of the conversion we can show that the expected value of the economic obligation is about $1,050 million, as entered in the Economic column in Exhibit 7.5.

Let's review. Recall that the stock market valued the aggregate company for $267,686 million, which we entered in the Economic column in Exhibit 7.5 in the total common shareholders' equity line. Now total economic liabilities plus convertible preferred plus common shareholders' equity amounts to $312,931 million. By the fundamental balance identity we know that total economic assets must be $312,931 million also. We enter this amount in the Economic column for the total asset row. Subtracting the total GAAP asset value of $22,357 million, we see that there is at least $290,574 million of economic asset value that has not been explained.

The unexplained amount is so large that the bulk of it must be Assets not Recognized by GAAP. As is apparent from any knowledge of Microsoft's business and a cursory examination of its balance sheet, most of Microsoft's economic assets are not recorded in its GAAP accounts. Cash and Short-Term Investments amount to about $14 billion of Microsoft's $22 billion in total assets on the balance sheet, or just about two-thirds of Microsoft's total GAAP assets are in Cash and Short-Term Investments. Surely, Cash and Short-Term Investments are not Microsoft's main *economic* asset!

Microsoft's main economic asset is the intellectual property it owns. In particular, the computer codes for Windows, Microsoft Office, and other software forms the most likely source of Microsoft's earnings and cash flows for a few more years. These economic assets should, whether recorded or not, generate income. GAAP will identify income that results from transactions with customers. In other words, Microsoft's GAAP income statement will eventually show the fruits of these unbooked assets.

Let's look at the income Microsoft earned in the year following June 30, 1998. Exhibit 7.6 provides Microsoft's income statement for the year beginning on June 30, 1998, and ending on June 30, 1999.

Exhibit 7.6

Microsoft Corporation
Income Statement

Microsoft Corporation
Income Statement
For the Year Ended June 30, 1999
(amounts in millions, except earnings per share)

Revenue	$19,747
Operating expenses:	
Cost of revenue	$ 2,814
Research and development	2,970
Sales and marketing	3,231
General and administrative	689
Other expenses	115
Total operating expenses	$ 9,819
Operating income	$ 9,928
Investment income	1,803
Gain on sale of Softimage, Inc.	160
Income before income taxes	$11,891
Provision for income taxes	4,106
Net income	$ 7,785

The preferred dividends were stated in Microsoft's 1999 10K.

Microsoft's net income for 1999 was $7,785 million. The convertible preferred shareholders were paid $28 million in dividends in 1999, leaving $7,757 million for the common shareholders. Common shareholders' accounting return on equity for 1999 can be calculated as follows:

$$\$7,757/\$15,647 = 0.501 = 50.1\%$$

An accounting rate of return of more than 50% should strike you as extremely high, but our analysis points to the reasons it is so high. Microsoft's enormous pool of economic assets generates income, which makes the numerator in the accounting return on equity ratio high. Yet most of these assets do not appear on its balance sheet and therefore are not reflected in Microsoft's GAAP shareholders' equity. This low number holds down the denominator of the accounting return on equity. A high ratio—GAAP income over GAAP shareholders' equity—results.

Let's suppose that as an investor, you bought a share of Microsoft common stock at its closing price of $108.375 on June 30, 1998. By June 30, 1999, this share grew in value to $180.375. Because Microsoft pays no dividends, your economic rate of return can be calculated as follows:

$$(\$180.375 - \$108.375)/\$108.375 = 0.664 = 66.4\%$$

This result exceeds the accounting rate of return:

$$66.4\% - 50.1\% = 16.3\%$$

This is quite a large amount for a difference in rates of return.

Microsoft most likely received good news during fiscal 1999 that was not captured by GAAP. Everything else constant, this factor would be reflected in Microsoft's market-to-book ratio being higher on June 30, 1999, than it was on June 30, 1998. Microsoft did not hold everything else constant, however. It fulfilled option obligations that caused shares to be issued at below-market prices. This effect overwhelmed the good news in Microsoft's economic return on equity and dragged the market-to-book ratio down to 16.78 on June 30, 1999.

We chose Microsoft because we knew its book and market values were likely to be significantly different. How did we know? We knew a little about Microsoft's economic assets, and we knew GAAP were not likely to capture them. One look at the balance sheet reaffirmed our intuition—the largest asset on Microsoft's balance sheet is Cash and Short-Term Investments. We strongly suspected that these were not Microsoft's main economic assets.

Review Questions

1. What if we estimated the liabilities not recognized by GAAP to be $75,000 million instead of $39,380 million? What would the value of the unexplained economic asset value be?

2. Is the analysis of a company like Microsoft easier or more difficult than a company like Harrodsburg? Explain.

3. Do you think the stock market aggregate valuation for a company is always correct? Why or why not? Under what circumstances would you expect it to be accurate?

Discussion

Why are book values different from market values? The key lies in the processes that generate the two values. Market values result from transactions between buyers and sellers. Book values derive from applying GAAP to the transactions and events of the period. The market valuation process and the GAAP valuation process serve different purposes, play different roles in the activity of the world's economies, and even are conducted by different people.

Market processes balance supply and demand. The only balancing process in the GAAP financials is the one required by ASSETS = LIABILITIES + EQUITIES. It's simply a numerical identity, not a balancing of competing assessments of value. People use GAAP financial statements because they are produced by a given set of rules and are checked, verified, and often backed by the reputation of a public accounting firm. These aspects are the strengths of GAAP.

So even for a company such as Microsoft, the GAAP financial statements can reveal important information. After all, the earnings generated by Microsoft's unbooked assets must be captured eventually in GAAP income. If we become aware of Microsoft's economic position and know how GAAP work, we can expect that Microsoft's accounting return on equity will remain very high for many years to come. When Microsoft issues financial statements, investors will be looking at its accounting return on equity and comparing it to a pretty high benchmark.

Chapter 16 discusses comparing statistics to benchmarks.

At least two good reasons explain why GAAP do not show the intellectual property, particularly the value of the computer codes for Windows, Microsoft Office, and other software that is Microsoft's main economic asset. The first: the research and development expenditures required to produce the computer code for Windows, Microsoft Office, and other software that likely constitutes most of this intellectual property presented an uncertain payoff potential at the time they were made. GAAP treat research and development costs as expenses, not assets, to limit managements' ability to overstate income by avoiding the recording of expenses. The second: many favorable events led the value of the software to far exceed the expenditures required to produce it. Microsoft got lucky, and GAAP did not recognize these fortunate events by recording their value. The GAAP approach is to let these good fortunes prove themselves in the generation of revenue.

Investors in the stock market, not willing to wait so long for proof, recognized these events by bidding up the price of Microsoft's stock.

You will want to keep these examples in mind as we study the details of GAAP for different assets and liabilities in Part 3 of this book. What requirements do GAAP impose before they recognize an item as an asset or liability? Are these requirements met by all assets that generate future benefits or all liabilities requiring a future sacrifice? Or is GAAP recognition limited relative to market value recognition?

Exactly how do GAAP calculate the adjustments for different types of assets and liabilities that they do recognize? Are these adjustments in line with changes in market values? What will be the effects of the differences between GAAP adjustments and market revaluations on future financial statements? These questions must be addressed in the context of specific types of assets and liabilities, because no single answer addresses them all. The devil, as they say, is in the details, and that is certainly true with accounting.

Conclusion

Making good use of accounting data requires understanding what is and what is not recognized in compiling them. We explore this distinction in the chapters that follow. We go through many specific areas such as receivables, inventories, long-lived assets, and long-term debt to gain a more refined insight into accounting recognition. To understand what the accounting reports, we must first understand what is happening economically; that is, we must have some way to judge what appropriate recognition might look like. We can then use that recognition to examine the strengths and weaknesses of various accounting techniques.

The next chapter begins this process by looking at receivables.

Key Terms

accounting return on equity *141*	**economic return on equity** *141*	**market-to-book ratio** *134*
book valuation *132*	**market capitalization** *131*	**restrictive recognition** *132*

PART 3

Topics in Financial Reporting

chapter 8

© GETTY IMAGES/EYE WIRE

Accounts Receivable

Telephone service, utilities like gas and electricity, and cable television are goods and services most of us routinely buy on account. When you pay these bills, you probably write a check that causes a bank to transfer cash; occasionally, you may take cash directly to those you owe.

The Yapese, whose money consisted of special heavy stones, found direct transfer of currency to settle their accounts too cumbersome. Therefore, they developed a rather unique approach of paying debts. They left the stones where they laid, and simply agreed that they now belonged to someone else. This practice came in especially handy for the one very precious stone that rolled into the ocean. Instead of risking their lives trying to get it back ashore, the Yapese decided that because everyone knew it was there, it was still available to settle debts. If you owned the stone in the ocean and built up a debt that you wanted to pay off, you simply told your creditor that he now owned the stone in the ocean. If we could only get Visa to accept such a payment!

Almost every organization sells its goods or services on credit. Virtually all business-to-business transactions are conducted on credit. Typically, cash payment for a credit sale is expected fairly soon, say within 60 or 90 days. **Accounts receivable** are the amounts owed by customers; typically, they are current assets.

This chapter focuses on accounts receivable—understanding why they exist and how they are accounted for in the financial statements.

We begin by discussing the nature of accounts receivable, after which we analyze their economic value. The time over which repayments are made and the probability of repayment are the major factors affecting the economic value of accounts receivable. GAAP for accounts receivable are directed primarily at the uncertainty of collection. In comparing GAAP with economic values, we see that GAAP ignore interest (the time value of money). Finally, we present some financial statistics used to assess the level of an organization's accounts receivable relative to its sales on account: receivables turnover and days-receivables held

Nature of Accounts Receivable

OBJECTIVE:
Learn to understand the definition of accounts receivable.

Organizations use accounts receivable to help customers finance purchases. Providing financing may be a profitable service in and of itself, but customers are usually allowed to purchase on account because it raises their propensity to buy. Any consultant, plumber, or attorney will confirm that it is virtually impossible to do business without extending clients the opportunity to pay their fees over a reasonable period.

An Example: Navigant Consulting, Inc.

Accounts receivable can be substantial fractions of an organization's booked assets. For example, look at the asset side of the 2000 and 2001 balance sheets for Navigant Consulting, Inc. (NCI), given in Exhibit 8.1 on page 154. NCI is "a management consulting firm to Fortune 500 and other companies, government agencies, law firms, financial institutions and regulated industries." NCI operates two primary lines of business: Financial & Claims Consulting and Energy & Water Consulting. Financial & Claims Consulting provides services that include data management, quality control, business and property valuation, and bankruptcy management. Energy & Water Consulting provides advice on

Exhibit 8.1

Navigant Consulting
Balance Sheet Excerpts

Notice the qualifier "net" on Accounts Receivable.

Accounts Receivable are 33% of total assets in 2001.

Accounts Receivable are 34% of total assets in 2000.

Navigant Consulting, Inc.
Consolidated Balance Sheets (Asset Side Only)
December 31, 2001 and 2000
(amounts in thousands)

ASSETS	2001	2000
Current assets:		
Cash and cash equivalents	$ 35,950	$ 48,798
Accounts receivable, net	52,412	55,012
Prepaid expenses and other current assets	4,804	3,776
Income tax receivable	—	476
Deferred income taxes	5,611	3,351
Total current assets	$ 98,777	$111,413
Property and equipment, net	20,648	19,328
Goodwill and intangible assets, net	35,455	27,523
Deferred income taxes	2,445	3,708
Other assets	1,501	1,510
Total assets	$158,826	$163,482

The booked assets of many consulting firms like NCI are primarily accounts receivable.

the production, generation, transmission, and distribution of network-based industries such as electric utilities.

At December 31, 2001, NCI had total assets of $158.8 million, $52.4 million of which were accounts receivable. Therefore, 33% ($52.4/$158.8) of the assets on NCI's 2001 balance sheet were accounts receivable.

Collectibility is the major business problem associated with accounts receivable. Every business that sells on account encounters problems collecting what it is owed. Some businesses, such as suppliers to large automobile manufacturers, have few uncollectible amounts. Other businesses, such as attorneys that represent individuals in civil litigation, have much larger problems with collections. We acknowledge our expectation that not all accounts receivable will be collected when we calculate their book value.

Collectibility can become a major problem for businesses that sell on account. Many businesses employ collection agencies who provide services, such as calling delinquent customers, in order to reduce this cost of doing business.

© GETTY IMAGES/PHOTO DISC

For example, NCI's Accounts Receivable at December 31, 2001, in Exhibit 8.1 are shown at a net amount of about $52.4 million. The total amount owed by customers is reduced by an allowance to reflect uncertainty about collections. The notes to NCI's financial statements, some excerpts from which are in Exhibit 8.2, provide more detail. We see that the $52.4 million has three parts: Billed Amounts, Engagements in Process, and an Allowance for Uncollectible Accounts.

Exhibit 8.2

Navigant Consulting
Footnote Excerpt

Gross receivables

Allowance for noncollections

Net receivables to appear on NCI's balance sheet in Exhibit 8.1

Excerpts from Notes to Financial Statements for NCI

4. ACCOUNTS RECEIVABLE:

At December 31, 2001 and 2000, the components of accounts receivable were as follows (amounts in thousands):

	2001	2000
Billed amounts	$41,814	$44,037
Engagements in process	20,546	20,496
Allowance for uncollectible accounts	(9,948)	(9,521)
Total	$52,412	$55,012

Engagements in process represent balances accrued by the Company for services that have been performed and earned but have not been billed to the customer. Billings are generally done on a monthly basis for the prior month's services. Engagements in process represent balances accrued by the Company for services that have been performed and earned but have not been billed to the customer. Billings are generally done on a monthly basis for the prior month's services.

The Allowance for Uncollectible Accounts at December 31, 2001, was about $9.9 million. This figure reduces the amount owed to NCI and provides the amount of $52.4 million shown on the balance sheet. Therefore, to determine how much its clients actually owed NCI (in millions)—the gross amount of Accounts Receivable:

Gross accounts receivable equal net accounts receivable plus the allowance for uncollectibles.

$$x = \text{Amount owed by customers}$$
$$x - 9.9 = 52.4$$
$$x = 52.4 + 9.9$$
$$x = 62.3 \text{ million}$$

(We could also calculate the gross amount customers owe by adding the Billed Amounts and Engagements in Process shown in Exhibit 8.2: $41.8 + $20.5 = $62.3 million.)

Why sell on credit if some customers don't pay? Because selling on credit boosts sales. Uncollectible accounts are just another cost of doing business. Obviously, if we knew who was not going to pay their bills before we made sales, we would not sell to them. If we had to be 100% sure someone would pay us before we sold to them then we would sell only to customers who paid in cash! Profits would suffer. As we will see, GAAP treat uncollectible accounts as expenses on the income statement, right along with the cost of goods sold, administrative expenses, and other costs of operations.

NCI's income statement in Exhibit 8.3 on page 156 includes Bad Debt Expense in General and Administrative Expenses, which total about $55.4 million in 2001.

Schedule II to NCI's 2001 10K gives us more detail and appears in Exhibit 8.4 on page 156. We see that NCI recorded an expense for bad debts of about $5.6 million in 2001. NCI wrote off—gave up on collecting specific accounts—about $5.2 million in 2001. Note that the amount of the expense is not the same as the amount written off. We explain this difference in detail in the section on GAAP for Accounts Receivable.

The NCI example illustrates the importance of accounts receivable as assets, and shows that expenses related to bad debts represent important expenses. Shortly, we explain how to compute bad debt expense, where the allowance for uncollectible accounts

Exhibit 8.3

Navigant Consulting
Income Statement

NCI includes Bad Debt Expense in General and Administrative Expenses. Other companies might include it in Other Expenses or even list it as a separate line item in the income statement.

Navigant Consulting, Inc.
Consolidated Statement of Income
For the Year Ended
December 31, 2001
(amounts in thousands)

	2001
Revenues	$235,580
Consulting services expense	152,007
Value Sharing Retention Program	11,296
Stock-based compensation—consultants	3,238
Gross margin	$ 69,039
General & administrative expenses	55,413
Depreciation expense	7,118
Amortization expense	5,700
All other expenses and income	8,403
Net loss before taxes	$ (7,595)
Income tax expense (benefit)	(2,284)
Net loss	$ (5,311)

Exhibit 8.4

Navigant Consulting
Schedule II in 2001 10K (excerpt)

NCI's Bad Debt Expense (included in General and Administrative Expenses)

Schedule II to 10K for NCI
Valuation and Qualifying Accounts (Excerpt)
(amounts in thousands)

Description	Balance at Beginning of Year	Charged to Expenses	Deductions*	Balance at End of Year
Year ended 12/31/01 Allowance for doubtful accounts	$9,521	$5,604	$5,177	$9,948

*Represents write-offs of bad debts.

comes from, and what a write-off (or charge-off) of an account receivable means. Before we go into the GAAP for these items in detail, we first examine the economic value of accounts receivable.

Economic Value of Accounts Receivable

OBJECTIVE:
Learn to analyze the economic value of accounts receivable.

Accounts receivable are straightforward assets. They simply represent the rights to receive cash payments in the future. Therefore, their economic value equals their expected net present value. At any point in time, the probabilities of eventual collection should be estimated based on all available information.

Consider the hypothetical example of Service Co., a provider of consulting and financial analyses. Service Co. signs contracts to provide a new consulting service to companies. The services will be completed on December 31, 2003, at which time Service Co. will pay all salaries and costs incurred to provide the services. This amount is $100,000. On December 31, 2003, they bill clients $125,000 for the services provided. Some clients will likely never pay Service Co. for the services. Those that do pay will do so on the last day of the year, December 31, 2004.

Service Co. expects to collect only $115,000 of the $125,000 owed to it. That is, Service Co. expects 8% of its billed amounts to be uncollectible:

$$\$125,000 \times 0.08 = \$10,000$$

Exhibit 8.5 displays Service Co.'s cash flows. The payment of salaries and costs on December 31, 2003, is an investment. It creates accounts receivable that are expected to pay off $115,000 on December 31, 2004.

Exhibit 8.5

Service Co.
Expected Cash Flows

Service Co. Expected Cash Flows **(amounts in thousands)**		
	Dec. 31, 2003	**Dec. 31, 2004**
Expected collections	$ 0	$115
Payments	(100)	0
Expected net cash flow	$(100)	$115

Exhibit 8.5 suggests a simple way to view Service Co.'s economics. Focus on the expected net cash flows: $100,000 goes out on December 31, 2003, and $115,000 is expected to come in on December 31, 2004. Again, this transaction is tantamount to Service Co. investing $100,000 in salaries and benefits on December 31, 2003. This investment creates an asset (accounts receivable) that gives off an expected net cash flow of $115,000 on December 31, 2004. On that date, Service Co.'s initial investment of $100,000 is expected to be returned along with $15,000 profit.

Remember: Economic value is determined by the net present value of expected cash flows.

Suppose the interest rate appropriate for Service Co. is 15% per year. From Chapter 6, we know that Service Co.'s value on December 31, 2003, is the expected net present value of its future cash flows.

$$-\$100,000 + (\$115,000)/(1.15) = \$0$$

Therefore, Service Co. expects to earn a normal economic rate of return of 15% on its investment in accounts receivable. Another way of saying it is that the $100,000 investment in accounts receivable in anticipation of a $115,000 payoff at the end of the year has a net present value of zero if the discount rate is 15%. Because it earns only a normal rate of return, Service Co. is neither a winner (value greater than zero) nor a loser (value less than zero).

Ex ante, Service Co. is neither an expected winner nor expected loser in this investment. Ex post, Service Co.'s fate will be determined by the actual amount of the receivables collected. If it collects only $114,000 it will lose relative to its cost of money; if it collects $118,000 it will earn more than its cost of capital.

Now let's think about the economic value of Service Co.'s accounts receivable on December 31, 2003. Nominally, it billed clients $125,000, but it does not expect to collect the full amount. It expects $10,000 of the $125,000 to go bad. Further, any collections it makes will occur on December 31, 2004; therefore, they must be discounted. The economic value of the accounts receivable is their expected net present value:

$$\text{Present value} = (\$125,000 - \$10,000)/1.15$$
$$= \$115,000/1.15$$
$$= \$100,000$$

So we see the three parts to the economic value of accounts receivable. First, there is the nominal amount owed by customers ($125,000). Second, the nominal amount of the receivable must be reduced for the expectation that some amounts will not be collected. That is, there is an allowance for bad debts ($10,000). With Service Co., this allowance takes the value of receivables from their nominal level of $125,000 down to their expected collections of $115,000. Third, the expected cash flows from the receivable should be discounted to get their expected net present value (the discount factor of 1/1.15). The discounting scales down the value of the $115,000 expected cash flow to $100,000 to reflect the timing of the cash flow (see Figure 8.1).

Figure 8.1

The Economic Value of Receivables

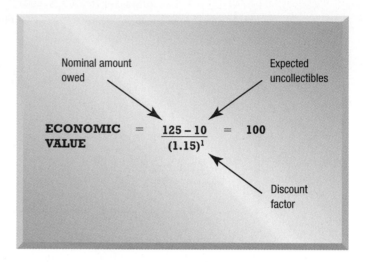

In the next section, we see that GAAP treatment for receivables requires an allowance for doubtful accounts but does not discount accounts receivable.

GAAP for Accounts Receivable

OBJECTIVE:

Learn to become familiar with GAAP for accounts receivable.

Accounts receivable initially are recorded in conjunction with the recognition of revenues. That is, we recognize the creation of the asset, accounts receivable, when we determine that a sale has been made and the customer owes the firm for it. For example, the notes to NCI's financial statements in Exhibit 8.6 reveal that NCI recognizes revenue when services are performed, except for some long-term contracts. NCI allows for amounts expected to be uncollectible.

Exhibit 8.6

Navigant Consulting Footnote Excerpt

> **Excerpts from Notes to Financial Statements for Navigant Consulting, Inc.**
>
> REVENUE RECOGNITION
>
>   The Company recognizes revenues as the related professional services are provided. Certain contracts are accounted for on the percentage of completion method, whereby revenues are recognized based upon costs incurred in relation to total estimated costs at completion. A provision is made for the entire amount of estimated losses, if any, at the time when they are known.

Revenue recognition criteria (discussed in Chapter 3)

Recall from Chapter 3 that three criteria must be met before we recognize revenue:

- The earnings process is substantially complete.
- An exchange has taken place.
- Collection is reasonably assured.

You might wonder how GAAP reconcile the requirement that collection is reasonably assured with the uncertainty of collections inherent in accounts receivable.

The accounting for receivables relies on the fact that the *aggregate* amount collected from a large number of accounts receivables is usually much more certain than the amount that will be collected from any one account.[1] For example, Service Co. may be fairly sure it is going to collect $115,000 of its $125,000 in accounts receivable, which is all GAAP require. They do not require that we be fairly certain of collecting $125,000. They do require that we be fairly sure of collecting somewhere close to $115,000. If the uncertainty about collection is large, GAAP will not allow a sale, and therefore a receivable, to be recognized in the first place. So all the GAAP we discuss next presume that the uncertainty about how much will be collected ultimately is fairly small, even though we are fairly certain that some accounts will be uncollectible.

After the initial decision to recognize revenue and a related receivable, the accounting for accounts receivable accomplishes three purposes. The accounting must do the following:

- Keep track of how much is owed by each individual customer.
- Provide a **contra-asset account** (an account that subtracts from the value of an asset), and **Allowance for Doubtful Accounts,** to allow the balance sheet to show accounts receivable at the amount that is expected to be collected.
- Record Bad Debt Expense to account for the effects on income of uncollectible accounts.

To keep track of the amounts owed by customers, GAAP for accounts receivable begin from the maximum possible collections. They track uncertainty about collections by treating expected uncollectible amounts as expenses and establishing an **Allowance for Doubtful Accounts,** a contra-account to Accounts Receivable. GAAP for accounts receivable ignore interest. GAAP also must record the cash ultimately collected. Any difference between expected uncollectibles and the actual amounts that ultimately prove to be uncollectible must be worked through the accounts.

Consider the Service Co. example from the previous section. When it bills its clients on December 31, 2003, Service Co. would recognize the revenue from the sales and the creation of accounts receivable with the following entry:

Accounts Receivable   125,000
　　Sales Revenue   125,000
12/31/2003 (To recognize revenue and to anticipate collection of the receivable.)

The total Accounts Receivable actually includes the sum of the amounts owed by each of Service Co.'s clients. So the detail underlying the $125,000 in Accounts Receivable consists of client-by-client records that show the services provided to each client, the amount billed, the date the bill was sent, and any payments made on account.

As we discussed, $125,000 is the maximum that Service Co. might collect. It expects to collect only $115,000. GAAP require Service Co.'s balance sheet to show the expected collections of $115,000, not the maximum collection of $125,000. Therefore, we establish a contra-asset account, Allowance for Doubtful Accounts, to allow for uncollectibles.

Similarly, recording Sales of $125,000 overstates the positive effect on income from this transaction. Actually, Service Co. expects to collect only $115,000 in cash. Although a good case can be made for the creation of a contra-revenue account to bring sales revenue down to expected collections, it is not standard practice. Instead, we treat expected uncollectibles as expenses and record them as follows:

Bad Debts Expense   10,000
　　Allowance for Doubtful Accounts   10,000
12/31/2003 (To record bad debt expense in anticipation of not collecting 100% of receivables.)

These two entries merit some additional attention. The entry to record the sale and accounts receivable reflects a *transaction*. The entry to record the bad debts expense and

> A **contra-asset account** is an account that offsets another account. Recall, Accumulated Depreciation is a contra-asset account to Property, Plant, and Equipment.
>
> **Allowance for Bad Debts, Allowance for Uncollectibles,** and **Allowance for Doubtful Accounts** are all different names companies use for the same contra-account.

> *Be sure you understand that accounts receivable is the total of amounts owed by each customer.*

---

[1]Insurance companies have long recognized this notion of aggregation when setting premiums.

the allowance for doubtful accounts reflects an *adjustment*. As we discussed in Chapter 6, this adjustment can be approached in two ways. One is to focus on matching the bad debts expense to sales. The other is to focus on establishing the proper allowance for doubtful accounts (that is, to make sure the net valuation of the receivables asset is as accurate as possible). We will discuss this concept in more detail later. For now, just be aware that the entry to record the bad debts expense and the allowance is an adjustment, and we need to pay attention to it.

To continue the Service Co. example, let's begin by assuming everything goes exactly as expected. On December 31, 2004, Service Co. collects $115,000 of the $125,000 it billed, and $10,000 is uncollectible. Service Co. then makes the following entries:

Cash 115,000
    Accounts Receivable 115,000

12/31/2004 (To recognize collection of cash from companies owing Service Co.)

Next, we show how to record recognition of the news about exactly which customers billed on December 31, 2004, will not pay. The receivables from them must be taken off the books, because they are no longer assets. When Service Co. knows that a specific customer is not going to pay, the receivable from that customer fails one of the crucial tests it must pass to qualify as an asset: the future benefit requirement. Therefore, that receivable must be *written off*.

Allowance for Doubtful Accounts 10,000
    Accounts Receivable 10,000

12/31/2004 (To write-off accounts that will not be collected.)

Exhibit 8.7 shows the T-accounts for the entries to Accounts Receivable and Allowance for Doubtful Accounts. The most important thing to notice about these accounts is that the write-off itself *does not affect the net accounts receivable*. A write-off lowers the balances in both Accounts Receivable and Allowance for Doubtful Accounts. It does not directly affect bad debts expense. Bad debts expense is determined by the entry that establishes (or adjusts) the balance in Allowance for Doubtful Accounts, not by an entry that writes off an actual bad debt.

Prior to write-off of accounts receivable:

Gross accounts
    receivable   x
    Less allowance . . .   (y)
Net accounts
    receivable . . . . .   x − y

After a write-off of say, $w, the accounts appear as follows:

Gross accounts
    receivable . . . .   x − w
    Less allowance . .   (y − w)
Net accounts
    receivable
    x − w − y + w = x − y

Exhibit 8.7

Service Co.
Accounts Receivable Transactions

Service Co.
Accounts Receivable Transactions

ACCOUNTS RECEIVABLE

1/1/03		0	115,000	Collections	12/31/04
			10,000	Write-off	12/31/04 **WRITE-OFF**
12/31/03 Sales		125,000			
		0			

ALLOWANCE FOR DOUBTFUL ACCOUNTS

			0		
WRITE-OFF 12/31/04 Write-off		10,000	10,000	Expense	12/31/03
			0		

In fact, establishing the Allowance for Doubtful Accounts lets us recognize the bad debts expense associated with the amounts billed in the period of the billing, instead of in the period when the accounts actually go bad. We use this account because we know, at the time of the billing, that some of the receivables will very likely go bad, but we don't know exactly which ones.

Suppose Service Co. continues to conduct business at a similar level. Every year it sells and bills $125,000 on the last day of the year and expects to collect $115,000 on December 31 of the following year and to write off $10,000 of accounts receivable. However, events do not always unfold according to expectations. For example, what if Service Co. collects only $112,000 on December 31, 2006, instead of the $115,000 that was expected. Worse still, Service Co. believes the dip in collections is likely to persist, and it expects 10% bad debts on sales in 2006 and beyond. Here are the entries Service Co. will make:

Cash 112,000
    Accounts Receivable 112,000
12/31/2006 (To recognize collection of cash from companies owing Service Co. from 2005 sales.)

Allowance for Doubtful Accounts 13,000
    Accounts Receivable 13,000
12/31/2006 (To write off accounts that will not be collected.)

Accounts Receivable 125,000
    Sales Revenue 125,000
12/31/2006 (To recognize revenue and to anticipate collection of the receivable.)

<table>
<tr><td>

METHOD ONE: Focus on the percentage of sales not expected to be collected.

Allowance for Doubtful Accounts (000s)

		10	12/31/05
12/31/06	13	12.5	12/31/06
		9.5	*Ending Balance*

(9.5 is the plug, or the number that drops out)

</td></tr>
</table>

Establishing an allowance for uncollectibles at December 31, 2006, and recognizing bad debts expense for the year ended December 31, 2006, raises an interesting issue. Two possibilities correspond to the two ways of approaching adjustments we discussed in Chapter 6.

If we focus on recording the bad debts expense associated with billings for 2006, we would record 0.10 × $125,000 = $12,500 in bad debts expense.

Bad Debts Expense 12,500
    Allowance for Doubtful Accounts 12,500
12/31/2006 (To record bad debt expense in anticipation of not collecting 100% of receivables.)

If we focus on leaving the Allowance for Doubtful Accounts with a balance sufficient to value the net accounts receivable at the expected amount of collections, we would adjust the balance in the Allowance for Doubtful Accounts so that the net receivable ends up at $112,500. That is, we would solve 125,000 − x = 112,500, and find that the ending balance in Allowance for Doubtful Accounts must be $12,500. Analyzing the account, we would determine that we must add $15,500 to it:

METHOD TWO: Focus on the ending balance in Allowance for Doubtful Accounts.

Bad Debts Expense 15,500
    Allowance for Doubtful Accounts 15,500
12/31/2006 (To record bad debt expense in anticipation of not collecting 100% of receivables.)

Allowance for Doubtful Accounts (000s)

		10	12/31/05
12/31/06	13	15.5	12/31/06
		12.5	*Ending Balance*

(15.5 is the plug, or the number that drops out)

Method two is worth studying further. Its bad debts expense of $15,500 is composed of two parts: One reflects expected uncollectibles on 2006 sales, and the other reflects the worse-than-expected collections on 2005 sales:

$$\$15,500 = \$12,500 + \$3,000$$

| **Bad debt expense** | **Bad debt expense on 2006 sales** | **Shortfall in collections of 2005 sales (relative to the allowance established)** |

Determining Bad Debt Expense and the Allowance for Bad Debts

Management must provide estimates of uncollectibles.

To this point, we simply assumed, for our calculations, that expected uncollectibles are known. For example, we assumed that Service Co. knew that 8% of its accounts would turn out to be uncollectible. In the terms used in Chapters 6, it is equivalent to assuming that the probabilities of collecting various amounts are known. Of course, these probabilities must come from somewhere and we need to know how expected uncollectibles are calculated. In practice, it is *management's responsibility* to estimate the expected uncollectibles. Managers may take any of the many approaches to perform this estimation. They all use some combination of the collection experience and knowledge of current economic conditions. In the **percent-of-sales method,** management asks what percentage of sales it expects will end up being uncollectible. In the Service Co. example, it recorded 8% of sales as bad debts expense, until experience in 2006 led it to reconsider.

Because receivables often consist of many relatively small accounts, errors in this estimation often wash out, so that actual uncollectibles end up being close to the percent of sales management estimates. If the balance in the Allowance for Doubtful Accounts grows too large because fewer debts are written off as being uncollectible than were estimated, the percentage of sales is lowered. If the balance in the allowance becomes too small because more debts are written off as being uncollectible than were estimated, the percentage is increased. The percent-of-sales method therefore smoothes the recording of bad debt expenses over time.

Aging is another method of estimating expected uncollectibles. Aging focuses directly on the balance of Accounts Receivable at the balance sheet date. The accounts comprising this balance are classified according to the length of time since they were posted. A typical aging of accounts receivable classifies them according to whether they are zero to 30 days old (i.e., the sale occurred less than 30 days before the balance sheet date), 31 to 60 days old, 61 to 90 days old, 90 to 120 days old, and more than 120 days old. Experience indicates that the likelihood of a collection problem increases with the age of the receivable.

For example, experience may show that the percentages given in Exhibit 8.8 provide good estimates of the amounts that will ultimately turn out to be uncollectible. Notice how the percentage estimated to be uncollectible starts at 0.5% for new sales and rises to 40% for accounts more than six months old. These percentages vary from industry to industry, but the table in Exhibit 8.8 offers a rough idea of how the likelihood of collection falls with the age of the account.[2]

Exhibit 8.8

Estimated Uncollectibles by Age of Receivable

Age of Receivable	Percentage Expected to Be Uncollectible
0–30 days	0.5%
31–60 days	2
61–90 days	10
91–120 days	25
More than 120 days	40

The idea of aging is to use the type of information in Exhibit 8.8 to calculate the required ending balance in the Allowance for Doubtful Accounts. For example, suppose on December 31, 2005, Uncollectible Company has $3,600,000 of receivables aged as in Exhibit 8.9. That is, $3,000,000 of the receivables is between 0 and 30 days old, $500,000 is between 31 and 60 days old, etc.

The aging method calculates the balance required in Allowance for Doubtful Accounts by multiplying each aged component of the receivables by the estimated percentage of

[2]The numbers in this table correspond roughly to those given in the "Annual Collectibility Survey," *Commercial Collection Agency Section of the Commercial Law League of America,* New Providence, NJ, April 1993.

Exhibit 8.9

Uncollectible Co.
Aged Accounts Receivable

Age of Receivable	Amount of Receivable (in 000s)
0–30 days	$3,000
31–60 days	500
61–90 days	50
91–120 days	30
More than 120 days	20
Total	$3,600

Allowance for Doubtful Accounts

	25.5	(balance prior to adjustment)
	20.0	(adjustment)
	45.5	(ending balance)

uncollectibles for that age. For example, we expect 0.5% of the $3,000,000 of the zero-to-30-day-old receivables to be uncollectible. Therefore, we must add

$$\$3,000,000 \times 0.005 = \$15,000$$

to the Allowance for Doubtful Accounts just to cover the receivables that are zero to 30 days old. This figure must be added to the amounts required for all the other age layers as shown in Exhibit 8.10 to determine the total required balance in the Allowance for Doubtful Accounts.

Exhibit 8.10

Calculation of Required Ending Balance in Allowance for Doubtful Accounts

Age of Receivable	Amount	Percent Estimated Uncollectible	Amount Estimated Uncollectible
0–30 days	$3,000	0.5%	$15.0
31–60 days	500	2	10.0
61–90 days	50	10	5.0
91–120 days	30	25	7.5
More than 120 days	20	40	8.0
Total	$3,600		$45.5

The entry Uncollectible Company must make depends on the balance in the Allowance for Doubtful Accounts before the adjustment. The aging tells us that the balance must *end up* at $45,500. Suppose that before adjustment, the balance in the Allowance for Doubtful Accounts is a credit of $25,500. Then the entry to adjust the Allowance for Doubtful Accounts and to record bad debt expense is

Bad Debt Expense 20,000
    Allowance for Doubtful Accounts 20,000

(To record bad debt expense in anticipation of not collecting 100% of receivables.)

Review Questions

1. Describe how the aging of receivables and the percentage-of-sales methods work to arrive at a balance in the Allowance for Doubtful Accounts.

2. Assume in the Service Co. example that $118,000 is collected on December 31, 2006, and that only 6% of accounts receivable are estimated to default in the future. Make the journal entries to record bad debt expense in 2006 and 2007 under each of the two methods. Show what the Allowance for Doubtful Accounts would look like under each of the methods.

Comparison of GAAP and Economic Value

OBJECTIVE:

Learn to relate GAAP for accounts receivable to their underlying economics.

Let's begin our comparison of GAAP and economic values by restating the Service Co. data including the unexpected shortfall of collections in 2006. Recall that $125,000 in sales is made on December 31 of any year. Until 2006, it is expected that 8% of the accounts receivable generated by these sales will go bad. In 2006 and beyond, it is expected that 10% of the accounts receivable generated by these sales will go bad. Collections occur on December 31 in the year following the sale and go exactly as expected except in 2006 when only $112,000 instead of the expected $115,000 is collected. The applicable interest rate is 15%. The data on accounts receivable, collections, and write-offs are given in Exhibit 8.11.

Exhibit 8.11

Service Co.
Collections Data (000s)

	December 31			
	2004	**2005**	**2006**	**2007**
Accounts receivable (gross)	$125	$125	$125	$125
Expected collections	115	115	115	112.5
Collections	115	115	112	112.5
Write-offs	10	10	13	12.5

As we already noted, one difference between GAAP accounting for accounts receivable and economic accounting is that GAAP ignores interest. This difference makes the market-to-book less than one for receivables (i.e., GAAP overstate economic value in this case). For example, in years in which the expected collections are $115,000, the economic value of the receivable at the beginning of the year is

$$\$115,000/(1.15) = \$100,000$$

In years in which the expected collections are $112,500, the economic value of the receivable at the beginning of the year is

$$\$112,500/(1.15) = \$97,830$$

The book value of Accounts Receivable depends on whether Service Co. uses the aging or percent-of-sales method for calculating Bad Debt Expense and the Allowance for Doubtful Accounts. With the percent-of-sales method, the Allowance for Doubtful Accounts is $10,000 at December 31, 2004 and 2005, and $9,500 at December 31, 2006 and 2007. Exhibit 8.12 displays these figures for the percent-of-sales method.

Exhibit 8.12

Service Co.
Net Accounts Receivable under
Percent-of-Sales Method (000s)

	December 31			
	2004	**2005**	**2006**	**2007**
Accounts receivable, gross	$125	$125	$125	$125
Allowance for doubtful accounts	(10)	(10)	(9.5)	(9.5)
Accounts receivable; net	$115	$115	$115.5	$115.5

As shown in Exhibit 8.13, the market-to-book ratios for Accounts Receivable are less than one at each December 31. These ratios reflect the lack of discounting in the book value. In addition, the market-to-book starts at 0.87, but falls to 0.85 at December 31, 2006, because the percent-of-sales method fails to give complete recognition to the unexpectedly low collections in 2006.

Exhibit 8.13

Service Co.
Market-to-Book Ratios for
Accounts Receivable under
Percent-of-Sales Method (000s)

	December 31			
	2004	**2005**	**2006**	**2007**
Market value of accounts receivable	$100.00	$100.00	$97.83	$97.83
Accounts receivable, net	$115.00	$115.00	$115.50	$115.50
Market value/Book value	0.87	0.87	0.85	0.85

The usual argument for failing to discount Accounts Receivable is that they are expected to be collected fairly quickly, so interest effects are minor. For example, we show in the next section that NCI's receivables are outstanding about 83 days on average. To make the calculations a little easier, let's round up to 90 days and call it three months. At 10% interest with monthly compounding, the present value of the $52.4 million in net accounts receivable that NCI had outstanding at December 31, 2004, amounts to $51.1 million on that date.

$$\$52.4/(1 + 0.10/12)^3 = \$51.1$$

In other words, the market-to-book ratio for NCI's receivables is about 96.75%.

$$\$51.1/\$52.4 = 0.975$$

With monthly compounding, we divide the annual rate by 12 and use the number of months as the number of compounding periods.

The picture is slightly different with the aging method. The Allowance for Doubtful Accounts is $10,000 at December 31, 2004 and 2005, and $12,500 at December 31, 2006 and 2007. Exhibit 8.14 displays these figures for the aging method.

Exhibit 8.14

Service Co.
Net Accounts Receivable under
Aging Method (000s)

	December 31			
	2004	**2005**	**2006**	**2007**
Accounts receivable, gross	$125	$125	$125	$125
Allowance for doubtful accounts	(10)	(10)	(12.5)	(12.5)
Accounts receivable, net	$115	$115	$112.5	$112.5

As shown in Exhibit 8.15, the market-to-book ratios for Accounts Receivable under aging are less than one at each December 31, but they are a constant 0.87. Aging keeps pace with all information about collections as it occurs, so no dip in market-to-book occurs in 2006.

Exhibit 8.15

Service Co.
Market-to-Book Ratios for
Accounts Receivable under Aging
Method (000s)

	December 31			
	2004	**2005**	**2006**	**2007**
Market value of accounts receivable	$100.00	$100.00	$97.83	$97.83
Accounts receivable, net	$115.00	$115.00	$112.50	$112.50
Market value/Book value	0.87	0.87	0.87	0.87

Returns on equity for receivables are close to their economic values, although they are classified slightly differently. With accounts receivable, GAAP lump interest revenue in with the original sales revenue (precisely because we do not discount the value of the accounts receivable). Recognition of the sale implicitly includes some interest. The

Another way of saying it is that percentage-of-sales results in smoother income statements, whereas aging leads to a more accurate balance sheet valuation of receivables.

interest really should be recognized in the period it is earned, not when the sale is made. The justification for being sloppy with interest here is that it should be a minor factor on accounts receivable, which are collected fairly quickly.

The recognition of bad debts expense also affects accounting return on equity, and the percent-of-sales and aging methods take a different approach. Percent-of-sales smoothes recognition of unexpectedly bad collections over several periods, whereas aging recognizes unexpectedly bad collections in the periods that information about collections becomes available. This difference is conceptually important, but in practice it should be minor for receivables.

GAAP accounting for accounts receivable results in book values and returns on equity that are fairly close to their economic values. The fact that each account is outstanding for only a short period of time mitigates the effects of ignoring interest. Usually, the estimation of expected uncollectibles is quite accurate because errors wash out over a large number of accounts.

Still, problematic differences between book and economic values are caused by the treatment of the uncertainty of collection. One problem lies in managements' incentives to provide accurate estimates. In practice, no one knows the expected uncollectibles—they must be estimated by management. Although management generally knows as much information as anyone regarding expected uncollectibles, management's incentives for accurate estimation are sometimes suspect. When the expectations of uncollectibles built into the book values differ substantially from those used to determine economic value, market-to-book ratios differ significantly from one.

Raising cash by selling receivables

In one case, estimating uncollectibles is perceived to be a serious problem: when receivables are factored. To raise cash, organizations sometimes sell or *factor* their accounts receivable. If the factoring is *without recourse*, the purchaser of the accounts receivable bears all the risk of uncollectibles.

Another piece of evidence that the estimates of uncollectibles built into book values can be too low comes from the banking industry. Banks allegedly are sometimes reluctant to recognize deteriorations in the likelihood of collecting on their loans. Bank examiners are constantly poring over the allowances for doubtful notes of banks with an eye toward making sure the allowances are sufficient to handle subsequent write-offs.

When organizations factor their receivables without recourse, they often do so at a substantial discount to the book value of the receivables (the discount is the cost of getting someone else to bear the risk of not being able to collect the receivables). This discount is generated largely by concerns over collectibility, not interest effects. The buyer of an account receivable without recourse, knowing that the seller is likely to have better information about collectibility, is understandably wary of any receivable offered for sale. Factoring with recourse, that is, giving the buyer the right to look to the seller for payment if an account is uncollectible, mitigates the effects of this wariness by providing the buyer with a guarantee. Another possibility is simply to bear the discount imposed by concerns over differences in the quality of information between buyer and seller. The discounts relative to book value when accounts receivable are factored shows that the book value is often based on an underestimate of expected uncollectibles.

Understating expected uncollectibles is not the only possibility. Sometimes, management has incentives to overstate expected uncollectibles. If expected uncollectibles are overstated, subsequent collections are likely to exceed the net book value of the receivables. This gain from the collection experience is most often recognized by lowering the bad debts expense for the period of the favorable collection experience. Management may have incentives to overstate expected uncollectibles in years of high reported profitability, so that bad debts expense can be understated some time in the future should profits dip. The overstatement of bad debts expense in one period provides a cushion to make profits look higher in future periods.

We conclude this chapter with a brief exploration of some of the common financial statistics used to assess accounts receivable.

OBJECTIVE:
Learn to become familiar with some common financial statistics related to accounts receivable.

Financial Statement Analysis of Accounts Receivable

Most organizations are sensitive to amounts they have tied up in accounts receivable. As we saw in the Total Toy Company example in Chapter 4, profitability does not mean

It is common practice to use an average, or a weighted average, in the denominator of a ratio that is a flow variable divided by a stock variable.

Receivables turnover equals *sales on account* divided by the average *accounts receivable.*

positive cash flows. Further, we saw in Chapter 6 how the time value of money works to make dollars received sooner worth more than dollars received later. Rapid collection of receivables provides a real payoff, then, in getting an organization's money quickly.

The problem of minimizing uncollectible amounts is also a factor. The best way to make sure an account does not end up uncollectible is to collect it! Careful attention to receivables balances is a virtual necessity in prudent financial management.

Financial analysts often compute a few ratios of financial statement numbers to assess the management of receivables. The most common ratio is **receivables turnover.** The idea is to assess the amount of receivables in light of the total sales of the organization. For example, NCI's revenues for 2001 were $235.6 million. Its average net accounts receivable outstanding was:

Accounts receivable, December 31, 2001 . . . . $52.4 million
Accounts receivable, December 31, 2000 . . . .   55.0 million
Average ($52.4 + $55.0)/2 . . . .   53.7 million

Accounts receivable turnover for NCI in 2001 was

$$\$235.6/\$53.7 = 4.39 \text{ times}$$

A more intuitive measure of the management of receivables is how long, on average, a receivable is held before it is collected. If NCI's receivables turned over 4.39 times during 2001, on average an account lasted

$$365/4.39 = 83 \text{ days}$$

Days Receivables Outstanding equals 365 days divided by the receivables turnover.

This lengthy period for an account to be outstanding is largely a reflection of NCI's business. Speeding collection of receivables would seem to offer a potentially large payoff for NCI, given the fraction of their assets represented by receivables and their long life.

Conclusion

This chapter explored GAAP for accounts receivable. Both time and uncertainty play a role in their economic values. GAAP require taking account of the uncertainty of collection by requiring recognition of bad debts expense and the establishment of a contra-asset account, Allowance for Doubtful Accounts. GAAP do not consider interest on accounts receivable.

GAAP book values are fairly close to economic values for receivables. The major difference between them is interest on accounts receivable, which could be significant when the receivables balance is expected to be large for a long time. As these differences go, however, the GAAP book values for receivables are fairly close to economic values.

Key Terms

accounts receivable *153*

aging *162*

allowance for bad debts *159*

allowance for doubtful accounts *159*

allowance for uncollectibles *159*

contra-asset account *159*

days receivables outstanding *167*

percent-of-sales *162*

receivables turnover *167*

chapter 9

© GETTY IMAGES/PHOTO DISC

Inventories

Craving a Coffee Coolata and wanting some donuts, a professor stopped by the local Dunkin' Donuts at about 11:45 P.M. one warm summer evening. Unfortunately, the Coffee Coolata machine had been shut down for the evening. Worse, they were out of donuts. One might understand not being able to get a Coffee Coolata. But no donuts? Makes you wonder why they were open!

In the jargon of inventory management, the professor encountered a stock-out problem. A stock-out problem occurs when inventory on hand is insufficient to meet demands. Stock-outs are costly—not only are professors left hungry and thirsty, but the store foregoes sales!—and most organizations keep inventories on hand to avoid them.

This chapter focuses on two aspects of inventories—understanding some of the economics of inventories and how they are accounted for in the financial statements.

We begin with a discussion of the nature of inventories, after which we analyze their economic value. Similar to investments in any assets, investments in inventories are expected to earn normal rates of return. The major uncertainties that can cause inventories to earn abnormal positive or negative rates of return include unexpected shifts in customers' demands, newly discovered uses for the inventoried item, and obsolescence.

GAAP for inventories are focused on determining the acquisition cost of inventory and its allocation between the cost of goods sold expense in the income statement and inventory asset on the balance sheet. GAAP cost allocation methods include last-in, first-out (LIFO), first-in, first-out (FIFO), and average cost. We explain these methods in this chapter.

Economic values do enter the accounting for inventories in a secondary way, however. GAAP treat changes in the economic value of inventories differently, depending on whether value increased or decreased. Increases in value over cost are ignored. Decreases must be recognized immediately, according to the lower-of-cost-or-market (LOCM) rule.

Finally, we present some common measures of an organization's investment in and use of inventories: inventory turnover and days inventory held.

Nature of Inventories

OBJECTIVE:
Learn to understand the definition of inventories.

Different kinds of inventories serve various purposes. An organization that sells directly to consumers, like a grocery store or a car dealer, holds inventories of the merchandise (*merchandise inventories*) its customers may want. A city in a snowy climate holds *supplies inventories* of salt and sand to put on icy roads. A manufacturer holds inventories of the raw materials (*raw materials inventories*) it consumes in the manufacturing process, as well as *work-in-process (WIP) inventories* of partially completed products. A manufacturer's *finished goods inventories* are completed items awaiting sale and shipment to customers. Accounting, consulting, and law firms carry *unbilled services,* which are analogous to a manufacturer's work-in-process inventory.

Organizations hold inventories to reduce the risk of incurring stock-out costs. Stock-out costs include lost sales because customers fill their demands elsewhere, delayed sales because customers' purchases are postponed, and increased costs because raw materials

Inventory management is an important determinant of profitability in many manufacturing companies.

© COURTESY OF SOUTH-WESTERN PUBLISHING

shortages disrupt production schedules. They may also hold work-in-process inventories to smooth out work in a multistage production process or to acquire raw materials at a particularly attractive price.

Holding inventories is costly for many reasons. Some inventories require explicit holding costs to store, preserve, or safeguard them. For example, Ben & Jerry's inventories of ice cream must be kept refrigerated. Inventory may spoil, get stolen, or become obsolete. Funds tied up in investments in inventory carry an opportunity cost; they could be invested in interest-earning opportunities instead of in inventories.

Optimal inventory policies involve trading off the costs and benefits of holding inventories. Over the years, improvements in information technology, production methods, and in the management of inventories have led to decreases in the inventory levels in many organizations. It is unlikely, however, that even the best management will eliminate all inventory holdings. Inventories will be significant assets for many organizations for a long time to come.

An Example: Maytag

Exhibit 9.1 contains a listing of the assets of the Maytag Corporation at the end of its 2001 and 2000 fiscal years, and Exhibit 9.2 on page 172 shows the consolidated statement of income for 2001. Exhibit 9.3 on page 172 contains excerpts from notes to Maytag's financial statements. Maytag manufactures and sells home and commercial appliances such as clothes washers and dryers, refrigerators, and vending machines. It has important investments in inventories. Of its approximately $1,370 million in current assets on December 31, 2001, about $448 million were inventories. That's almost 33% of current assets in inventories. Maytag's total assets were about $3,156 million. So inventories account for more than 14% of the total assets on Maytag's balance sheet at December 31, 2001.

The excerpted notes (Exhibit 9.3) tell how Maytag accounts for inventories. We will learn about these methods when we present GAAP later in this chapter. The notes also

Exhibit 9.1

Maytag
Balance Sheet Excerpt

Inventories account for 32.7% of Maytag's current assets at December 31, 2001, and 30.2% of current assets at December 31, 2000.

Maytag Corp.
Consolidated Balance Sheets (asset side only)
(amounts in thousands)

Assets	December 31	
	2001	**2000**
Current assets		
Cash and cash equivalents	$ 109,370	$ 6,073
Accounts receivable, less allowance for doubtful accounts (2001—$24,121; 2000—$15,583)	618,101	476,211
Inventories	447,866	325,313
Deferred income taxes	63,557	45,616
Other current assets	40,750	51,895
Discontinued current assets	89,900	171,451
Total current assets	$1,369,544	$1,076,559
Noncurrent assets		
Deferred income taxes	$ 227,967	$ 110,393
Prepaid pension cost	1,532	1,526
Intangible pension asset	101,915	49,889
Other intangibles, less allowance for amortization (2001—$123,395; 2000—$112,790)	296,909	272,431
Other noncurrent assets	62,548	42,910
Discontinued noncurrent assets	60,001	251,154
Total noncurrent assets	$ 750,872	$ 728,303
Plant, property, and equipment		
Land	$ 20,854	$ 19,616
Buildings and improvements	352,447	320,545
Machinery and equipment	1,812,446	1,607,006
Construction in progress	146,335	84,980
	$2,332,082	$2,032,147
Less accumulated depreciation	1,296,347	1,168,085
Total plant, property, and equipment	$1,035,735	$ 864,062
Total assets	$3,156,151	$2,668,924

show that Maytag, like most manufacturing firms, holds many different types of inventories. Finished goods accounts for most of Maytag's total inventories.

Part 1 of this text described how cost of goods sold is recognized when an item in inventory is sold. Manufacturing firms, like Maytag, sell their finished goods to customers and use raw materials and supplies in creating work-in-process and, ultimately, finished goods. The use of raw materials or supplies in making products is the transformation of one type of asset into another; therefore, it does not result in the recognition of an expense.

Cost of goods sold is the major expense for most companies. Maytag's Cost of Sales, at about $3.3 billion, is by far its largest expense in 2001.

With such large investments in inventories that generate such large expenses, it is important for many companies to understand their economic value. We explore the economic value of inventories in the next section.

Exhibit 9.2

Maytag
Income Statement

As an inventory item is sold, the cost of the item is recognized as an expense, usually called Cost of Goods Sold. Maytag calls this expense Cost of Sales.

Maytag Corp.
Consolidated Statement of Income
Year Ended December 31, 2001
(amounts in millions)

Net sales	$4,323.7
Cost of sales	(3,320.2)
Gross profit	$1,003.5
Selling, general, and administrative expenses	(704.6)
Special charges	(9.8)
Operating income	$ 289.1
Interest expense	(64.8)
Loss on securities	(7.2)
Other—net	(5.0)
Income from continuing operations before income taxes, minority interests, extraordinary item and cumulative effect of accounting change	$ 212.1
Income taxes	(30.1)
Minority interests	(14.5)
Loss from discontinued operations	(110.9)
Extraordinary item—loss on early retirement of debt	(5.2)
Cumulative effect of accounting change	(3.7)
Net income	$ 47.7

Exhibit 9.3

Maytag
Notes

Notice that Maytag carries four types of inventories.

The "excess of FIFO cost over LIFO" is often called the LIFO reserve. We will see its usefulness later.

Excerpts from Maytag Corporation Notes

Inventories are stated at the lower of cost or market. Inventory costs are determined by the last-in, first-out (LIFO) method for approximately 91 percent and 90 percent of the Company's inventories at December 31, 2001 and 2000, respectively. Costs for other inventories have been determined principally by the first-in, first-out (FIFO) method.

. . .

Inventories consisted of the following:

	December 31	
(amounts in thousands)	**2001**	**2000**
Raw materials	$ 62,587	$ 42,393
Work in process	76,524	60,588
Finished goods	382,925	303,249
Supplies	9,659	7,451
Total FIFO cost	$531,695	$413,681
Less excess of FIFO cost over LIFO	83,829	88,368
Inventories	$447,866	$325,313

Economic Value of Inventories

OBJECTIVE:
Learn to analyze the economic value of inventories.

The economic value of inventories is driven by the expected future cash flows they produce. The difficulty of assessing these expected cash flows depends in part on the kind of inventory. For example, merchandise inventories that will quickly be sold to customers may have a predictable future cash flow. It is more difficult to estimate the expected cash flows from raw material inventory that will be input to a production process and become part of a finished good sold to customers. Also, the expected cash flows from some inventories are derived from cost savings. For example, inventories of supplies that help keep production on schedule generate cash flows in the form of cost savings, not direct inflows to the organization.

Regardless of whether it is direct or indirect and easy to estimate or difficult to estimate, the value of inventories still ultimately depends on future cash flows. Like any investment, the investment in inventories must be expected to earn at least a normal rate of return. Let's take a simple case of Widget Co., a hypothetical retailing firm that buys widgets in one period and sells them in the next. It has no costs or revenues other than those for widgets. Initially, widgets can be purchased for $1 each. The business is expected to last three years. Exhibit 9.4 shows the expected timing of widget purchases and sales over the 3-year period. It also shows the expected purchase and selling prices for widgets over that time period. For simplicity (it will make finding present values easier), let's assume all units after the initial purchase are bought on December 31, and all sales take place on December 31.

Exhibit 9.4

Widget Company
Purchases and Sales of Widgets

Date	1/1/03	12/31/03	12/31/04	12/31/05
Units purchased	100 @ $1	120 @ $1.05	100 @ $1.10	0
Units sold	0	100 @ $1.10	100 @ $1.20	120 @ $1.20

Suppose Widget Co. investments are expected to earn at least 10%, which is Widget Company's cost of capital (the cost it must pay to obtain funds of all kinds). If it earned less than 10%, it would be best not to invest the money because it would not recover its cost of capital.

Exhibit 9.5 calculates the net cash inflows and outflows for each of the periods for which Widget Co. plans to be in the resale widget business.

Exhibit 9.5

Widget Company
Expected Future Cash Flows

Date	1/1/03	12/31/03	12/31/04	12/31/05
Cash receipts	$ 0	$ 110	$ 120	$144
Cash disbursements	(100)	(126)	(110)	(0)
Net cash flow	$(100)	$ (16)	$ 10	$144

We assume all its purchases are made for cash, and all its sales are for cash. Widget Co. spends $100 for widgets on January 1, 2003 (100 widgets × $1 per widget). It expects to sell 100 widgets on December 31, 2003, for $1.10 per widget, but then it must immediately purchase another 120 widgets at $1.05 each to restock its inventory. So on December 31, 2003, Widget Co. has expected cash receipts of $110 from customers and cash disbursements of $126 to suppliers. The cash flow for each year is similarly computed.

REMEMBER: Companies invest in assets that have positive net present values.

Does it make sense economically for Widget Co. to be in this 3-year widget business? To answer that question, we must compute the net present value (NPV) of all the net cash flows using the cost of money, 10%. If the net present value is greater than or equal to zero, then we know the business is expected to at least return the cost of capital, and Widget Co. should enter into the business. As shown in Exhibit 9.6 on page 174, the NPV is slightly greater than zero and Widget Co. should invest in the inventory.

Exhibit 9.6

Widget Company
Net Present Value Computation

$$\text{NPV} = -\$100 - \$16/(1.1) + \$10/(1.1)^2 + \$144/(1.1)^3$$
$$= \$1.91 > 0$$

Because NPV is greater than zero Widget Company should invest.

With this background, let us now explore how GAAP treat inventories. For simplicity, we confine the discussion initially to merchandise inventories purchased for cash.

GAAP for Inventories

OBJECTIVE:

Learn to become familiar with GAAP for inventories.

GAAP for merchandise inventories is keyed off the sequence of purchases of the inventory items. For example, Widget Co. spends a total of $336 ($100 + $126 + $110 in Exhibit 9.5) on inventory.

GAAP determine two things:

*Fundamental Inventory
Balance Equation*

   Beginning Inventory
+ *Purchases*
− *Cost of Goods Sold*
= *Ending Inventory*

- The balance sheet values for inventories (dollar value in the balance sheet associated with inventory assumed to be not yet sold)
- The cost of goods sold (cost of inventory items assumed to be sold to generate revenues of a period)

You can see these values in the inventory equation: Beginning inventory + purchases − cost of good sold = ending inventory. Thus, for a given sequence of purchases, GAAP will tell us how to describe the amounts that remain in inventory and the amounts that are cost of goods sold.

Note that the beginning inventory balance of the period is known going into the period, and the amount of purchases will be tabulated as the company goes through the period. Thus, if we can compute the value of ending inventory, the cost of goods sold will be the amount that balances the inventory equation. In other words, once the ending inventory value is computed, cost of goods sold equals beginning inventory plus purchases minus ending inventory.

Periodic versus Perpetual Inventory Systems

*Spending money to make
money is only part of the
inventory management
equation.*

The previous description of the computation of ending inventory and cost of goods sold is referred to as the **periodic inventory method.** The ending inventory quantity is determined by an actual physical count of goods on hand as of the balance sheet date. The ending inventory value is determined by multiplying the units counted by an appropriate unit price. Cost of goods sold is then determined using the inventory balance sheet equation.

In a periodic inventory system, every time an item is sold a journal entry is made to recognize sales revenue and the receipt of cash or the creation of an account receivable.

Cash or Accounts Receivable . . .   xxx
     Sales Revenue   xxx

(This entry is made every time an item is sold.)

The entry to record the cost of goods sold is made once, at the end of the period, after the inventory has been counted and valued.

The **periodic inventory method** computes ending inventory and cost of goods sold only at regular intervals, not continuously.

Cost of Goods Sold . . . . zzz
    Inventory . . . . zzz
(This entry is made at the end of the period once.)

Given that items may be purchased for inventory during the period at many different unit costs that also may be different from the unit costs of the beginning inventory, a flow assumption (which costs are associated with goods sold and which remain in inventory) must be made in order to compute ending inventory value.

A **perpetual inventory system** records the cost of goods sold at the time of a sale.

In a **perpetual inventory system,** a journal entry records the cost of goods sold at the time of the sale (we do not wait until the end of the period). Perpetual inventory systems maintain updated values for inventories. The knowledge of what items were sold and what remain in inventory is useful in planning the amount of inventory to be purchased or produced in the future. In perpetual systems a physical count of inventory will still be taken at the end of the period. This inventory count enables a company to see the amount of inventory shrinkage from theft and other factors. The more timely inventory information needed by a perpetual inventory system requires more record keeping, which is not too burdensome in this electronic age. Even in a perpetual system, though, some assumptions must be made about how costs flow through accounts.

The remainder of this chapter will focus on periodic inventory systems to compute the ending inventory value and cost of goods sold for the period. Three principle inventory flow assumptions are used—FIFO, LIFO, and average cost.

FIFO (First-In, First-Out)

FIFO assigns amounts to costs of goods sold in the order of purchase.

First-in, first-out (FIFO) assigns amounts to costs of goods sold in the order of purchases. That is, the first items purchased for inventory are the first ones assumed to be sold for purposes of constructing financial statements. For Widget Co., FIFO assigns $100 to cost of goods sold in 2003, $105 in 2004, and $131 in 2005. This convention implies Widget Co.'s inventories are assigned a book value of $126 at December 31, 2003, $131 at December 31, 2004, and $0 at December 31, 2005. FIFO for Widget Co. generates the inventory T-account in Exhibit 9.7.

Exhibit 9.7

Widget Company Inventory Account under FIFO Flow Assumtion

Inventory (FIFO)				
1/1/03	Beginning balance	0		
1/1/03	Purchase (100 @ $1)	100	100	Transfer to CGS (100 @ $1)
12/31/03	Purchase (120 @ $1.05)	126		
12/31/03	Balance (120 @ $1.05)	126		
12/31/04	Purchase (100 @ $1.10)	110	105	Transfer to CGS (100 @ $1.05)
12/31/04	Balance (20 @ $1.05 + 100 @ $1.10)	131	131	Transfer to CGS (20 @ $1.05 + 100 @ $1.10)
12/31/05	Balance	0		

Again, at the end of 2003, 220 units were available for sale during the year. The oldest 100 units purchased for $1 each (the first ones into the inventory) are assumed to be the ones sold during the year. This assumption leaves the 120 units purchased for $1.05 each remaining in inventory. These units become the beginning inventory for the next year. Be sure you understand how all of the other numbers were generated in Exhibit 9.7.

FIFO results in increasing book values of inventory on Widget Co.'s balance sheets from December 31, 2003, to December 31, 2004, as shown in Exhibit 9.8 on page 176. The income statements using FIFO are given in Exhibit 9.9.

Exhibit 9.8

Widget Company
Inventory Values Using FIFO

	12/31/03	12/31/04	12/31/05
Inventory balance	$126	$131	$0

Exhibit 9.9

Widget Company
Net Incomes Using FIFO

	2003	2004	2005
Revenues	$110	$120	$144
Cost of goods sold	100	105	131
Net income (pretax)	$ 10	$ 15	$ 13

LIFO (Last-In, First-Out)

LIFO assigns amounts to cost of goods sold in the reverse order of purchases.

Last-in, first-out (LIFO) assigns amounts to cost of goods sold in the reverse order of purchases. That is, the last items purchased are assumed to be the first items sold. For Widget Co., LIFO assigns $105 to cost of goods sold in 2003, $110 in 2004, and $121 in 2005. Contrast this method with the first period, 2003, calculation of cost of goods sold under LIFO with FIFO. Under FIFO the oldest 100 units were assumed to be sold. Under LIFO the last ones in, the $1.05 per unit ones, were the ones assumed to be sold. This approach leaves an inventory value of $121 at the end of 2003. The cost of goods sold in 2005 is a bit trickier. Because no purchases are made in 2005, LIFO can assign the cost of beginning inventory in 2005 only as cost of goods sold. This process involves reaching all the way back to the purchases of the first period, the only goods still available for sale.

This method implies that Widget Co.'s inventories are assigned a book value of $121 at December 31, 2003, $121 at December 31, 2004, and $0 at December 31, 2005. LIFO for Widget Co. generates the inventory T-account shown in Exhibit 9.10.

Exhibit 9.10

Widget Company
Inventory Account under LIFO
Flow Assumption

	Inventory (LIFO)			
1/1/03	Beginning balance	0		
1/1/03	Purchase (100 @ $1)	100		
12/31/03	Purchase (120 @ $1.05)	126	105	Transfer to CGS (100 @ $1.05)
12/31/03	Balance (20 @ $1.05 + 100 @ $1)	121		
12/31/04	Purchase (100 @ $1.10)	110	110	Transfer to CGS (100 @ $1.10)
12/31/04	Balance (20 @ $1.05 + 100 @ $1.00)	121	121	Transfer to CGS (20 @ $1.05 + 100 @ $1.00)
12/31/05	Balance	0		

The value of $121 in inventory (attributable to the unsold purchases of the first period) is called a LIFO layer. As long as inventory levels do not decrease, this LIFO layer comprised of older costs will always remain on the balance sheet (see Exhibit 9.11). If Widget Co. purchases more than it sells, under the LIFO assumption current unit costs will find their way into cost of goods sold.

Exhibit 9.11

Widget Company
Inventory Values Using LIFO

	12/31/03	12/31/04	12/31/05
Inventory balance	$121	$121	$0

Net incomes for the three years under the LIFO assumption are shown in Exhibit 9.12.

Exhibit 9.12

Widget Company
Net Incomes Using LIFO

	2003	2004	2005
Revenues	$110	$120	$144
Cost of goods sold	105	110	121
Net income (pretax)	$ 5	$ 10	$ 23

The **average cost method** uses the weighted average cost of the beginning inventory and purchases to assign costs to the ending inventory and cost of goods sold.

Average Cost

The **average cost method** usually results in cost of goods sold and inventory values somewhere between those computed using LIFO and FIFO. It finds the average cost per unit of the beginning inventory and purchases for the period. It then uses this average cost to assign values to cost of goods sold and ending inventory. For example, the average cost of widgets is $1.0273 in 2003 (see Exhibit 9.13).

Exhibit 9.13

Widget Company
Average Cost per Unit in 2003

Date	Units Purchased	Cost per Unit	Total Cost
1/1/03	100	$1.00	$100
12/31/03	120	1.05	126
Total	220		$226
Average cost: $226/220 units = $1.0273 per widget rounded			

The average cost flow assumption uses the $1.0273 cost per unit to compute cost of good sold (100 × 1.0273) and ending inventory (120 × 1.0273) in 2003. In 2004, the average cost method starts with the beginning inventory and averages its cost with the purchases in 2004 (see Exhibit 9.14).

Exhibit 9.14

Widget Company
Average Cost per Unit in 2004

Date	Units Purchased	Cost per Unit	Total Cost
1/1/04	120 (Beg. Inv.)	$1.0273	$123.28
12/31/03	100	1.10	110.00
Total	220		$233.28
Average cost: $233.28/220 units = $1.0603 per widget			

These average cost computations lead to the inventory values and costs of good sold depicted in Exhibit 9.15 on page 178.

Exhibit 9.15

Widget Company
Inventory Account under the
Average Cost Flow Assumption

Inventory (average cost)				
1/1/03	Beginning balance	0		
1/1/03	Purchase (100 @ $1)	100		
12/31/03	Purchase (120 @ $1.05)	126	102.73	Transfer to CGS (100 @ $1.0273)
12/31/03	Balance (120 @1.0273)	123.28		
12/31/04	Purchase (100 @ $1.10)	110		
			106.03	Transfer to CGS (100 @ $1.0603)
12/31/04	Balance (120 @ $1.0603)	127.24		
			127.24	Transfer to CGS (120 @ $1.0603)
12/31/05	Balance	0		

Average cost assigns the same costs per unit to inventory and cost of goods sold. Average cost shows the book value of inventory on Widget Co.'s balance sheets from December 31, 2003, to December 31, 2005, as shown in Exhibit 9.16.

Exhibit 9.16

Widget Company
Inventory Values Using
Average Cost

	12/31/03	12/31/04	12/31/05
Inventory balance	$123.28	$127.24	$0

Net incomes for the three years under the average cost assumption are shown in Exhibit 9.17.

Exhibit 9.17

Widget Company
Net Incomes Using Average Cost

	2003	2004	2005
Revenues	$110.00	$120.00	$144.00
Cost of goods sold	102.73	106.03	127.24
Net income (pretax)	$ 7.27	$ 13.97	$ 16.76

FIFO, LIFO, and average cost for Widget Co. are compared in Exhibit 9.18. Because all three methods provide alternative ways of treating what we assume are the same purchases, they all get a total cost of goods sold over the period from January 1, 2003, to December 31, 2005, of $336. As a result, the total net income from January 1, 2003, to

Exhibit 9.18

Widget Company
Comparison of Inventory
Methods

Date	Purchases	Inventory at Date			Cost of Goods Sold for Year Ended at Date		
		FIFO	LIFO	Average	FIFO	LIFO	Average
1/1/03	100						
12/31/03	126	126	121	123.28	$100	$105	$102.73
12/31/04	110	131	121	127.24	105	110	106.03
12/31/05	0	0	0	0	131	121	127.24
Total all years	336				$336	$336	$336.00

December 31, 2005, under all three methods is $38. The methods differ only in the way they assign these totals to periods.

> ### Review Questions
>
> 1. Define LIFO, FIFO, and average cost.
>
> 2. In Exhibit 9.4, assume that the 120 units purchased on December 31, 2003 cost $0.95 per unit instead of $1.05. (Assume all other numbers remain the same.) Is the investment in inventory still a positive net present value project? Recompute net income and ending inventory under FIFO and LIFO for each of the three years.

Lower-of-Cost-or-Market (LOCM)

Specific item identification provides an alternative way to compute inventory and cost of goods sold values.

Frequently, sellers of high-value, low-volume items, or items with unique identifications, such as serial numbers on cars, use specific item identification in doing inventory accounting.

Cost of goods sold is recorded as the cost of the specific items sold and ending inventory is the cost of the specific items remaining in inventory.

LOCM is also used with specific item identification inventory accounting.

Regardless of the method used to determine the amount assigned to ending inventory, GAAP require that it never be greater than the inventory's market value. This is called the ***lower-of-cost-or-market (LOCM)*** rule for inventories. If the prices for inventoried items progress as expected, LOCM wouldn't have much impact. For increasing prices, such as in the Widget example, all methods would result in book values of inventory less than market. For decreasing prices, such as those that have occurred for many electronic components, FIFO would have inventory values close to market, and most firms facing decreasing inventory prices use FIFO.[1]

LOCM's biggest impact comes when unexpected decreases in prices occur. Suppose on December 31, 2003, immediately after Widget Co. made its purchase at $1.05 per unit, the market price of widgets falls unexpectedly to $1.02. If Widget Co. uses LIFO, its inventory would have a book value of $121, which is less than its market value of $122.40 (120 units × $1.02). LOCM has no impact in this case.

If Widget Co. uses FIFO or average cost, LOCM requires that the book value of the inventory be reduced. For example, under FIFO, Widget Co.'s inventory has a book value of $126. A write-down of $3.60 is required to bring the book value of the inventory down to its market value of $122.40. This reduction in book value could be portrayed as an increase in cost of goods sold. The journal entry for this treatment is

    Cost of Goods Sold 3.60
        Inventory 3.60

Alternatively, the decline in market value could be set out separately, as a loss on revaluation of inventory. The journal entry is

    Loss on LOCM Write-Down 3.60
        Inventory 3.60

Once inventory is written down, this lower book value is considered its cost from that point forward; that is, the "lower-of-cost-or-market" rule is more accurately "lower-of-book-value-or-market-value." After a LOCM write-down, the book value of the inventory is its (now lower) market value. The book value of inventory is never increased under GAAP.

Comparison of GAAP and Economic Values

OBJECTIVE:
Learn to relate GAAP for inventories to the underlying economics of inventories.

The LOCM rule guarantees that the book values of inventories cannot be greater than their market values. That is, LOCM mechanically guarantees that market-to-book ratios

---

[1]The choice between LIFO and FIFO is affected by the **LIFO conformity rule,** which is a tax rule requiring companies that use LIFO for calculating income taxes to also use LIFO for financial reporting purposes.

for inventory items are at least 1. If prices are falling, the LOCM rule pushes market-to-book ratios toward 1. LOCM also pushes toward prompt recognition of losses from declines in inventory values in the periods in which the losses occur.

The more interesting case happens when prices rise. Because LIFO assigns the most recent costs to cost of goods sold, it can result in inventory book values being calculated using old and low prices. This approach could be a significant factor in pushing market-to-book ratios above 1.

If Widget Co. uses LIFO and prices continue to increase over time, the market-to-book ratio for its inventory will also increase over time. Exhibit 9.19 shows Widget Company's market-to-book ratios for 2003 and 2004. Both LIFO and FIFO are shown.

Exhibit 9.19

Market-to-Book Ratios under LIFO and FIFO

	2003	2004
Market value of inventory	$126 (120 @ $1.05)	$132 (120 @ $1.10)
Book value of inventory (LIFO)	$121	$121
Book value of inventory (FIFO)	$126	$131
Market value to book value (LIFO)	1.04	1.09
Market value to book value (FIFO)	1.0	1.008

Notice that market-to-book ratios are closer to 1 for FIFO than they are for LIFO. Indeed, if prices continue to rise the LIFO market-to-book ratio would continue to rise.

This unrecorded increase in value does two things to the accounting return on the inventory investment. First, until the inventory is decreased, the investment in inventory generally shows a lower accounting rate of return under LIFO than under FIFO. Second, when the inventory is liquidated, the accounting rate of return is very large under LIFO because cost of goods sold is calculated using old costs. Exhibit 9.20 shows the progression of accounting rates of return for Widget Company under both LIFO and FIFO.

Exhibit 9.20

Accounting Rates of Return under LIFO and FIFO

	2003	2004	2005
Beginning book value of inventory (FIFO)	100	126	131
Net income (FIFO)	10	15	13
Net income/Beginning book value (FIFO)	0.10	0.119	0.099
Beginning book value of inventory (LIFO)	100	121	121
Net income (LIFO)	5	10	23
Net income/Beginning book value (LIFO)	0.05	0.083	0.19

The proponents of LIFO's depiction of the economics usually argue that until the LIFO layer is liquidated, the cost of goods sold under LIFO accurately reflects opportunity cost (that is, the cost that appears in the income statement is closer to the dollar amount that actually has to be expended to replenish the inventory). Consider Widget Company's sale of 100 units on December 31, 2003. When it sells 100 units on that day, it must replace those units by buying at $1.05 each. The economic income on this transaction, it is argued, is much closer to the $5 shown under LIFO than the $10 shown under FIFO.

This logic seems sound, as far as it goes. The real problem is not LIFO's calculation of cost of goods sold, but in the failure to recognize the holding gains on inventory. The expected increase in the value of inventory is what makes Widget Company's investment in inventory pay off. It is not until the inventory is liquidated that this increase in value is finally realized. Until then, any cash inflows must be reinvested.

Widget Co.'s market-to-book values for inventory under FIFO are close to 1 in each year. This result is caused by our assumption that enough units are purchased on December 31 of each year to cover all, or almost all, the inventory held on that day. Therefore, the unit costs reflected in Widget Co.'s inventory all, or almost all, come from the balance sheet date. Generally, organizations make purchases throughout the year, and the unit costs reflected in the inventory include some from early in the year. This activity would lead the market-to-book to be more than 1, even under FIFO.

Review Questions

1. Compute the equivalent of Exhibit 9.19 and Exhibit 9.20, using average cost figures. Explain how these numbers relate to the LIFO and FIFO numbers.

2. If prices continually fall over time, which inventory flow assumption, LIFO or FIFO, provides market-to-book ratios closer to 1?

Financial Statement Analysis of Inventory

OBJECTIVE:
Learn to become familiar with some common financial statistics related to inventories.

Maytag's sales revenue amounted to $4.3 billion in 2001, and its cost of goods sold was $3.3 billion.

It had a gross profit of $4.3 − $3.3 = $1.0 billion, and its gross profit percentage is thus 1.0/4.3 = 23%.

Maytag's inventory turnover ratio is 3.3/0.4 = 8.25 times.

The days inventory held is 365/8.25, which is 44.2 days.

Some important financial statistics involve inventories. *Gross profit percentage* is sales minus cost of goods sold, all divided by sales. It is the starting point in many financial analyses, because it represents what is left of $1 of sales that can be used for other expenses and for a profit.

An organization's investment in inventories is often assessed by *inventory turnover* and *days inventory held.* These financial statistics are analogous to those for accounts receivable, except that the amount of inventory is related to cost of goods sold. Inventory turnover is cost of goods sold divided by average inventory. Days inventory held is 365 divided by inventory turnover.

These financial statistics are affected by the method used to account for inventories. A common chore in financial statement analysis requires converting the accounting results of a firm that uses LIFO so they can be compared with a competitor that uses FIFO. This conversion is possible because organizations that use LIFO are required to disclose, directly or indirectly, what their inventories would have been had they used FIFO. For example, the notes to Maytag Corp.'s financial statements excerpted in Exhibit 9.3 contain a representative disclosure that relates FIFO and LIFO inventories. Maytag uses primarily LIFO to calculate the book values of its inventories. The notes show that the FIFO value of Maytag's inventories on December 31, 2001, was about $531.7 million. The excess of FIFO over LIFO was about $83.8 million, leaving the LIFO value of inventories at about $447.9 million.

Notes such as Maytag's typically do not explain the difference in cost of goods sold between LIFO and FIFO, but we can figure it out. The key lies in understanding the "Excess of FIFO Cost over LIFO." Many organizations call the excess of FIFO cost over LIFO the *LIFO reserve.*

Regardless of the inventory method, the basic equation for the inventory account remains the same. Let BI denote beginning inventory, COGS denote cost of goods sold, and EI denote ending inventory.

$$BI + \text{Purchases} - COGS = EI$$

Because we are interested in cost of goods sold, we solve for COGS.

$$COGS = \text{Purchases} - (EI - BI)$$

We want to understand the difference between the cost of goods sold under LIFO and FIFO. Let's use a subscript to denote the accounting method; BI_{FIFO} is the beginning inventory under FIFO, $COGS_{LIFO}$ is cost of goods sold under LIFO, and so on. Note that purchases are the same under either method, so we don't need a subscript for them.

$$COGS_{LIFO} = Purchases - (EI_{LIFO} - BI_{LIFO})$$
$$COGS_{FIFO} = Purchases - (EI_{FIFO} - BI_{FIFO})$$

Therefore

$$COGS_{LIFO} - COGS_{FIFO} = (EI_{FIFO} - BI_{FIFO}) - (EI_{LIFO} - BI_{LIFO})$$
$$= (EI_{FIFO} - EI_{LIFO}) - (BI_{FIFO} - BI_{LIFO})$$
$$= Ending\ LIFO\ reserve - Beginning\ LIFO\ reserve$$

Recall that Maytag calls its LIFO reserve Excess of FIFO Cost over LIFO.

The difference between cost of goods sold under LIFO and cost of goods sold under FIFO equals the amount of change in the LIFO reserve. Exhibit 9.21 shows that Maytag's LIFO reserve was $83.8 million on December 31, 2001, and $88.4 million on December 31, 2000. The change in Maytag's LIFO reserve is shown in Exhibit 9.21.

Exhibit 9.21

Change in Maytag's LIFO Reserve

LIFO reserve on 12/31/01	$ 83.8
Less LIFO reserve on 12/31/00	(88.4)
Change in LIFO reserve	$ (4.6)

Plugging this figure into the formula for the difference in cost of goods sold, we see that Maytag's cost of goods sold would be $4.6 million higher under FIFO.

$$COGS_{LIFO} - COGS_{FIFO} = (4.6)$$
$$COGS_{FIFO} = COGS_{LIFO} + 4.6$$

Because revenues and other expenses do not change, pretax income under FIFO would be $4.6 million lower. Using the LIFO reserve and the relationship between the cost of goods sold under LIFO and FIFO, we could compute Maytag's gross margin percentage, inventory turnover, and days inventory held as if Maytag had used FIFO.

Conclusion

GAAP for inventories are based on the flow of purchases. FIFO, LIFO, and average cost are all GAAP that assign costs of all goods available for sale (beginning inventories plus purchases) to ending inventories and cost of goods sold. We assumed a flow of purchases independent of the GAAP method used in order to clearly explain how the methods work, rather than to be accurate in any assumptions about purchasing behaviors. Firms sometimes make purchases at the end of an accounting period to avoid liquidating a LIFO layer. As we will discuss further in Chapter 14 on income taxes, inventory accounting is one of the few places where GAAP and tax accounting sometimes are required to be the same. Avoiding liquidation of a LIFO layer can save taxes.

In the next chapter, we continue our exploration of GAAP by exploring accounting for marketable securities.

Key Terms

average cost method *177*

days inventory held *181*

finished goods inventories *169*

first-in, first-out (FIFO) *175*

gross profit percentage *181*

inventory turnover *181*

last-in, first-out (LIFO) *176*

LIFO conformity rule *179*

LIFO reserve *181*

lower-of-cost-or-market (LOCM) *179*

merchandise inventories *169*

periodic inventory method *174*

perpetual inventory system *175*

raw materials inventories *169*

supplies inventories *169*

unbilled services inventories *169*

work-in-process inventories (WIP) *169*

chapter 10

© GETTY IMAGES/EYE WIRE

STOC

Marketable Securities

In an era of poorly developed capital markets, many people would keep their extra cash in jars under their beds. This strategy may physically safeguard the currency, but it doesn't generate much of a return on investment. Keeping money in jars would have cost Microsoft about $1 billion in interest in 1998, not to mention the cost of the jars!

Most companies, including Microsoft, invest excess cash in financial instruments called marketable securities. This chapter focuses on marketable securities.

1. Their nature and economic value

2. How they are accounted for

3. How accounting relates to their economic value.

4. Common financial statistics, based on accounting numbers, related to them

After discussing the nature of marketable securities, we analyze their economic value. Marketable securities are investments, and they are expected to earn a normal rate of return. The major uncertainties that can cause marketable securities to earn an abnormal positive or negative rate of return include unexpected good or bad news about the investment's payoffs. GAAP are focused on the economic values of marketable securities, but sometimes treat the income and losses on marketable securities in a peculiar way.

Finally, we present a common measure of an organization's investment in marketable securities: the quick ratio. We also discuss how transactions in marketable securities can be used to manage reported GAAP net income.

Nature of Marketable Securities

Marketable securities are stocks, bonds, and other financial instruments that organizations hold in lieu of holding cash. There are many reasons why organizations choose to hold marketable securities. First, they may be expected to earn a higher rate of return than cash in a bank account would earn. Second, if good markets exist for the securities, it is quick and cheap to turn them into cash. Third, an investment in marketable securities is passive; that is, it requires management attention only in deciding what securities to buy and sell, not in operating an entity.

An Example: Merrill Lynch

Consider Merrill Lynch & Co., Inc., the asset side of whose balance sheet is shown in Exhibit 10.1 on page 186. As a global organization, Merrill Lynch provides investment, financing, insurance, and other products and services. Merrill Lynch's clients include individual investors, small and large businesses, governments, and financial institutions.

Like many financial institutions, Merrill Lynch has enormous total assets: almost $420 billion as of December 28, 2001. Further, as is typical for a large financial institution, Merrill Lynch holds many different kinds of financial assets that are determined by the specialized and technical nature of its business.

Of Merrill's assets, $92.9 billion are Trading Assets that Merrill trades for a profit. Merrill has Marketable Investment Securities of $77.8 billion. These marketable investment securities consist of liquid (i.e., easily converted into cash) debt and equity securities. The **debt securities** include bonds issued by corporations, municipalities, and the

Exhibit 10.1

Merrill Lynch & Co.
Balance Sheet Excerpt

Merrill Lynch & Co., Inc.
Consolidated Balance Sheets (asset side only)
(amounts in millions)

Assets	December 28, 2001	December 29, 2000
Cash and cash equivalents	$ 11,070	$ 23,205
Cash and securities segregated for regulatory purposes or deposited with clearing organizations	4,467	6,092
Receivables under resale agreements and securities borrowed transactions	124,632	114,581
Marketable investment securities	77,820	49,251
Trading assets, at fair value	92,883	91,514
Securities pledged as collateral	12,084	9,097
Securities received as collateral	3,234	—
Other receivables (net of allowance for doubtful accounts of $81 in 2001 and $68 in 2000)	54,950	76,913
Investments of insurance subsidiaries	3,983	4,002
Loans, notes, and mortgages (net of allowance for loan losses of $425 in 2001 and $176 in 2000)	19,005	17,472
Other investments	5,869	4,938
Equipment and facilities (net of accumulated depreciation and amortization of $4,910 in 2001 and $4,658 in 2000)	2,873	3,444
Goodwill (net of accumulated amortization of $924 in 2001 and $720 in 2000)	4,071	4,407
Other assets	2,478	2,284
Total assets	$419,419	$407,200

Our main concern in this chapter is marketable securities that are reported here.

For Merrill, trading assets include operating assets, similar to inventories for a retailer.

Merrill's insurance subsidiaries report marketable securities here.

Some miscellaneous marketable securities are included here.

U.S. government. The two important characteristics of debt securities are a maturity date and an upper bound on the promised payments (interest and repayment of principal). For example, a home or a car loan specifies the total amount the lender is entitled to receive and gives a set of payments that result in the debt being repaid over a definite period of time. Specification of the total to be repaid puts an upper bound on what the lender can receive. Specification of the time at which the debt is to be repaid in full gives the obligation a maturity date.

Equity securities represent a residual claim against the assets of the company. Examples include common and preferred stocks.

Merrill Lynch's marketable investment securities also include **equity securities.** Equity securities include the common stock of corporations. Common stock has neither a maturity date nor an upper bound on payments. It is an ownership claim on an entity that gives the holder the rights to all financial returns in excess of what is required to meet the entity's obligations. Ownership can be sold or can be rendered moot by bankruptcy, but it has no maturity date.

Good markets provide a place to buy and sell many types of debt and equity securities. For example, many corporations' common stocks are traded on the New York Stock Exchange, the American Stock Exchange, Nasdaq, or in stock markets in London, Hong Kong, Tokyo, or elsewhere. These markets are "good" in the sense we discussed in Chapter 1. They have many buyers and sellers and low transactions costs. Up-to-the-minute prices for many common stocks traded on these markets are available on the Internet.

All these markets exist because people wish to profit from trading and holding securities. The profit can come from two sources:

1. Dividend or interest payments received under the terms of the security
2. Increases in the market value of the security

Of course, market values of securities can decrease, as well as increase, so holding marketable securities can result in losses as well as gains.

Exhibit 10.2 shows an excerpt from Merrill Lynch's income statement. Interest and dividend payments Merrill receives from the issuers of the marketable securities it holds are recognized as Interest and Dividends. Gains and losses from holding some types of marketable securities are included in Principal Transactions. We will see when we study GAAP which types of marketable securities generate gains and losses that end up in such an income statement account.

Exhibit 10.2

Merrill Lynch & Co.
Income Statement Excerpt

Interest and dividends are included here.

Gains and losses on marketable securities are included in Principal Transactions.

Merrill Lynch & Co., Inc. Consolidated Statements of Earnings (revenues only) Year Ended Last Friday in December (amounts in millions)	
Revenues	**2001**
Commissions	$ 5,266
Interest and dividends	20,143
Principal transactions	3,930
Investment banking	3,539
Asset management and portfolio service fees	5,351
Other	528
Total revenues	$38,757

Obviously, for an organization like Merrill Lynch, marketable securities constitute important assets and the revenues generated by them are crucial in affecting net income. Although common principles underlie the economic value of the different kinds of marketable securities and the income they generate, their accounting treatment can be significantly different. Before getting into the GAAP for them, we discuss their economic values.

Economic Value of Marketable Securities

OBJECTIVE:

Learn to analyze the economic value of marketable securities.

Like accounts receivable, marketable securities are straightforward assets. Through some combination of interest payments, dividend payments, and increases in value to be captured by sale, marketable securities are *expected* (however sometimes they will not!) to increase their holder's wealth.

Although many sophisticated theories in finance explain the economic value of debt and equity securities, we require only the basic idea that the economic value at any point in time is equal to the present value of the expected future cash flows. For example, on January 1, 2004, suppose MS Co. buys a marketable security that is expected to pay off $1,000 on December 31, 2007. If the interest rate appropriate for this security is 8% (that is, you will not buy it unless you believe your return will be at least 8% in every year you hold it), it has an economic value on January 1, 2004, of:

$$\$1,000/(1 + 0.08)^4 = \$735.03$$

Exhibit 10.3

Economic Value of Marketable Security

8% Interest Rate, Events Unfold as Expected				
Date	1/1/04	12/31/04	12/31/05	12/31/06	12/31/07
Value	$735.03	$793.83	$857.34	$925.93	$1,000.00

If you don't understand exactly how we got the numbers in Exhibit 10.3, review the present value section in Chapter 6.

A company that is strapped for cash may sell zero-coupon bonds and not have to pay interest on them until they repay the principal—often many years in the future.

A **zero-coupon bond** is a bond that does not promise any regular interest payments.

If everything proceeds as expected, this initial value of $735.03 will grow at 8% per year until it eventually reaches $1,000 on December 31, 2007. Exhibit 10.3 shows this progression.

This same economic analysis applies in many possible cases. This marketable security might be a **zero-coupon bond**; that is, one that does not promise any regular interest payments. The bond contract promises only a lump return at its maturity date. In this example, the bond promises a payment of $1,000 on its maturity date, December 31, 2007. If investors demand an 8% return on the investment in this bond, it will sell for $735.03 on January 1, 2004. Zero-coupon bonds are commonplace.

The marketable security might be a common stock that pays no dividends but is expected to be worth $1,000 on December 31, 2007. If investors demand an 8% return on the investment in this common stock, it will sell for $735.03 on January 1, 2004.

Whether the marketable security is a debt or equity security might affect the assessments of its expected payoff and the appropriate rate of return it should earn, but it does not affect the underlying principles that determine its economic value. If only GAAP were that simple!

GAAP for Marketable Securities

OBJECTIVE:

Learn to become familiar with GAAP for marketable securities.

How a company (investor) accounts for investments in the marketable securities of other companies (investees) is a function of the size of the investment and the intentions of the investor. In this chapter we describe the accounting for such investments in cases where the investment is small and the intention is to earn a return on otherwise idle cash.

Corporate long-term investment objectives might be active or passive. Passive, non-control investors seek dividends and the sale of stock at a profit—similar to the investment of idle cash in the short run. Active corporate investors seek control over other corporations for strategic objectives. They may wish to acquire distribution channels, protect raw material sources, increase their scale of operations, or diversify risk by moving into other businesses. Particularly when an active investor acquires a large share of the investee's stock (greater than 20% of it) the accounting will be much different from what is described in this chapter. We consider the accounting for long-term investments in Chapter 15.

GAAP for short-term, marketable securities begin by classifying them into three categories: trading, available-for-sale, and held-to-maturity. Held-to-maturity securities are those debt securities that the entity intends to hold until maturity. Trading securities are either debt or equity securities that the entity intends to use to generate trading profits. Available-for-sale securities are either debt or equity securities that do not qualify as either trading securities or held-to-maturity securities. This residual category ends up being the largest for many firms. For example, as shown in Exhibit 10.4, the notes to Merrill Lynch's financial statements reveal that available-for-sale securities constitute about $4.1 billion of its $4.6 billion in marketable securities at December 25, 2001.

A **trading security** is a debt or equity security purchased as part of a conscious management decision to try to generate profits through buying and selling securities.

Trading Securities

GAAP for a **trading security** are conceptually the simplest—they follow economic values exactly. At each balance sheet date, the market value of trading securities is

Exhibit 10.4

Merill Lynch & Co.
Notes to Consolidated Financial
Statements (excerpt)

Merrill Lynch & Co., Inc. Notes to Consolidated Financial Statements (excerpt) (amounts in millions)		
Marketable Investment Securities	**2001**	**2000**
Available-for-sale	$70,320	$48,483
Held-to-maturity	7,460	632
Trading	40	136
Total	$77,820	$49,251

Unrealized holding gains or **losses** represent the difference in the current market price of the security from the acquisition cost of the security. These securities have not been sold, however.

A gain or loss is realized when the securities actually are sold at a profit or loss.

determined. An adjustment is made to bring the book value into agreement with the market value. If increases in book values are required, they are taken as **Unrealized Holding Gains** and reported on the income statement. If decreases in book values are required, they are taken as **Unrealized Holding Losses** on Marketable Securities and reported on the income statement.

Suppose MS Co. classifies the marketable security in Exhibit 10.3 as a trading security, and that events unfold as expected (required interest rates and required returns do not change). Suppose it buys the security on January 1, 2004, for cash. It records the transaction with the following entry:

Marketable Securities—Trading 735.03
    Cash 735.03
(To record the purchase of a marketable security classified as trading.)

On December 31, 2004, MS Co. would find that its security has a market value of $793.83. It must make the following adjustment:

Market value of security	$ 793.83
Unadjusted book value of security	(735.03)
Adjustment required	$ 58.80

The entry would appear as follows:

Marketable Securities—Trading 58.50
    Unrealized Gain on Marketable Security—Trading 58.50
(To record the unrealized appreciation on the marketable security—trading.)

REMEMBER: This unrealized gain will show up on the income statement of MS Co.

Unrealized Gain on Marketable Securities—Trading is a temporary account that is closed to Retained Earnings. Exhibit 10.5 shows the T-accounts, Marketable Securities—Trading and Unrealized Gain on Marketable Securities—Trading.

Exhibit 10.5

T-Accounts for Marketable
Securities—Trading Example

Marketable Securities—Trading			Unrealized Gain on Marketable Securities—Trading		
Dr.	Cr.		Dr.	Cr.	
Purchase on 1/1/04 735.03				58.80	Credit for the adjustment
Required adjustment 58.80		Closing 58.80			
Balance on 12/31/04 793.83				0	Post-closing balance

Now suppose that something unexpected happens in 2005, and the market value of the security is $875 on December 31, 2005, instead of the expected $857.34. MS Co. must make the following adjustment:

NOTE: The adjustment compares the current market price to the current book value.

Market value of security	$ 875.00
Unadjusted book value of security	(793.83)
Adjustment required	$ 81.17

The entry would appear as follows:

Marketable Securities—Trading 81.17
    Unrealized Gain on Marketable Security—Trading 81.17

(To record the unrealized appreciation on the marketable security—trading.)

Exhibit 10.6 shows the T-accounts, Marketable Securities—Trading and Unrealized Gain on Marketable Securities—Trading.

Exhibit 10.6

T-Accounts for Marketable Securities—Trading Example

Marketable Securities—Trading				Unrealized Gain on Marketable Securities—Trading		
	Dr.	Cr.			Dr.	Cr.
Purchase on 1/1/04	735.03					Credit for the adjustment
						81.17
Required adjustment on 12/31/04		58.80		Closing	81.17	
						Post-closing balance
Balance on 12/31/04	793.83					0
Required adjustment on 12/31/05	*81.17*					
Balance on 12/31/05	875.00					

For trading securities, the balance sheet reflects market values, and all gains or losses are reflected in income.

Suppose that on January 3, 2006, MS Co. sold this security for $880. It would make the following journal entry:

This entry removes the asset account, records the receipt of cash, and recognizes a gain in the amount of the difference. (Keep in mind that some of the gains from holding this security were recorded in earlier years.)

Cash 880.00
    Marketable Securities—Trading 875.00
    Gain on Marketable Security—Trading 5.00

(To record the sale of the marketable security—trading.)

Review Questions

1. In the MS Co. example just completed, what is the total profit on this security transaction? What were all of the cash flows? Which periods saw profits?

2. Suppose instead that market value of the security is $790 on December 31, 2005. Make the required adjusting entry. Suppose the security is sold for $810 on January 3, 2006. Make the required journal entry.

Available-for-Sale Securities

An **available-for-sale security** is a debt or equity marketable security that is not classified as trading or held-to-maturity.

GAAP for an **available-for-sale security** are conceptually muddy—they follow economic values, but treat holding gains and losses as equity adjustments, not as income items. At each balance sheet date, the market value of available-for-sale securities is determined. An adjustment is made to bring the book value into agreement with the market value. If increases in book values are required, they are taken as Unrealized Holding Gains on Marketable Securities—Available-for-Sale. If decreases in book values are required, they are taken as Unrealized Holding Losses on Marketable Securities—Available-for-Sale. Neither unrealized holding gains nor losses on available-for-sale securities are reported on the income statement.

Suppose MS Co. classifies the marketable security in Exhibit 10.3 as an available-for-sale security, and that events unfold as expected. Suppose it buys the security on January 1, 2004, for cash. It records the transaction with the following entry:

Marketable Securities—Available-for-Sale 735.03
    Cash 735.03

(To record the purchase of a marketable security classified as available-for-sale.)

The following entry would be made to record the adjustment to market value on December 31, 2004.

Marketable Securities—Available-for-Sale 58.50
    Unrealized Gain on Marketable Security—Available-for-Sale 58.50

(To record the unrealized appreciation on the marketable security—available-for-sale.)

Unrealized Gain on Marketable Securities—Available-for-Sale is a permanent account that appears on the balance sheet. Exhibit 10.7 shows the T-accounts, Marketable Securities—Available-for-Sale and Unrealized Gain on Marketable Securities—Available-for-Sale.

Exhibit 10.7

T-Accounts for Marketable Securities—Available-for-Sale Example

Marketable Securities— Available-for-Sale			Unrealized Gain on Marketable Securities— Available-for-Sale		
	Dr.	Cr.		Dr.	Cr.
Purchase on 1/1/04	735.03		Credit for the adjustment		58.80
Required adjustment on 12/31/04	58.80				
Balance on 12/31/04	793.83		Balance on 12/31/04		58.80
Required adjustment on 12/31/05	*81.17*		Credit for the adjustment		*81.17*
Balance on 12/31/05	875.00		Balance on 12/31/05		139.97

As before, assume the market value of the security is $875 on December 31, 2005, instead of the expected $857.34. MS Co. must make the $81.17 adjustment.

Marketable Securities—Available-for-Sale 81.17
    Unrealized Gain on Marketable Security—Available-for-Sale . . . 81.17

(To record the unrealized appreciation on the marketable security—available-for-sale.)

Exhibit 10.8

Merrill Lynch & Co.
Consolidated Balance Sheets
(shareholders' equity section)

Merrill Lynch & Co., Inc.
Consolidated Balance Sheets (shareholders' equity section)
(amounts in millions)

Common Stockholders' Equity	December 28, 2001	December 29, 2000
Shares exchangeable into common stock	62	68
Common stock (par value $1.33 1/3 per share; Authorized: 3,000,000,000 shares; issued: 962,533,498 shares)	$ 1,283	$ 1,283
Paid-in capital	4,209	2,843
Accumulated other comprehensive loss (net of tax)	(368)	(345)
Retained earnings	16,150	16,156
	$21,336	$20,005
Less: Treasury stock, at cost (2001: 119,059,651 shares; 2000: 154,578,945 shares)	977	1,273
Unamortized employee stock grants	776	853
Total common stockholders' equity	$19,583	$17,879

Accumulated unrealized gains and losses on available-for-sale securities are reported here.

For available-for-sale securities, the balance sheet reflects market values, but holding gains and losses are *not* reflected in income. They are reported on the balance sheet in the shareholders' equity section, but they are not included in Retained Earnings.

For Merrill Lynch, the accumulated holding gains and losses on marketable securities classified as available-for-sale are reflected in the Accumulated Other Comprehensive income amount of ($368) in the shareholders' equity section of its balance sheet. This category is shown in Exhibit 10.8.

Suppose, as before, that on January 3, 2006, MS Company sold this security for $880. They would make the following journal entry:

In the case of available-for-sale securities, the entire gain or loss shows up in income in the year in which the security is disposed of.

Cash	880.00	
Unrealized Gain on Marketable Security— Available-for-Sale	139.97	
Marketable Securities—Available-for-Sale		875.00
Gain on Marketable Security—Available-for-Sale		144.97

(To record the sale of the marketable security—available-for-sale.)

In this case, because Unrealized Gain on Marketable Security—Available-for-Sale is a permanent account, it must be eliminated. Notice that the entire gain, $144.97, will enter into the income statement in 2006 because none of this amount was previously reported in income.

Review Questions

1. Explain the timing difference between when total profit or loss shows up in the income statements when the security is a trading security versus when it is an available-for-sale security.

2. Suppose instead that the market value of the security is $790 on December 31, 2005. Make the required adjusting entry. Suppose the security is sold for $810 on January 3, 2006. Make the required journal entry (assuming it is an available-for-sale marketable security).

Held-to-Maturity Securities

Held-to-maturity securities are debt securities that the holder intends to keep until they mature.

Amortized cost is used to account for held-to-maturity securities.

Held-to-maturity securities must be debt securities, because only they have maturity dates. GAAP for held-to-maturity securities follow economic values only if events progress exactly as expected. The accounting jargon for the method used to account for held-to-maturity securities is **amortized cost.** The amortized cost method begins with historical cost and the expected rate of return at the time the securities were purchased.

At each balance sheet date, the book value of held-to-maturity securities is determined by adjusting their cost as if the rate of return in effect when the securities were purchased remains in effect. For example, suppose MS Co. classifies the marketable security in Exhibit 10.3 as a held-to-maturity security, and that events unfold as expected. Suppose it buys the security on January 1, 2004, for cash. It records the transaction with the following entry:

Marketable Securities—Held-to-Maturity 735.03
    Cash 735.03

(To record the purchase of a marketable security classified as held-to-maturity.)

Regardless of the market value of the security on December 31, 2004, MS Co. would adjust the security's value by the interest on its beginning balance $735.03 \times 0.08 = \$58.80$. This adjustment would bring the balance in Marketable Securities—Held-to-Maturity to $793.83. The other side of the entry would be Interest Revenue as follows:

Marketable Securities—Held-to-Maturity 58.80
    Interest Revenue 58.80

(To record interest revenue, computed using the interest rate from the time of purchase, on held-to-maturity securities.)

Exhibit 10.9 shows the T-accounts, Marketable Securities—Held-to-Maturity and Interest Revenue.

Exhibit 10.9

T-Accounts for Marketable Securities—Held-to-Maturity Example

Marketable Securities— Held-to-Maturity			Interest Revenue		
Dr.	Cr.			Dr.	Cr.
Purchase on 1/04 735.03					*58.80* Adjustment
Required adjustment *58.80*		Closing 58.80			Post-closing
Balance on 12/31/04 793.83				0 balance	

Now suppose that something unexpected happens in 2005, and the market value of the security is $875 on December 31, 2005, instead of the expected $857.34. The accounting for held-to-maturity securities does not recognize this unexpected event. Instead, it proceeds as if the value of the security is steadily increasing at 8% per year. The book value of the held-to-maturity security is adjusted by the interest on the beginning balance of $793.83 \times 0.08 = \$63.51$ on December 31, 2005. This adjustment would bring the balance in the held-to-maturity securities account to $857.34 with the following entry:

Marketable Securities—Held-to-Maturity 63.51
    Interest Revenue 63.51

(To record interest revenue, computed using the interest rate from the time of purchase, on held-to-maturity securities.)

Exhibit 10.10 shows the T-accounts, Marketable Securities—Held-to-Maturity and Interest Revenue.

Exhibit 10.10

T-Accounts for Marketable Securities—Held-to-Maturity Example

Marketable Securities— Held-to-Maturity				Interest Revenue		
	Dr.	Cr.			Dr.	Cr.
Purchase on 1/1/04	735.03					63.51 Adjustment
				Closing	63.51	
Required adjustment on 12/31/04		58.80				Balance on 0 12/31/05
Balance on 12/31/04	793.83					
Required adjustment on 12/31/05		63.51				
Balance on 12/31/05	857.34					

For held-to-maturity securities, the balance sheet does not reflect market values, except by chance. Interest revenue is reflected on the income statement, but the amount reflected is only what was originally expected. Unexpected events are not acknowledged in the accounts.

Review Questions

1. Complete the following table. In each box, explain in words the accounting treatment for the security—explain how it affects both the balance sheet and income statement.

	Held-to-Maturity	Available-for-Sale	Trading
Debt security			
Equity security			

Comparison of GAAP and Economic Values

OBJECTIVE:

Learn to relate GAAP for marketable securities to the underlying economics of these securities.

GAAP for marketable securities range from exactly following economic values for trading securities, to a historical cost-based approach for held-to-maturity securities. Available-for-sale securities are treated with a half-measure. The balance sheet is "marked-to-market" (i.e., the balance sheet shows market values), but the unrealized holding gains and losses are not included in the calculation of net income.

Marketable securities available-for-sale is not the only item that receives inconsistent treatment between the balance sheet and income statement. Assets denominated in foreign currencies also generate currency translation gains and losses that are held off the income statement. As a result, another accounting statement is more in line with economics—the statement of comprehensive income. ***Comprehensive income*** is actually what best matches our introduction of balance sheets, income statements, and their articulation in Part 1. However, common usage still refers to the conventional income statement when using the phrase "net income."

Exhibit 10.11 gives Merrill Lynch's statement of comprehensive income. It shows that several sources give rise to items that bypass the income statement, including foreign

Exhibit 10.11

Merrill Lynch & Co.
Comprehensive Income

Merrill Lynch & Co., Inc.
Consolidated Statements of Comprehensive Income
(amounts in millions)

	Year Ended December 2001
Net Earnings	$ 573
Other Comprehensive Income	
Foreign currency translation adjustment:	
Foreign currency translation gains	127
Income tax expense	(120)
Total	7
Net unrealized losses on investment securities available-for-sale:	
Net unrealized holding losses arising during the period	(51)
Reclassification adjustment for gains included in net earnings	(19)
Net unrealized losses on investment securities	(70)
Adjustments for:	
Policyholder liabilities	(10)
Deferred policy acquisition costs	(13)
Income tax benefit	37
Total	(56)
Other items	26
Total other comprehensive loss	(23)
Comprehensive income	$ 550

These foreign currency items are beyond the scope of this book.

This section reports the unrealized gains (losses) on available-for-sale securities.

These adjustments are beyond the scope of this book.

currency translations, net unrealized holding gains (losses) on investment securities available-for-sale, and adjustments for policyholder liabilities.

The Total Other Comprehensive Loss of $23 million (from Exhibit 10.11) explains the increase in accumulated other comprehensive loss (net of tax) in the stockholders' equity section as follows:

Accumulated Other Comprehensive Loss
(net of tax)

	Dr.	Cr.
Balance on 12/29/00	345	
Other comprehensive loss in 2001	23	
Balance on 12/28/01	368	

By selling available-for-sale securities with unrealized holding gains, an organization can boost its net income, but not its comprehensive income.

Unrealized holding gains on held-to-maturity securities can be realized by selling the security. Because these holding gains are also not counted in comprehensive income, transactions in held-to-maturity securities could be used to manipulate reported net income. For example, on December 31, 2005, MS Co. would have marketable securities with a book value of $857.34, but a market value of $875 if it classified its marketable security as held-to-maturity. *Any time a disparity arises between the market value of an asset or liability and its book value, engaging in a transaction involving the asset or liability can trigger an income effect.* MS Co. could sell its held-to-maturity securities for $875. Because its book value would be only $857.34, a gain of $875.00 − $857.34 = $17.66 would be brought onto the income statement.

MS Co. could choose to continue to hold this marketable security. Embedded unrealized holding gains and losses, therefore, give management an *option* as to when to recognize the gain by engaging in a transaction. The relation between accounting and economic values affects management's ability to manipulate (*manage* is the more polite term) the reported accounting results. This is valuable knowledge for anyone who will base important decisions on accounting reports.

Financial Statement Analysis of Marketable Securities

OBJECTIVE:
Learn to become familiar with some common financial statistics related to marketable securities.

The **quick ratio** is the total of assets that can be converted quickly into cash divided by current liabilities.

Marketable securities can be exchanged into cash readily and constitute an important resource for meeting current liabilities. One common financial statistic involving marketable securities is the **quick ratio.** The quick ratio is the total of assets that can be converted quickly into cash divided by current liabilities. The quickly converted assets are usually cash, marketable securities, and accounts receivable.

Merrill Lynch's balance sheet is not classified in a convenient way to calculate the quick ratio, so let's illustrate with AOL's position at June 30, 1997, as given previously in Exhibit 5.1. The relevant parts of AOL's balance sheets are repeated in Exhibit 10.12. We see that AOL's current assets totaled about $323.5 million on June 30, 1997. Of that amount, about $124.3 + $0.3 + $65.3 + $26.1 = $216.0 million are in cash, short-term investments (i.e., marketable securities), and receivables. AOL's current liabilities totaled $554.5 million. The quick ratio of 0.39 is calculated as follows:

$$\$216.0/\$554.5 = 0.39$$

Exhibit 10.12
AOL, Inc.
Balance Sheet Excerpt

America Online, Inc.
Consolidated Balance Sheets
(Current Assets and Current Liabilities Only)
(amounts in thousands)

	June 30, 1997	June 30, 1996
Current assets:		
Cash and cash equivalents	$124,340	$118,421
Short-term investments	268	10,712
Trade accounts receivable	65,306	49,342
Other receivables	26,093	23,271
Prepaid expenses and other current assets	107,466	65,290
TOTAL CURRENT ASSETS	$323,473	$267,036
Current liabilities:		
Trade accounts payable	$ 69,703	$105,904
Other accrued expenses and liabilities	297,298	127,876
Deferred revenue	166,007	37,950
Accrued personnel costs	20,008	15,719
Current portion of long-term debt	1,454	2,435
TOTAL CURRENT LIABILITIES	$554,470	$289,884

Quick assets (Cash and cash equivalents through Other receivables)

Total current liabilities (TOTAL CURRENT LIABILITIES)

Conclusion

GAAP for marketable securities are some of the more complicated areas of accounting to learn. GAAP partly follow economic values but diverge in important ways for available-for-sale and held-to-maturity securities. As such, GAAP for marketable securities provide a good lesson in the importance of knowing the accounting rules instead of trying to presume them.

In the next chapter, we continue exploring GAAP when we turn to GAAP for long-term assets.

Key Terms

amortized cost *193*

available-for-sale security *190*

comprehensive income *194*

debt securities *185*

equity securities *186*

held-to-maturity securities *192*

marketable securities *185*

quick ratio *196*

trading security *188*

unrealized holding gains *189*

zero-coupon bond *188*

chapter 11

© GETTY IMAGES/PHOTO DISC

Long-Lived Assets

In a February 18, 1998, letter to the chairperson of the U.S. House of Representatives Committee on the Budget, the U.S. General Accounting Office (GAO) reported the results of an audit of the Federal Aviation Administration (FAA) fiscal 1996 balance sheet. The FAA is charged with ensuring "safe, orderly, and efficient air travel throughout the United States."

The GAO reported that a large fuel storage tank and several buildings at the Air Route Traffic Control Center in Miami, Florida, were included in the FAA asset accounts. The only problem is that these assets no longer existed—they had been demolished! In Cleveland, Ohio, the auditors found $12 million in assets, including a medical trailer and a daycare center, which were not included in the accounts. Let's just hope the FAA radar is better at keeping track of air traffic than its accounting system is at keeping track of assets!

In order to conduct business, most companies rely on assets that generate benefits over many periods of time. This chapter focuses on long-lived assets, and it has five main goals.

1. To discuss the nature of long-lived assets

2. To analyze economic values of long-lived assets

3. To present GAAP for long-lived assets

4. To explore how the economics of long-lived

assets are or are not reflected in GAAP accounting

5. To describe some common financial statistics related to long-lived assets

After discussing the nature of long-lived assets, we analyze their economic value. Long-lived assets are an investment and are expected to earn a normal rate of return. Companies generally use long-lived assets in combination with other assets in producing or distributing products and services. The major uncertainties that can cause long-lived assets to earn an abnormal positive or negative rate of return include unexpected good or bad news about the demand for an organization's products and services, the prices of important inputs that must be used in combination with the long-lived assets, and the invention of better production methods or technologies (the long-lived asset becomes obsolete).

GAAP are focused on the historical cost of long-lived assets, and estimate changes in the economic values of long-lived assets in a peculiar way. We will show how GAAP disclosures can be used to deduce some facts about an organization's investment in long-lived assets. However, much of the important information about the economic value of long-lived assets must be obtained from sources outside of the financial statements.

Nature of Long-Lived Assets

OBJECTIVE:
Learn to understand the definition of tangible and intangible long-lived assets.

Long-lived assets are the land, buildings, equipment, intellectual property, brands, copyrights, patents, and so on, that generate benefits for organizations over long periods of time. Long-lived assets may be either tangible or intangible. *Tangible* long-lived assets, like land and buildings, have a physical existence. *Intangible* long-lived assets, like brands, intellectual property, and the rights conveyed by patents and copyrights, do not have a physical existence.

Long-lived assets are critically important for many organizations. Buildings typically are expected to provide benefits for several decades. To make their products, manufacturers require machinery and equipment that often can be used for many years. Increasingly,

The Quaker Oats Company's brand name—one of its prime intangible assets—boosts consumer sales of its diverse product line.

as we saw in Chapter 7, intangible assets like Microsoft's intellectual property are the most important generators of value.

An Example: Quaker Oats

Consider the asset side of the 1996 balance sheet for The Quaker Oats Company given in Exhibit 11.1. Quaker is an international food and drink manufacturer and distributor. After listing its current assets, Quaker shows its Property, Plant, and Equipment and then its Intangible Assets. These two categories of noncurrent assets (long-lived assets) make up $1,200.7 + $2,237.2 = $3,437.9 million of Quaker's $4,394.4 million in total assets at December 31, 1996.

Quaker's Property, Plant, and Equipment consists of Land, Buildings and Improvements, and

Exhibit 11.1

Quaker Oats
Consolidated Balance Sheets

Property—Net comprises 27.3% of Quaker's total assets on December 31, 1996.

Intangible Assets—Net of Amortization comprises 50.9% of Quaker's total assets on December 31, 1996.

The Quaker Oats Company and Subsidiaries
Consolidated Balance Sheets (asset side only)
(amounts in millions)

	December 31	
Assets	**1996**	**1995**
Current Assets		
Cash and cash equivalents	$ 110.5	$ 93.2
Trade accounts receivable—net of allowances	294.9	398.3
Inventories		
Finished goods	181.8	203.6
Grains and raw materials	62.1	69.7
Packaging materials and supplies	31.0	33.4
Total inventories	$ 274.9	$ 306.7
Other current assets	209.4	281.9
Total current assets	$ 889.7	$1,080.1
Property, plant and equipment		
Land	$ 29.6	$ 26.0
Buildings and improvements	389.5	398.4
Machinery and equipment	1,524.2	1,521.6
Property, plant, and equipment	$1,943.3	$1,946.0
Less accumulated depreciation	742.6	778.2
Property—Net	$1,200.7	$1,167.8
Intangible assets—Net of amortization	2,237.2	2,309.2
Other assets	66.8	63.3
TOTAL ASSETS	$4,394.4	$4,620.4

Machinery and Equipment. Land may be damaged by pollution, but we usually think of it as lasting forever. Buildings and machinery, however, wear out. The Accumulated Depreciation of $742.6 million reduces the gross amount of $1,943.3 for Property, Plant, and Equipment to account for the effects of wear and tear on buildings, improvements, machinery, and equipment. It puts the book value of Quaker's Property, Plant, and Equipment at $1,200.7 million.

The use of long-term assets other than land generates depreciation and amortization expenses. These expenses often are not shown as one line item on income statements. Rather, they are included in various other categories of expenses. Exhibit 11.2 shows that depreciation and amortization expenses are included in Quaker's Cost of Goods Sold and Selling, General, and Administrative Expenses.

Exhibit 11.2

Quaker Oats
Income Statement

Depreciation and amortization on assets used for production end up as part of Cost of Goods Sold.

Depreciation and amortization on sales and administrative assets are included in Selling, General, and Administrative Expenses.

Quaker's statement of cash flows in Exhibit 11.3 shows that the total depreciation and amortization included in this income statement amount to $200.6 million.

If you don't remember how depreciation and amortization are added back in the indirect method cash flow statement, review Chapter 4.

The Quaker Oats Company and Subsidiaries Consolidated Statements of Income Year Ended December 31, 1996 (amounts in millions)	
Net Sales	$5,199.0
Cost of goods sold	2,807.5
Gross profit	$2,391.5
Selling, general, and administrative expenses	1,981.0
Gains on divestitures and restructuring charges—net	(113.4)
Interest expense	106.8
Interest income	(7.4)
Foreign exchange loss—net	8.9
Income before income taxes	$ 415.6
Provision for income taxes	167.7
Net Income	$ 247.9

Even though the total depreciation and amortization is not shown on Quaker's income statement, we can find it on the cash flow statement if Quaker uses the indirect method. Fortunately, they do use the indirect method; Exhibit 11.3 on page 202 shows how the cash flow statement reveals $200.6 million in total depreciation and amortization expenses for Quaker.

The notes to Quaker's financial statements excerpted in Exhibit 11.4 on page 202 explain the methods and assumptions used to calculate depreciation. Buildings and improvements are expected to have useful lives between 20 and 50 years. Useful lives for Quaker's machinery and equipment range from 3 to 17 years.

We should also point out that the balance sheet presentation of Quaker's Intangible Assets is a bit different from the presentation for Property, Plant, and Equipment. Whereas the cost of Property, Plant, and Equipment is shown separately from its Accumulated Depreciation, the cost and accumulated amortization for Intangible Assets are shown in one line: Intangible Assets—Net of Amortization. Even though intangible assets may not physically wear out, their potential to provide benefits usually declines over time. Patents and copyrights expire. Brands may eventually lose their value. Amortization adjusts the gross book value of intangible assets down to their book value. More detail can be found in Quaker's notes (see Exhibit 11.5 on page 202).

As indicated in Quaker's notes in Exhibits 11.4 and 11.5, cost provides the starting point in the accounting for long-lived assets. Determination of cost can be complicated. For example, long-lived assets may be either *purchased* or *self-constructed*. Purchased, tangible assets usually have fairly determinable acquisition costs. However, after acquisition the market for a used, long-lived asset may be thin. For example, few potential buyers are

Exhibit 11.3

Quaker Oats
Cash Flow Statement Excerpt

The depreciation and amortization add-back is $200.6 million. It is not unusual to obtain total depreciation and amortization from the statement of cash flows in this manner.

The Quaker Oats Company and Subsidiaries
Consolidated Statements of Cash Flows (operating activities only)
Year Ended December 31, 1996
(amounts in millions)

Cash Flows from Operating Activities

Net income	$ 247.9
Adjustments to reconcile net income to net cash provided by operating activities:	
Depreciation and amortization	200.6
Deferred income taxes	14.3
Gains on divestitures—net of tax of $54.6	(81.8)
Restructuring charges	23.0
Loss on disposition of property and equipment	29.0
Decrease (increase) in trade accounts receivable	62.6
Decrease (increase) in inventories	19.6
Decrease (increase) in other current assets	65.1
(Decrease) increase in trade accounts payable	(53.7)
(Decrease) increase in other current liabilities	(164.2)
Change in deferred compensation	21.5
Other items	26.5
Net Cash Provided by Operating Activities	$ 410.4

Exhibit 11.4

Quaker Oats
10K Excerpt (PP&E note)

The Quaker Oats Company
Notes to 1996 Financial Statements (excerpts)

Property and Depreciation—Property, plant, and equipment are carried at cost and depreciated on a straight-line basis over their estimated useful lives. Useful lives range from 20 to 50 years for buildings and improvements and from three to 17 years for machinery and equipment.

Exhibit 11.5

Quaker Oats
10K Excerpt

These amounts are shown on the balance sheets on December 31, 1996 and 1995.

The Quaker Oats Company
Notes to 1996 Financial Statements (excerpts)

Intangibles—Intangible assets consist principally of excess purchase price over net tangible assets of businesses acquired (goodwill) and trademarks. Goodwill is amortized on a straight-line basis over periods not exceeding 40 years.

Intangible assets, net of amortization, and their estimated useful lives consist of the following:

(amounts in millions)	Estimated Useful Lives (in years)	1996	1995
Goodwill	10 to 40	$1,887.1	$1,893.2
Trademarks and other	2 to 40	586.8	588.4
Intangible assets		$2,473.9	$2,481.6
Less accumulated amortization		236.7	172.4
Intangible assets—net of amortization		$2,237.2	$2,309.2

likely to want much of Quaker's used machinery and equipment. Some of Quaker's land may be in desirable locations, but some is probably in locations that make it mostly useful only to Quaker.

Intangible assets may be difficult to sell independently of selling the whole organization. A brand such as Coca-Cola may offer limited use, except in marketing a specific soft drink. Intellectual property like expertise may not be transferable to another organization.

Self-constructed, intangible assets represent an especially difficult challenge. It may be unclear what constitutes their acquisition cost. In fact, it may be unclear whether they even exist. An organization may know it spent money trying to establish a brand, but whether its expenditures will generate any future benefits may be highly uncertain. Markets for self-constructed, intangible assets often do not exist.

Although these distinctions (tangible versus intangible, purchased versus self-constructed) pose special problems for GAAP, they pose no special *conceptual* issues to economic valuation. Economic value is still determined by the present value of expected future net cash flows.

Economic Value of Long-Lived Assets

OBJECTIVE:
Learn to analyze the economic value of long-lived assets.

Unlike accounts receivable and marketable securities, long-lived assets are not straight-forward assets. Land, buildings, equipment, and intellectual property may generate future benefits, but the process by which this occurs is often complex. For example, Quaker may buy land, upon which it builds a food-processing plant, in which it puts food-processing equipment, with which it processes grains it purchases in commodities markets, that it then packages, sells to retail grocers on account, and, finally, collects cash to settle these accounts. Investments in long-lived assets are recouped through the usage of those assets to generate future cash flows.

The linkage between a particular long-lived asset and the future expected cash flows it generates might be indirect, however, those future expected cash flows still determine its economic value. We use an example to illustrate the issues.

Line Painter Co. will begin operations on January 1, 2004. Line Painter raises $1,000 cash by selling shares of stock to investors. These investors require a rate of return of 10% annually and the interest rate that can be earned on bank deposits is also 10%. Line Painter will paint the stripes and lines on highways. A machine can do this job, but the machine requires an operator, who must be paid a salary of $90 on December 31 of each year. The machine will paint for five years. At the end of the fifth year, it is completely worn out and worthless; that is, it has no salvage value. The machine is expected to paint enough highways to produce $327.42 in sales revenue each year, all of which is collected in cash on December 31 of each year. No inventory is required. The states, counties, and cities that hire Line Painter supply the paint. The machine is trouble free during its useful life and requires no maintenance. Line Painter will pay no annual dividends, but, at the end of its fifth year, when the machine is worthless, Line Painter will distribute all remaining cash in the bank as a **liquidating dividend.** We will assume no taxes are assessed or due.

A **liquidating dividend** is a distribution to shareholders of the remaining assets of a business when that business ceases operations.

REMINDER: Economic value of an asset is the present value of the future cash flows it will generate.

How much should this machine cost when Line Painter buys it on December 31, 2003? The tempting answer is "whatever people are willing to pay for it." So what should people be willing to pay for it?

Chapter 6 described how the economic value of anything equals the present value of its future expected net cash inflows. In this case, the expected net cash inflows in each year equal $327.42 − $90.00 = $237.42. Thus, the value of the machine should be the present value at 10% of $237.42 received at the end of each of the next consecutive five years. Thus, the following equation calculates the value of the machine at December 31, 2003:

$$\sum_{t=1}^{5} \frac{\$237.42}{(1.1)^t} = \$900.00$$

If the machine sold for more than $900, Line Painter would be better off putting its $900 in the bank at 10% instead of getting into the line painting business. If the machine sold for less than $900, competitors would be drawn into the line painting business because the investment would yield more than 10%. This competition would force the price of the painting machine up or the revenues from painting down until an investment in the line painting business was expected to earn 10%.

So let's assume Line Painter pays $900 cash for the machine on December 31, 2003. Note that the value of the machine changes each year. In fact, its value declines each year because at the end of each year, one less year of future net cash flows remains. The value of the machine at the end of each of the five years is calculated as follows:

Dec. 31, 2004	Dec. 31, 2005	Dec. 31, 2006	Dec. 31, 2007	Dec. 31, 2008
$\sum_{t=1}^{4} \dfrac{\$237.42}{(1.1)^t}$ $= \$752.59$	$\sum_{t=1}^{3} \dfrac{\$237.42}{(1.1)^t}$ $= \$590.43$	$\sum_{t=1}^{2} \dfrac{\$237.42}{(1.1)^t}$ $= \$412.05$	$\dfrac{\$237.42}{(1.1)^1}$ $= \$215.84$	$\dfrac{\$0}{(1.1)^0}$ $= \$0$

Economic depreciation for a period is the change in economic value from the beginning to the end of a period.

We calculated the economic value of the machine at December 31 of each year from 2004 to 2008. The change in the economic value of the machine from the beginning of the year to the end of the year is the **economic depreciation** of the asset for that year. For Line Painter, economic depreciation for each year is as follows (allow for some rounding error):

2004	2005	2006	2007	2008
$900.00	$752.59	$590.43	$412.05	$215.84
$752.59	$590.43	$412.05	$215.84	$0.00
= $147.41	= $162.16	= $178.38	= $196.21	= $215.84

At the end of the machine's life, it is fully depreciated, that is, its value is zero. Also note that the sum of the economic depreciation across the five years is $900, which is the machine's original cost:

$$\$147.41 + \$162.16 + \$178.38 + \$196.21 + \$215.84 = \$900.00$$

Note well that the machine's economic depreciation reflects the fall in the value of the machine. Although it may be correlated with the machine's physical deterioration, the fall in the value of the machine occurs because it will generate less remaining cash flow. Less cash flow means less economic value. It is the flow of economic value out of the machine that causes depreciation.

If the discount rate is zero, the economic value of the machine will equal the total future net cash flows.

The impact of the time value of money is evident in this example. It results in two specific effects. First, the economic value of the machine is always smaller than its total future net cash flows. Second, economic value declines in this example at an increasing rate, causing the economic depreciation to be greater with each passing year. Both of these effects go away if we set the discount rate to zero (you can do the calculations to verify this assumption). Further, the way the economic value of the machine progresses through time is a function of the *pattern* of cash flows it produces. Economic depreciation can be increasing, decreasing, or level over time, depending on the interest rate and the pattern of cash flows.

The principles underlying the economic value of a long-lived asset do not depend on whether the asset is tangible or intangible, or whether it was purchased or self-constructed. For example, if Line Painter Co. used an intangible asset instead of a machine, our analysis would be unchanged, but we would have used some different terminology. In particular, we would have described the decline in the value of an intangible asset as amortization, not depreciation. The concepts remain the same.

Application of GAAP for long-lived assets, however, *does depend* on whether the asset is tangible or intangible, and whether it was purchased or self-constructed. We explore GAAP for long-lived assets in the next section.

GAAP for Long-Lived Assets

OBJECTIVE:

Learn to become familiar with GAAP for long-lived assets.

GAAP for fixed assets specify three things:

1. Whether to recognize that an asset has been created in an accounting sense.
2. If an asset is to be recognized, the book value to enter on the balance sheet.
3. The allocation of the cost of the asset to the periods that it will benefit; that is, the determination of when the cost of the asset will show up as an expense in the income statement.

Capitalization versus Expense

An internally developed patent, which all agree brings future benefit, is not listed formally as an asset in the balance sheet because of difficulty in measuring the development cost of the patent.

The act of recognizing an accounting asset by setting up an asset account is called **capitalization.** Tangible assets, whether purchased or self-constructed, are always recognized. Intangible assets may or may not be recognized. Purchased intangible assets are more likely to be recognized under GAAP than self-constructed intangibles, which are virtually never recognized. This rough guide to capitalization is shown in Exhibit 11.6.

Exhibit 11.6

Rough Guide to GAAP Decision to Capitalize an Expenditure

	Expenditure made to:	
	Purchase "an Asset"	Self-Construct "an Asset"
Tangible	Recognized	Recognized
Intangible	May not be recognized (e.g., advertising, R&D)	Almost never recognized

In the case of advertising, although the cost may be known, the exact nature of the future benefit is uncertain and is almost never recorded as an asset.

Some specifics may help clarify recognition issues around intangible assets. For example, purchased patents are recognized, but patents developed in-house are not. The costs of developing in-house patents are expensed as incurred. Advertising costs, except for the costs of some direct response advertising campaigns, are not recognized as assets. They are expensed as incurred. The costs of training personnel may create economically valuable expertise, but they are not recognized as assets.

Valuation

Costs related to an asset incurred subsequent to acquisition are capitalized if the future service potential of the asset increases through extension of its service life, enhancement of the quality of the asset's output, or enlargement of the capacity of the asset.

Capitalized interest is the cost of interest that is not expensed in a period, but rather is put into the cost of an asset (i.e., Interest Expense is not debited, but an asset is instead). This approach is usually used when the borrowing that caused the interest is related directly to the construction of the asset (e.g., a construction loan).

Recognized, purchased, long-lived assets, whether tangible or intangible, initially are recorded at their cost. The basic idea is that cost provides the best estimate of the value of the asset at the time it was acquired. The cost of a **purchased asset** includes all those costs required to get the asset ready for its intended use. These costs include transportation, installation, and testing. For purchased assets, determining cost is not difficult. The determination of cost for many self-constructed assets, however, is often difficult.

Recognized, **self-constructed assets** are also recorded at the total of all costs required to ready the asset for use, but that amount is often complicated to determine. For example, nuclear power plants were among the most costly assets ever constructed by any organization other than a government. Construction was incredibly complex, time-consuming, and occurred during periods of high interest rates. Some nuclear power generating plants never were allowed to begin producing power, and others began operation only after long delays. For many plants, interest costs incurred during construction were the largest single factor in the cost of the plant.

The cost of some self-constructed intangible assets is so difficult to determine that no attempt is made to do so, and the costs are expensed as incurred. For example, software firms spend a great deal of money attracting and training a capable work force, but these costs are not recorded as assets. They are recorded as expenses in the periods incurred.

Depreciation

Depreciation is the systematic allocation of the cost of a tangible asset to the periods that it benefits.

Amortization is the systematic allocation of the cost of an intangible asset to the periods that it benefits.

The final area of GAAP for long-lived assets concerns how the cost of an asset will be assigned to the periods benefited by the asset. GAAP provide guidelines for allowable **depreciation** policies for tangible assets and **amortization** policies for intangibles. GAAP require that depreciation or amortization be recorded over the useful life of the asset. The *useful life* of an asset is the time period over which the asset's benefits will be felt.

GAAP are quite liberal about the precise way in which depreciation is to be assigned to periods. In practice, we lack precise knowledge of the pattern of cash flows from an asset. Therefore, GAAP do not require that economic depreciation be recorded. Instead, GAAP allow any "systematic and rational" method.

GAAP begin with the depreciable cost of the asset. Depreciable cost is the asset's cost less salvage value.

Units-of-Production Depreciation

A method tied to the physical use of the asset may be systematic and rational. For example, Line Painter Co. could depreciate its machine on the basis of the length of lines painted each year. Suppose the machine's useful life is 20,000 miles of lines. If the machine painted 5,000 miles of lines one year, then 25% of its capacity was used that year:

$$\frac{5,000}{20,000} = 0.25$$

Thus, $225, or 25% of the depreciable cost of $900, would be recorded as depreciation expense that year ($225 = 0.25 × $900). This method of depreciation is called *units-of-production,* and it is the only GAAP method that might result in increasing depreciation charges over time. An asset's economic value is not guaranteed, however, to decline in exact proportion to physical usage, so units-of-production depreciation is equal to economic depreciation only by chance.

Straight-Line Depreciation

The vast majority of businesses use straight-line depreciation in their financial statements.

Most GAAP depreciation methods achieve their "systematic and rational" status by their algorithmic nature. For example, *straight-line depreciation* takes a fixed percentage of the asset's depreciable cost each year as depreciation expense for the year. Line Painter's machine had a useful life of five years and no salvage value, so straight-line depreciation would take 0.20 (1/5 × 100) of the machine's cost as depreciation expense each year. Straight-line depreciation would assign $900 × 0.20 = $180 as depreciation expense each year.

Sum-of-Years'-Digits Depreciation

No matter which method is used to compute depreciation expense for the period, the journal entry to record it follows the form:

Dep. Expense . . . XXX
  Accum. Depreciation . . XXX

Sum-of-years'-digits is another method that uses depreciation rates based only on an asset's useful life. It is an *accelerated depreciation* method that assigns more depreciation to earlier rather than to later years. If an asset is expected to have a useful life of n years, sum-of-years'-digits depreciation assigns depreciation expense the first year as follows:

$$\frac{n}{\sum_{i=1}^{n} i} \times \text{Depreciable cost of the asset}$$

Depreciation expense the second year is assigned as follows:

$$\frac{n-1}{\sum_{i=1}^{n} i} \times \text{Depreciable cost of the asset}$$

Depreciation for subsequent years is assigned in a similar manner. For Line Painter, the depreciation expense assigned to each year is given in Exhibit 11.7.

Exhibit 11.7

Line Painter Co.
Sum-of-Years'-Digits Depreciation

Year	Digit	Depreciation Rate	Depreciable Cost	Depreciation Expense
2004	1	5/15	$900	$300
2005	2	4/15	900	240
2006	3	3/15	900	180
2007	4	2/15	900	120
2008	5	1/15	900	60
Sum	15	1		$900

Declining Balance Depreciation

Double-declining balance depreciation with salvage value: the DDB rate is still applied to the remaining book value, but would switch to the straight-line method or stop if the remaining book value would be below salvage value.

Finally, ***declining balance depreciation*** takes a multiple of the straight-line depreciation applied to the *remaining book value* of the asset as depreciation expense in any period. It continues to take this amount as depreciation expense *until straight-line depreciation on the remaining depreciable balance over the remaining useful life exceeds that charge.* For example, the straight-line rate for Line Painter's machine is 0.20. Double-declining balance depreciation would take $2 \times 0.20 = 0.40$ of the remaining book value of the asset as depreciation expense, until straight-line depreciation on the remaining balance, over the remaining useful life, is greater. The calculations are shown in Exhibit 11.8.

Exhibit 11.8   Line Painter Co., Double-Declining Balance Depreciation

Year	Remaining Book Value	Declining Balance Rate	Declining Balance Depreciation	Straight-Line on Remaining Balance	Depreciation Expense
2004	$900	$2 \times 20\% = 40\%$	$360.00	$\dfrac{\$900}{5} = \$180.0$	$360.0
2005	540	40	216.00	$\dfrac{\$540}{4} = \$135.0$	216.0
2006	324	40	129.60	$\dfrac{\$324}{3} = \$108.0$	129.6
2007	194.4	40	77.76	$\dfrac{\$194.4}{2} = \$97.2$	97.2
2008	97.2	40	38.88	$\dfrac{\$194.4}{2} = \$97.2$	97.2
Sum					$900.0

Notice in Exhibit 11.9 that in 2007 the calculation switches to straight-line depreciation on the remaining depreciable balance over the remaining useful life (97.2 is greater than 77.76).

Exhibit 11.9 on page 208 shows the book value of Line Painter's machine under straight-line, sum-of-years'-digits, and double-declining balance depreciation.

Review Questions

1. An asset with a useful life of five years and an acquisition cost of $600 has a salvage value of $100. Compute depreciation expense for each of the five years, assuming (a) straight-line depreciation, (b) DDB depreciation, and (c) sum-of-year's-digits depreciation.

Exhibit 11.9

Line Painter Co.
Book Value of Machine

*RULE OF THUMB: Acceler-
ated depreciation methods
depreciate about 2/3 of the
amount to be depreciated over
the first half of the useful life
of the asset.*

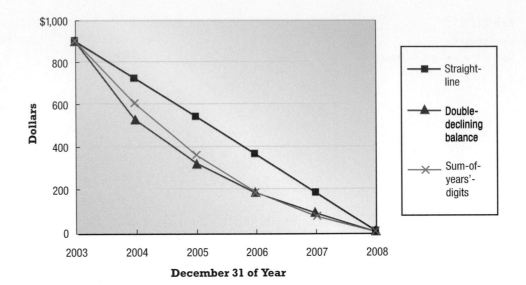

December 31 of Year

2. How does the presentation for tangible and intangible assets differ in the balance sheet?

3. What is economic depreciation? Under what conditions might economic depreciation be appreciation?

4. Why do you think most businesses use straight-line depreciation?

Comparison of GAAP and Economic Values

OBJECTIVE:

Learn to relate GAAP for long-
lived assets to the underlying
economics of these assets.

Exhibit 11.10 shows the economic and book values of the machine so that we can compare them. As you can see, the economic values and book values of Line Painter's machine begin at $900 and end at $0. The paths they take to go from $900 to $0 differ, however. In this example, if everything proceeds as expected, the book value of the machine is never greater than its economic value.

If GAAP record depreciation expense too early, market-to-book ratios of the assets will be pushed over 1.

Exhibit 11.10

Line Painter Co.
Book and Economic Value
of Machine

*In most financial statements,
the economic values of long-
term, fixed assets are generally in excess of their book
values.*

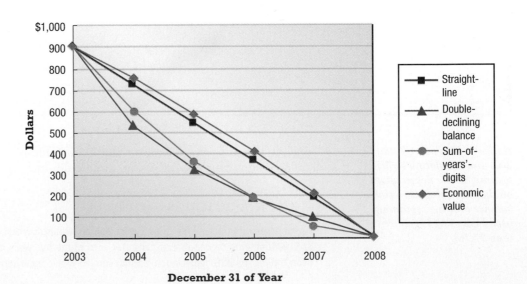

December 31 of Year

Changing Expectations

But that's if everything goes as expected. Really interesting things happen if a surprise occurs during the asset's life. For example, suppose that unexpected increases in state budgets for highway construction generate revenues in 2006 of $400 instead of the $327.42 that was expected. Further suppose that these increased revenues will continue through December 31, 2008.

This unexpected good news increases the value of the painting machine. At December 31, 2006, we would expect the economic value of the machine to be

Dec. 31, 2006	Dec. 31, 2007	Dec. 31, 2008
$\sum_{t=1}^{2} \dfrac{\$310.00}{(1.1)^t}$	$\dfrac{\$310.00}{(1.1)^1}$	$\dfrac{\$0}{(1.1)^0}$
$= \$538.02$	$= \$281.82$	$= \$0$

You might recall that the value of the machine on December 31, 2006, was expected to be $412.05. So, in addition to the unexpectedly high revenues in 2006, Line Painter Co. shows an abnormal gain of $538.02 − $412.05 = $125.97 on the painting machine.

In the United States, GAAP do not recognize increases in the value of long-lived assets. In spite of the good economic news, Line Painter's books would proceed as if no favorable news about the value of the painting machine had been received. Exhibit 11.11 shows the book values, the originally expected economic values, and the realized economic values in the case of this new scenario.

Exhibit 11.11

Line Painter Co.
Book, Expected, and Realized
Economic Values of Machine

Note the widening gap between economic value and accounting value after the good news becomes known.

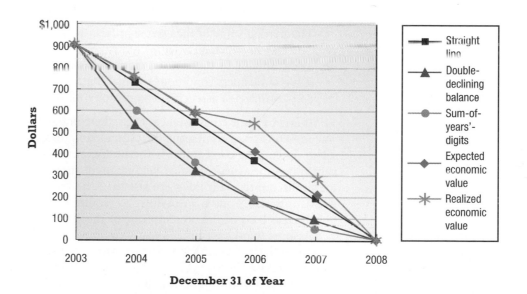

Only if the asset were sold would any recognition of its increase in value be made. If Line Painter's machine were sold at the end of 2007, it should sell for its economic value of ($400 − $90)/(1.1) = $281.82. Under straight-line depreciation, the book value of the asset would be $900 − (4 × $180) = $180. Therefore, Line Painter would recognize an accounting gain on the sale of $281.82 − $180 = $101.82. The journal entry to record this transaction would be as follows:

Cash	281.82	
Accumulated Depreciation	720.00	
Equipment		900.00
Gain on Sale of Equipment		101.82

The gain of $101.82 would be reported in the income statement, most likely in a category such as Other Gains and Losses. Note that the gain would be even larger if Line Painter used double-declining balance depreciation. The book value of the machine at the end of 2007 under double-declining balance is $97.20. Thus, the reported gain would be $281.82 − $97.20 = $184.62.

Asset Impairment

What if the cash flows unexpectedly declined, instead of increased? For example, assume that in 2006, cash revenues fall to $200 and information suggests they will stay at $200 for the rest of the asset's useful life. The economic value of the asset at December 31, 2006, would be ($200 − $90)/(1.1) + ($200 − $90)/(1.1)² = $190.91. If Line Painter used straight-line depreciation and sold the asset at the end of 2006, it would record the loss on sale of equipment with the following journal entry:

Cash	190.91	
Accumulated Depreciation	540.00	
Loss on Sale of Equipment	169.09	
Equipment		900.00

The loss would be reported on the income statement in a category such as Other Gains and Losses.

Following conservatism in accounting principles, we don't always record the good economic events until we are absolutely sure of them (or realize them in a transaction). The bad economic events are likely to be recorded when we are reasonably sure they will happen.

Would Line Painter's financial statements reflect this change in value without selling the asset? The answer is maybe. GAAP require the recognition of **asset impairment** charges under certain conditions. Firms are required to review an asset for impairment whenever circumstances suggest the asset's revenue-generating ability may have declined significantly. Examples of such circumstances include the following:[1]

- The market value of the asset significantly decreases.
- The way in which an asset is used changes.
- The company forecasts losses from the asset's continued use.
- Adverse business conditions or legal matters affect the asset.
- Self-constructed assets cost significantly more than originally estimated.

If any of these circumstances exist, the company must perform an impairment test. The test consists of comparing the estimated *undiscounted* future cash flows from the asset to its current book value. If the undiscounted cash flows are greater than its book value, then the asset is deemed *not* impaired, and no entries are made in the accounts. If the undiscounted cash flows are less than the book value of the asset, then the asset is deemed impaired and a write-down is required. The book value of the asset then must be reduced to equal the present value of the expected future cash flows.

ASSET IMPAIRMENT TEST: Are the undiscounted future cash flows less than the current book value of the asset? If not, do nothing. Do not change the value of the asset on the books.

If yes, write down the carrying value of the asset to its economic value (the present value of its future cash flows).

Assume that Line Painter's yearly cash revenues fall to $290 in 2006 and are expected to remain there through 2008. The undiscounted sum of future cash revenues at the end of 2006 is $400[($290 − $90) × 2]. If Line Painter employs straight-line depreciation, the book value of the machine at the end of 2006 is $360. Thus, because the undiscounted cash flows of $400 are greater than $360, no impairment charge would be recorded. Note that no impairment is recorded even though the economic value of the asset has fallen below its book value. (Verify that the economic value is now $347.12.) In this case, the impairment test prevents the book value from being updated to economic value.

Now let's assume that the yearly cash revenues fall to $220 in 2006 and are expected to remain at that level for 2007 and 2008. The undiscounted sum of future cash revenues at the end of 2006 is ($220 − $90)(2) = $260. This amount is well below the straight-line book value of $360. Thus, the machine would be deemed impaired. The present value of the remaining cash flows is now expected to be [($220 − $90)/(1.1)] + [($220 − $90)/(1.1)²] = $225.62. The impairment charge recorded would be $360 − $225.62 = $134.38. The machine's book value would be reduced to $225.62 by the following entry:

[1]See *SFAS No. 121*, "Accounting for the Impairment of Long-Lived Assets."

Impairment Loss	134.38	
Accumulated Depreciation		134.38

or

Impairment Loss	134.38	
Accumulated Depreciation	540.00	
Equipment	225.62	
Equipment		900.00

An equally good journal entry would be to have just one aggregate credit of Equipment for $674.38.

Once an impairment is recognized, a new depreciation schedule that depreciates the asset's remaining book value over its remaining useful life must be determined.

Recognizing an impairment causes the book value of the asset to be equal to its economic value. Because the impairment test employs undiscounted cash flows, however, economic values must fall significantly before an impairment charge is triggered. The test removes some volatility from impairment charges that might occur if the impairment test were based on discounted cash flows. Because future cash flows must be estimated, it would be easy to determine whether their discounted value had fallen below book value if one wished to record an impairment charge (Why would someone want to record an impairment charge?). However, the rules requiring that assets be reviewed for impairment when certain circumstances exist help to prevent managers from avoiding asset impairment charges altogether (Why would someone want to avoid an impairment charge?).

In 1996, Quaker Oats performed an impairment test on the assets of its Snapple beverage unit. Exhibit 11.12 contains the note explaining that an impairment test was performed, and that Snapple's long-lived assets passed. Although no impairment was recognized, Quaker sold Snapple in March 1997 for a loss of about $1.4 billion!

Exhibit 11.12

Quaker Oats
10K Excerpt (asset impairment)

The Quaker Oats Company
Notes to the 1996 Financial Statements (excerpts)

The Company has evaluated the recoverability of Snapple beverages long-lived assets, including intangible assets, as of December 31, 1996 pursuant to Financial Accounting Standards Board (FASB) Statement #121. In performing its review for recoverability, the Company compared the estimated undiscounted future cash flows to the carrying value of Snapple beverages long-lived assets, including intangible assets. The carrying value of Snapple beverages long-lived assets at December 31, 1996 was $1.7 billion. As the estimated undiscounted future cash flows exceeded the carrying value of long-lived assets, the Company was not permitted or required to recognize an impairment loss.

Although the Company's latest evaluation of recoverability has not resulted in the recognition of an impairment loss, given the disappointing performance of the business, management expects to update its assessment during 1997. Accordingly, the Company's estimate of undiscounted future cash flows to be generated by Snapple beverages could change in the near term. A change that results in recognition of an impairment loss would require the Company to reduce the carrying value of Snapple beverages to fair market value, which is significantly below the current carrying value of the long-lived assets.

Financial Statement Analysis of Long-Lived Assets

OBJECTIVE:
Learn to recognize common financial statistics related to long-lived assets.

Given the tenuous connection between book and economic values for long-lived assets, it is not surprising that most financial statement analyses of these items focus on gaining a physical, not an economic, understanding. For example, we know from Exhibit 11.4 that Quaker uses straight-line depreciation, and from Exhibit 11.1, that it showed accumulated depreciation of $742.6 million as of December 31, 1996. That accumulated depreciation figure was related to Quaker's Buildings and Improvements of $389.5 million and its Machinery and Equipment of $1,524.2 million. These assets total $389.5 + $1,524.2 = $1,913.7 million. Because this total is the historical cost of Quaker's assets, we know that they are about 39% depreciated, determined as follows:

$$\frac{742.6}{1,913.7} = 0.388$$

Quaker uses useful lives of 20 to 50 years for its buildings, so applying this percentage suggests that the age of Quaker's buildings and improvements falls between 0.388×20 years = 7.76 years and 0.388×50 years = 19.4 years. Quaker's machinery and equipment are between 0.388×3 years = 1.16 years and 0.388×17 years = 6.6 years.

Review Questions

Suppose a company begins operations and purchases a long-lived depreciable asset for $300. The asset has a useful life of three years and has no salvage value.

1. Compute depreciation expense for each of the years of the asset's useful life under straight-line depreciation; compute under DDB depreciation.

2. Make the corresponding journal entries for each of the numbers computed in both depreciation methods.

3. Which method of depreciation will show the highest net income in year 1?

4. Suppose the company continues to purchase one asset every year for the next 10 years. What will be the depreciation expense for the company in year 4 if it uses straight-line depreciation? DDB depreciation?

Conclusion

Accounting for long-lived assets has long been governed by allocation of historical costs in a predictable fashion. The various depreciation techniques—straight-line, declining-balance, units-of-production, and sum-of-years-digits—are all algorithmic ways of spreading an asset's historical cost over time. This approach leads to book values equaling economic values only by chance.

The advent of impairment rules reflects a significant change in attitude. The impairment rules require adjusting the book values to be in line with economic values under certain conditions. For assets with thin markets, this exercise is delicate, requiring numerous estimates of future cash flows and interest rates. It will be interesting to see whether future accounting policy makers widen the application of the impairment rules, or restrict them.

This completes our exploration of assets and their related revenues and expenses. In the next chapter, we take up liabilities and their related revenues and expenses.

Key Terms

accelerated depreciation *206*

amortization *206*

asset impairment *210*

capitalization *205*

declining balance depreciation *207*

depreciation *206*

economic depreciation *204*

intangible assets *199*

liquidating dividend *203*

long-lived assets *199*

purchased asset *205*

self-constructed assets *205*

straight-line depreciation *206*

sum-of-years'-digits depreciation *206*

tangible assets *199*

units-of-production depreciation *206*

useful life *206*

Appendix 11.1: Economic Value of Line Painter Co.

One can think about the economic value of Line Painter in at least two ways. As we know, the economic value of anything is the present value of its expected future net cash inflows. Therefore, we can find the economic value of Line Painter by finding the present value of the net cash inflows we would receive if we owned Line Painter.

Recall that Line Painter pays no annual dividends, but it will pay a liquidating dividend of all cash in the bank at the end of 2008. So, the value of Line Painter at any point in time should be the present value of this liquidating dividend. To find the value, we need to determine how much cash Line Painter will have in the bank at the end of 2008. Recall that Line Painter raised $1,000 cash from stock investors and spent $900 of that on December 31, 2003, to purchase the machine, leaving $100 in the bank. The bank account pays 10% interest each year on the beginning balance. At the end of 2008, it will accumulate to

$$(\$100)(1.1)^5 = \$161.05$$

Line Painter brings in $327.42 − $90.00 = $237.42 cash each year from operating the machine. Because Line Painter pays no annual dividend, taxes, or other expenses, this cash amount goes into Line Painter's bank account each year. Thus, the first year's $237.42 earns four years of interest, the second earns three years of interest, and so on.

Exhibit 11.A1

Line Painter Co.
Accumulation of Cash

	At December 31 of Year				
	2004	**2005**	**2006**	**2007**	**2008**
Beginning balance	$100.00	$347.42	$619.58	$ 918.96	$1,248.28
Interest @ 10%	10.00	34.74	61.96	91.90	124.83
Cash from operations	237.42	237.42	237.42	237.42	237.42
Ending balance	$347.42	$619.58	$918.96	$1,248.28	$1,610.53

Another way to look at this accumulation of the cash flows from operating the machine is as follows:

$$(\$237.42)(1.1)^4 + (\$237.42)(1.1)^3 + (\$237.42)(1.1)^2 + (\$237.42)(1.1) + \$237.42$$

$$= \$237.42\left(\sum\nolimits_{t=0}^{4} (1.1)^t\right)$$

$$= \$1,449.47$$

Line Painter's cash in the bank and, therefore, its liquidating dividend at December 31, 2008, is $161.05 + $1,449.47 = $1,610.52. The value of Line Painter at December 31, 2003, would be

$$\$1,610.52/(1.1)^5 = \$1,000$$

The simplest approach of all would be to recognize that all of Line Painter's assets return 10% annually. At the beginning of the 5-year period, it has $1,000 in assets. Therefore, at the end of the 5-year period, it should have exactly ($1,000)(1.1)^5 in asset value. Verify that this number is $1,610.52.

Similar calculations at the end of each year yield the following economic values.

12/31/04	12/31/05	12/31/06	12/31/07	12/31/08
$1,610.52/	$1,610.52/	$1,610.52/	$1,610.52/	$1,610.52/
$(1.1)^4$	$(1.1)^3$	$(1.1)^2$	$(1.1)^1$	$(1.1)^0$
= $1,100.00	= $1,210.00	= $1,331.00	= $1,464.11	= $1,610.52

The economic value of the firm at December 31, 2003, is a clue to another path to the same answer. Note that the economic value of the machine at December 31, 2003, is

$900 and the cash in the bank is $100. The economic value of cash is always just the amount of cash. Thus, we can simply add together the values of the individual assets—in this case the machine and cash in the bank—and get the economic value of the firm. Note that the cash in the bank at December 31, 2004, is $100(1.1) + $237.42 = $347.42. Adding to this the value of the machine yields the value of Line Painter; that is, $347.42 + $752.58 = $1,100.00.

Exhibit 11.A2

Line Painter Co.
Economic Value

	At December 31 of Year					
	2003	**2004**	**2005**	**2006**	**2007**	**2008**
Cash	$ 100.00	$ 347.42	$ 619.58	$ 918.96	$1,248.28	$1,610.52
Machine[2]	900.00	752.58	590.43	412.05	215.84	0
Economic value of Line Painter Co.	$1,000.00	$1,100.00	$1,210.01	$1,331.01	$1,464.12	$1,610.52

[2]See page 204 for computations of the values of the machine.

chapter 12

© GETTY IMAGES/PHOTO DISC

Long-Term Liabilities

In this chapter you will learn:

1 To understand the definition of long-term liabilities

2 To analyze the economic value of long-term liabilities

3 To become familiar with GAAP for long-term liabilities

4 To relate GAAP for long-term liabilities to the underlying economics of these liabilities

5 To become familiar with some common financial statistics related to long-term liabilities

There is an old saying that if you owe a bank $1 million, the bank owns you. But if you owe a bank $10 million, you own the bank! As we will see in this chapter and the next, this saying contains an element of truth: debt and equity are more alike than typically is acknowledged. This chapter begins our study of GAAP for the sources of long-term capital.

Most companies rely on long-term liabilities to acquire funds that will be repaid over time. This chapter focuses on long-term liabilities.

After discussing the nature of long-term liabilities, we analyze their economic value. Liabilities are probable sacrifices of resources in the future. The keys to their economic values are the probabilities that particular amounts will have to be sacrificed and the ordering of the sacrifices through time. Similar to the process for valuation of assets, we use our familiar tool of discounted expected value to calculate the economic values of liabilities.

Just as assets are expected to earn normal rates of return, liabilities are expected to require the payment of a normal rate of return. And just as assets can generate abnormal returns, so can liabilities be settled for unexpectedly low or high amounts. The two major sources of uncertainty for liabilities can cause their payments to be abnormally low or high: interest rate risk (changes in the levels of interest rates over time) and default risk (the risk that principal and interest will not be repaid).

GAAP for liabilities are based on information available at the time the transaction that gave rise to the liability occurred; that is, GAAP for liabilities are largely historically based. Changes in the value of liabilities because of changes in interest rates or default risks typically are not recognized under GAAP. This implies that the book values of liabilities shown on GAAP balance sheets can be quite different from their economic values.

The chapter concludes by exploring some common financial statistics used to assess an entity's dependence on debt-financing: times interest-earned and debt-to-equity ratios.

Nature of Long-Term Liabilities

OBJECTIVE:
Learn to understand the definition of long-term liabilities.

Long-term liabilities are the loans, leases, mortgages, deferred compensation arrangements, bonds, and credit agreements that organizations use to delay sacrifices of resources over long periods of time. The largest long-term liabilities typically are financial instruments that organizations use to raise money to transact business.

Long-term liabilities that are financial instruments usually specify a schedule of payments, restrictions on the actions of the borrower, and creditor and debtor rights in both normal times and if the borrower defaults.

General Characteristics of Financial Instruments

The **financial instruments** (agreements, contracts) between borrowers and lenders that give the borrowers use of the lenders' money over a period of time typically specify four things:

1. A schedule of payments, or a formula for computing the payments, that the borrower promises to make to the lender
2. A set of restrictions on the borrower's actions or financial conditions, the violation of which puts the borrower in *default*
3. A definition of the borrower's and lender's rights if there is no default
4. A definition of the lender's and borrower's rights if the borrower defaults

Some common terms are used to specify these four contract areas found in debt instruments. We discuss each part in turn.

Schedule of Payments

Many debt instruments promise a schedule of periodic payments equal to a coupon rate times the face value of the instrument. These payments are promised at specified dates between the ***date of issuance*** and the maturity date. The **face value** is a nominal amount printed on the face of the instrument and is paid from the borrower to the lender at the **maturity date**. The **coupon rate** is a percentage that is applied to the face value to determine the periodic payments.

The face value, maturity date, and coupon rate constitute a *contractual language* that describes the cash flows the issuer of the instrument promises to pay the holders. For example, on January 1, 2001, a note might be issued with a face value of $1,000 and a maturity date of December 31, 2006. The bond carries a coupon rate of 5.0%.

These features describe the cash that the issuer of the note promises to pay the holders. The issuer promises to pay the holder $1,000 on December 31, 2006. Further, the issuer promises to pay the holder $50 per year in coupon payments until the bond is paid off on December 31, 2006:

$$\$1,000 \times 0.05 = \$50$$

Now some potential for confusion arises. Common practice is for notes to make coupon payments semiannually. The 5% coupon rate really means that the issuer promises to pay the holder $25 twice per year:

$$^1/_2(\$1,000 \times 0.05) = \$25$$

Because the date of issuance of the note is January 1, we assume the coupon payments are made on June 30 and December 31 through December 31, 2006. On the maturity date, December 31, 2006, the note also promises to pay the holder the face value of $1,000. Exhibit 12.1 lists all the promised payments from January 1, 2001, to December 31, 2006. Figure 12.1 on page 218 portrays the important features of the note's terms graphically.

The **face value, maturity date,** and **coupon rate** describe the cash flows of the debt instrument.

We cannot overemphasize that the coupon rate determines only the cash to be received by the note holder, not the interest earned. For example, a zero-coupon bond has no periodic coupon payments, but its holder earns interest by paying less than the face value for the bond.

Exhibit 12.1

Hypothetical Note

Promised Payments of Hypothetical Note	
Date	**Promised Payment**
June 30, 2001	$ 25
December 31, 2001	25
June 30, 2002	25
December 31, 2002	25
June 30, 2003	25
December 31, 2003	25
June 30, 2004	25
December 31, 2004	25
June 30, 2005	25
December 31, 2005	25
June 30, 2006	25
December 31, 2006	25
December 31, 2006	1,000

Figure 12.1 Cash Payments Promised to the Holder of a Hypothetical Note with $1,000 Face Value, 5% Coupon Rate, Maturing on December 31, 2006

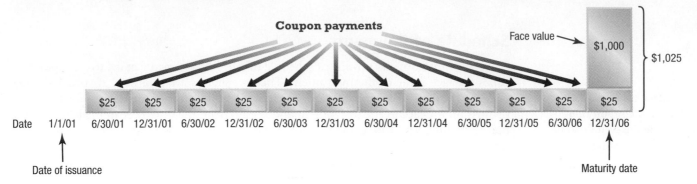

Some debt instruments contain **floating rates.** A floating rate is a rate that may change over time. Many floating rate agreements tie the promised periodic payments to the **London interbank offer rate (LIBOR).** For example, a floating rate note might require the borrower to pay the lender the LIBOR rate on June 30 of each year plus one percentage point times the face value of the note.

> **LIBOR** is the interest rate that most international banks charge one another for overnight loans.

In many situations, the issuers and purchasers of notes are concerned primarily with their promised cash flows. As we will see, GAAP are keyed primarily to the promised cash flows of a liability and do not capture the other features of notes. It is important, however, to understand these other features so we can be alert to them. We should recognize that the other terms of liabilities, such as restrictions on the borrower's actions and priority in bankruptcy, can become active at crucial times such as periods of extreme financial distress.

Restrictions on the Borrower's Actions or Financial Condition

> **Covenants** are restrictions on the borrower's actions or financial condition.

Restrictions on the borrower's actions or financial condition are called **covenants.** For example, many financial instruments contain dividend covenants that restrict the ability of corporate borrowers to pay dividends. This restriction provides the lender with some assurance that the borrower will not distribute all the borrowed funds, leaving the lender holding an empty shell of a corporation. Other covenants may require the borrowed funds to be put to specific uses, such as expanding manufacturing capacity or building a new showroom. Covenants that restrict the borrower's actions are called **negative covenants** because they prohibit things. Borrowers can always adhere to negative covenants simply by obeying them.

> **Negative covenants** prohibit some actions by the borrower.

Some covenants require the borrower to maintain specified financial statistics within a limited range. One common focus of these covenants is the current ratio, which is the ratio of current assets to current liabilities. For example, a covenant might require the borrower to maintain a current ratio greater than one. Another common focus is the debt-to-equity ratio, which is the ratio of long-term debt to shareholders' equity. A covenant might require the debt-to-equity ratio to be no greater than two. These types of covenants are called **positive covenants** because they specify some positive result that must be achieved. Borrowers cannot always adhere to positive covenants, even with the best of intentions, because their financial results might be influenced by factors beyond their control.

> **Positive covenants** specify some result that must be achieved.

> **Technical default** results from the failure to maintain the requirements of a positive covenant.

Failure to make the promised payments or violation of a negative covenant puts the borrower in default. Failure to maintain the requirements of a positive covenant puts the borrower in **technical default.** Lenders will often bargain with borrowers in technical default to work out the problems with the debt without enforcing default conditions or penalties.

Rights of the Borrower and Lender in the Absence of Default

Some debt agreements grant the borrower or lender rights beyond the required payments, even in the absence of default. For example, some bonds are callable. **Callable bonds** allow the *issuer* to repurchase them from the holder at specified times for specified prices. **Convertible bonds** allow the *holder* to convert the bond into some other type of financial instrument, for example, common stock, in specified conditions on specified terms.

Rights of the Borrower and Lender in Default

Debt instruments give their holders certain rights if the borrower defaults. Usually, lenders get some decision-making or control authority upon default. In a corporate bankruptcy, where the corporation does not have enough resources to pay all its debts, borrowers may get complete ownership of the corporation.

Many common financial instruments provide the lender with specific collateral or security. **Collateral** or security is assets that the lender can seize if the borrower defaults. Home mortgages have the house as collateral. Car loans have the automobile as collateral. **Unsecured notes** rely on the general creditworthiness of the borrower for their repayment.

Many instruments specify their seniority. **Seniority** specifies the order in which claims are to be paid if default occurs. *Senior debt* must be paid before junior or *subordinated debt.*

Recourse gives the lender the right to look to another party for repayment, if the borrower defaults. Many municipalities in the United States have separate entities for their airports but allow the airport authority to issue bonds that have recourse to the city. If the airport authority defaults, the holders of these bonds can look to the city for repayment.

Collateral is assets that secure the value of the debt instrument in case of borrower default.

Unsecured notes are debt instruments that rely on the general creditworthiness of the borrower.

Classification of Long-Term Financing Instruments

Long-term financing instruments can be classified by whether they have fixed terms, variable terms, or are executory. A financial instrument with fixed terms specifies completely all payments to be made under the instrument. A financial instrument with variable terms gives the rules by which the required payments will be calculated, but the exact amounts are not known until either some choices are made or until some contingencies are resolved. An **executory instrument** imposes duties on both parties to the transaction. Exhibit 12.2 shows how various long-term financing instruments are classified using this framework.

An **executory instrument** imposes duties on both parties to a transaction.

Exhibit 12.2 Classification of Long-Term Financing Instruments

| FIXED TERMS | VARIABLE TERMS | | EXECUTORY |
	Choices	Contingencies	
Standard bank loans	*Issuer:* Callable bonds, Revolving credit agreements	*Amount:* Pensions, Other postretirement employment benefits (OPEBs)	Leases
Many corporate bonds and notes			
Fixed rate mortgages	*Holder:* Convertible bonds, Redeemable bonds	*Terms:* Floating rate notes	

An Example: Northwest Airlines

As an example of a company that has many different types of long-term liabilities, consider Northwest Airlines at December 31, 2001. According to its 10K, Northwest operates the fourth largest airline in the world. It serves more than 145 cities in 24 countries and, in 2001, people boarded Northwest airplanes more than 54.1 million times.

Exhibit 12.3 provides the liabilities section of Northwest's balance sheet. We have highlighted three types of items:[1] Long-Term Debt, Long-Term Obligations under Capital Leases, and Long-Term Pension and Postretirement Health Care Benefits. Both current and noncurrent accounts are associated with long-term debt and obligations under capital leases. **Current maturities of long-term debt** indicates the amount of long-term debt that must be repaid over the coming year. **Long-term debt** indicates the amount of obligations due after the coming year. Therefore, Northwest's obligations under its long-term debt at December 31, 2001, are (in millions):

Many long-term obligations have a related short-term component listed in the current liabilities section.

Current maturities of long-term debt	$ 223
Long-term debt (noncurrent portion)	4,828
Total obligations under long-term debt	$5,051

We will discuss capital leases in more detail later in the chapter. For now, we note that capital leases are debt agreements that package acquisition of an asset with a financing arrangement. Current obligations under capital leases indicates the amount of payments due in the coming year under some of Northwest's leases. Long-term obligations under capital

Exhibit 12.3

Northwest Airlines
Liabilities Section of
Balance Sheet

Northwest Airlines Corporation
Consolidated Balance Sheets (Liabilities section only)
(in millions, except share data)

	DECEMBER 31	
CURRENT LIABILITIES	**2001**	**2000**
Air traffic liability	$ 1,275	$ 1,307
Accrued compensation and benefits	737	549
Accounts payable	691	592
Collections as agent	298	112
Accrued aircraft rent	253	229
Other accrued liabilities	476	476
Current maturities of long-term debt	223	191
Current obligations under capital leases	193	62
Total current liabilities	$ 4,146	$ 3,518
LONG-TERM DEBT	$ 4,828	$ 3,051
LONG-TERM OBLIGATIONS UNDER CAPITAL LEASES	$ 393	$ 494
DEFERRED CREDITS AND OTHER LIABILITIES		
Long-term pension and postretirement health care benefits	$ 1,749	$ 882
Deferred income taxes	1,005	1,353
Other	546	558
Total deferred credits and other liabilities	$ 3,300	$ 2,793
MANDATORILY REDEEMABLE PREFERRED SECURITY OF SUBSIDIARY WHICH HOLDS SOLELY NON-RECOURSE OBLIGATION OF COMPANY (Redemption value 2001, $530; 2000, $610)	$ 492	$ 558
Total long-term liabilities	$ 9,013	$ 6,896
Total liabilities	$13,159	$10,414

Current Maturities of Long-Term Debt and Current Obligations under Capital Leases are both related to long-term obligations.

This aggregates the standard types of long-term debt. Exhibit A12.1.1 in Appendix 12.1 gives the details.

Long-term liabilities that arose under some leases.

Long-term liabilities from pension and other retirement benefits.

[1]Deferred income taxes are the subject of Chapter 14, so we do not discuss them here.

leases give the amount of the obligations due after the coming year. Therefore, Northwest's obligations under its capital lease arrangements at December 31, 2001, are (in millions):

Current obligations under capital leases	$193
Long-term obligations under capital leases	393
Total obligations under capital leases	$586

Long-term pension and postretirement health care benefits are long-term liabilities for promised pension payments and health care benefits to workers in retirement. Given the time spans involved, the uncertainties involving how many workers will survive and stay employed at Northwest long enough to qualify for these benefits, and the uncertainty of future health care costs, these obligations are difficult to estimate. GAAP for them are quite complex, and we will leave them for your future study.

Appendix 12.1 provides more detail on Northwest's liabilities by exploring the notes to its financial statements.

Interest expense is the primary income statement item associated with long-term liabilities. Exhibit 12.4 gives Northwest's income statement for 2001. The two deductions

Exhibit 12.4

Northwest Airlines Income Statement

Northwest Airlines Corporation
Consolidated Statement of Operations
(in millions, except per share amounts)

	DECEMBER 31 2001	2000
OPERATING REVENUES		
Passenger	$ 8,417	$ 9,653
Cargo	720	857
Other	768	730
Total operating revenues	$ 9,905	$11,240
OPERATING EXPENSES		
Salaries, wages and benefits	$ 3,963	$ 3,610
Aircraft fuel and taxes	1,727	1,872
Depreciation and amortization	690	617
Aircraft maintenance materials and repairs	669	640
Other rentals and landing fees	533	513
Commissions	500	663
Aircraft rentals	447	423
Other	2,244	2,333
Total operating expenses	$10,773	$10,671
OPERATING INCOME (LOSS)	$ (868)	$ 569
OTHER INCOME (EXPENSE)		
Airline Stabilization Act funds	$ 461	—
Interest expense	(369)	$ (350)
Interest capitalized	29	23
Interest of mandatorily redeemable preferred security holder	(25)	(27)
Investment income	66	62
Earnings of affiliated companies	(5)	92
Other, net	41	66
Total other income (expense)	$ 198	$ (134)
INCOME (LOSS) BEFORE INCOME TAXES	$ (670)	$ 435
Income tax expense (benefit)	(247)	179
NET INCOME (LOSS)	$ (423)	$ 256

Two categories of interest expense. Northwest probably separates them because of the special nature of the mandatorily redeemable security.

for interest in Northwest's calculation of its net income can be found in Interest Expense and Interest of Mandatorily Redeemable Preferred Security Holder.

Conclusion

The financial instruments that generate liabilities are varied and complex. Further, financial engineers are constantly inventing new types of financial instruments. We now want to consider the economic value of long-term liabilities and then GAAP for them. We cannot consider every kind of long-term liability in this introductory text. Therefore, in the next section, we will discuss the economic value of bonds with fixed terms.

Economic Value of Long-Term Liabilities

OBJECTIVE:

Learn to analyze the economic value of long-term liabilities.

We explore the economic value of liabilities with the case of a long-term liability with fixed terms. We continue the example of the basic corporate bond with a $1,000 face value, a 5% coupon rate, and cash flows as shown in Exhibit 12.1 and Figure 12.1. We assume that all promised payments will surely be made. Recall, the bond is issued on January 1, 2001, and matures December 31, 2006. Coupon payments are made semiannually each June 30 and December 31 during the life of the bond.

When the bond is offered to the market, investors bid in terms of the total amount they are willing to pay for the bond. Suppose investors offer $859.22 for our example bond. Implicit in this price is an interest rate that the market applies in discounting the bond's future cash flows. We will need to determine this **implicit interest rate.**

The annual economic (market) rate of return to the holders of the bond is 8.16% since $(1.04)(1.04) = 1.0816$.

It means that an 8% annual rate of return compounded semiannually is equivalent to a simple rate of return of 8.16% per annum.

The task is to determine the interest rate that makes the present value of the future cash flows of the bond equal to $859.22. Of the many ways to figure out the implicit interest rate, the easiest is probably to use trial and error on different interest rates in a spreadsheet program. Exhibit 12.5 verifies that the price of $859.22 is consistent with a yield of 8%, compounded semiannually. The market determined that an 8% rate (4% every six months) generates an appropriate return for the holders of this bond.

Exhibit 12.5

Present Value of Bond

$\dfrac{\$25}{1.04} = \$24.04$

$\dfrac{\$25}{(1.04)^4} = \$21.37$

$\dfrac{\$1,025}{(1.04)^{12}} = \$640.21$

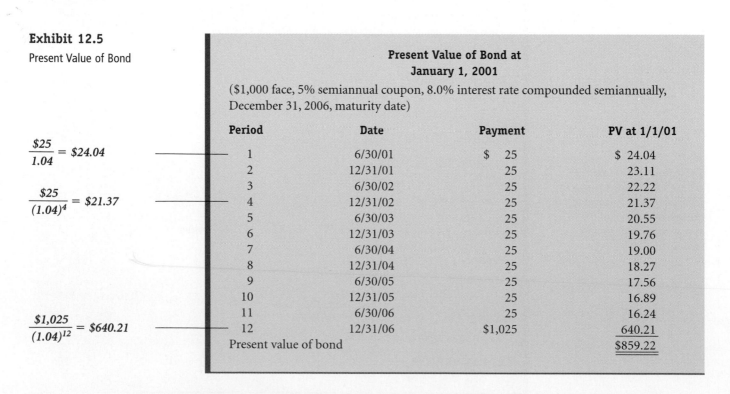

**Present Value of Bond at
January 1, 2001**

($1,000 face, 5% semiannual coupon, 8.0% interest rate compounded semiannually, December 31, 2006, maturity date)

Period	Date	Payment	PV at 1/1/01
1	6/30/01	$ 25	$ 24.04
2	12/31/01	25	23.11
3	6/30/02	25	22.22
4	12/31/02	25	21.37
5	6/30/03	25	20.55
6	12/31/03	25	19.76
7	6/30/04	25	19.00
8	12/31/04	25	18.27
9	6/30/05	25	17.56
10	12/31/05	25	16.89
11	6/30/06	25	16.24
12	12/31/06	$1,025	640.21
Present value of bond			$859.22

The trading floor on a major exchange is a busy place.

We need some terminology about the difference between the price of the bond and its face value. When a bond sells for less than its face value, we say that it sells at a **discount**. The discount on this bond is:

Face value of bond	$1,000.00
Market value of bond	(859.22)
Discount	$ 140.78

When a bond sells for more than its face value, we say it sells at a **premium**.[2]

Just as with an asset, the value of the liability at any point in time is the present value of the remaining cash flows. For example, if the interest rate stays at 8.0% compounded semiannually, the value of the bond over its life will be as shown in Exhibit 12.6. The value of the bond on January 1, 2004 (or on December 31, 2003, just after the coupon payment), would be $921.37, which is equivalent to a discount on the bond of $78.63:

Face value of bonds	$1,000.00
Discount on bonds	(78.63)
Market value of bonds	$ 921.37

The market rate on this bond with semiannual coupon payments would usually be called 8%, even though 8% compounded semiannually provides an annual rate of return of 8.16%. So we see that accountants aren't the only ones with confusing terminology— finance professionals do it, too!

Exhibit 12.6 Present Values of Bond

Present Values of Bond
($1,000 face, 5% semiannual coupon, 8.0% interest rate compounded semiannually, December 31, 2006, maturity date)

Date of Cash Flow	Amount of Cash Flow	Present Value of Cash Flow on Date						
		Jan. 1	December 31					
		2001	2001	2002	2003	2004	2005	2006*
6/30/01	$ 25	$ 24.04						
12/31/01	25	23.11						
6/30/02	25	22.22	$ 24.04					
12/31/02	25	21.37	23.11					
6/30/03	25	20.55	22.22	$ 24.04				
12/31/03	25	19.76	21.37	23.11				
6/30/04	25	19.00	20.55	22.22	$ 24.04			
12/31/04	25	18.27	19.76	21.37	23.11			
6/30/05	25	17.56	19.00	20.55	22.22	$ 24.04		
12/31/05	25	16.89	18.27	19.76	21.37	23.11		
6/30/06	25	16.24	17.56	19.00	20.55	22.22	$ 24.04	
12/31/06	25	15.61	16.89	18.27	19.76	21.37	23.11	
12/31/06	1,000	624.60	675.56	730.69	790.32	854.80	924.56	$1,000.00*
		$859.22	$878.33	$899.01	$921.37	$945.54	$971.71	$1,000.00*

*After last coupon payment, but just before retirement.

[2]If the market determined the interest rate on the example bond to be 3%, the bond would sell for a premium.

Figure 12.2

Economic Value of Bond [$1,000 face, 5% coupon (2 1/2% semiannual), 8.0% interest compounded semi-annually]

NOTE: At maturity the value of the bond is the face amount, $1,000.

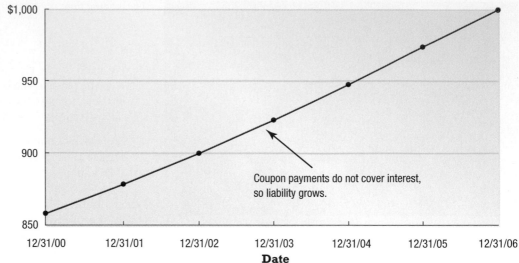

Coupon payments do not cover interest, so liability grows.

Date

The evolution of the value of the bond is plotted in Figure 12.2. Note how the value increases over time. The same thing that causes the bond to sell at a discount in the first place causes the value to increase over time: the coupon payments do not cover all the required interest.

Let's go through this example in detail. Economic interest expense in the first six months of the bond's life is 4% of the initial obligation:

$$\$859.22 \times 0.04 = \$34.37$$

This amount is $9.37 more than the coupon:

$$\$34.37 - \$25.00 = \$9.37$$

Therefore, the value of the obligation grows by $9.37 to $868.59.

Economic interest expense in the next six months would be 4% of the obligation at the beginning of that six-month period:

$$\$868.59 \times 0.04 = \$34.74$$

This amount is $9.74 more than the coupon:

$$\$34.74 - \$25.00 = \$9.74$$

Therefore, the value of the obligation grows by $9.74 to $878.33. This amount is the same value for the bond we got in Exhibit 12.6 at December 31, 2001, except for rounding error. If the market still priced the bond to yield 8% compounded semiannually, on December 31, 2001, the bond would sell for $878.34, which amounts to a discount of $121.66:

Face value of bonds	$1,000.00
Discount on bonds	(121.66)
Market value of bonds	$ 878.34

Let's tie together the computations on interest expense and the behavior of the discount on the bonds. Earlier, we showed that the discount fell from $140.78 to $121.66 over the first year, a decline of $19.12. Except for rounding, it is the same amount we get when we add the shortfall of coupon payments under interest expense for the first year:

	Interest Expense	Coupon Payment	Excess of Interest Expense over Coupon Payment
First six months	$34.37	$(25.00)	$ 9.37
Second six months	34.74	(25.00)	9.74
Total for first year	$69.11	$(50.00)	$19.11

This example demonstrates how the increase in the value of the obligation is the same as the fall in its discount. Both amounts are equal to the difference between the coupon payments and the interest expense on the bond. As we see in the next section, this concept is the key to understanding GAAP for this example bond.

GAAP for Long-Term Liabilities

We introduce GAAP for liabilities by continuing the bond example. In fact, the previous section on economic value contains all the work needed to understand GAAP for the example bond. GAAP views the issuance of the bond as borrowing $859.22 at 8% interest, compounded semiannually, and records the value of the liability and the interest expense just as we calculated for economic values.

The only slight complication is the use of a contra-liability account, Discount on Bonds Payable, to keep track of the liability. When the bond is sold for $859.22, we make the following entry:

Cash	859.22	
Discount on Bonds Payable	140.78	
Bonds Payable		1,000.00

Discount on Bonds Payable is a contra-liability account that is netted against the bonds payable account to show the liability on the balance sheet. The liabilities section of the balance sheet on the date of issuance of the bonds would contain a liability of:

Bonds payable	$1,000.00
Less discount on bonds payable	(140.78)
Bonds payable, net	$ 859.22

Intuitively, what happens is that after 6 months, the bondholder is owed 4% interest. The bond contract lets the issuer pay the holder $9.37 less than what is owed for interest. Therefore, the amount of the issuer's obligation to the bondholder increases by $9.37.

After the date of issuance, we must account for two things each year: the coupon payments and interest expense. It is convenient to take care of both these things at the time the coupon payments are made. For example, consider the first coupon payment. Cash goes down by $25.00. If we record interest expense of 4% of 859.22, or $34.37, at the same time, the amount we need to balance the entry is the amount of the increase in the obligation. We recognize the increase in the obligation by decreasing, or *amortizing*, the discount. Here's the entry:

Interest Expense	34.37	
Discount on Bonds Payable		9.37
Cash		25.00

Continuing with the entry for the second coupon payment, we have:

Interest Expense	34.74	
Discount on Bonds Payable		9.74
Cash		25.00

In total, over the first year we record $50.00 in coupon payments, $69.11 in interest expense, and increase the liability by $19.11 by amortizing the Discount on Bonds Payable. These entries leave the amount of the liability on the balance sheet at $878.33:

Bonds payable	$1,000.00
Less discount on bonds payable	(121.67)
Bonds payable, net	$ 878.33

This is the same as the economic value of the bond at the end of the first year of its life, as shown in Exhibit 12.6.

So we see that GAAP follow the economic value logic we presented in the previous section. To minimize the possibility of confusion about the discount amortization, Exhibit 12.7 on page 226 contains all the calculations that drive the accounting entries.

GAAP Interest Expense and Liability Value for Example Bond

($1,000 face, 5% semiannual coupon, 8.0% interest rate compounded semiannually, December 31, 2006, maturity date)

From	To	Beginning Balance	Interest Expense	Coupon Payment	Discount Amortization	Ending Balance
1/1/01	6/30/01	$859.22	$ 34.37	$ 25.00	$ 9.37	$ 868.59
7/1/01	12/31/01	868.59	34.74	25.00	9.74	878.33
1/1/02	6/30/02	878.34	35.13	25.00	10.13	888.47
7/1/02	12/31/02	888.47	35.54	25.00	10.54	899.01
1/1/03	6/30/03	899.01	35.96	25.00	10.96	909.97
7/1/03	12/31/03	909.97	36.40	25.00	11.40	921.37
1/1/04	6/30/04	921.37	36.85	25.00	11.85	933.22
7/1/04	12/31/04	933.22	37.33	25.00	12.33	945.55
1/1/05	6/30/05	945.55	37.82	25.00	12.82	958.37
7/1/05	12/31/05	958.37	38.33	25.00	13.33	971.70
1/1/06	6/30/06	971.71	38.87	25.00	13.87	985.58
7/1/06	12/31/06	985.58	39.42	25.00	14.42	1,000.00
Totals			$440.76	$300.00	$140.76	

Exhibit 12.7

GAAP
Interest Expense and Liability
Value for Example Bond

Note how the discount amortization accelerates through time, which is caused by the increasing interest expense relative to the constant coupon payment.

Notice how over the life of the bond, the total discount of $140.76 is completely amortized (there is $0.02 of rounding error), and the total interest expense of $440.76 is equal to the coupon payments of $300 plus the amortized discount of $140.76. The liability for the bond ends up at $1,000 just before it is retired.

All this accounting goes forward regardless of what happens to the market value of the bond. GAAP take the interest rate implied by the initial issuance of the bond and make all subsequent interest expense and discount amortization entries using that interest rate. We will explore the possibility that the market rate might change in the *Comparison of GAAP and Economic Values* section.

Before turning to that analysis, we need to discuss two additional GAAP topics. First, to round out our treatment of GAAP, we should discuss a liability that is more complex than the coupon bond example we focused on. We choose to discuss leases briefly because they are commonly encountered.

The second thing we should discuss is the retirement of liabilities. Just as with retiring assets, the difference between the book value and the market value of a liability can generate a gain or loss.

Operating and Capital Leases

Leases are executory contracts (exchanges of promises to do things in the future). GAAP usually do not recognize obligations arising out of such contracts as liabilities.

In many industries, **leases** are important methods of acquiring assets, and it is worthwhile to spend some time discussing them.

The key to understanding leases is to recognize the difference between purchasing and renting. Think about the different ways people acquire housing. Most students are tenants who rent a room or an apartment. In exchange for making monthly payments, the tenant receives the shelter and convenience of the dwelling. Usually, a formal rental document, or lease, spells out the rights and duties of the landlord and the tenant.

Other people buy their houses. Most people don't have enough spare cash to buy their houses outright, so they obtain a mortgage from a lending institution. The lending institution supplies the money for the buyer's purchase. In exchange, the buyer makes monthly payments to the lender. The buyer also receives the shelter and convenience of the dwelling. So think of the difference between renting and buying from the point of view of the person needing housing. Both buying and renting require monthly payments and give access to a dwelling.

The big difference between buying and renting comes at the end of the transactions. After making the last mortgage payment, the purchaser of a house owns it. A tenant who has made the last lease payment has to move out. This difference may not be important because the provisions of a lease can make it a virtual purchase. For example, consider "leasing" a house from a bank with a lease whose term and payments are identical to those of a mortgage on the house. Include in the lease a clause that gives the tenant the right to buy the house for $1 at the end of its term. This agreement is a lease only in the title of the document recording it. For all practical purposes, it is a purchase using a mortgage.

Operating leases are not treated as liabilities.

Why is this distinction important? A lease that is considered a rental agreement is called an **operating lease.** The only accounting entries made are to record periodic rent expense. No asset or liability is recognized.

Capital leases are executory contracts for which the underlying obligation is shown as a liability.

A lease that is considered a purchase is called a **capital lease,** and it is recorded as a purchase under GAAP. Recording a purchase involves recognizing an asset (the cost of the thing being leased) and a liability (the obligation to pay all of the future lease payments) and recording periodic depreciation or amortization expense on the asset and interest expense on the liability. The classification of a lease as an operating or capital lease affects the assets and liabilities shown on the balance sheet and the classification (and the timing) of the expenses shown on the income statement.

A lease may or may not create a liability under GAAP. GAAP specify criteria for deciding whether a lease is a capital lease that creates a liability or an operating lease, which does not. Satisfaction of any one of the following three criteria requires treating a lease as a capital lease.

1. The lease lasts for at least 75% of the expected useful life of the leased property.
2. The present value of the lease payments is at least 90% of the value of the property.
3. The lease contains a bargain purchase clause that allows the lessee to buy the asset at below market price at any time during the lease.

Financing Option 3 in Appendix 12.2 is just like a capital lease with level lease payments.

If a lease meets any of these criteria and must be treated as a capital lease, the lessee must record a liability equal to the present value of the payments under the lease and an asset of equal value. Interest expense is assessed on the book value of the liability at the rate in effect at the time the lease was signed. The leased asset is depreciated if it is tangible or amortized if it is intangible. The depreciation or amortization is calculated using one of the standard GAAP methods discussed in Chapter 11.

If the lease is an operating lease, no journal entry would be made when the lease was entered into. At the end of each year a journal entry would be made to record Rent (Lease) Expense and Cash would be credited (decreased) by the same amount. We will further explore capital leases in the *Financial Statement Analysis of Long-Term Liabilities* section of this chapter.

Retirement of Long-Term Liabilities

Retiring long-term liabilities is just like retiring an asset. Their book value must be eliminated, and the consideration given up must be recorded. Any difference between the book value of the liabilities retired and the consideration given up is a gain or loss.

If the debt is retired at its maturity, no gain or loss exists. The amount owed at maturity is the face value of the debt, and GAAP ensure that the amount of the liability in the accounts is equal to the face value at the maturity date. For instance, if the example $1,000, 5% coupon bond with maturity date of December 31, 2006, is retired on its maturity date, the book value of the bond is $1,000 (see Exhibit 12.7), and the discount is fully amortized. The entry to record the retirement is

Bonds Payable 1,000.00
    Cash 1,000.00

If a bond is retired at a date other than its maturity date, a gain or loss may be incurred. To signal its special nature, which we discuss more fully in the next section, the gain or loss on retirement of debt is treated in a special way. These gains and losses are separated from other income items and are clearly labeled as extraordinary gains and losses.

For example, suppose the bond whose book values are reported in Exhibit 12.7 is retired at the close of business on January 1, 2004, by buying it from its holder on the bond market for $873.11. (You will see where this number comes from in the next section.) From Exhibit 12.7, the bond has a book value on January 1, 2004, of $921.37. This book value is the difference between the face value of $1,000 and the discount, so we know the book value of the discount at January 1, 2004, must be

Face value of bond	$1,000.00
Less discount on bond payable on 1/1/04	X
Book value of liability on 1/1/04	$ 921.37

Solving for X, we see that the discount on January 1, 2004, must be $78.63. Therefore, the entry to retire the bond is

Bonds Payable	1,000.00	
Discount on Bonds Payable		78.63
Cash		873.11
Gain on Retirement of Bonds		48.26

On the other hand, if the bond was retired on January 1, 2004, by purchasing it in the market for $1,000, a loss would be recorded through the following entry:

Bonds Payable	1,000.00	
Loss on Retirement of Bonds	78.63	
Discount on Bonds Payable		78.63
Cash		1,000.00

Although these entries are used to record the retirement of bonds, whether the retirement is good or bad for the firm retiring the bonds is not clear. We address this issue in the next section, which compares the GAAP and economic values.

Review Questions

1. Give the entry to record the issuance for $95 of a bond with a $100 face value.

2. Give the entry to record the issuance for $105 of a bond with a $100 face value. Use an account called Premium on Bonds Payable to record the difference between the face value and the amount received.

3. Suppose the coupon on the bond in step 2 is 8% payable semiannually. Suppose the market rate of interest implicit in the price of $105 is 6% compounded semiannually. Give the entry to record the payment of the first coupon and the interest expense over the first six months of the bond's life. Show how the account Premium on Bonds Payable is amortized.

4. Why are some leases recorded like purchases with financing combined?

5. What are the two types of leases recognized by GAAP, and what tests are used to distinguish between them?

6. Explain how a gain or loss on retirement of bonds arises.

OBJECTIVE:
Learn to relate GAAP for long-term liabilities to the underlying economics of these liabilities.

Comparison of GAAP and Economic Values

As long as the interest rate remains unchanged, the book value of a long-term liability with fixed terms equals its market value. Therefore, the market-to-book ratio of the bond is 1, as long as the interest rate does not change from the date of its issuance.

Recall: The bond was issued on January 1, 2001, and matures on December 31, 2006. The coupon rate is 5% (paid semiannually at the rate of 2.5%) and the bond was originally sold for $859.22. The interest rate implicit in this price is 8% compounded semiannually.

The interesting issues arise when interest rates change, so let's consider a couple of scenarios for the example bond with $1,000 face value from the previous sections. Suppose the interest rate appropriate for the bond unexpectedly changes to 5%, compounded semiannually, on January 1, 2004. The bond would then sell for its face value of $1,000 because the market interest rate just exactly coincides with the coupon rate. That is, the value of the bond in the market would jump *up* from $921.37 to $1,000.00 when the interest rate *falls* from 8% (compounded semiannually) to 5% (compounded semiannually). If the borrower wanted to retire the bond, it would have to come up with $921.37 to repurchase the bond just before the interest rate falls, but it would have to pay $1,000.00 just after the interest rate falls. The evolution of the economic value of the bond with this unexpected fall in interest rates is plotted in Figure 12.3.

Figure 12.3

Economic Value of Bond [$1,000 face, 5% coupon, initially sold to yield 8% (compounded semiannually), market drops to 5% (compounded semiannually)]

NOTE: On 12/31/03 the market value of the bond jumps to par, $1,000, because the market rate equals the coupon rate.

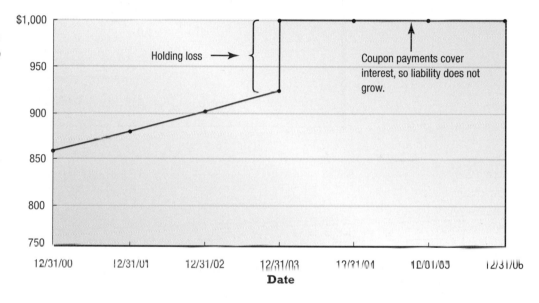

Because the bond is a liability, the fall in the interest rate generates a holding loss for its issuer. Think of it this way. The issuer in effect borrowed at 8%. If it would have waited, it could have borrowed at 5%. The promised payments of a 5% coupon and a $1,000 face would have brought $1,000 in the bond market if the interest rate were 5%. No discount would have been applied because the coupon payments cover the required interest, and the borrower would have received more cash for the same promised payments.

Another way to say it is that the borrower must pay the loan back with more expensive current dollars.

What if, instead of falling to 5%, the interest rate *rose* unexpectedly from 8% (compounded semiannually) to 10% (compounded semiannually) on January 1, 2004? As verified in Exhibit 12.8 on page 230, the value of the bond in the market would *fall* on January 1, 2004, to $873.11. (Now you see where we got this number in the last section!) If the borrower wanted to retire the bond just after this interest rate increase, it would have to come up with only $873.11 to buy back the bond on the market (even though it has the liability listed at $921.37 in its balance sheet).

The evolution of the economic value of the bond with this unexpected increase in interest rates is plotted in Figure 12.4 on page 230.

Another way to say it is that the borrower must pay the loan back with cheaper current dollars.

Because the bond is a liability, the increase in the interest rate generates a holding gain for its issuer. Think of it this way: The issuer in effect borrowed at 8%. If the issuer waited, it would borrow at 10%. The promised coupon payments would bring in less cash from the bond market, and a greater gap would separate the amount of the coupon payments from the required interest. The bond would sell for a deeper (i.e., bigger) discount.

An inverse relation, then, characterizes the relationship between the changes in interest rates and the value of bonds in the market. This relation presents implications for borrowers and for users of financial statements. As discussed in the previous section, GAAP for bonds do not keep up with changing interest rates. A change in the interest

Exhibit 12.8

Present Values of Bond

Present Values of Bond

($1,000 face, 5% semiannual coupon, 10% interest rate compounded semiannually, December 31, 2006, maturity date)

Date of Cash Flow	Amount of Cash Flow	Present Value of Cash Flow on Date			
		Jan. 1	December 31		
		2004	2004	2005	2006*
6/30/04	$ 25	$ 23.81			
12/31/04	25	22.68			
6/30/05	25	21.60	$ 23.81		
12/31/05	25	20.57	22.68		
6/30/06	25	19.59	21.60	$ 23.81	
12/31/06	25	18.66	20.57	22.68	
12/31/06	1,000	746.20	822.70	907.03	$1,000.00*
		$873.11	$911.36	$953.52	$1,000.00*

*After last coupon payment, but just before retirement.

Figure 12.4

Economic Value of Bond [$1,000 face, 5% semiannual coupon, 8% followed by 10% (compounded semiannually) market rate of interest, matures 12/31/06]

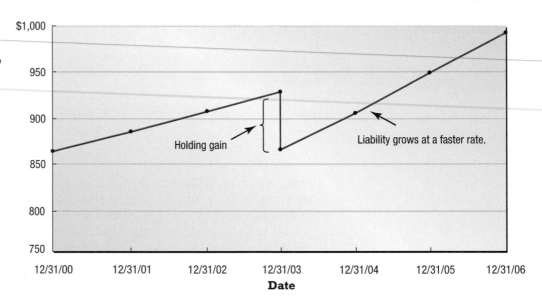

rate, therefore, opens a gap between the bond's market value and its book value. This shift in interest rates causes the market-to-book ratio of the bond to move away from 1 and opens the opportunity to recognize accounting gains or losses by retiring the bond.

We should keep in mind that we are talking about the bond from the borrower's point of view. A market-to-book ratio of less than 1 is good news for the borrower. A market-to-book ratio of more than 1 is bad news. If interest rates fall, the market-to-book of the bond will go above 1. It is bad news for the borrower, because it indicates that a lower rate could have been obtained by waiting to borrow. If interest rates rise, the market-to-book of the bond will go below 1. It is good news for the borrower, because it indicates that a lower rate was obtained by borrowing earlier.

Again, consider an unexpected fall in interest rates to 5% on January 1, 2004. We noted that the bond would then sell for its face value of $1,000. Its book value, however, would be $921.37. If the bond were retired, a loss on retirement of bonds of $78.63 would be recorded as shown in the section on GAAP. As mentioned earlier, the loss on retirement of bonds gets special treatment on the income statement. It is pulled out and labeled *extraordinary.*

If all retirements of bonds resulted in losses, a requirement to label them as extraordinary would be unlikely. However, consider what would happen if the example bond was retired after its interest rate rose to 10% on January 1, 2004. We showed how to record the gain of $48.26 in the section on GAAP (see page 228).

But is capturing this gain really a good thing for the issuer? Although an issuer may have good reasons to retire bonds, we need to think about the economics behind this transaction. Suppose that the borrower simply issued another bond to raise the cash necessary to retire the example bond. The market would charge an interest rate of 10% on this new borrowing. The net effect would be that the borrower would take out a loan of $873.11 at 10% to buy back a promised stream of cash outflows that should be discounted at 10% to yield a present value of $873.11! Does that sound circular? It is! No gain, economically speaking, results from the exchange of cash flow streams with the same present value. GAAP records a gain only because it failed to record the cause of the situation, which is the change in the interest rate. The borrower is better off for having borrowed at 8% instead of 10%, but that benefit accrues when the interest rate changes, not when the bonds are retired. GAAP, however, do not count things that way.

By ignoring the effects of the change in interest rates, GAAP create a gap (pun intended!) between book values and market values. Anytime such a disparity exists, it can be closed by engaging in a transaction. When interest rates rose dramatically in the 1970s, the market value of corporate bonds fell. Some companies borrowed to retire bonds in order to show a gain on their books. To do so, they paid investment bankers fees to execute the borrowing and retirement transactions. The costs of these transactions impose a loss on shareholders. But GAAP recorded a gain on the transaction. To call attention to this problem, the FASB required reporting gains and losses on the retirement of bonds as extraordinary items.

GAAP's failure to keep up with changing interest rates for liabilities also affects accounting returns on equity. To work through this issue, look again at Figure 12.3. With fixed terms, the bond's market value and its book value must get to $1,000 just before its retirement. When interest rates fall unexpectedly, the borrower realizes a holding loss on bonds. But interest expense is then less in subsequent periods. GAAP make up for their failure to recognize the holding loss by recognizing too much interest expense in the remaining periods of the bond's life.

Reexamine Figure 12.4; again, because the bond has fixed terms, both its market and book values must get to $1,000 just before its retirement. If interest rates increase, GAAP's failure to recognize the holding gain must be offset by recognizing too little interest expense in the remaining periods of the bond's life.

These complications are only a few of the many involving liabilities. Investment bankers and others are busily cooking up all kinds of hybrid and derivative securities, and it is beyond the scope of this book to cover them in more detail. We have, however, laid out the basic issues involving accounting for liabilities.

In the next section, we consider some of the financial statistics that are used in analyzing liabilities.

So even though many of these "exchanges" were economically neutral, when transactions costs (which may be substantial) are considered these exchanges were not in the economic best interests of shareholders.

Financial Statement Analysis of Long-Term Liabilities

OBJECTIVE:

Learn to become familiar with some common financial statistics related to long-term liabilities.

Many important financial statistics involve long-term liabilities and interest expense. **Times-interest-earned** is earnings before interest and taxes divided by interest expense. It gives an indication of whether earnings are sufficient to at least pay the interest on debt. Times-interest-earned for Northwest Airlines for 2000 can be calculated from its income statement given in Exhibit 12.4.[3] We see that interest expense, including interest

[3]We do not use 2001 because Northwest had a loss that year.

on the preferred redemable stock, was $393 million ($368 million + $25 million), whereas Income Before Income Taxes was $435 million. Earnings before taxes and interest was

$$\$435 + \$393 = \$828 \text{ million}$$

Times-interest-earned is

$$\frac{\text{Net income before interest and taxes}}{\text{Interest expense}} = \frac{\$828}{\$393} = 2.11 \text{ times}$$

Northwest could have paid 2.11 times the interest it actually did in 2000 without reporting a net loss.

Times-interest-earned is an indication of how the flow of resources from operations compares to the flow of resources required to pay interest on debt.

Measures of the stock of liabilities include the ratio of debt to equity. The **debt-to-equity ratio** is calculated in various ways. One common method is to divide noncurrent liabilities by stockholders' equity. The equity section of Northwest Airlines' balance sheet is given in Exhibit 12.9.

The larger the amount of interest-bearing liabilities in the balance sheet, the more difficult it will be for the company to meet the interest payments.

Exhibit 12.9

Northwest Airlines
Equity Section of Balance Sheet

Northwest Airlines Corporation		
Consolidated Balance Sheets (Equities section only)		
(in millions, except share data)		
	DECEMBER 31	
PREFERRED REDEEMABLE STOCK	**2001**	**2000**
(Liquidation value 2001—$228; 2000—$233)	227	232
COMMITMENTS AND CONTINGENCIES		
COMMON STOCKHOLDERS' EQUITY (DEFICIT)		
Common stock, $0.01 par value; shares authorized— 315,000,000; shares issued (2001—110,344,796; 2000—110,088,522)	1	1
Additional paid-in capital	1,451	1,459
Accumulated deficit	(518)	(94)
Accumulated other comprehensive income (loss)	(305)	(5)
Treasury stock (2001—25,136,582 shares; 2000—26,994,364 shares)	(1,060)	(1,130)
Total common stockholders' equity (deficit)	(431)	231
Total equities (deficit)	(204)	463

Generously counted!

Even by including the preferred redeemable stock, Northwest's book equity is negative at December 31, 2001, and a very small $463 million at December 31, 2002. From Exhibit 12.3, Northwest's total long-term liabilities at December 31, 2000, were $10,414 million. This would give it a debt-to-equity ratio of:[4]

$$\$10,414/\$463 = 22.5$$

[4]Although it serves to demonstrate the calculations and to show us that the debt-to-equity ratio can get very large because equity can be small (or negative!), Northwest's debt-to-equity ratio is not very representative. Minnesota Mining and Manufacturing (3M) has a more typical debt-to-equity ratio. On December 31, 1999, 3M had total noncurrent liabilities of $3,788 million and total shareholders' equity of $6,289 million. This gives a debt-to-equity ratio of $3,788 ÷ $6,289 = 0.602.

*"Tricks" that keep financial obligations off of the balance sheet are referred to as **off-balance-sheet financing.***

Our treatment of Northwest's preferred redeemable stock is highly suspect. This sounds more like debt than equity, but we have included it in equity and excluded it from debt. Northwest's leases are also a source of concern. For leases classified as capital leases, a liability for the lease payments is put on the balance sheet and interest expense is recognized. For leases classified as operating leases, no liability is put on the balance sheet and no interest expense is recorded. The GAAP classification of leases as capital or operating is crude. Financial engineers easily can design leases that fail the tests for a capital lease by a small margin. These leases may be more like capital leases in reality but classified as operating leases for GAAP purposes. Fortunately, required disclosures about leases can help us out here.

Exhibit 12.10 contains excerpts from Note 4—Leases to Northwest's financial statements. Aside from showing the payments required under capital leases, the disclosure also provides the minimum payments required under noncancelable operating leases. As you can see from Exhibit 12.10, Northwest has far more commitments under noncancelable operating leases than it does under capital leases.

Figure 12.10

Northwest Airlines
Excerpt from Note 4

Excerpt from Note 4—Leases to Northwest Airlines' Financial Statements

At December 31, 2000, future minimum lease payments under capital leases and noncancelable operating leases with initial or remaining terms of more than one year were as follows (in millions):

	Capital Leases	Operating Leases
2001	$106	$ 655
2002	280	668
2003	87	650
2004	62	641
2005	51	622
Thereafter	146	5,924
	$732	$9,160
Less sublease rental income		(516)
Total minimum operating lease payments		$8,644
Less amounts representing interest	(176)	
Present value of future minimum capital lease payments	$556	
Less current obligations under capital leases	(62)	
Long-term obligations under capital leases	$494	

In analyzing financial statements, particularly when it comes to a question of solvency, it is important to look for obligations not on the balance sheet. Footnotes in the financial statements often provide clues to information that may not be directly disclosed.

We can use these disclosures to include recognition of a liability under noncancelable operating leases in Northwest's financial statements. To put the commitments under noncancelable operating leases on the same footing as capital leases, we estimate the present value of the minimum payments given in Exhibit 12.10. We need to use the information on capital leases to form an estimate of the interest rate to use in calculating a present value.

The capital lease information gives us a series of payments starting in 2001 that have a present value of $556 million. We will have to cope with the fact that the payments

Exhibit 12.11

Note Excerpt

Excerpt from Note 4—Leases to Northwest Airlines' Financial Statements

. . . Expiration dates range from 2002 to 2009 for aircraft under capital leases, and from 2001 to 2023 under operating leases.

after 2005 are not given year-by-year, but simply are listed as "Thereafter." However, some information in Note 4 that will help is given in Exhibit 12.11.

Although we don't know exactly the amount of the payments from 2006 onward, we can put some bounds on them. One extreme would be to assume that all the payments will be made in 2006. Alternatively, we could assume that the "Thereafter" payments occur evenly in each year from 2006 through 2009. We can use a spreadsheet program to solve for the interest rate that gives each stream of payments a present value of $556 million. We could use an estimate of the interest rate between these two values. Exhibit 12.12 provides the details.[5] The calculations there suggest that an estimated interest rate of 9.2% would be pretty close.

Exhibit 12.12

Estimation of Interest Rate for Lease Capitalization

	CASE 1		CASE 2	
Year	Payment	Present Value	Payment	Present Value
2001	$106.0	$ 96.75	$106.0	$ 97.36
2002	280.0	233.29	280.0	236.22
2003	87.0	66.16	87.0	67.42
2004	62.0	43.04	62.0	44.13
2005	51.0	32.31	51.0	33.34
2006	146.0	84.44	36.5	21.92
2007			36.5	20.13
2008			36.5	18.49
2009			36.5	16.98
Total present value		$555.99		$555.99
Interest rate		9.56%	Interest rate	8.87%

Exhibit 12.13 shows two estimates of the present value of the payments under non-cancelable operating leases using 9.2% as the interest rate. The low estimate is $4,341.8 million for the assumption that the "Thereafter" payments are spread equally from 2006 through 2023. The high estimate is $6,004.2 million for the assumption that all the "Thereafter" payments must be made in 2006. The truth is somewhere in between, but $5,200 million is not a bad guess. We should think about that a bit—it is $5.2 billion! Adding this amount to their liabilities of $10,414 million would give Northwest total long-term liabilities of

$$\$10,414 + \$5,200 = \$15,614$$

Northwest's already astronomical debt-to-equity ratio at December 31, 2000, would go to

$$\frac{\$15,614}{\$463} = 33.7$$

[5]This estimation can be done either by trial and error on the interest rate or with a built-in function, such as Excel's **Goal seek** or **Solver.**

Exhibit 12.13

Present Value of Operating Lease Payments

Estimates of Present Value of Operating Lease Payments
Interest Rate 9.2%

Year	Case 1 Payment	Case 1 Present Value	Case 2 Payment	Case 2 Present Value
2001	$ 655.0	$ 599.82	$655.0	$ 599.82
2002	668.0	560.18	668.0	560.18
2003	650.0	499.17	650.0	499.17
2004	641.0	450.78	641.0	450.78
2005	622.0	400.57	622.0	400.57
2006	5,924.0	3,493.65	329.1	194.09
2007			329.1	177.74
2008			329.1	162.77
2009			329.1	149.05
2010			329.1	136.49
2011			329.1	125.00
2012			329.1	114.46
2013			329.1	104.82
2014			329.1	95.99
2015			329.1	87.90
2016			329.1	80.50
2017			329.1	73.72
2018			329.1	67.50
2019			329.1	61.82
2020			329.1	56.61
2021			329.1	51.81
2022			329.1	47.47
2023			329.1	43.47
Estimated liability		$6,004.20		$4,341.80

Conclusion

GAAP for long-term debt follow economics, as long as interest rates are constant. The liability shown on a GAAP balance sheet for a standard debt instrument with fixed terms is the present value of its future cash flows. Interest expense is the interest rate times the beginning balance of the liability.

When interest rates change, GAAP do not. This creates a disparity between the book values of liabilities and their economic values. Engaging in a transaction can close this disparity and result in a gain or loss on the income statement. Such gains and losses must be classified as "extraordinary" in the United States.

The financial instruments and transactions that create long-term liabilities can be quite complex. Financial engineers are constantly inventing new tools for raising money, and we can expect GAAP to be ever-evolving in this area. That evolution just makes it more important than ever to do our best at understanding how the economic values of liabilities behave, how book values are calculated, and how the book and economic values are related.

In the next chapter, we focus on equities. Equities are alternatives to debt for raising funds to be used over the long haul. Equity instruments also can be quite complex, and we will introduce some of the complexities in addition to covering the basics.

Key Terms

callable bonds *219*

capital lease *227*

collateral *219*

convertible bonds *219*

coupon rate *217*

covenants *218*

current maturities of long-term debt *220*

date of issuance *217*

debt-to-equity ratio *232*

default *217*

discount on bonds *223*

executory instrument *219*

face value *217*

financial instruments *216*

floating rates *218*

implicit interest rate *222*

leases *226*

LIBOR *218*

long-term debt *220*

long-term liabilities *216*

maturity date *217*

negative covenants *218*

off-balance-sheet financing *233*

operating lease *227*

positive covenants *218*

premium on bonds *223*

recourse *219*

senior debt *219*

seniority *219*

subordinated debt *219*

technical default *218*

times-interest-earned *231*

unsecured notes *219*

zero-coupon bonds *217*

Appendix 12.1: More Detail on Northwest's Liabilities

Let us look more closely at Northwest Airlines' liabilities. We begin with a brief discussion of its current liabilities, then move to its long-term debt.

Current Liabilities

Even though Exhibit 12.3 (the liabilities section of Northwest's balance sheet) shows its current liabilities, we did not discuss them much in the body of the chapter. Recall from Chapter 2 that current liabilities are liabilities that must be discharged within one year of the balance sheet date. Northwest's current liabilities reflect the nature of its business. *Air Traffic Liability* represents tickets for air travel that consumers bought and paid for but have not yet used. Northwest has an obligation to either carry the holders of those tickets to their destinations or refund the tickets. *Accrued Compensation and Benefits, Accrued Aircraft Rent,* and *Other Accrued Liabilities* represent amounts for goods and services that Northwest consumed but for which it has not yet paid. *Accounts Payable* represents goods and services that Northwest bought on credit from the suppliers of those goods and services. *Collections as Agent* represents amounts that Northwest collected as a representative of another organization, such as another airline. Northwest must remit these amounts to that other organization. We already discussed *Current Maturities of Long-Term Debt* and *Current Obligations under Capital Leases.*

As we saw in Part 1 of this book, the accounting for current liabilities mainly involves making appropriate adjustments to recognize and value them. Except for the current portion of long-term obligations, explicit recognition of interest expense on current liabilities is typically not done. The idea is that current liabilities are outstanding for such a short period of time that interest is immaterial.

Exhibit A12.1.1

Northwest Airlines
Note Explaining Composition Of
Long-Term Debt and Short-Term
Borrowings

Excerpts from Note 3 to Northwest Airlines' Financial Statements
NOTE 3—LONG-TERM DEBT AND SHORT-TERM BORROWINGS
Long-term debt consisted of the following (in millions,
with interest rates as of December 31, 2000):

	DECEMBER 31	
	2001	2000
Unsecured notes due 2004 through 2039, 8.5% weighted-average rate	$1,291	$ 990
Revolving Credit Facilities due 2005, 4.1%	962	—
Pass-through trust certificates due through 2019, 7.8% weighted-average rate	820	579
Equipment pledge notes due through 2013, 4.1% weighted-average rate	654	300
Secured notes due through 2009, 3.2% weighted-average rate	339	349
Aircraft notes due through 2016, 6.0% weighted-average rate	315	331
NWA Trust No. 2 aircraft notes due through 2012, 9.8% weighted-average rate	230	241
Sale-leaseback financing obligations due through 2020, 9.9% imputed rate	219	223
NWA Trust No. 1 aircraft notes due through 2006, 8.6% weighted-average rate	141	161
Other	80	68
Total debt	5,051	3,242
Less current maturities	223	191
Long-term debt	$4,828	$3,051

Long-Term Liabilities

Let us look at the components of long-term debt a bit closer. Exhibit A12.1.1 contains excerpts from Northwest's financial statements' Note 3—Long-Term Debt and Short-Term Borrowings.

As is suggested by Exhibit A12.1.1, long-term liabilities come in quite complex forms. Northwest's long-term liabilities include Unsecured Notes, Revolving Credit Facilities, Secured Notes, Aircraft Notes, and Sale-Leaseback Financing Obligations.

Unsecured Notes

Unsecured notes are most likely standard financial instruments with fixed face values, maturity dates, and coupon rates. These bonds and notes are unsecured, therefore no specific assets would go to the note holder should Northwest default. The holders of unsecured bonds and notes are relying on Northwest's general ability to repay its debts (creditworthiness) for their repayment. Northwest lists its liability at December 31, 2001, under Unsecured Notes as $1,291 million with a weighted average interest rate of 8.5%. Exhibit A12.1.2 on page 238 contains more information about these notes from Note 3.

Revolving Credit Facilities

A *revolving credit facility,* or *revolver,* is an agreement that allows the borrower to acquire and repay funds repeatedly, as long as the net amount outstanding remains less than a specified maximum. Northwest has borrowed $962 million under such arrangements, at an interest rate of 4.1%. Other information in Note 3 to Northwest's financial statements about these revolvers is given in Exhibit A12.1.2.

Northwest has several types of secured notes. *Secured Notes* give the holder the rights to take specific Northwest assets should Northwest default. Exhibit A12.1.1 shows that

Exhibit A12.1.2

Note Explaining Revolving
Credit Facilities

Excerpts from Note 3 to Northwest Airlines' Financial Statements

The Company's unsecured credit facilities were amended on October 23, 2001. The amended secured credit agreement consists of (i) a $725 million revolving facility ($13 milion of which has been utilized as letters of credit as of December 31, 2001) available until October 2005, and (ii) a $250 million 364-day revolving credit facility expiring in October 2002 and renewable annually at the option of the lenders; however, to the extent any portion of the $250 million facility is not renewed for an additional 364-day period, the Company may borrow up to the entire non-renewed portion of the facility and such borrowings would then mature in October 2005. This credit agreement is secured by the Company's Pacific route system and certain aircraft. Borrowings under these secured credit facilities currently bear interest at a variable rate equal to the three-month London Interbank Offered Rate ("LIBOR") plus 2.0% (4.1% at December 31, 2001). Commitment fees are payable by the Company on the unused portion of the revolving credit facilities at a variable rate equal to .35% per annum at December 31, 2001, and are not considered material.

Exhibit A12.1.3

Northwest Airlines
Note Explaining Credit Covenant

Excerpts from Note 3 to Northwest Airlines' Financial Statements about Covenants

The credit agreement contains certain financial covenants, including limitations on indebtedness . . ., equity redemptions and dividends, as well as requirements to maintain a certain level of liquidity. . . . At December 31, 2001, the Company was in compliance with the covenants of all of its credit agreements.

Northwest has Secured Notes, Aircraft Notes, and Equipment Pledge Notes. These notes have fixed terms and include aircraft and equipment as collateral. For example, aircraft and other assets with a total book value of $4.6 billion at December 31, 2001, are pledged as collateral.

Some of Northwest's financial instruments contain covenants. Exhibit A12.1.3 outlines some of these restrictions.

Leases get separate disclosure in Northwest's financial statements. Northwest Airlines has both operating and capital leases. Exhibit A12.1.4 contains excerpts from the Northwest financial statements' Note 4—Leases.

Exhibit A12.1.4

Northwest Airlines
Note Explaining Leases

Excerpts from Note 4 to Northwest's Financial Statements

On December 31, 2001, the Company leased 129 of the 428 aircraft it operates. Of these, 21 were capital leases and 108 were operating leases.

The capital leases result in the recognition of assets and liabilities on Northwest's balance sheet. We showed on page 221 that Northwest's liabilities in Exhibit 12.3 include total obligations under capital leases that amount to $586 million. Exhibit A12.1.5 shows the asset side of Northwest's balance sheet. We see that flight equipment under capital leases has a net book value of $565 million at December 31, 2001.

Exhibit 12.4 shows Northwest's income statement. Operating leases generate rent expense that is included in Other Rentals and Landing Fees and Aircraft Rentals. Capital leases generate interest expense and amortization that is included in Depreciation and Amortization.

Exhibit A12.1.5

Northwest Airlines
Balance Sheet—Assets

Northwest Airlines Corporation
Consolidated Balance Sheets (Asset side only)
(amounts in millions)

	DECEMBER 31	
ASSETS	2001	2000
CURRENT ASSETS		
Cash and cash equivalents	$ 2,512	$ 693
Restricted short-term investments	100	35
Accounts receivable, less allowance (2001—$20; 2000—$16)	512	534
Flight equipment spare parts, less allowance (2001—$121; 2000—$131)	273	313
Deferred income taxes	122	108
Maintenance and operating supplies	64	103
Prepaid expenses and other	207	228
Total current assets	$ 3,790	$ 2,014
PROPERTY AND EQUIPMENT		
Flight equipment	$ 7,015	$ 6,498
Less accumulated depreciation	1,981	1,896
	$ 5,034	$ 4,602
Other property and equipment	$ 1,886	$ 1,826
Less accumulated depreciation	854	794
	$ 1,032	$ 1,032
Total property and equipment	$ 6,066	$ 5,634
FLIGHT EQUIPMENT UNDER CAPITAL LEASES		
Flight equipment	$ 846	$ 846
Less accumulated amortization	303	281
Total flight equipment under capital leases	$ 543	$ 565
OTHER ASSETS		
Intangible pension asset	$ 943	$ 375
International routes, less accumulated amortization (2001—$333; 2000—$310)	634	657
Investments in affiliated companies	213	836
Other	766	796
Total other assets	$ 2,556	$ 2,664
Total Assets	$12,955	$10,877

The leased assets are shown here.

Appendix 12.2: Comparison of Alternative Forms of Financing

Financing arrangements can be quite varied with respect to interest rate, length of time, priority of claims against assets, and so on. To put some of this into perspective, consider the following example. On January 1, 2003, an insurance company offers a manufacturing company a loan of $100 at an annual rate of 6% interest (we keep the numbers simple to minimize computations) with three repayment options:

- *Option 1:* The manufacturing company pays the insurance company $6 interest at the end of each of the next three years and repays the principal amount of the loan, $100, at the end of the third year.

- *Option 2:* The manufacturing company pays the insurance company $119.10 at the end of the third year and nothing before that time.
- *Option 3:* The manufacturing company pays the insurance company $37.41 at the end of each of the next three years and nothing else.

The loan is clearly a liability. It promises future cash payments at definite dates in definite amounts, and its issuance is a transaction. For each of the options, GAAP must determine the amount of the liability shown on each balance sheet from the time the loan is issued until it is retired. GAAP also need to specify the amount of interest expense to be reflected in each income statement for periods from the issuance of the loan until its retirement.

First, let us note that the present value (PV) of each of the three repayment options at 6% interest is $100, which indicates they all correspond to a 6% loan.

It is unlikely in practice that 6% would be the market rate of interest in all three of the alternatives. Not all are of equal risk from the perspective of the lender. Option 2 is the most risky (since the lender has to wait until the end of three years to get anything back). Option 3 is the least risky in that sense.

$$\begin{aligned}
\text{Option 1: PV} &= (6)/(1.06) + (6)/(1.06)^2 + (6)/(1.06)^3 + (100)/(1.06)^3 \\
&= (6)/(1.06) + (6)/(1.124) + (6)/(1.191) + (100)/(1.191) \\
&= 5.66 + 5.34 + 5.04 + 83.96 \\
&= 100 \\
\text{Option 2: PV} &= (119.10)/(1.06)^3 \\
&= (119.10)/(1.191) \\
&= 100 \\
\text{Option 3: PV} &= (37.41)/(1.06) + (37.41)/(1.06)^2 + (37.41)/(1.06)^3 \\
&= (37.41)/(1.06) + (37.41)/(1.124) + (37.41)/(1.191) \\
&= 35.29 + 33.28 + 31.41 \\
&= 100
\end{aligned}$$

For each of the three options we will show how GAAP record the liability and associated interest cost.

Option 1: Bond Sold at Par

This option is just like a bond sold at par value. The entry to record the loan on January 1, 2003, is as follows:

Cash	100	
Loan Payable		100

On December 31 of 2003, 2004, and 2005, the following journal entry is made to record interest at a rate of 6% and to record the cash outflow to pay the interest:

Interest Expense	6	
Cash		6

Interest expense for the first year is 6% of $100, or $6. Because it is paid in full (in the exact amount) when due, the loan obligation remains at $100 on the balance sheet.

The last year, on December 31, 2005, the following journal entry is made to record repayment of the face amount of the loan:

Loan Payable	100	
Cash		100

GAAP for the loan follow the economics exactly in recording the value of the liability on the balance sheet and interest expense on the income statement, as long as the interest rate remains at 6%. GAAP view the issuance of the loan as borrowing $100 at 6%. Unlike the economic value, however, GAAP lock these data in place in its calculations until the loan is retired. Changes in interest rates are ignored when doing the accounting for the loan.

Option 2: The Zero-Coupon Bond

This option resembles a zero-coupon bond where the borrower receives a loan up front and pays no interest or principal until maturity, when it is paid in one lump sum.

The entry to record the loan on January 1, 2003, is as follows:

Cash 100
    Loan Payable 100

Remember that we are doing accrual accounting. The borrower had use of the money during the year and the cost of that use, whether currently paid or not, is the $6 interest charge that must show up as expense in 2003.

On December 31, 2003, interest on the loan must be recorded. Throughout the year, the borrower had use of $100 and it is a 6% loan. Therefore, interest expense for the year is $6, and the following journal entry is made:

Interest Expense 6
    Loan Payable 6

In the previous entry, because the interest was not currently paid, the credit entry is to the long-term obligation to show that it must be paid in the future. Thus, the amount of the loan payable obligation going into the second year, 2004, is now $106. During the second year, the borrower effectively has use of $106 of the lender's money. Thus, the interest calculation at the end of the second year is $0.06 \times \$106$, or $6.36. On December 31, 2004, the following entry is made:

Interest Expense 6.36
    Loan Payable 6.36

Using similar logic, at the end of 2005 just before the obligation is paid, the following entry is made:

Going into 2005, the amount of the obligation has grown to $100 + $6 + $6.36, or $112.36. Interest Expense is now 0.06 of this amount, or $6.74.

Interest Expense 6.74
    Loan Payable 6.74

Finally, when the full obligation is finally repaid at the end of 2005, the following journal entry is made:

Loan Payable 119.10
    Cash 119.10

In computing interest expense on any fixed-rate obligation, the amount of the expense is always the historical rate of interest (the market rate of interest in effect when the loan was entered into), multiplied by the book value of the obligation at the beginning of the period.

Option 3: The Mortgage

This option resembles a standard mortgage and many leases. The entry to record the loan on January 1, 2003, is as follows:

Cash 100
    Loan Payable 100

Again, under this option, interest expense must be recorded on December 31, 2003. Once again it will be $6 because the borrower had use of $100 for the year at 6% interest. Under this option, however, the borrower is contractually committed to pay the lender $37.41. Because only $6 is owed at this point for interest, the additional $31.41 must be a repayment of principal. The following entry is made on December 31, 2003:

Interest Expense 6.00
Loan Payable 31.41
    Cash 37.41

Procedurally, the "plug" is always to decrease Loan Payable (i.e., we compute Interest Expense first and the entry to Loan Payable is what is needed to make the debits equal the credits).

During 2004 the borrower only had use of $100 − $31.41, or $68.59, of the lender's money. Therefore, Interest Expense for 2004 is $4.12 ($0.06 \times \$68.59$). At the end of 2004, the following journal entry is made:

Interest Expense 4.12
Loan Payable 33.29
    Cash 37.41

Verify that at the end of 2005 the following journal entry will be made:

```
Interest Expense  ................................   2.12
Loan Payable  ....................................  35.29
    Cash  .........................................        37.41
```

Note that after this journal entry and the last cash payment of $37.41 is made, the balance in the loan payable account is zero. This option is just like a fixed-rate home mortgage. A level payment is made each month, most of which is interest in the early years of the loan. Part of each payment goes to reduce principal. These repayments of principal get larger through time as less and less of the fixed payment is for interest.

Exhibit A12.2.1 shows the amount of expense for each of the years and the amount of the balance sheet liability for each of the three options. Figure A12.2.1 depicts the liability on the balance sheet over the life of the three options.

Note how the obligation remains constant when the interest due for any year is paid in full. When interest is not paid in full (the zero-coupon bond being the extreme case where none of the interest is paid until the end) the obligation grows through time and the interest expense increases through time. When part of the principal is repaid annually, the obligation book value decreases and the interest expense decreases through time.

Exhibit A12.2.1

Interest Expense and Obligation Value under the Three Options

Interest Expense and Obligation Value Under the Three Options	Jan.1 2003	December 31 2003	December 31 2004	December 31 2005
Option 1: Bond at par:				
Interest expense for the year		6.00	6.00	6.00
Book value of the obligation	100.00	100.00	100.00	100.00
Option 2: Zero-coupon bond				
Interest expense for the year		6.00	6.36	6.74
Book value of the obligation	100.00	106.00	112.36	119.10
Option 3: Mortgage				
Interest expense for the year		6.00	4.12	2.12
Book value of the obligation	100.00	68.59	35.30	0.00

Figure A12.2.1

Book Values of Liability Under Options 1, 2, and 3

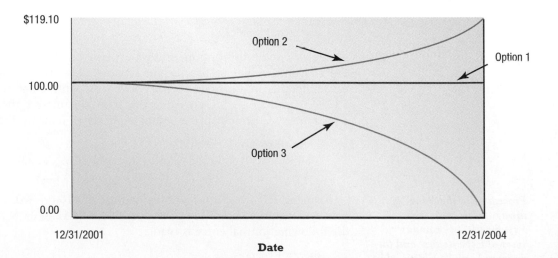

chapter 13

© PHILIP JAMES CORWIN/CORBIS

Equities

Over the past twenty years, junk bonds (sometimes referred to as "toxic waste") have often been used to finance corporate takeovers and management buyouts. Junk bonds are debt instruments that carry high rates of interest because they are risky. Often, smaller companies with poor investment ratings use them as an alternative to expensive and dilutive stock offerings or bank loans with many restrictive covenants on corporate activities.

In case of default, bondholders are given control of the company, and they take whatever resources are left (even if it's nothing!). So what is the ultimate junk bond? It is a bond that carries an infinite interest, is immediately in default, and results in the bondholders owning the issuing company. But wait! That's just common stock!

The point is that distinguishing debt from equity can be difficult, yet GAAP treatment of the two is different. We studied debt in the last chapter and focus on equities in this chapter. This chapter discusses the following:

1. The nature of equities and their economic value

2. How GAAP account for some typical transactions involving stock

3. Some standard financial statistics related to common stock

We begin by defining equities and discussing the idea of ownership that underlies them. We then discuss the distinction between debt and equity, present some different kinds of equity, and provide some example disclosures. A new statement, the statement of changes in shareholders' equity, is presented and discussed. Because equity is a residual and we will discuss its economic value in great length in Chapter 16, we offer only a brief discussion of the economic value of equities now. In contrast to many of the chapters in this part of the book, the section on the GAAP treatment of equity presents quite a few entries that affect the equity section. We will present GAAP for issuances and retirements of equity, dividend payments (both cash and stock), and the conversion of one type of equity into another. We conclude the chapter by examining some financial statement analysis issues involving equities: earnings per share and the treatment of employee stock options.

Nature of Equities

Equities are the financial instruments that specify ownership claims to the corporation. The **corporate charter**, a legal document establishing the corporation under the laws of the jurisdiction of incorporation, specifies the types of equities and their terms (further defined in the stock contract), as well as the number of their shares that may be issued. The charter may also give the shares a **stated**, or **par value**.

In the United States, the states have jurisdiction over the laws of incorporation, and state laws differ in the status granted to par value. According to some state laws, corporations cannot pay cash dividends that reduce the value of shareholders' equity below the total par value of the stock. Other states place no such constraint on cash distributions to shareholders.

Ownership

Because equities are ownership claims, we should discuss the concept of ownership. Owners of a corporation have three important rights:

1. The right to control how the corporation uses its assets, what liabilities it incurs, what strategic and operating policies it adopts, and so on.

2. The right to receive the benefits produced by the corporation after all other providers of capital (such as bondholders) have been paid what they are contractually obligated to receive in the form of cash dividends or increases in the value of their ownership claims.

3. The right to transfer the ownership of the corporation to someone else.

The reality for most large corporations is that management or a nominating committee of the board proposes new directors.

Equity holders can exert their rights to control how the corporation is operated in several ways. The most direct and powerful way is through the ability to nominate and elect candidates to the group that holds the authority to run the company: the **board of directors.** Also, equity holders can propose and vote on **shareholder resolutions** that mandate or prohibit specific policies or behavior of corporate officers. Equity holders also have the right to vote on whether the corporation is allowed to issue other forms of equity that might interfere with their rights to control the corporation and to enjoy its benefits.

The corporate charter may authorize equity securities that carrry different voting rights. Although the variations are almost endless, one common practice for a family-held company, like Ford Motor Company or the World Wrestling Entertainment, is to issue different classes of common stock with different voting powers. For example, Note 12 to the World Wrestling Entertainment's fiscal 2000 annual report (Exhibit 13.1) shows that it has two different classes of common stock that are not equal in number. There are 56.667 million shares of Class B common stock and only 11.5 million shares of Class A common stock. Only Class A common stock is publicly traded. The McMahon family owns all the Class B common. Therefore, even if each share of common stock has one vote, because the Class B common stock outnumbers the Class A common stock by almost 5 to 1, the holders of the Class B common stock effectively control the World Wrestling Entertainment. Even though each share of Class A and Class B common stock has an equal residual claim, each type of sharcholder does not have the same say in the governance of the company.

Exhibit 13.1
WWE
Shareholders' Equity Note

> **Note 12 from WWE 2000 Annual Report**
> 12. Stockholders' Equity
> . . . On April 30, 2000, the Company had 56,667,000 shares of Class B common stock and 11,500,000 shares of Class A common stock outstanding.

The WWE Class B stock is entitled to ten votes per share.

Preferred stock, in the event of bankruptcy, has a senior claim against the assets of the firm relative to common shareholders, but junior to bondholders.

Dividends on preferred stock, as with common stock, are not expenses of the company. They are returns of capital.

A variety of methods can be used to limit the voting rights of a class of equity other than to outnumber it. Some types of equity simply carry no voting rights at all under the corporate charter. Others grant limited voting rights only in special circumstances; still others come with "super" voting rights (WWE Class B common shares for example).

For example, it is not unusual to see **preferred stock** issued with no voting rights. Preferred stock offers some advantages, however. Holders of preferred stock have the right to receive dividends before dividends can be paid to the voting common shareholders. Preferred shareholders may be promised payments specified as a percentage of the par value of the preferred, much like debt holders. For example, a 10%, $100 par value preferred share typically promises the holder payment of $5 semiannually.

This arrangement does not mean that preferred stock is really debt. One big difference between preferred stock and debt revolves around what happens when the promised payments are not made. Preferred shareholders, unlike debt holders, have no right to push the corporation into bankruptcy should they not be paid. In this sense, the payments to preferred shareholders are more like dividends than interest, but the line certainly can get blurry. We will discuss this issue further in the next subsection, where we compare debt and equity.

The holders of ordinary common stock have no rights to receive any payments from the corporation. In case of liquidation, common shareholders receive whatever is left after all other debt and equity holders have been paid. Often, dividends are paid regularly on common stock, even though it is not a legal necessity to do so. These dividends constitute part of the benefit of owning the company that the common shareholders enjoy.

The right to dispose of the corporation is the last kind of right the owners possess. Most corporations issue common shares that are freely transferable. These shares are often traded in public markets, such as the New York Stock Exchange, the American Stock Exchange, or the Nasdaq. The right to sell common stock allows its holders to capture increases in the value of their shares. This **capital gain** is another benefit to ownership enjoyed by common shareholders. Their total benefit is therefore their dividends plus their capital gains.

Of course, sometimes the "gains" are actually losses!

OBJECTIVE:
Learn to understand more about the distinction between debt and equity.

Equity, Debt, and Hybrid Financial Instruments

Many forms of equity and debt are hybrid combinations of the features of a basic common stock and a basic bond. To understand these hybrid combinations, let's compare the relevant features of debt and equity (see Exhibit 13.2).

Exhibit 13.2

Features of Debt and Equity

Pure Debt:	Hybrids:	Pure Equity:
• Fixed maximum payments	• Preferred	• No maximum payments

• Entitlement to payments	• Convertible
	  • Redeemable
	  • Cumulative
		• No entitlement to payments

• Seniority over stock in bankruptcy	• Options/warrants	• Residual claim—i.e., lowest seniority
• No control or decision rights	• Convertible bonds	• Decision rights

Four main features differentiate the extremes of debt and common equity. First, debt agreements specify the payments due to their holders. Making the payments discharges the debt. Therefore, a debt agreement determines the maximum payment that a debt holder is entitled to receive. There is no maximum payment to holders of equity. Second, debt holders are entitled to the payments specified in the debt agreement, with legal recourse if the promised payments are not made, that is, if default occurs. Third, in default the debt holders have the right to get paid before any payments are made to equity holders. Debt has seniority over equity. Fourth, equity holders hold the decision rights in a corporation, as long as no default has occurred.

The bottom line is that common equity offers more decision control over an organization, and debt holders have stronger rights to cash payments.

Preferred stock is a hybrid that is usually closer to equity, but has many features of debt. It may have limited or no voting (decision) rights. It may specify a dividend "entitlement" expressed as a percentage of par value. The par value of the preferred stock acts like the face value of debt. Also, the "entitlement" to payments is not a legally enforceable right, but preferred dividends must be paid before any common dividends are paid.

Preferred stock may be **redeemable,** which means it can be exchanged with the corporation for cash equal to its par value. The par value of a redeemable preferred stock works like the face value of a debt instrument.

Preferred stock takes priority after debt but before common stock. The rights to preferred dividends may be **cumulative,** meaning that any skipped dividends must be paid before any dividend is paid on common stock. Further, the corporate charter often grants the preferred shareholders the right to elect a certain number of directors, should preferred dividends lag too far behind. With the right combination of accumulation, redemption, and voting rights, a preferred stock essentially can be equivalent to debt.

To confuse matters further, some types of equity instruments are **convertible** into other types of equity, often common stock. The purest type of convertible instrument is an **option** or **warrant.** A stock option or a warrant (two names for the same thing) is

Stock options are traded on stock exchanges, but the company does not issue them. Those options are contracts between individual investors making "bets" on the future movements of stock prices.

the right to buy common stock at a specified price, called the **exercise price,** any time up to some specified date, called the **expiration date.**[1] For example, an option may give its holder the right to buy one share of common stock for $25 at any date on or before January 31, 2010. Many corporations routinely issue options to employees, particularly top executives, as a form of compensation and as an incentive device.

Bonds and preferred stock also can contain conversion rights. For example, Exhibit 13.3 shows that USX Corp., a steel and oil company, has preferred stock that is convertible into a specific class of its common stock that tracks the value of its steel operations (Steel Stock). The conversion price is $46.125 per share.[2]

Exhibit 13.3

USX Corporation
Equity Note Excerpt

USX Corp. 1999 Annual Report

Excerpts from Note 24

24. PREFERRED STOCK

   6.50% CUMULATIVE CONVERTIBLE PREFERRED STOCK . . . - As of December 31, 1999, 2,715,287 shares (stated value of $1.00 per share; liquidation preference of $50.00 per share) were outstanding. The 6.50% Preferred Stock is convertible at any time, at the option of the holder, into shares of Steel Stock at a conversion price of $46.125 per share of Steel Stock, subject to adjustment in certain circumstances. . . .

Stock ownership can give investors a say in a corporation's future.

© GETTY IMAGES/PHOTO DISC

Remember, the cost of debt and equity are treated differently in the financial statements. Interest is an expense in the income statement but dividends are not.

Conversion rights and the ability to create financial instruments with features in between those of pure debt and pure equity make it difficult to classify some financial instruments as either debt or equity. Yet, GAAP require it. Furthermore, the GAAP classification drives many aspects of the accounting. For example, if a security is classified as debt, the payments to its holders are accounted for and accrued as time passes, and the costs are deemed to be expenses. The payments to the holders of a security that

[1]Many different kinds of options are available. An American option, which allows the holder to buy any time up to a specified date, is what we defined here. European options give the holder the right to buy common stock only at the expiration date.

[2]On November 10, 2000, USX Steel Stock (ticker symbol X) closed at $14.50 per share. The 6.5% preferred (ticker symbol X-A) closed at $33.938 per share.

is classified as equity are accounted for as dividends and are accrued only when declared. If a debt security is retired at a cost different from its book value, a gain or loss is recorded. The retirement of an equity security is treated as a return of funds to investors. Investment bankers work hard at exploiting GAAP's need to classify financial instruments as debt or equity by clever design of hybrids and show no signs of stopping any time soon.

An Example: 3M

Fortunately, many corporations issue only one class of equity: pure common stock. It does not mean, however, their shareholders' equity accounts are simple, even though it may look that way initially. For example, consider the balance sheet for the Minnesota Mining and Manufacturing Company (also known as 3M) given in Exhibit 13.4. Its organization suggests that the equity holders own what is left. Given the balance sheet identity:

$$\text{Assets} = \text{Liabilities} + \text{Equities}$$

the book value of stockholders' equity is really a plug figure. As we saw in Chapter 2, once assets and liabilities are specified and their book values determined, the book value of

Authorized, issued, and outstanding are three terms relating to equities. Authorized refers to the number of shares that the charter or stock contract allows to be issued. Issued is the number of shares that were sold to the public, and outstanding refers to the number of shares still publicly owned (the company may have repurchased some of the issued stock).

Exhibit 13.4

3M Company
Balance Sheet

Minnesota Mining and Manufacturing Company and Subsidiaries Consolidated Balance Sheet At December 31 (amounts in millions)		
Assets	**1999**	**1998**
Current assets		
Cash and cash equivalents	$ 387	$ 211
Other securities	54	237
Accounts receivable—net	2,778	2,666
Inventories	2,030	2,219
Other current assets	817	886
Total current assets	$ 6,066	$ 6,219
Investments	$ 487	$ 623
Property, plant and equipment—net	5,656	5,566
Other assets	1,687	1,745
Total	$13,896	$14,153
Liabilities and Stockholders' Equity		
Current liabilities		
Short-term debt	$ 1,130	$ 1,492
Accounts payable	1,008	868
Payroll	361	487
Income taxes	464	261
Other current liabilities	856	1,114
Total current liabilities	$ 3,819	$ 4,222
Long-term debt	1,480	1,614
Other liabilities	2,308	2,381
Stockholders' equity—net; Shares outstanding—1999: 398,710,817; 1998: 401,924,248	6,289	5,936
Total	$13,896	$14,153

3M combines all its shareholders' equity accounts into one line on its balance sheet. The statement of changes in stockholders' equity provides the details.

stockholders' equity follows. 3M's financial statements encourage this view by showing Stockholders' Equity in one line on its balance sheet. At December 31, 1999, 3M had about 398.7 million shares of common stock **outstanding,** or in the hands of investors. The book value of those shares was $6,289 million, or about $15.77 per share:

$$\frac{\$6,289}{398.7 \text{ shares}} = \$15.77 \text{ per share}$$

On December 31, 1998, 3M's Stockholders' Equity was $5,936 million with about 401.9 million shares outstanding—a book value of about $14.77 per share.

Statement of Changes in Shareholders' Equity

OBJECTIVE:

Learn to become familiar with the statement of changes in shareholders' equity.

Stockholders are quite interested in the book value of their equity. Both the composition of the book value of equity at any point in time and the changes in equity over time can be studied to reveal important facts about the status and progress of an organization's economic situation. We already encountered three basic components of shareholders' equity. The equity accounts at any point consist of the following:

- Equity raised through the issuance of financial instruments such as common stock (Common Stock, Additional Paid-In Capital)
- Equity built through undistributed earnings (Retained Earnings)
- Equity arising from accounting adjustments that bypass the income statement (Holding Gains or Losses on Available-for-Sale Securities)

Exhibit 13.5 on page 250 shows the detail behind 3M's stockholders' equity account. It is taken from 3M's Statement of Changes in Stockholders' Equity and comprehensive income, and its format takes a bit of getting used to. The components of Stockholders' Equity are listed across the columns. The rows show the balances at given points in time and changes to those balances. Because this statement explains an equity account, positive amounts (increases) are credits, and negative amounts (decreases) are debits.

We see that 3M's Stockholders' Equity is comprised of Common Stock and Capital in Excess of Par, Retained Earnings, Treasury Stock, Unearned Compensation ESOP, and Accumulated Other Comprehensive Income. The balance at December 31, 1999, of Stockholders' Equity of $6,289 million given in the last row of the total column is the sum of the other columns on that same row:

Common stock and capital in excess of par	$ 296
Retained earnings	10,741
Treasury stock	(3,833)
Unearned compensation ESOP	(327)
Accumulated other comprehensive income	(588)
Stockholders' equity at December 31, 1999	$ 6,289

Common Stock and Capital in Excess of Par arise from the issuance of common shares. Retained Earnings is accumulated, undistributed net income. Treasury Stock is a contra-equity account that we will study in detail in the section, *GAAP for Equities*. We will see that it adjusted the value of Common Stock and Capital in Excess of Par and Retained Earnings downward for shares that have been reacquired by 3M.

Unearned Compensation ESOP and Accumulated Other Comprehensive Income represent accounting adjustments that bypass the income statement (ESOP stands for Employee Stock Ownership Plan). They are analogous to the holding gains or losses on available-for-sale marketable securities. Balance sheet accounts are adjusted, but instead of closing the offsetting accounts to Income Summary and, ultimately, Retained Earnings, they are left open and must appear in the stockholders' equity section of the balance sheet. These accounts arise from entries that are due more to

Minnesota Mining and Manufacturing Company and Subsidiaries
Excerpts from Consolidated Statement of Changes in
Stockholders' Equity and Comprehensive Income

(amounts in millions, except per-share amounts)	Total	Common Stock and Capital in Excess of Par	Retained Earnings	Treasury Stock	Unearned Compensation ESOP	Accumulated Other Comprehensive Income
Balance at December 31, 1998	$5,936	$296	$ 9,980	$(3,482)	$(350)	$(508)
Net income	1,763		1,763			
Cumulative translation adjustment—net	(176)					(176)
Minimum pension liability adjustment—net	(30)					(30)
Debt and equity securities, unrealized gain—net	126					126
Total comprehensive income	$1,683					
Dividends paid ($2.24 per share)	(901)		(901)			
Amortization of unearned compensation	23				23	
Reacquired stock (9.0 million shares)	(825)			(825)		
Issuances pursuant to stock option and benefit plans (5.7 million shares)	373	___	(101)	474	___	___
Balance at December 31, 1999	$6,289	$296	$10,741	$(3,833)	$(327)	$(588)

Exhibit 13.5

3M Company
Excerpts from Consolidated
Statement of Changes in Share-
holder's Equity

compromises in the accounting policy-making process than to the fundamental ideas of how income statements and balance sheets ought to fit together. They are items that indeed do affect the residual claim but GAAP keep them out of the income statement.

The display of the line *comprehensive income* is required by GAAP in order to allow us to see what income would be if (most) of these items were counted in income. For 3M in 1999, we see that its GAAP net income was $1,763 million, and its total comprehensive income is $1,683 million (which includes net income). As we might expect, comprehensive income was less than GAAP net income. Accounting policymakers are not under pressure to bypass the income statement for items that tend to increase income.

The columns in the statement of changes in shareholders' equity show the balances in the various equity accounts and the reasons for their changes between December 31, 1998, and December 31, 1999. This statement is equivalent to showing the T-accounts. For example, Retained Earnings had a balance of $9,980 at December 31, 1998. Three things affected 3M's Retained Earnings: net income, dividends, and issuances pursuant to stock option and benefit plans. The earning of net income increased Retained Earnings by $1,763. The declaration of dividends reduced Retained Earnings by $901. Issuances of common stock under stock option and benefits plans, which we will discuss in more detail later, reduced Retained Earnings by $101. In T-account form, we have:

Every column in the statement of changes in shareholders' equity refers to a T-account.

Retained Earnings

	Dr.	Cr.	
		9,980	Beginning balance
Dividends	901	1,763	Net income
Issuances for stock option and benefit plans	101		
		10,741	Ending balance

The statement of changes in stockholders' equity provides a great deal of information about the equity accounts. It can help us unwind many of the entries that were made and thus uncover the events that transpired during the period. However, as discussed in Chapter 7, the book value of equity can be quite different from its market value. Before we get into the GAAP for equity transactions in more detail, we discuss the economic value of equities.

Economic Value of Equities

The economic value of equities is derived from the stream of cash flows they provide to their holders. These cash flow streams are usually some combination of dividends and the expected proceeds of the eventual sale of the equity. For example, even though Microsoft pays no dividends, its shareholders expect to receive cash upon the sale of their shares. The amount that a share of Microsoft will fetch at any future date is quite uncertain, so risk is involved in an investment in Microsoft common. Nonetheless, financial theory says that it's the cash flow stream, and its attendant risk, that drives the value of Microsoft's common stock.

The cash flows provided by hybrid securities can take complex forms, particularly when conversion features are involved. For example, suppose an option holder keeps an option until the date it expires. The cash flow to the option holder is a function of the exercise price of the option and the price of the stock on that date. If the stock price is below the exercise price when the option expires, the option holder will not exercise the option and the cash flow is zero. If the stock price is above the exercise price at the expiration date, the option holder will exercise the option and will get a net cash flow equal to the difference between the stock price and the exercise price.

We will leave to Chapter 16 and finance courses a more in-depth discussion of the economic value of equities. The important point at this juncture is the kind of analysis of the economic value of equity that we did in Chapter 7. There we looked at the economic value of equities in terms of the economic assets and liabilities of the entity. Because equity is a residual claim, all our work on the economic values of specific assets and liabilities in Chapters 8 through 12 can be aggregated to generate insights into the economic value of the equity that is a claim on the ownership of those assets and liabilities.

We proceed to look at GAAP for equities.

GAAP for Equities

GAAP for pure equities involve recording their issuance, retirement, increases through earnings, and decreases from dividend distributions. GAAP for hybrid securities that are more complex forms of equities involve recording their conversion and redemption, as well as issuance and retirement.

Issuance and Retirement

Most often, corporations issue equity to raise cash for investment and operating purposes. We covered the basics of the issuance of equity for cash in Chapter 2. For example, if

10,000 shares of $0.10 par value common stock are issued for $50,000 cash, we debit Cash and credit Common Stock for the total par value of the stock issued ($1,000) and Additional Paid-In Capital for any remaining amount needed ($49,000):

Cash	50,000	
Common Stock		1,000
Additional Paid-In Capital		49,000

Retiring common stock is a bit trickier because the amount the corporation must pay to reacquire its shares will almost never exactly equal their book value. For example, suppose USX wants to retire five million of its Steel Shares. These shares have a par value of $1 per share and a book value of about $17 per share. Suppose the market value on the date USX reacquires the stock is $20 per share. There are two things we should note here. First, and most importantly, USX *cannot have a gain or loss from transacting in its own shares.* Reacquiring its own shares is a transaction with its owners, not an income-producing transaction. Second, a treatment consistent with the way we accumulate the equity accounts would reduce Common Stock by the par value of the shares and Additional Paid-In Capital by the amount put in when the shares were initially sold. Any difference between the repurchase price and the original sale price would go to Retained Earnings. For example, suppose the Steel Shares were initially sold for $10 ($1 went into Common Stock and $9 went into Additional Paid-In Capital for each share sold). The entry to retire the shares would be:

If you have any uncertainty about the criteria for separating income from capital transactions, review Chapter 3.

An alternative would be to debit Common Stock for $5 million and Additional Paid-In Capital for $95 million.

Common Stock	5,000,000	
Additional Paid-In Capital	45,000,000	
Retained Earnings	50,000,000	
Cash		100,000,000

Treasury Stock

We would go to the trouble to make this journal entry for a major retirement of stock, but what about more minor transactions like those required to obtain shares of stock to distribute under executive stock options? A management stock option plan typically requires the corporation to purchase its shares on the market to provide to the manager upon exercise of the option. Many companies are constantly buying and reissuing shares of their own common stock.

Although the essence of these transactions is retirement and reissuance of common stock, a short-cut accounting technique is usually applied to these transactions: the **treasury stock method.** The treasury stock method treats the purchases of an entity's own stock as building a sort of inventory. This inventory is an accounting fiction only, and it is certainly not an asset. It is a contra-equity.

Companies cannot own themselves (cannot have an asset account for their own stock), nor can they show gains or losses from trades in their own stock.

An example might help. Exhibit 13.5 gives 3M's statement of changes in shareholders' equity. We see that Treasury Stock was a $3,833 million *reduction* in shareholders' equity at December 31, 1999. That's because Treasury Stock is a contra-equity.

The statement of changes in shareholders' equity shows us all the activity in 3M's treasury stock account. In T-account form, the statement shows:

Treasury Stock

	Dr.	Cr.	
Beginning balance	3,482		
Reacquired stock (9.0 million shares)	825		
		474	Issuances pursuant to stock option and benefit plans (5.7 million shares)
Ending balance	3,833		

Get in the habit of checking your understanding of an accounting number by validating it in another part of the statements whenever possible.

3M purchased (reacquired) 9.0 million shares of treasury stock that were worth $825 million. More than likely, 3M reacquired this stock by paying cash for it in the market. If so, we could expect to see it reflected in the financing section of the statement of cash flows, which is shown in Exhibit 13.6. Indeed, the cash flow statement reveals that 3M actually paid $825 million to reacquire this stock. So, Treasury Stock is listed on the balance sheet at cost. Here is 3M's entry for reacquiring its stock in 1999:

Treasury Stock 825
    Cash 825

Exhibit 13.6

3M

Partial Cash Flow Statement

Cash spent for treasury stock

Cash raised from treasury stock

Minnesota Mining and Manufacturing Company and Subsidiaries
Consolidated Statement of Cash Flows (Financing Activities Section Only)
Years ended December 31
(amounts in millions)

	1999	1998	1997
Cash Flows from Financing Activities			
Change in short-term debt—net	$ (164)	$ 55	$ 705
Repayment of long-term debt	(179)	(129)	(565)
Proceeds from long-term debt	2	645	337
Purchases of treasury stock	(825)	(618)	(1,693)
Reissuances of treasury stock	390	292	355
Dividends paid to stockholders	(901)	(887)	(876)
Distributions to minority interests	(51)	(96)	(22)
Net cash used in financing activities	$(1,728)	$(738)	$(1,759)

No attempt was made to identify pieces of Common Stock, Additional Paid-In Capital, and Retained Earnings to reduce. It was all lumped together in the treasury stock contra-equity account.

3M's issuances of treasury stock are harder to decipher, but we can make some progress. We see from the statement of cash flows that cash brought in (when Treasury Stock was reissued) was $390 million. We see from the statement of changes in shareholders' equity that Retained Earnings was debited for $101 million and Treasury Stock credited for $474 million. As is often the case in analyzing financial statements, we cannot quite tie all the numbers down here—we are missing a credit of $17 million:

As in a company's financial statements, all parts of an item must be examined to determine how the entire structure fits together.

Cash 390
Retained Earnings 101
    Treasury Stock 474
    ??? 17

What are our choices for the missing account(s)? It could be an asset account, a liability account, or an equity account. It is unlikely that the missing account is an asset or a liability. If it were an asset, then 3M somehow would have reduced its assets in the course of issuing treasury shares. Not likely. Similarly, the missing account is not likely to be a liability. How could 3M have created a liability by issuing treasury shares?

Therefore, the remaining $17 million most likely is associated with an equity account. The statement of changes in shareholders' equity is a big help with this possibility because it shows all the changes in the equity accounts. Again, let's go through the possibilities in a systematic way. The statement shows no increases in Common Stock and Capital in Excess of Par, so those accounts cannot be affected by this entry. The entry already affects Retained Earnings and Treasury Stock. So there are only two possibilities left: Unearned Compensation—ESOP (Employee Stock Ownership Plan) or Accumulated Other Comprehensive Income. Because the description of this entry in the statement of changes in shareholders' equity is "Issuances Pursuant to Stock Option and Benefit Plans," and because these plans involve the compensation of employees, it is most reasonable to suppose that the $17 million is part of the $23 million listed as Unearned Compensation—ESOP. The entry was probably:

Cash	390	
Retained Earnings	101	
Treasury Stock		474
Unearned Compensation—ESOP		17

The important point is that Retained Earnings is debited for $101 million in the reissuance. This $101 million is the difference between the amount 3M paid to reacquire the stock and the amount it received upon reissuance ($474 − $390) plus the amount of unearned compensation ($17), which was likely reduced by the issuance of common stock to the ESOP. By convention, 3M uses Retained Earnings to absorb this difference.[3] *It is not a loss.* 3M cannot make or lose money by buying and selling its own ownership claims.

Conversion

If we consider options as the purest form of a convertible security, we have just seen the entry that records a conversion—the conversion (exercise) of employee stock options. So let's look at another example—the conversion of preferred stock that does not involve cash. It is just an exchange of certificates. Suppose the holders of 1 million shares of USX's 6.5%, $1 par value convertible preferred stock choose to convert their preferred shares into Steel Shares. Exhibit 13.3 gives the terms of the conversion: $46.125 per share. Assuming that exactly one share of preferred is traded for one share of common we must transfer balances from the preferred accounts to the common stock accounts. Also assume that the par value of the common is $0.50 per share. The entry to accomplish this is (in millions):

If the balance in Additional Paid-In Capital—Preferred was insufficient to make this journal entry, the difference would be taken up by reducing Retained Earnings.

6.5% Convertible Preferred Stock	1.000	
Additional Paid-In Capital—Preferred	45.125	
Common Stock		0.500
Capital in Excess of Par		45.625

Distributions to Shareholders

Distributions of assets to shareholders usually occur in the context of regular dividend payments, whether the stock is common or preferred. The declaration of cash dividends by the board of directors is recorded by debiting Retained Earnings and crediting Dividends Payable. For example, we see from the statement of shareholders' equity in Exhibit 13.5 that 3M declared $901 million in dividends in 1999.[4] The entry made at the time of declaration was

The declaration of the dividend by the board of directors instantaneously creates the liability.

Retained Earnings	901	
Dividends Payable		901

[3]It is also common to use Additional Paid-In Capital to absorb the difference.

[4]The statement of changes in shareholders' equity actually says, "Dividends Paid" not dividends declared. Because dividends declared in the year are what should go in this statement, 3M's labeling them in this statement as dividends paid is technically incorrect. However, we will see from the statement of cash flows that 3M paid all the dividends that it declared.

The financing section of the statement of cash flows given in Exhibit 13.6 shows that 3M actually paid all $901 million of the dividends it declared. 3M's payment of dividends was recorded by debiting Dividends Payable and crediting Cash:

Dividends Payable	901	
Cash		901

The timing of the recording of the liability, Dividends Payable, reflects the fact that shareholders are entitled to receive dividends *only after they have been declared by the board of directors.* This timing issue applies even to cumulative preferred stock. No adjustments are made to accrue the dividends on any stock, even though the terms of the preferred stock agreement may call for the payment of regular dividends according to a specific formula. As equity holders, preferred shareholders have no right to litigate for the failure to pay promised dividends until the board has declared those dividends. Of course, we do accrue interest on debt, and here is one place where the classification of a particular financial instrument as being equity instead of debt invokes a whole different set of accounting conventions.

Stock Splits and Stock Dividends

Why would a corporation bother to split its stock? One company that doesn't is Berkshire Hathaway on its Class A shares. Whereas most shares on the NYSE sell for less than $100 each, Berkshire Hathaway Class A shares sold for prices between $40,800 and $65,600 each between November 1999 and November 2000!

Corporations sometimes recalibrate shareholders' equity by splitting their stock. A *2-for-1 split* would give each shareholder one additional share for each share owned. If the stock had a par of $1.00 before the split, it would have a par of $0.50 afterward.

All a **stock split** does is redescribe the shareholders' equity, which, other things equal, should cause the market value of the shares to fall proportionally. A stock split simply cuts the total equity "pie" into more pieces. No accounting entry is required to record a stock split, although the number of shares outstanding and their par value listed on the balance sheet in the description of the stock must be changed accordingly.

Amazon.com is a big contrast to Berkshire Hathaway. Here are a few excerpts from Note 9 to Amazon's 1999 annual report:

> On April 18, 1997, the Company effected a 3-for-2 common stock split.
>
> . . .
>
> On June 1, 1998, the Company effected a 2-for-1 stock split . . .
>
> . . .
>
> On January 4, 1999, the Company effected a 3-for-1 stock split . . .
>
> . . .
>
> On September 1, 1999, the Company effected a 2-for-1 stock split . . .

So two shares on April 17, 1997, became three shares in the first split, which split into six shares, which split into 18 shares, which split into 36 shares on September 1, 1999!

Usually a distribution of stock that is 20–25% or less is referred to as a stock dividend. Anything more than that is usually called a split.

A **stock dividend** is a small stock split. In a 5% stock dividend, shareholders receive 1.05 shares for each share they own. Although this move has the same appearance as a stock split, GAAP do require an entry for a stock dividend. Because no assets or liabilities are affected by a stock split, neither is total shareholders' equity. The only thing we could do is reclassify the equity, which is what is required by GAAP. In a stock dividend, we must reclassify some Retained Earnings into Common Stock and Additional Paid-In Capital. The par value is not changed in a stock dividend. The amount of the reclassification is determined by the market price of the stock on the day the split takes effect.

For example, suppose 3M declared a 10% stock dividend on a date when it had 400 million shares outstanding of $0.75 par common stock that was selling for $9 per share. 3M would reclassify:

$$400 \text{ million} \times \$9 \times 10\% = \$360 \text{ million}$$

of equity. The entry would debit Retained Earnings and credit Common Stock and Capital in Excess of Par:

This entry is often referred to as capitalizing Retained Earnings.

Retained Earnings	360	
Common Stock		30
Capital in Excess of Par		330

Conclusion

This section presented the basic entries involving equities. The entries themselves aren't too hard, but two aspects of them need special mention. The first is the distinction between debt and equity. We already discussed the differences in accounting that follow from classifying a financial instrument as debt versus equity, but we will emphasize them again. Debt is counted as an obligation and shown as a liability on the balance sheet, its interest is accrued, and its costs are interest expenses that reduce income. Equity is counted as a residual ownership piece, its dividends are not accrued until declared, and its costs are dividends that do not reduce income.

The second thing that should be discussed is the issuance of equity for consideration other than cash. Corporations have long issued equity as part of acquisitions of other businesses, which we study in detail in Chapter 15, and to corporate executives as a part of their compensation plans. "New economy" companies often issue equity to compensate the suppliers of goods and services to the corporation. The difficulty raised any time equity is issued in exchange for something other than cash is how to value it. If either the equity issued or the thing being acquired has a readily determinable market value, then we can use that value to drive the accounting.

As an example of issuances of equity for other than cash, look at the excerpts from Amazon.com's 1999 10K given in Exhibit 13.7. The excerpts show the supplemental cash flow information from the statement of cash flows and Note 1 to the financial statements. Amazon received the equities of some of its customers in lieu of cash. It placed a "fair value" on those securities of about $54.4 million. Because the transactions were not for cash, this fair value should be considered an estimate in analyzing Amazon's financial condition. Presumably, the issuing companies also recorded an estimate of the value of their issuing equity to Amazon.

Exhibit 13.7

Amazon.com
10K Excerpt

Amazon.com, Inc.
Excerpts from 1999 Annual Report
From the Consolidated Statements of Cash Flows
(amounts in thousands)

	December 31,		
	1999	**1998**	**1997**
. . .			
Supplemental Cash Flow Information			
Fixed assets acquired under capital leases	$ 25,850	$ —	$3,463
Fixed assets acquired under financing agreements	5,608	—	1,500
Stock issued in connection with business acquisitions	774,409	217,241	—
Equity securities of other companies received for non-cash revenue for advertising and promotional services	54,402	—	—
Cash paid for interest, net of amounts capitalized	59,688	26,629	326

Revenue Recognition

. . .

During 1999, the Company recorded approximately $5.8 million of revenue associated with noncash transactions whereby the Company received equity securities of other companies in exchange for advertising and promotional services to be provided for a fixed period of time. The Company recorded the fair value of the consideration on the date received, $54.4 million, and is recognizing revenue ratably over the term of the agreements as the advertising and promotional services are provided.

Review Questions

1. Give the entry for a corporation that issues 10 shares of common stock with a par value of $5 per share in exchange for $75.

2. Is the purchase of treasury stock like the retirement of shares? Why or why not?

3. What kind of account is Treasury Stock, and where does it appear on the balance sheet?

4. Can a corporation make a profit buying and selling treasury stock? Why or why not?

5. Give the entries to record the declaration and payment of $75 in dividends.

6. How would the conversion at par of bonds with a $100 face value into equity affect a corporation's balance sheet?

7. How does a 3-for-2 stock split affect a corporation's balance sheet and income statement?

Financial Statement Analysis of Equities

OBJECTIVE:

Learn to become familiar with some common financial statistics related to common stock.

We discussed the market-to-book ratio and return on equity in Chapter 7. Here, we explore two more topics in the financial statement analysis of equities: earnings per share and employee stock options.

Earnings per Share

In valuing a corporation's equity securities, investors often find it useful to look at the corporation's **earnings per share (EPS)** of common stock. EPS is a measure of earnings divided by a measure of the number of shares outstanding.

$$EPS = \frac{A \text{ measure of earnings}}{A \text{ measure of the number of shares outstanding}}$$

You might be wondering why we say, "a measure of earnings" instead of just "net income," and "a measure of the number of shares outstanding" instead of just "shares outstanding." Suppose EPS Company has $0.10 par value common stock. It begins the year on January 1 with 10,000 shares outstanding and then issues 7,500 additional shares on May 1. At December 31 it has 17,500 shares outstanding, but not all of those were outstanding for the entire year. Exhibit 13.8 on page 258 shows the number of shares outstanding at the end of each month. Ten thousand shares were outstanding for four months of the year, and 17,500 shares were outstanding for eight months of the year. The measure of earnings we put in the numerator, however, is the flow of resources generated over the entire year.

The easy way to handle the changing number of shares over the year is to compute the weighted average number of shares outstanding (WA). The weights are the number of months the shares were outstanding. In this case, we have

$$WA = (10,000 \times 4/12) + (17,500 \times 8/12)$$

$$= 15,000 \text{ shares}$$

If all equities were simply common stock, the calculation of earnings per share would be simple: net income divided by the weighted average number of common shares outstanding. Suppose EPS Company had net income of $150,000 for the year. Let's label our calculation **basic earnings per share,** which results in the following:

$$\text{Basic EPS} = (\$150,000)/(15,000 \text{ shares})$$

$$= \$10.00 \text{ per share}$$

The presence of other types of equities muddies up this situation. What should we do if a corporation has preferred stock? What about stock options and other convertible securities?

Exhibit 13.8
EPS Company Shares
Outstanding

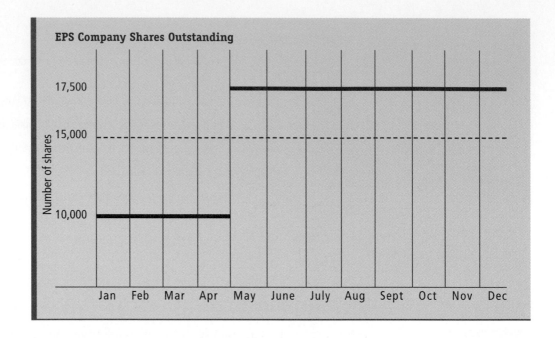

A better name would be net
income applicable to com-
mon. *Dividends are paid in
cash, not GAAP income.
Using the word* available
*suggests net income could be
paid out, which it cannot.
Unfortunately,* net income
available to common *is*
accepted usage.

First, let's consider preferred stock. The earnings per share we are computing is earnings per share of common stock. The existence of preferred stock does not affect the denominator (the number of shares of common stock). But what about the earnings?
Preferred dividends must be paid before common shareholders can be paid any dividends. Also, preferred dividends are *not* deducted in the computation of net income. **Net
income available to common shareholders,** then, is not the total amount of net income,
but rather *net income minus dividends on preferred stock.*

Again suppose EPS Company had net income for the year of $150,000. Now sup-
pose also that it declared and paid preferred dividends of $15,000. Net income available
to common is then

Net income	$150,000
Preferred dividends	(15,000)
Net income available to common shareholders	$135,000

The calculation of basic earnings per share is then

$$\text{Basic EPS} = (\$150,000 - \$15,000)/(15,000 \text{ shares})$$
$$= (\$135,000)/(15,000 \text{ shares})$$
$$= \$9.00 \text{ per share}$$

*The computation of diluted
earnings per share is a complicated task. In general
many examples of debt, preferred stock and rights can
ultimately turn into common
stock (e.g., convertible preferred, convertible debt, war-
rants). GAAP provide
detailed rules about how to
adjust the numerator and
denominator of the diluted
earnings per share computation. They also provide many
tests to determine if a particular financial instrument
should enter into the computation of EPS.*

Stock options and other convertible securities present more complications for the
calculation of earnings per share. Suppose EPS Company has outstanding options to purchase 5,000 shares of common stock at $20 per share. Further suppose the shares of EPS
Company sell for $90 per share. Clearly, the holders of these options are extremely likely
to exercise them. For all practical purposes, 5,000 more shares are outstanding than those
indicated simply by looking at the common shares that are actually outstanding. The exercise of the options will *dilute* the ownership claims of the existing holders of EPS Company's shares. It is reasonable, then, to change the number of shares in the denominator
of the earnings per share calculation to reflect the exercise of the options. To alert everyone to the fact that we have assumed the options will be exercised, let's label this earnings per share calculation **diluted earnings per share.**

$$\text{Diluted EPS} = (\$150,000 - \$15,000)/(15,000 + 5,000 \text{ shares})$$
$$= (\$135,000)/(20,000 \text{ shares})$$
$$= \$6.75 \text{ per share}$$

EPS Company's situation is fairly obvious because the stock price is so far above the exercise price of the options. But what if the exercise price of the options was $88 instead of $20? It is much less apparent whether the options will eventually be exercised. Perhaps our original calculation of basic earnings per share might be the most relevant.

GAAP handle this dilemma by requiring presentation of both basic and diluted earnings per share. Both must be presented on the face of the income statement. Exhibit 13.9 gives the total net income, basic EPS, and diluted EPS for 3M for the year ended December 31, 1999.

There is not much difference between basic and diluted earnings per share for 3M (1.1%), but that's not the case for many of the profitable "new economy" companies. For example, Microsoft's basic earnings per share for 1999 was $1.54 per share. Its diluted earnings per share was $1.42. That $0.12 per share difference is 7.8% of basic earnings per share.

Exhibit 13.9

3M Company
Income Statement Excerpt

Minnesota Mining and Manufacturing Company and Subsidiaries Excerpts from Consolidated Statement of Income Year Ended December 31, 1999	
Net income (millions)	$1,763
Weighted average common shares outstanding (millions)—basic	402.0
Earnings per share—basic	$4.39
Weighted average common shares outstanding (millions)—diluted	406.5
Earnings per share—diluted	$4.34

Employee Stock Options

If the assumed conversion of a security would increase diluted earnings per share, that security is called antidilutive. *Antidilutive securities are excluded from the calculation of diluted earnings per share. If a company has a net loss, even options that would be profitable for the holder to exercise are antidilutive, since by increasing the number of shares in the denominator, they would reduce the loss per share.*

Many corporations, especially high-technology start-ups, give corporate executives many stock options for compensation and motivation purposes. GAAP allow these transactions to be treated as equity transactions and do not require recording compensation expenses. For example, suppose EPS Company's stock options were issued pursuant to an executive compensation plan. As long as the stock price equaled, or was lower than, the exercise price at the time the options were issued, EPS Company is not required to make any entry to record the fact that the executives were given a valuable right.

So let's suppose that the stock price on the date EPS Company issues the 5,000 options was $20 per share. Recall that the exercise price is also $20 per share. Further, suppose standard financial methods for valuing these options estimate them to be worth $1 per share, and they are exercisable immediately.

One allowable GAAP treatment is to record compensation expense of $5,000 at the time the options are issued:

Compensation Expense	5,000	
Stock Options Granted		5,000

where Stock Options Granted is an equity account. If the executives exercised these options at a later date, the entry recording the exercise would be

Cash	100,000	
Stock Options Granted	5,000	
Common Stock ($0.10 par)		500
Additional Paid-In Capital		104,500

Some argue that an option with an exercise price equal to the stock price at the date the option is issued is value-less. This argument is incor-rect. Aside from the strong theoretical arguments that the right to buy stock at a fixed price is valuable, op-tions with exercise prices equal to (and even less than) the market price of the stock are sold for positive prices in options markets. Also, can anyone seriously contend that these options could be withheld from executives without stimulating a protest from them?

GAAP do not require this treatment, however. GAAP allow EPS Company to make no entry at the time these options are issued. The entry at the time the options are exercised would be

Cash	100,000	
Common Stock		500
Additional Paid-In Capital		99,500

However, if EPS Company chooses not to record compensation expense at the time the options are issued, as most companies do, it is required to present footnote disclosures that reveal what its net income would be (pro forma) if it had recorded compensation expense. These disclosures, along with the presentation of diluted earnings per share, help financial analysts understand the financial implications of outstanding stock options.

For example, Exhibit 13.10 contains excerpts from the notes to Microsoft's 1999 financial statements. They show that, had compensation expense been recorded for stock options granted, its net income would have been $7,074 million instead of the $7,757 that was reported. Further, diluted earnings per share would have been $1.29 per share, instead of the $1.42 per share that was reported.

Exhibit 13.10

Microsoft Corporation
Annual Report Excerpts

Microsoft Corporation Stock Options
Excerpts from 1999 Annual Report

The Company follows Accounting Principles Board Opinion 25, *Accounting for Stock Issued to Employees*, to account for stock option and employee stock purchase plans.

An alternative method of accounting for stock options is SFAS 123, Accounting for Stock-Based Compensation. Under SFAS 123, employee stock options are valued at grant date using the Black-Scholes valuation model, and compensation cost is recognized ratably over the vesting period. Had compensation cost for the Company's stock option and employee stock purchase plans been determined based on the Black-Scholes value at the grant dates for awards, pro forma income statement ... 1999 would have been as follows:

Year Ended June 30, 1999

	Reported	Pro Forma
Revenue	$19,747	$19,747
Operating expenses:		
Cost of revenue	$ 2,814	$ 3,024
Research and development	2,970	3,504
Sales and marketing	3,231	3,448
General and administrative	689	822
Other expenses	115	115
Total operating expenses	$ 9,819	$10,913
Operating income	$ 9,928	$ 8,834
Investment income	1,803	1,803
Gain on sale of SoftImage, Inc.	160	160
Income before income taxes	$11,891	$10,797
Provision for income taxes	4,106	3,723
Net income	$ 7,785	$ 7,074
Preferred stock dividends	28	28
Net income available for common shareholders	$ 7,757	$ 7,046
Diluted earnings per share	$ 1.42	$ 1.29

Conclusion

The fundamental accounting identity

$$\text{Assets} = \text{Liabilities} + \text{Equities}$$

requires that we distinguish liabilities from equities. That distinction affects our calculation of income because the costs of raising funds from liabilities are treated as expenses, while the dividends paid to equity holders are treated as transactions with owners.

If all the financial instruments that firms use to raise funds were simple, the accounting for debt and equity would be fairly easy. However, financial instruments with complicated features can be difficult to classify as debt or equity. This complexity creates havoc for the application of the fundamental accounting identity and the calculation of income. Further, the addition of conversion features really complicates things, because a given financial instrument can start its life as debt and then be morphed into equity.

We highlighted the basic issues involved in accounting for debt and equity and discussed many of the complexities. Debt and equity analyses, however, often involve extensive analysis of footnote disclosures, disclosures from proxy statements, and the examination of other sources of information about the exact terms of the financial instruments that have been issued by the entity of interest.

Key Terms

basic earnings per share *257*

board of directors *245*

capital gain *246*

comprehensive income *250*

convertible *246*

corporate charter *244*

cumulative *246*

diluted earnings per share *258*

earnings per share (EPS) *257*

exercise price *247*

expiration date *247*

net income available to common shareholders *258*

option *246*

outstanding *249*

par value *244*

preferred stock *245*

redeemable *246*

shareholder resolutions *245*

stated value *244*

stock dividend *255*

stock split *255*

treasury stock method *252*

warrant *246*

chapter 14

© GETTY IMAGES/PHOTO DISC

Income Taxes

Two things are widely known as unavoidable: death and taxes. We can leave the discussions of death to medical and religious books. But for an accounting text, we have avoided taxes as long as we can. It's time we faced the issue of taxes head on. This chapter focuses on income taxes and the impact they have on economic values and GAAP for them.

Taxes generate benefits for organizations, but they are indirect. Taxes pay for roads, courts, national defense, the establishment and maintenance of a system of commercial laws, and many other benefits that all organizations enjoy. An organization's enjoyment of these public goods is not connected to the payment of any particular amount of taxes. Only governments own the assets that generate these benefits, which are not the types of benefits accounted for by GAAP.

The accounting for income taxes reflects the effects of taxes on the book values of assets and liabilities. We begin our exploration of the accounting for income taxes by examining tax disclosures and explaining why tax accounting principles (TAP) are different from GAAP. We then show how the economic value of assets and liabilities is affected by income taxes. We have ignored these effects up to this point, but they are crucial to understanding accounting and economic value. We then discuss GAAP for income taxes and compare economic values to GAAP. Finally, we discuss how to analyze GAAP accounting for income taxes.

Nature of Income Taxes

An **income tax** is a tax determined by taking a percentage of an income calculation.

Tax accounting principles (TAP) are the rules used to compute taxable income.

Taxes come in many different forms. Most taxes can be described in terms of the bases for their computation. For example, a sales tax is calculated by taking a percentage of a sales price. A property tax is calculated by taking a percentage of an appraised value of property. A value-added tax is calculated by taking a percentage of the value added by a manufacturing or distribution process.

Our focus is income taxes. **Income taxes** are calculated by taking a percentage of some calculation of income. The phrase "some calculation of income" might seem unduly guarded, but it is not. Special rules govern the calculation of taxable income. **Taxable income** (not GAAP income) is the basis for an income tax. Special rules specify the allowable accounting methods for calculating taxable income, and they are not the same as the GAAP we have studied. In the United States, GAAP are set by common practice—the rulings of the FASB, SEC, and related bodies. **Tax accounting principles (TAP)** are set by the Internal Revenue Service and by Congress in the form of tax laws it enacts. In many other countries, the International Accounting Standards Board (IASB) or a similar body sets GAAP, whereas governmental authorities that have jurisdiction over funding set TAP. The degree of similarity between GAAP and TAP in countries varies widely. GAAP and TAP are the same in Germany, but many significant differences distinguish GAAP from TAP in the United States.

Differences between GAAP and TAP create a problem for GAAP. Taxes are important determinants of the economic values that GAAP are trying to capture in the financial statements. In the United States, the corporate income tax rate in 2002 was 35 percent for most large corporations, and income taxes represent a significant cost of doing business.

An Example: Northwest Airlines

For example, look at Northwest Airlines' income statements shown in Exhibit 14.1 on page 264. For the year ended December 31, 1997, Northwest showed income tax expense of $378.8 million. That's more than the $358.9 million in its expense for aircraft rentals that year. In 1998, a benefit of $144.5 million was ascribed to income taxes.

Exhibit 14.1

Northwest Airlines
Income Statements

Northwest Airlines Corporation
Consolidated Statements of Operations
(in millions, except per share amounts)

	YEAR ENDED DECEMBER 31		
Operating Revenues	**1998**	**1997**	**1996**
Passenger	$7,606.5	$ 8,822.1	$8,598.3
Cargo	633.5	789.4	745.8
Other	804.8	614.3	536.4
	$9,044.8	$10,225.8	$9,880.5
Operating Expenses			
Salaries, wages and benefits	$3,260.6	$ 3,023.9	$2,709.4
Stock-based employee compensation	—	—	242.8
Aircraft fuel and taxes	1,097.1	1,393.8	1,396.9
Commissions	691.9	855.2	868.4
Aircraft maintenance materials and repairs	761.0	620.4	556.2
Other rentals and landing fees	450.4	456.7	454.0
Depreciation and amortization	427.0	396.0	377.7
Aircraft rentals	345.1	358.9	346.3
Other	2,203.1	1,963.7	1,875.0
	$9,236.2	$ 9,068.6	$8,826.7
OPERATING INCOME (LOSS)	$ (191.4)	$ 1,157.2	$1,053.8
Other Income (Expense)			
Interest expense	$ (328.9)	$ (244.7)	$ (269.8)
Interest capitalized	16.8	10.6	7.3
Interest of mandatorily redeemable preferred security holder	(22.5)	(24.3)	(27.2)
Investment income	79.3	68.0	71.2
Foreign currency gain (loss)	(21.5)	1.8	19.1
Other, net	38.2	16.0	18.0
	$ (238.6)	$ (172.6)	$ (181.4)
INCOME (LOSS) BEFORE INCOME TAXES AND EXTRAORDINARY ITEM	$ (430.0)	$ 984.6	$ 872.4
Income tax expense (benefit)	(144.5)	378.8	336.3
INCOME (LOSS) BEFORE EXTRAORDINARY ITEM	$ (285.5)	$ 605.8	$ 536.1
Loss on extinguishment of debt, net of taxes	—	(9.3)	—
NET INCOME (LOSS)	$ (285.5)	$ 596.5	$ 536.1

The tax expense/benefit line is large in the income statement.

As we will see shortly, the key to this discussion will be in understanding that, for the same transactions, assets get used up and liabilities get incurred at different rates in the financial statements than in the tax statements. For example, the same asset may be depreciated at a faster or slower rate for tax purposes than in the financial statements.

Taxes also show up on balance sheets. Northwest's balance sheets in Exhibit 14.2 show deferred income taxes in both assets and liabilities sections. Deferred income taxes assets are $114.3 million at December 31, 1998, and deferred income taxes liabilities are $1,112.7 million. Combining these two amounts, we see that Northwest's net deferred tax liability as of December 31, 1998, was $998.4 million:

Deferred income taxes (liabilities)	$1,112.7
Less deferred income taxes (assets)	(114.3)
Net deferred taxes	$ 998.4

Exhibit 14.2 Northwest Airlines Corporation Balance Sheet

Northwest Airlines Corporation
Consolidated Balance Sheets
(amounts in millions)

Assets	December 31 1998	December 31 1997	Current Liabilities	December 31 1998	December 31 1997
CURRENT ASSETS			Air traffic liability	$ 1,107.2	$1,222.5
Cash and cash equivalents	$ 480.0	$ 740.4	Accounts payable	682.6	504.9
Short-term investments	47.9	437.7	Accrued compensation and benefits	504.2	376.5
Accounts receivable, less allowance			Accrued aircraft rent	207.7	207.5
(1998—$23.5; 1997—$21.2)	664.7	664.8	Accrued commissions	150.3	183.9
Flight equipment spare parts, less			Other accrued liabilities	424.0	439.7
allowance (1998—$158.8;			Current maturities of long-term debt	319.2	227.4
1997—$148.9)	386.6	376.1	Current obligations under capital leases	57.6	55.9
Deferred income taxes	114.3	84.8	Short-term borrowings	8.9	53.7
Prepaid expenses and other	176.6	294.0		$ 3,461.7	$3,272.0
	$ 1,870.1	$2,597.8	LONG-TERM DEBT	$ 3,681.5	$1,841.9
PROPERTY AND EQUIPMENT			LONG-TERM OBLIGATIONS		
Flight equipment	$ 6,168.4	$5,246.7	UNDER CAPITAL LEASES	$ 597.3	$ 649.4
Less accumulated depreciation	1,485.8	1,295.6			
	$ 4,682.6	$3,951.1	DEFERRED CREDITS AND OTHER LIABILITIES		
Other property and equipment	$ 1,654.5	$1,489.0	Deferred income taxes	$ 1,112.7	$1,161.5
Less accumulated depreciation	678.6	612.4	Long-term pension and post-		
	$ 975.9	$ 876.6	retirement health care benefits	500.1	407.3
	$ 5,658.5	$4,827.7	Other	579.4	674.1
				$ 2,192.2	$2,242.9
FLIGHT EQUIPMENT UNDER CAPITAL LEASES			MANDATORILY REDEEMABLE PREFERRED		
Flight equipment	$ 873.3	$ 907.1	SECURITY OF SUBSIDIARY WHICH HOLDS		
Less accumulated amortization	263.3	270.0	SOLELY NON-RECOURSE OBLIGATION OF		
	$ 610.0	$ 637.1	COMPANY—NOTE F (Redemption value		
			1998—$631.8; 1997—$551.0)	$ 564.1	$ 486.3
OTHER ASSETS					
Investments in affiliated			REDEEMABLE STOCK		
companies	$ 675.9	$ 185.9	Preferred, liquidation value		
International routes, less accumulated			(1998—$263.7; 1997—$311.3)	$ 260.7	$ 306.2
amortization (1998—$263.4;			Common	—	848.5
1997—$239.9)	704.3	727.8		$ 260.7	$1,154.7
Other	762.0	359.9			
	$ 2,142.2	$1,273.6	COMMON STOCKHOLDERS' EQUITY (DEFICIT)		
	$10,280.8	$9,336.2	Common stock, $.01 par value; shares		
			authorized—315,000,000; shares issued		
			and outstanding (1998—108,953,764;		
			1997—103,780,875)	$ 1.1	$ 1.0
			Additional paid-in capital	1,444.6	1,273.6
			Accumulated deficit	(648.5)	(362.2)
			Accumulated other comprehensive loss	(68.1)	(101.8)
			Treasury stock (1998—28,978,351; 1997—		
			6,800,000 shares repurchased and		
			18,177,874 shares to be repurchased)	(1,205.8)	(1,121.6)
				$ (476.7)	$ (311.0)
				$10,280.8	$9,336.2

The appearance of income taxes as both benefits and expenses on the income statement and as both assets and liabilities on the balance sheet may be puzzling. The accounting for taxes is tied to the accounting for the assets and liabilities on the balance sheet. We will see how accounting assets and liabilities can generate **deferred tax liabilities** and **deferred tax assets.** Similarly, we will see how income taxes can come to be shown as expenses in some cases and benefits in others in an income statement. To see how these things can occur, we must go into some detail about TAP. Before doing so, however, it is helpful to examine the parts of Notes A and J of the Northwest financial statements given in Exhibit 14.3. They will give us some clue as to the ways in which tax accounting is different from financial accounting.

Exhibit 14.3

Excerpts from Notes to Northwest Airlines' Financial Statements

Description of accounting for deferred taxes

Consequence of faster depreciation under TAP than under GAAP

Consequence of more expenses taken under GAAP than under TAP

This figure agrees with the net deferred tax liability reported on the balance sheet.

Excerpts from Notes A and J to Northwest Airlines' Financial Statements

From Note A:

INCOME TAXES: The Company accounts for income taxes utilizing the liability method. Deferred income taxes are primarily recorded to reflect the tax consequences of differences between the tax and financial reporting bases of assets and liabilities.

From Note J:

The net deferred tax liabilities listed below include a current net deferred tax asset of $114.3 million and $84.8 million and a long-term net deferred tax liability of $1.11 billion and $1.16 billion as of December 31, 1998 and 1997, respectively.

Significant components of the Company's net deferred tax liability were as follows (in millions):

	December 31	
Deferred Tax Liabilities:	**1998**	**1997**
Financial accounting basis of assets in excess of tax basis	$1,489.4	$1,452.0
Expenses other than depreciation accelerated for tax purposes	313.0	309.4
Other	15.9	12.4
Total deferred tax liabilities	$1,818.3	$1,773.8
Deferred Tax Assets:		
Pension and postretirement benefits	$ 84.7	$ 128.3
Expenses accelerated for financial reporting purposes	547.9	409.3
Leases capitalized for financial reporting purposes	80.4	105.1
Alternative minimum tax credit carryforwards	103.2	54.4
Other tax credit carryforwards	3.7	—
Total deferred tax assets	819.9	697.1
Net deferred tax liability	$ 998.4	$1,076.7

Intuitively, you can think of a deferred tax liability as an obligation to pay tax in the future, and a deferred tax asset as a prepaid tax.

Note A says it all: "Deferred income taxes are primarily recorded to reflect the tax consequences of differences between the tax and financial reporting bases of assets and liabilities." The liability method is an accounting approach used to compute and create deferred taxes. We examine this approach later.

The amounts in Note J provide detail for the balance sheet. The total net deferred tax liability of $998.4 agrees with the total on the balance sheet.

Several of the descriptions from Note J are particularly revealing. For example, the first explanatory line under Deferred Tax Liabilities is "Financial accounting basis of assets in excess of tax basis." The second line is "Expenses other than depreciation accelerated for tax purposes." Under Deferred Tax Assets, we find "Expenses accelerated for financial reporting purposes." These descriptions hint at what GAAP accounting for taxes is really all about. Rather than trying to present a separate set of financial statements for tax accounting, GAAP try to give us enough information (through the deferred tax accounts) to enable us to see what would have to be changed in order to generate the tax statements. These disclosures also hint that the main differences between tax and financial reporting arise because of timing differences. Items of revenue and expense are likely to appear in both tax and financial reports in the same amounts, but in different periods.

Up to this point, we have not introduced TAP at all. To understand GAAP accounting for income taxes in more detail, we must first introduce some of the main TAP rules that are different from GAAP. These differences drive the GAAP creation of deferred tax.

Tax Accounting Principles (TAP)

Any discussion of TAP should begin by noting that the purposes of tax accounting are different from the purposes of financial reporting governed by GAAP. The primary purpose of TAP is to raise revenues for the government. TAP determine taxable income, which in turn determines the income taxes to be paid. TAP are also used as political and macroeconomic tools to modify behavior in the economy. For example, by giving special treatment to investments in specific types of assets or assets in specified locations, TAP depreciation rules can be used to encourage or discourage investments in the assets affected by the tax rules.

Like GAAP, the application of TAP produces an income statement and balance sheet. The income calculated on a TAP income statement is taxable income. Revenues in TAP, unfortunately, are called **income,** and expenses are called **deductions.** The values on a TAP balance sheet are called the **tax bases** of the assets and liabilities. TAP are decidedly not aimed at yielding taxable income that reflects economic performance, or tax bases that reflect economic values. Taxable income and tax bases of assets and liabilities determine an entity's tax payments, nothing more.

Let us briefly survey a few areas of TAP and show how they compare to GAAP for the same transactions.

Marketable Securities

See Chapter 10 for the GAAP rules for marketable securities.

TAP do not require recognition of gains or permit recognition of losses on marketable securities until those gains or losses are realized through a transaction. In contrast, for marketable securities classified as trading securities, GAAP require unrealized gains and losses to appear in the income statement.

Depreciation

See Chapter 11 for a discussion of GAAP rules for depreciation.

TAP allow much more accelerated depreciation over shorter lives than do GAAP. Recall that GAAP require an asset's depreciable cost to be written off in a systematic and rational manner over the asset's useful economic life. Depreciable cost includes an allowance for a reasonable salvage value. Allowable GAAP methods include units-of-production, straight-line, sum-of-years'-digits, and declining balance.

TAP depreciation is guided by the **Modified Accelerated Cost Recovery System (MACRS).** Regardless of the best estimate of useful economic life, the MACRS classifies all property into one of eight categories:

MACRS Class	Examples
3-year property	Small tools, assets used in research and development
5-year property	Automobiles, computers, trucks and office equipment
7-year property	Office furniture, manufacturing equipment, and all property not in any other class
10-year property	Mobile homes
15-year property	Roads
20-year property	Sewer systems
27.5-year property	Residential real property
39-year property	Nonresidential real property

Half-year convention: the double-declining-balance rate for a 5-year life is twice $\frac{1}{5}$, or 40%. One-half of 40% is 20%, the rate applied to the asset for the first year it is acquired.

MACRS depreciation rates approximate double-declining balance depreciation with a switch to straight-line for property in classes of 10 or fewer years. MACRS also uses a **half-year convention,** in which any asset purchased during a year is treated as if it were purchased at the middle of the year. MACRS depreciation rates for 3-, 5-, and 7-year property are as follows:

Year	3-Year Property	5-Year Property	7-Year Property
1	33.33%	20.00%	14.29%
2	44.44	32.00	24.49
3	14.81	19.20	17.49
4	7.42	11.52	12.49
5		11.52	8.93
6		5.76	8.93
7			8.93
8			4.45
Total	100.00%	100.00%	100.00%

Postretirement Benefits Other Than Pensions

In general, TAP are geared much more to actual cash flows than are GAAP.

In addition to pensions, many organizations promise workers other benefits in retirement. GAAP require the obligations for these benefits and the associated expenses to be recorded in the periods in which the benefits are earned. TAP do not allow recognition

Financial reporting methods factor in taxes due on employee's postretirement benefits, a sum that can be significant.

If the deferred tax amount is $14.4 billion and GM's tax rate is 35%, then the actual amount of the benefit is about $14.4/0.65 = $22.1.

of these obligations and prohibit taking deductions for these obligations as workers earn them. Instead, TAP allow deductions only when benefits are actually paid.

The exact calculations required by GAAP for postretirement benefits other than pensions are beyond the scope of this book. It is worth noting, however, that the tax effects of the difference between GAAP and TAP recognition for these items can be quite substantial. For example, these benefits were the largest single item in explaining GM's deferred taxes in fiscal 1999. The deferred taxes associated with postretirement benefits other than pensions for GM in that year were about $14.4 billion. Even though GM's total assets were a whopping $274.7 billion, $14.4 billion is still quite a substantial amount.

Asset Impairments

TAP do not allow deductions for asset impairments. As we saw in Chapter 11, GAAP do.

Net Operating Loss Carryforwards/Carrybacks

The period over which taxable income is calculated affects the taxes paid, and fairness requires we make some provisions for smoothing things out across time. For example, consider a U.S. company subject to the federal statutory tax rate of 35%. Suppose this company has income of exactly zero in each of three years. Then, it will pay no tax:

Year	Taxable Income	Taxes Owed (@ 35%)
1	0	0
2	0	0
3	0	0
Total	0	0

Now suppose the company's taxable income over the three-year period adds up to exactly zero, but that it is not zero in each year. Suppose the taxable income is $60,000 one year, *negative* $100,000 the next, and $40,000 the third year. Although it still adds up to exactly zero profits over the three-year period, this pattern of taxable income would result in $35,000 in tax payments if there were no ability to utilize the $100,000 loss to offset tax payments in the first and third years:

Year	Taxable Income	Taxes Owed (@ 35%)
1	60	21
2	(100)	?
3	40	14
Total	0	35 ± ?

The government sensibly has chosen to allow taxpayers to use losses to recoup past taxes, a **loss carryback,** and to use any remainder to offset future taxes—a **loss carryforward.** In the second year, the taxpayer is allowed to use $60,000 of the $100,000 tax loss as a tax loss carryback to obtain a refund of the $21,000 in taxes it paid in the first year. The remaining $40,000 of the $100,000 loss can be used as a tax loss carryforward to offset future income. It then can use the $40,000 tax loss carryforward to offset $40,000 of taxable income in the third year:

In Year 2, $60 of the loss is carried back to the previous year's income of $60, and the $21 taxes paid for Year 1 are refunded to the company. The other $40 of loss in Year 2 can be carried forward and used to offset future gains.

In Year 3, the $40 of earned income is offset by the $40 loss carried forward from Year 2, and no taxes are paid.

Year	Taxable Income	Taxes Owed (@ 35%)
1	60	21
2	(100)	(21)
3	40	0
Total	0	0

Because they generate future benefits in the form of tax savings, tax loss carryforwards may lead to assets that are reported on GAAP balance sheets.

Warranties

Just as with postretirement benefits other than pensions, TAP do not allow the deduction of a warranty expense until the cash is paid. GAAP for warranties is aimed at recording warranty liabilities and matching warranty expense to sales in the proper period, regardless of when the cash expenditures for fulfilling the warranties actually occur.

Inventories

Inventory accounting is the one area where, in certain instances, the TAP and GAAP treatments are required to be identical.

Inventories are one of the few places where GAAP and TAP *must,* in some circumstances, agree. We mentioned the LIFO conformity rule in Chapter 9. This rule requires any company using LIFO for tax purposes also to use LIFO in the preparation of its financial statements. It is conceivable that an organization could use LIFO for GAAP reporting and FIFO for TAP reporting, but we know of no actual instances of it.

Lease Transactions

Leases are often used to affect tax payments. Here are some of the issues: Suppose Taxpayer A owns a depreciable asset that Taxpayer B can put to more profitable use. Taxpayers A and B can arrange a transaction in at least two ways that will allow B to use the asset. One possibility is for B to buy the asset from A. Taxpayer A may even loan B the money to make the purchase. Arranged this way, Taxpayer A may have a gain or loss on the sale of the asset plus interest revenue on money loaned to B. Taxpayer B will have depreciation deductions plus interest expense on money borrowed from A.

Another possibility is for B to lease the asset from A. Arranged this way, A will have rental income, and B will have rent expense. Taxpayer A retains ownership, so no gain or loss is recognized from a sale of the asset, and A continues taking deductions for depreciation.

See Chapter 11 for a discussion of the treatment of leases in the financial statements.

As we discussed in Chapter 11, the provisions of leases determine whether a given lease transaction is treated as an *operating lease* or as a de facto purchase under GAAP. Treating a lease as a purchase is called treating it as a *capital lease.*

TAP also make distinctions between operating leases and capital leases. The criteria TAP use to classify leases as capital leases are similar to, but not exactly the same as, the criteria used under GAAP. Taxpayers sometimes use these differences to structure leases that are classified as operating leases under GAAP, but are classified as capital leases under TAP. Because they are accounted for differently under GAAP and TAP, deferred tax consequences will result.

*Two basic categories of items are treated differently in the TAP statements and the GAAP statements: **temporary (timing) difference** items and **permanent difference** items.*

The TAP and GAAP treatments of depreciation and lease transactions differ in terms of the timing of recognition of expenses, but not in the total amounts recognized over time. These items create **temporary (timing) differences** between GAAP and TAP books. Other items cause **permanent differences** between the two sets of books. These items are recognized on one set of books, but never recognized on the other. For example, interest on municipal bonds is not included in taxable income;[1] it is included in GAAP income. Expenditures for fines imposed for violations of the law are never deductible under TAP, but must be counted as expenses under GAAP. Both the proceeds from and expenditures for life insurance on key employees are not recognized under TAP, but must be recognized under GAAP.

Deferred tax items relate only to temporary (timing) difference items. Permanent difference items do not create deferred tax accounts.

Items that cause permanent differences between TAP and GAAP books do not give rise to tax assets or liabilities on GAAP balance sheets.

Example of TAP Financial Statements

An example of how TAP determine income statements and balance sheets will be useful. The fundamentals of accounting presented in Chapters 1 through 4 continue to be the

---

[1]Making interest on municipal bonds tax exempt lowers the interest rates investors demand on these bonds. This feature makes acquiring funds cheaper for municipalities, which is the typical justification for exempting interest on municipal bonds from taxation.

foundation for the construction of financial statements, whether under GAAP or TAP. The basic relationships between income statements and balance sheets presented in Chapters 2 and 3 hold just as well with TAP as with GAAP. The techniques of debits and credits are just as applicable to keeping records under TAP as they are to keeping records under GAAP. TAP affect which events are recognized and exactly how they are portrayed through time, not the underlying relationships among the resulting financial statements.

On July 1, 2004, NetService incorporates by issuing 10,000 shares of no par common stock for $100 per share. This event is recorded under TAP the same way it would be under GAAP (amounts in $1,000s):

GAAP:
Cash	1,000	
Common Stock		1,000

TAP:
Cash	1,000	
Common Stock		1,000

Also on July 1, NetService signs an employment contract with a manager and buys office equipment for $750,000. Again, the GAAP and TAP entries would be the same. No entry is required to recognize the employment contract under either GAAP or TAP.

GAP:
Office Equipment	750	
Cash		750

Will be depreciated on a straight-line basis.

TAP:
Office Equipment	750	
Cash		750

Will be depreciated according to MACRS.

On July 1, NetService invests $100,000 of its remaining cash in tax-exempt municipal bonds. These bonds were purchased at face value. They pay interest at 4% per year, compounded semiannually and paid on December 31 and June 30. Initial recording of the bonds is identical under GAAP and TAP.

GAAP:
Municipal Bonds	100	
Cash		100

Will show interest on bonds as revenue.

TAP:
Municipal Bonds	100	
Cash		100

Will not show interest on bonds as revenue.

Between July 1 and December 31, 2004, NetService performs services for which it bills $245,000. NetService guarantees its services and expects to incur $10,000 in costs on December 31, 2005, to fulfill these guarantees.

Both TAP and GAAP would record the sale, but, unlike GAAP, TAP do not allow recording any expenses for fulfilling the guarantee until those costs are paid. The entries under GAAP and TAP are:

GAAP:
Accounts Receivable	245	
Revenue		245

Adjusting entries for warranties and bad debt expense will be required.

TAP:
Accounts Receivable	245	
Revenue		245

No adjusting entry for warranties or bad debt expense will be required.

Between July 1 and December 31, 2004, NetService collects $220,000 of the $245,000 owed by customers. NetService expects to incur $1,000 in bad debts on the $25,000 still owed by its customers.

Both TAP and GAAP record the collection, but TAP do not allow recording of any expenses for bad debts until the accounts are written off.

	Cash	220
GAAP:	Accounts Receivable	220
	Will adjust for bad debt expense.	
	Cash	220
TAP:	Accounts Receivable	220
	Will not recognize bad debt expense. Will wait until write-off.	

Municipal bond interest is a permanent difference item.

On December 31, NetService receives its interest payment of $2,000 ($100,000 times 0.04/2) from the municipal bonds. This receipt is not revenue under TAP. Similar to an increase in the value of a marketable security available-for-sale under GAAP, interest from tax-exempt municipal bonds increases TAP equity without being counted in the TAP income statement. GAAP count it as revenue.

GAAP:	Cash	2
	Interest Revenue (Income statement account)	2
TAP:	Cash	2
	Tax-Exempt Revenue (Shareholders' equity account)	2

Between July 1 and December 31, NetService pays its workers $75,000 for services rendered. These payments fully compensate all workers for all amounts earned between July 1 and December 31. This expense is recorded identically under both GAAP and TAP.

GAAP:	Wage Expense	75
	Cash	75
TAP:	Wage Expense	75
	Cash	75

The accounting process under TAP is the same as for GAAP. Therefore, after the transactions are recorded, the TAP books must be adjusted and closed. This process begins by preparing the unadjusted trial balance given in Exhibit 14.4. (Some accounts are

Exhibit 14.4

NetService
TAP Unadjusted Trial Balance

NetService TAP Unadjusted Trial Balance
As of December 31, 2004
(amounts in thousands)

	DR	CR
Cash	$ 297.0	
Accounts Receivable	25.0	
Municipal Bonds	100.0	
Office Equipment	750.0	
Bad Debt Expense	0.0	
Warranty Expense	0.0	
Depreciation Expense	0.0	
Wages Expense	75.0	
Tax Expense	0.0	
Allowance for Doubtful Accounts		$ 0.0
Accumulated Depreciation		0.0
Taxes Payable		0.0
Warranty Liability		0.0
Common Stock		1,000.0
Retained Earnings		0.0
Tax Exempt Revenues		2.0
Revenues		245.0
Totals	$1,247.0	$1,247.0

included in the unadjusted trial balance that are not necessary to prepare TAP financial statements. These accounts are there to help you learn more about how TAP differ from GAAP.) At this point, we will finish only the TAP statements. We will come back to the GAAP statements in a later section.

Just as we did in Chapter 3, we go through the list of accounts to determine if any adjustments are necessary.

- *Cash* requires no adjustment.
- *Accounts Receivable* requires no adjustment.
- *Municipal Bonds* requires no adjustment. TAP carry investments at cost and do not write them up or down to their market values.
- *Office Equipment* requires no adjustment. (We will have to adjust Accumulated Depreciation in a moment.)
- *Bad Debts Expense* and the *Allowance for Doubtful Accounts* require no adjustment. TAP recognize bad debt expense only when an account is written off, so the balance in Allowance for Doubtful Accounts under TAP is always zero. In turn, accounts receivable on a TAP balance sheet are overstated relative to their economic value.
- *Warranty Expense* and *Warranty Liability* require no adjustment. TAP recognize warranty expense only when costs to fulfill warranties are incurred. The balance in Warranty Liability is always zero under TAP.
- *Depreciation Expense* and *Accumulated Depreciation* require an adjustment to recognize MACRS depreciation under TAP. Office equipment is 5-year property, so we take 20% of its cost as depreciation expense in the year it was purchased.

TAP:
Depreciation Expense 150.0
    Accumulated Depreciation 150.0

Note that this amount is proper under TAP regardless of the useful economic life and salvage value of the office equipment. TAP depreciation adjustments are governed by TAP depreciation rules, namely MACRS. GAAP and the actual economic depreciation on the assets are irrelevant.

- *Wages Expense* requires no adjustment.
- *Tax Expense* and *Taxes Payable* require an adjustment. The purpose of TAP is to determine the income taxes due, (i.e., Taxes Payable). To compute the adjustment, we calculate NetService's taxable income. Taxable income is the net income before tax using TAP and is computed as follows:

Revenues	$ 245.0
Wages expense	(75.0)
Depreciation expense	(150.0)
Taxable income	$ 20.0
Income tax at 35%	$ 7.0

TAP:
Tax Expense 7.0
    Taxes Payable 7.0

These adjustments are all that are required. We should now close NetService's TAP books with the following entry:

TAP:
Revenues 245.0
    Depreciation Expense 150.0
    Wages Expense 75.0
    Taxes Expense 7.0
    Retained Earnings 13.0

We can now prepare financial statements under TAP. The TAP income statement shown in Exhibit 14.5 on page 274 does not have much use. The only TAP income calculation that is important is the one of taxable income, because it determines taxes payable. The TAP balance sheet shown in Exhibit 14.6 on page 274, however, is

Exhibit 14.5

NetService
TAP Income Statement

NetService TAP Income Statement
For the Six Months Ended December 31, 2004
(amounts in thousands)

Revenues	$ 245.0
Depreciation expense	(150.0)
Wages expense	(75.0)
Taxable income	$ 20.0
Income tax expense	(7.0)
Income after taxes	$ 13.0

Exhibit 14.6

NetService
TAP Balance Sheet

NetService TAP Balance Sheet
As of December 31, 2004
(amounts in thousands)

Assets	
Cash	$ 297.0
Accounts receivable	25.0
Municipal bonds	100.0
Total current assets	$ 422.0
Office equipment	$ 750.0
Less: Accumulated depreciation	(150.0)
Office equipment, net	$ 600.0
Total assets	$1,022.0
Liabilities	
Taxes payable	$ 7.0
Shareholders' Equity	
Common stock	1,000.0
Retained earnings	13.0
Tax exempt revenue	2.0
Total liabilities and shareholders' equity	$1,022.0

important. It gives the tax bases of assets and liabilities that serve as the starting point for the GAAP accounting for deferred taxes that we will explain later.

Review Questions

1. Does TAP produce an income statement and a balance sheet?

2. Can debit and credit techniques be used to record transactions under TAP?

3. What governs TAP depreciation, and how is it different from GAAP?

4. What is an operating loss carryback?

5. What is an operating loss carryforward?

6. What is the LIFO conformity rule?

7. Are leases treated the same under GAAP and TAP?

Economic Value of Deferred Income Taxes

OBJECTIVE:

Learn to analyze how income taxes impact the economic value of a firm's assets and liabilities.

Income taxes help pay for public goods, which an organization does not control and can consume independently of its income tax payments. Income taxes themselves do not have an economic value to an organization. However, income taxes affect the economic values of other assets and liabilities. The payments for income taxes depend on the amounts realized from the organization's other assets and liabilities. If an organization's assets produce no taxable income, the organization will owe no income tax. If an organization does not have liabilities that require it to pay out cash, it will have no deductions from them that reduce its income taxes.

The starting point in understanding the economic value of income taxes is, therefore, the economic values of an organization's assets and liabilities. The economic values of assets and liabilities are functions of the expected cash flows they produce. These expected cash flows should be the *after-tax* cash flows generated by an asset or required by a liability. After all, the purchaser of an asset gets to keep only the after-tax cash flow, so it is what determines the asset's economic value to the company.

Example of Deferred Tax Liability Creation: Depreciation

On December 31, 2003, a company purchases a fixed asset for $256.90 in cash. The asset is classified as 3-year property and, under MACRS, will be depreciated according to the following rates over four years: 33.33%, 44.44%, 14.81%, and 7.42%, respectively. The company has sufficient other taxable income in every year and can use depreciation in each of the four years to lower its taxable income and therefore save cash payments for income taxes. The company pays income taxes at a rate of 35% of pretax income. The company requires a rate of return of 6.5% after taxes.

The depreciation will shield $85.63 of income from taxation, saving the company $29.97 in tax payments.

The asset is expected to generate before-tax cash flow of $100 in the years 2004, 2005, and 2006. In 2003 the company will have a cash outflow to purchase the asset. But under MACRS it will also have $256.90 × 0.3333 = $85.63 of depreciation expense in year 2003 pretax TAP income. This incremental depreciation will lower the company's cash outflow for taxes by 0.35 × $85.63 = $29.97. So the net cash outflow in 2003, when the asset is purchased, is $256.90 − $29.97 = $226.93.

In 2006 the asset will generate $100 of pretax cash inflow. In that year there will be 0.0742 × $256.90 = $19.06 in depreciation. Therefore incremental taxable income from this asset will be $100.00 − $19.06 = $80.94. The incremental tax bill for this asset will be 0.35 × $80.94 = $28.33. The net cash inflow in 2006 is thus $100 less $28.33 in income taxes, or $71.67. Exhibit 14.7 shows the net cash flows from this asset, taking into account the impact of depreciation on tax payments.

Exhibit 14.7

Calculation of Example Asset's After-Tax Cash Flows

Year	2003	2004	2005	2006
(a) Before-tax cash flow	$ 0.00	$ 100.00	$100.00	$100.00
(b) Depreciation deduction	(85.63)	(114.17)	(38.05)	(19.06)
(c) Taxable income (loss) from asset [(a) − (b)]	(85.63)	(14.17)	61.95	80.94
(d) Income tax benefit (expenditure) @ 35% [0.35 of (c)]	29.97	4.96	(21.68)	(28.33)
(e) Initial cost of the asset	(256.90)	0	0	0
(f) After-tax cash flow (equals before—tax cash flow adjusted for the tax payments) [(a) + (d)]. In year 2003 the cost of the asset (e) is subtracted.	$(226.93)	$ 104.96	$ 78.32	$ 71.67

Considering the impact of taxes, the company essentially makes an investment of $256.90 at the end of 2003 in exchange for an immediate tax savings of $29.97 and a positive cash flow stream of $104.96, $78.32, and $71.67 in the subsequent three years. In fact, at 6.5%, this asset's stream of cash flows equals $256.90 in present value (PV) terms.

$$PV = \$29.97 + \$104.96/1.065 + \$78.32/(1.065)^2 + \$71.67/(1.065)^3$$
$$= \$29.97 + \$98.55 + \$69.05 + \$59.33$$
$$= \$256.90$$

It will be useful to rewrite the cash flows from the asset in a way that separates the effects of the depreciation on taxes. The after-tax cash flow in any year is the gross cash flow, minus taxes on the gross cash flow (that adds up to the after-tax cash flow ignoring depreciation), plus the dollar amount of the taxes saved by the depreciation deduction. The dollar amount of taxes saved by the depreciation adjustment is called the **depreciation tax shield.** To see this effect, notice that the after-tax cash flow in 2005 in Exhibit 14.7 is

$$\$78.32 = \$100.00 - \$21.68$$
$$= \$100.00 - (\$100.00 - \$38.05) \times 35\%$$
$$= \$100.00 - (\$100.00 \times 35\%) + (\$38.05 \times 35\%)$$
$$= \$100.00 - \$35.00 + \$13.32$$

| *Pretax cash flow from asset* | *Taxes on pretax cash flow, excluding the effect of depreciation* | *Reduction in taxes from depreciation deduction* |

Exhibit 14.8 verifies that the expected after-tax cash flows from the asset can be decomposed to isolate the effects of depreciation on taxes.

Exhibit 14.8

Decomposition of After-Tax Cash Flow

Separation of Depreciation's Effect on Taxes in Example Asset's After-Tax Cash Flows				
Year	**2003**	**2004**	**2005**	**2006**
Pretax cash flow	$ 0	$100.00	$100.00	$100.00
Less taxes on pretax cash flow	0	(35.00)	(35.00)	(35.00)
After-tax cash flow ignoring the effect of depreciation deductions [equals (1–35%) × pretax cash flow]	$ 0	$ 65.00	$ 65.00	$ 65.00
Depreciation tax shield (equals 35% of MACRS depreciation)	29.97	39.96	13.32	6.67
After-tax cash flow	$29.97	$104.96	$ 78.32	$ 71.67

The economic value of the asset can, therefore, be thought of as having three parts: (1) the discounted value of the expected gross cash flows, (2) the discounted value of the expected taxes on the gross cash flows, and (3) the discounted value of the depreciation tax shield. Exhibit 14.9 shows how this decomposition applies to the example asset.

The value of the asset is then the sum of the values of two sub-assets and a sub-liability. The gross cash flows are an asset. The taxes are a liability. The depreciation tax shield is an asset.

This discussion indicates in a general way that the economic values of assets and liabilities can give rise to tax assets and tax liabilities. The precise way deferred tax assets

Exhibit 14.9

Economic Value of an Asset with Income Taxes

Three Parts of Economic Value of an Asset with Income Taxes	
Present value of gross cash flows	$264.85
Present value of taxes on gross cash flows (a tax liability)	(92.70)
Present value of depreciation tax shield (a tax asset)	84.75
Total value of asset	$256.90

and liabilities arise under GAAP, however, is more complicated than this analysis of economic values suggests. We will do one other short example before going to the next section, which presents GAAP for deferred income taxes.

Example of Deferred Tax Asset Creation: Warranties

Consider the guarantee issued by NetService in conjunction with the sale of its services. Recall that NetService bills its clients $245,000 for services rendered between July 1 and December 31, 2004. NetService expects to incur $10,000 in costs to fulfill the guarantees for these services in 2002.

This $10,000 in expected warranty costs does not include its effect on income taxes. Suppose the warranty costs turn out to be exactly as expected. When NetService pays these warranty costs, TAP recognize them in the computation of taxable income. The effect is to lower taxable income by $10,000. This effect lowers NetService's taxes due by 35% of $10,000, or $3,500. The net effect of the guarantee on NetService's after-tax cash flows is $6,500: A $10,000 outflow less $3,500 in tax savings. The economic value of the warranty liability on December 31, 2004, is then the present value of $6,500 to be paid one year hence. Suppose the interest rate is 10%. The economic value of the warranty liability is (in thousands):

$$\$6.5/1.1 = \$5.91$$

To better understand the economics and the impact of taxes, it is useful to rewrite the calculation of the present value of the expected warranty costs by separating the warranty costs and the tax effects:

$$\$6.5/1.1 = (\$10.0 - \$3.5)/1.1 = \$10.0/1.1 - \$3.5/1.1$$

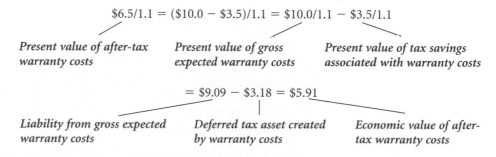

Present value of after-tax warranty costs   *Present value of gross expected warranty costs*   *Present value of tax savings associated with warranty costs*

$$= \$9.09 - \$3.18 = \$5.91$$

Liability from gross expected warranty costs   *Deferred tax asset created by warranty costs*   *Economic value of after-tax warranty costs*

The present value of the tax savings reduces the cash flow associated with the warranty liability. The tax effect, then, is a future benefit associated with the gross expected warranty costs. The economic value of the warranty liability consists of the economic value of the liability for gross expected warranty costs, less the economic value of a deferred tax asset created by these costs.

With this understanding of the basic economics of what is happening, let's look at the GAAP accounting treatment of taxes. We will see that, except for discounting, GAAP attempt to capture the basic economics of income taxes.

Recall that when we discussed accounts receivable in Chapter 8 we saw that GAAP failed to capture the time value of money as well.

GAAP for Deferred Income Taxes

GAAP for deferred income taxes are focused on differences between the GAAP and TAP balance sheets. We introduce GAAP for deferred income taxes in the context of the NetService example from the previous section where we already recorded the basic transactions for the year.

Go back and review the basic transactions for NetService (*Example of TAP Financial Statements*) in the *Nature of Income Taxes* section of this chapter. The unadjusted trial balance for the GAAP financial statements appears in Exhibit 14.10.

Exhibit 14.10

Net Service
GAAP Unadjusted Trial Balance

NetService GAAP Unadjusted Trial Balance As of December 31, 2004 (amounts in thousands)		
	DR	**CR**
Cash	$ 297.0	
Accounts Receivable	25.0	
Municipal Bonds	100.0	
Office Equipment	750.0	
Bad Debts Expense	0.0	
Warranty Expense	0.0	
Depreciation Expense	0.0	
Wages Expense	75.0	
Tax Expense	0.0	
Allowance for Doubtful Accounts		$ 0.0
Accumulated Depreciation		0.0
Taxes Payable		0.0
Warranty Liability		0.0
Common Stock		1,000.0
Retained Earnings		0.0
Interest Revenues		2.0
Revenues		245.0
Totals	$1,247.0	$1,247.0

Just as we did in Chapter 3, we go through the list of accounts to determine whether any adjustments are necessary.

- *Cash* requires no adjustment.
- *Accounts Receivable* requires no adjustment. *Bad Debt Expense* and *Allowance for Doubtful Accounts* will be adjusted shortly.
- *Municipal Bonds* might require adjustment. GAAP carry investments at market values. For simplicity, assume the market value of the bond is $100,000, so no adjustment is required.
- *Office Equipment* requires no adjustment. (We will adjust Accumulated Depreciation in a moment.)
- *Bad Debts Expense* and the *Allowance for Doubtful Accounts* require an adjustment. GAAP require recognition of bad debt expense when it is incurred, regardless of when an account is written off. GAAP also require establishing an Allowance for Doubtful Accounts to bring net accounts receivable on the GAAP balance sheet into line with their economic value. Recall, NetService expects $1,000 in uncollectible accounts as of December 31, 2004. The entry to set up the allowance and record the expense is

GAAP:
Bad Debt Expense 1.0
  Allowance for Doubtful Accounts 1.0

- GAAP require adjustment of *Warranty Expense* and *Warranty Liability.* Warranty Expense is recorded as incurred, and a warranty liability is established to reflect the obligation to pay warranty costs in the future. Recall, NetService expects warranty costs to be $10,000. The entry is

GAAP: Warranty Expense 10.0
              Warranty Liability 10.0

- *Depreciation Expense* and *Accumulated Depreciation* require an adjustment to recognize depreciation under GAAP. The useful economic life of the office equipment is expected to be five years, with no salvage value. NetService uses straight-line depreciation for GAAP purposes. Depreciation for one-half year is

It is acceptable to use the half-year convention for GAAP as well.

GAAP: Depreciation Expense 75.0
              Accumulated Depreciation 75.0

- *Wages Expense* requires no adjustment.
- *Tax Expense* and *Taxes Payable* require an adjustment. Our earlier calculations using TAP showed NetService owed $7,000 in taxes. Therefore, we know that Taxes Payable must be adjusted so that its balance ends up being $7,000.

If there is uncertainty about whether a deferred tax asset will be realized—e.g., if it is unlikely that there will be sufficient taxable income to use future deductions—then a contra-asset **valuation allowance** *must be established to reduce the net value reported on the balance sheet.*

Tax expense is more complicated. Think about the Warranty Liability recorded under GAAP. It is recorded at its gross amount of $10,000. However, when that liability is paid, it will generate tax benefits because its payments are tax deductible. As discussed in the previous section on the economic value of deferred taxes, the net outflow associated with the Warranty Liability is only $6,500: the gross of $10,000 less a $3,500 tax benefit. GAAP require that we record a Deferred Tax Asset to reflect this tax benefit.

Similarly, Allowance for Doubtful Accounts was established to offset part of the book value of Accounts Receivable. With this account, the appropriate Bad Debts Expense can be recognized and Accounts Receivable (net) on the GAAP balance sheet is more in line with economic value. Allowance for Doubtful Accounts is not allowed under TAP. When Accounts Receivable is ultimately realized at its net value, TAP will allow deductions for bad debts. In essence, Allowance for Doubtful Accounts of $1,000 has an associated tax benefit of $350, and GAAP require recognition of a Deferred Tax Asset to reflect these tax benefits.

Accumulated Depreciation also reduces the book value of an asset (Office Equipment in this case). However, there is Accumulated Depreciation on *both* the GAAP and TAP sets of books. In fact, Accumulated Depreciation under TAP is greater than it is under GAAP, because Depreciation Expense in 2001 is greater under TAP than under GAAP.

If TAP depreciation is greater than GAAP depreciation in some years, it must be less in others. After all, the total depreciation must add up to the cost of the asset under either system. TAP Accumulated Depreciation is $75,000 higher than GAAP in 2004, because TAP has recorded $75,000 *more* Depreciation Expense than GAAP through 2004. Therefore, TAP will record $75,000 *less* Depreciation Expense over the remaining depreciable life of the asset after 2004. Smaller depreciation deductions mean higher taxes. Therefore, GAAP require recording a Deferred Tax Liability of 35% of $75,000 associated with the accumulated depreciation account.

Tax Expense is now the plug in the entry to record the Deferred Tax Assets, the Deferred Tax Liability, and Taxes Payable:

GAAP: Deferred Tax Asset—Warranties 3.50
           Deferred Tax Asset—Bad Debts 0.35
           Tax Expense 29.40
              Deferred Tax Liability 26.25
              Taxes Payable 7.00

Note that if we were to take out the $2 of interest revenue, which is a permanent difference item, pretax net income would be $84. Now the tax rate, 35%, times $84 just equals tax expense of $29.4. GAAP accounting does a good job of matching an appropriate amount of taxes to GAAP income, which isn't always the case, but it is a good rule of thumb.

These adjustments are all that are required. We should now close NetService's GAAP books with the following entry:

GAAP:

Revenues	245.0	
Interest Revenue	2.0	
Depreciation Expense		75.0
Wages Expense		75.0
Bad Debts Expense		1.0
Warranty Expense		10.0
Taxes Expense		29.4
Retained Earnings		56.6

We can now prepare financial statements under GAAP. The GAAP income statement is shown in Exhibit 14.11. Notice how tax expense under GAAP better reflects the tax effects of the GAAP income calculation than does the $7,000 in taxes owed for 2004.

The GAAP balance sheet is shown in Exhibit 14.12.

Exhibit 14.11

NetService
GAAP Income Statement

NetService GAAP Income Statement
For the Six Months Ended December 31, 2004
(amounts in thousands)

Revenues	$245.0
Interest revenue	2.0
Total revenues	$247.0
Depreciation expense	(75.0)
Wages expense	(75.0)
Bad debts expense	(1.0)
Warranty expense	(10.0)
Income tax expense	(29.4)
Income after taxes	$ 56.6

GAAP versus TAP Accounts for NetService and the GAAP Tax Adjustments

The comparison between the GAAP and TAP balance sheets reveals a lot about how GAAP accounting for income taxes works. Exhibit 14.13 shows the amounts reflected in the GAAP and TAP balance sheets for all accounts except the ones for deferred taxes.

The GAAP adjustment for deferred income taxes is tied to the asset and liability accounts where there is a difference between the GAAP and TAP values. In other words, the GAAP adjustment is required on accounts whose book values differ from their tax bases. Three of these accounts can be found in the NetService example: Accounts Receivable, net; Office Equipment, net; and Warranties Payable.

The differences between the equity accounts are also revealing. The difference of $43,600 in Retained Earnings reflects the difference in cumulative income recognized by GAAP and TAP. The GAAP Retained Earnings, being a residual amount, already includes the GAAP adjustments for deferred taxes. Therefore, no further tax adjustment for that account is needed.

The difference in the tax-exempt revenue accounts of $2,000 also does not give rise to a deferred tax adjustment. Recall that the tax-exempt revenue account arises under TAP because interest on the municipal bonds is not taxable. Therefore, it is not counted as income under TAP. Interest on the municipal bonds is counted as income under GAAP. This difference in GAAP and TAP accounting for tax-free municipal bonds is a permanent difference between the two systems. A permanent difference between GAAP and

Exhibit 14.12

NetService
GAAP Balance Sheet

NetService GAAP Balance Sheet
As of December 31, 2004
(amounts in thousands)

ASSETS

Cash	$ 297.00
Accounts receivable, net of an allowance for doubtful accounts of $1.0	24.00
Municipal bonds	100.00
Deferred tax assets	3.85
Total current assets	$ 424.85
Office equipment	$ 750.00
Less accumulated depreciation	(75.00)
Office equipment, net	$ 675.00
Total assets	$1,099.85

LIABILITIES

Taxes payable	$ 7.00
Warranties payable	10.00
Deferred tax liability	26.25
Total liabilities	$ 43.25

SHAREHOLDERS' EQUITY

Common stock	$1,000.00
Retained earnings	56.60
Total shareholders' equity	$1,056.60
Total liabilities and shareholders' equity	$1,099.85

Exhibit 14.13

NetService
Comparison of GAAP and TAP
Balance Sheets

Comparison of NetService's GAAP and TAP
Balance Sheets
As of December 31, 2004
(amounts in thousands)

Account	GAAP Balance Sheet (book value)	TAP Balance Sheet (tax basis)	Difference
ASSETS (except Deferred taxes):			
Cash	$ 297	$ 297	$ 0
Accounts receivable, net	24	25	(1)
Municipal bonds	100	100	0
Office equipment, net	675	600	75
LIABILITIES (except Deferred taxes):			
Taxes payable	$ 7	$ 7	$ 0
Warranties payable	10	0	10
EQUITIES:			
Common stock	$1,000	$1,000	$ 0
Retained earnings	56.6	13	43.6
Tax-exempt revenue	0	2	(2)

TAP is not simply a matter of the timing of recognition. It is a difference in what will ever get recognized. The $2,000 of interest on the tax-exempt municipal bonds will never be included in taxable income; therefore, the GAAP and TAP tax-exempt revenue accounts will always be different.

Contrast this permanent difference in Tax-Exempt Revenue with the temporary difference in Warranties Payable. A temporary difference between GAAP and TAP is a difference that eventually will go away. Suppose NetService stops issuing warranties after December 31, 2004. Eventually, all the warranties will be settled. Then, the GAAP warranties payable account will reach a zero balance, which is the TAP balance.

Similarly, the receivables eventually will either be collected or written off. The office equipment will be fully depreciated at the end of its useful life. Then, GAAP Accounts Receivable, net and Office Equipment, net will have the same account balances as their TAP counterparts, namely, zero.

Another way to view it is to recognize that the $10 of warranty expense was not allowed in current taxable income and therefore $3.5 more in taxes was paid than if it was in taxable income. From the perspective of the accrual GAAP statement, we have prepaid the taxes.

Deferred tax adjustments are required in the case of temporary differences between GAAP and TAP asset and liability accounts. A temporary difference reflects different timing in GAAP and TAP accounting, and a deferred tax adjustment tries to put the GAAP books on an accrual basis with respect to taxes. Think about Warranties Payable. GAAP has recognized $10,000 of Warranties Expense and the associated Warranties Payable. TAP will not recognize the expense until the warranties are paid. GAAP recognition of $10,000 overstates the liability, because of the eventual tax deductibility of the warranty payments. The deferred tax adjustment corrects for this difference in timing of recognition.

Review Questions

1. What are temporary differences between GAAP and TAP?

2. What are permanent differences between GAAP and TAP?

3. Why do deferred tax assets arise under GAAP?

4. Why do deferred tax liabilities arise under GAAP?

Comparison of GAAP and Economic Values for Deferred Income Taxes

OBJECTIVE:
Learn to analyze whether GAAP for income taxes correctly capture the economic impact of taxes.

This difference between GAAP and economic values begins with GAAP's failure to update the basic asset value to its real economic value and is exacerbated by the treatment of taxes.

Let's begin comparing GAAP with economic values by thinking about NetService's warranty liability and associated deferred tax asset. The first thing we might notice is GAAP's lack of discounting. GAAP's failure to discount in valuing the deferred tax asset flows from its prohibition on discounting the warranty liability. Once we have recorded the warranty liability at its undiscounted amount of $10,000, the GAAP for deferred taxes will lead us to record the deferred tax asset of $3,500.

For purchased assets, such as NetService's office equipment, the comparison between GAAP and economic values is more complex. The GAAP deferred tax accounts are not aimed at separating the value of an asset into its three relevant economic parts: the present value of its gross cash flows, a liability for taxes on those cash flows, and the present value of a depreciation deduction. The GAAP deferred tax accounts just reflect differences in GAAP and TAP depreciation. Neither GAAP nor TAP depreciation reflects the fall in the value of the asset, except by chance. Therefore, the GAAP value of the asset and associated deferred taxes will not reflect the economic value of the asset, except by chance.

Because the deferred tax accounts relate to the amounts of other assets and liabilities on the balance sheet, comparing the GAAP values with the economic values of necessary deferred taxes gets us entangled in all the comparisons between GAAP and economic values for those assets and liabilities. If GAAP do not reflect economic values of the underlying assets and liabilities, then GAAP for deferred taxes will not reflect the economic values of associated tax effects.

This chapter has only scratched the surface of tax treatment under GAAP. The uncertainty of the timing differences ever reversing and the deferred taxes ever being realized creates practical problems in applying GAAP that are beyond the scope of this book.

OBJECTIVE:

Learn to analyze GAAP-related tax disclosures.

These comparative differences make understanding the economic significance of the deferred tax assets and liabilities especially difficult. As a result, the accounting for deferred taxes historically has been one of the most controversial areas of GAAP.

Analysis of Deferred Income Taxes

The complex and tangential connection between GAAP and economic values for deferred taxes makes crisp, meaningful analysis of deferred taxes a tough, if not impossible, task. Not a lot of commonly used financial ratios involve the deferred tax accounts. The GAAP disclosures do provide, however, some practical information to those willing to dig it out and reflect on it.

For example, the values in the deferred tax asset accounts reflect tax effects of items that have been counted for expenses for GAAP but have not yet been deducted under TAP. We might ask why a company would use this approach: Why are expenses for GAAP in excess of those for TAP? Sometimes, as with warranties, the answer is simple. GAAP require recognition while TAP prohibit it. But the amount of the deferred tax asset is tied to the amount of the warranty, which involves management estimates. If the deferred tax asset is extremely large, perhaps management overestimated warranty expenses. This overestimation will lower income in periods in which excess expense has been recorded, but it will raise income in later periods in which warranty costs turn out to be less than the book value of their associated liability. Thus, warranty expenses might be used to create hidden reserves of accounting benefits, and the deferred tax accounts might give the analyst a clue about these hidden reserves.

Conversely, the values in deferred tax liability accounts reflect tax effects of items that have been expensed more quickly under TAP than under GAAP. Large balances in deferred tax liability accounts raise the question as to whether GAAP expenses have been too low. Has income been overstated?

The deferred tax asset and deferred tax liability accounts also tell us something about the effectiveness of a company's tax planning policies. Economically, we would like to see a for-profit organization deferring its tax payments as long as possible. No interest accrues on legally deferred tax payments, so postponing tax payments amounts to getting an interest-free loan from the government. All well-run major corporations try to manage their tax payments in ways most advantageous to them, and a large balance in deferred tax liability accounts may reflect their success in doing so.

Conclusion

GAAP for income taxes are controversial and complex. They involve reconciling two sets of accounting principles: GAAP and TAP. If both GAAP and TAP reflect economic value for an asset or a liability, then the book value for that asset equals its tax basis, and no deferred taxes will be recognized. If either GAAP or TAP fail to reflect economic values, then either the book value or tax basis does not reflect economic values, and the difference between them will not reflect economic values. It is the Catch 22[2] of deferred taxes.

We are getting close to the end of this book and to your introduction to accounting. The last topic we will cover before again turning to financial statement analysis involves intercorporate investments. In today's economic environment most firms are structurally complex. The modern firm is a group of many firms and large divisions operating under one corporate umbrella. Companies are continually investing and divesting themselves of

---

[2]Catch 22 is the title of a novel by Joseph Heller about the absurdity of war. It is based on the Air Force rule about being discharged for reasons of insanity. One must apply for an insanity discharge. But since every sane person would want such a discharge, and only an insane person would not, the act of applying demonstrates the sanity of the applicant. All applications are, therefore, denied.

large divisions or entire companies. Many large companies merge (combine operations) with other companies. The next chapter provides an overview of the accounting for mergers and acquisitions and for major long-term investments that one corporation makes in another corporation.

Key Terms

deductions *267*

deferred tax assets *266*

deferred tax liabilities *266*

depreciation tax shield *276*

half-year convention *268*

income (in TAP) *267*

income tax *263*

loss carryback *269*

loss carryforward *269*

Modified Accelerated Cost Recovery System (MACRS) *267*

permanent differences *270*

tax accounting principles (TAP) *263*

tax bases *267*

taxable income *263*

temporary (timing) differences *270*

valuation allowance *279*

chapter 15

AOL Time Warner

© REUTERS NEW MEDIA INC./CORBIS

Active Investments in Corporations

Few types of business transactions attract the public's attention like an active investment of one major corporation in another. Unlike the investments in common stock we covered in Chapter 10, "*Marketable Securities,*" a corporation making an active investment seeks to affect or control the operations of the investee. For the employees of the investee corporation, considerable anxiety is often associated with a transaction in which another corporation gains an active influence over day-to-day activities. No doubt this effect on people's work lives is one reason the public's attention is drawn to these transactions.

The amounts involved in these active investments also attract attention. For example, America Online acquired Time Warner in a deal valued at $181.6 billion! Chase Manhattan merged with several companies, most recently with J. P. Morgan in a deal valued at $31 billion. This and other mergers helped boost the total assets of the combined entity, J. P. Morgan Chase & Co., to more than $715 billion!

A lot of colorful language also surrounds business combinations. There are poison pills, white knights, corporate raiders, vulture investors, greenmail, and golden parachutes. Personalities are celebrated, in both positive and negative ways. Jack Welch of GE was a folk-hero in part from his reputation of acquiring companies and imprinting them with a GE formula for profitability. Warren Buffet is portrayed as the savvy investor that acquires the right companies for his holding company, Berkshire Hathaway. "Chainsaw" Al Dunlop of Sunbeam was vilified as a corporate raider who acquired valuable businesses and slashed their work forces in the name of cost-savings and efficiency. His aggressive pursuit of oil companies made T. Boone Pickens of Mesa Petroleum a hero to some and a villain to others.

The most controversial aspect of business combinations often involves whether the combination is a *purchase* of one business by another, or a merger in which the operations of the businesses are combined in a more egalitarian way. Many people employed by firms that have merged perceive that there is really no such thing as a merger of equals—that one company's methods and, more importantly, its employees will dominate the merged businesses. A recent cartoon in the *New Yorker* captures this skepticism. It pictures a group of executives entering a bank lobby and announcing, "Don't anybody move: this is a merger."[1]

Regardless of public perceptions of business combinations, they are an indisputable fact of life in modern capitalist economies. The result is that most modern corporations consist of many separate entities, called **subsidiaries,** under one corporate umbrella. A subsidiary is a corporation that is controlled by another corporation, called the **parent.** We will see that when the accounts of the subsidiary are folded together with those of the parent, that subsidiary has been consolidated for financial reporting purposes. For example, the 2001 financial statements of the General Motors Corporation (GM) reported on 342 **consolidated subsidiaries** that it owned or in which it had majority interests. The performance of another 74 companies, of which GM owned between 20 and 50 percent, was also included in the report. This behavior is typical of most corporations. They continue to invest and divest themselves of new companies and divisions, some created internally and others purchased.

This chapter focuses on the active investments that corporations make in other corporations. It discusses the nature of such investments and the underlying economics of such transactions.

---

[1] *The New Yorker*, January 8, 2001, p. 36.

It outlines GAAP for active investments and then relates GAAP to the underlying economics. The chapter ends with a brief discussion of how GAAP for active investments affect some of the standard financial ratios we have looked at throughout this book.

Nature of Active Investments

OBJECTIVE:
Learn to understand the nature of active investments in corporations.

Recall that Chapter 10 discussed passive investments in securities.

Many corporations try to increase their profitability by investing in the common stock of other corporations. These investments can be either passive or active in nature, depending on the intention of corporate management.

The objective of a **passive investment** is to earn a return on cash not immediately needed for current operations, without getting involved in the running of the investee. Typically, the amount of stock acquired is not large enough to enable the investor to have a significant influence over the affairs of the investee corporation. We have already covered the accounting for passive investments in common stock in Chapter 10, "*Marketable Securities.*"

The purpose of an **active investment** is to obtain influence over another corporation in order to affect its operations. An active investor might want to affect the operations of another corporation for the following reasons:

- To increase the efficiency of its present operations (e.g., by purchasing another company in the same line of business)
- To gain access to raw material sources, distribution services, or markets (e.g., by purchasing a company that increases their control of vertical operations from the raw material to the sale of the product)
- To exploit its expertise to improve the operations of an inefficiently run investee

Active investments in corporations raise a fundamental issue that we haven't mentioned since Chapter 2—the entity concept. The entity is the person or organization about which accounting's financial history is written. But if one corporation owns 100% of another, what's the right entity? You might say the answer is obvious: it is the owning corporation with all its subsidiaries folded in. But what if the ownership percentage is only 95%? What if it is 40%?

When corporations own all or parts of other corporations, the guiding GAAP notion is to report on the relevant *economic* entity, regardless of the particular legal structure of ownership. In the case of General Motors in 2001 that we mentioned earlier, the accounts of 342 subsidiaries were consolidated with those of GM for financial reporting purposes. **Consolidation** means that the amounts in each account represent the total amounts applicable to GM and all its consolidated subsidiaries; that is, the inventories listed on the consolidated balance sheet are those of GM and the 342 consolidated subsidiaries.

What happens if the percentage of ownership falls to a level where the investing corporation has significant influence, but not full control, of the investee? An ownership interest in the common stock of a corporation is a **minority interest** if it is less than or equal to 50% of the total stock outstanding. Not all minority interests are capable of providing significant influence over the operations of the investee. Small minority interests are generally presumed to be passive investments and are accounted for as available-for-sale marketable securities (Chapter 10). Small is defined conventionally as any minority interest less than 20%. For ownership interests between 20% and 50%, a different method of accounting called the equity method will be used. The equity method calls for listing the investment in the subsidiary as a line item in the assets. However, unlike an available-for-sale security, an **equity method** investment is not marked-to-market. The consolidation method is used for investments in which the ownership interest exceeds 50% of the common stock of the investee. The consolidation method presents sums of the assets, liabilities, and equity of the consolidated entity in one consolidated balance sheet.

An Example: Xerox Corporation

Xerox Corporation's balance sheets for 2001 and 2000[2] are given in Exhibit 15.1. First, we should note that the balance sheets are called *consolidated* balance sheets. This title tells us that Xerox has some subsidiaries whose accounts are included in the totals in these balance sheets. Exhibit 15.2 contains the explanation in Xerox's own words, but it

Exhibit 15.1

Xerox
Consolidated Balance Sheets

The cash, receivables, inventories, and other accounts of the parent and all consolidated subsidiaries are included in these totals (the same for the liabilities).

Investments in Affiliates, at equity is the result of the equity method of accounting for investments for which Xerox owns between 20% and 50%.

Goodwill, net arises in the process of making active investments.

Minorities' Interests in Equity of Subsidiaries arises from consolidating subsidiaries of which Xerox owns less than 100%.

Xerox Corporation
Consolidated Balance Sheets
(amounts in millions)

	December 31, 2001	December 31, 2000 Restated
Assets		
Cash and cash equivalents	$ 3,990	$ 1,750
Accounts receivable, net	1,896	2,269
Finance receivables, net	3,922	4,392
Inventories	1,364	1,983
Deferred taxes and other current assets	1,428	1,078
Total Current Assets	$12,600	$11,472
Finance receivables due after one year, net	5,756	6,406
Equipment on operating leases, net	804	1,266
Land, buildings and equipment, net	1,999	2,527
Investments in affiliates, at equity	632	1,270
Intangible and other assets, net	4,453	3,763
Goodwill, net	1,445	1,549
Total Assets	$27,689	$28,253
Liabilities and Equity		
Short-term debt and current portion of long-term debt	$ 6,637	$ 3,080
Accounts payable	704	1,050
Accrued compensation and benefits costs	724	645
Unearned income	244	233
Other current liabilities	1,951	1,536
Total Current Liabilities	$10,260	$ 6,544
Long-term debt	10,128	15,557
Postretirement medical benefits	1,233	1,197
Deferred taxes and other liabilities	2,018	1,925
Total Liabilities	$23,639	$25,223
Deferred ESOP benefits	(135)	(221)
Minorities' interests in equity of subsidiaries	73	87
Obligation for equity put options	—	32
Company-obligated, mandatorily redeemable preferred securities of subsidiary trusts holding solely subordinated debentures of the Company	1,687	684
Preferred stock	605	647
Common stock, including additional paid-in capital	2,622	2,231
Retained earnings	1,031	1,150
Accumulated other comprehensive loss	(1,833)	(1,580)
Total Liabilities and Equity	$27,689	$28,253

[2]The numbers for 2000 are labeled "restated" because Xerox was forced to change its accounting for certain transactions in that year.

Consolidated balance sheets comprise the financial information of a parent company and its subsidiaries, just the way a manufactured product features many component parts.

also contains an interesting qualification. It states that "all significant **intercompany accounts** and **transactions** have been eliminated." That statement tells us, for example, that if one Xerox subsidiary owes another Xerox subsidiary $50 million, the consolidated balance sheet eliminates these accounts, instead of showing a receivable and a payable for $50 million. Xerox is telling us it doesn't double-count.

Xerox also has some active investments that it does not consolidate. The account Investments in Affiliates, at equity, captures Xerox's stake in these investments. Exhibit 15.3 contains excerpts from Xerox's notes that give more details. We can see that most of the total comes from Xerox's investment in Fuji Xerox, a joint venture between Xerox and Fuji Photo Film.

Goodwill arises in the course of making active investments. Usually, acquisition of an entire corporation involves paying more than the book value of the acquired company, which is apparent from the fact that, as we have often discussed, typical market-to-book ratios are above 1. Partly, this ratio results from things like the lower-of-cost-or-market rule and the asset impairment rule, which require assets to be written down and prohibit

Exhibit 15.2

Xerox
10K Note

Xerox Corporation
(Note excerpts)

Basis of Consolidation.

The consolidated financial statements include the accounts of Xerox Corporation and all of its controlled subsidiary companies (collectively the Company). All significant intercompany accounts and transactions have been eliminated. References herein to "we" or "our" refer to Xerox and consolidated subsidiaries unless the context specifically requires otherwise.

Exhibit 15.3

Xerox
10K Note

Xerox Corporation
(Note excerpts)

Basis of Consolidation.

Investments in business entities in which the Company does not have control, but has the ability to exercise significant influence over operating and financial policies (generally 20 to 50 percent ownership), are accounted for by the equity method.

Upon the sale of stock by a subsidiary, we recognize a gain or loss in our Consolidated Statements of Operations equal to our proportionate share of the increase or decrease in the subsidiary's equity.

Investments in Affiliates, at Equity

Investments in corporate joint ventures and other companies in which we generally have a 20 to 50 percent ownership interest at December 31, 2001 and 2000, follow:

These numbers appear on the 2001 and 2000 balance sheets.

	2001	2000
Fuji Xerox	$532	$1,160
Other investments	100	110
Investments in affiliates, at equity	$632	$1,270

them from being written up. However, you may recall from Chapter 7 on financial statement analysis that limited recognition of assets is a bigger issue than conservative adjustments of recognized assets. Microsoft's large market-to-book ratio was more the result of GAAP's failure to recognize all its assets than it was the result of conservative adjustments.

In the context of acquisitions, this means that the acquiring firm typically pays more for the acquired firm than the market value of its identifiable net assets. The premium over the market value of identifiable net assets is labeled goodwill. Exhibit 15.4 contains Xerox's explanation of its goodwill. As you can see from Xerox's discussion, the accounting for goodwill has changed. Previously, it was amortized over long periods, generally 25 to 40 years. Now, goodwill will no longer be amortized. Instead, it will be tested for impairment based on an impairment test similar to the one discussed in Chapter 11.

Exhibit 15.4

Xerox
Goodwill and Intangible
Assets Note

Note that Equity in the Net Income of Unconsolidated Subsidiaries increases Xerox's net income, whereas Minorities' Interests in Earnings of Subsidiaries reduces it, which is not at all obvious in Xerox's presentation of its income statement as faithfully reproduced in Exhibit 15.5.

**Xerox Corporation
(Note excerpts)**

Goodwill

SFAS No. 142 addresses financial accounting and reporting for acquired goodwill and other intangible assets subsequent to their initial recognition. This statement recognizes that goodwill has an indefinite useful life and will no longer be subject to periodic amortization. However, goodwill is to be tested at least annually for impairment, using a fair value methodology, in lieu of amortization.

The last item on the balance sheet we want to discuss is Minorities' Interests in Equity of Subsidiaries. We will see that this account arises because Xerox owns less than 100% of some of the subsidiaries that it consolidates. Because the asset side of Xerox's consolidated balance sheet shows 100% of the assets of all the consolidated companies, Xerox must acknowledge that others own interests in these assets. That is what the minorities' interests in equity of subsidiaries account does.

Let's move to Xerox's income statement, shown in Exhibit 15.5. Just as in the balance sheet, all items on the income statement relate to the totals of the parent and all consolidated subsidiaries. Two items on the income statement relate specifically to Xerox's active investments. Equity in the Net Income of Unconsolidated Affiliates is Xerox's share of the earnings of its active investments that are accounted for using the equity method. The revenues and expenses of these unconsolidated subsidiaries are not included in the line items of the consolidated income statement, so this item is the way Xerox's share of their net income gets recognized.

Xerox's share of the earnings of its unconsolidated subsidiaries, however, is only half the story. What about minority shareholders' portion of the earnings of subsidiaries that have been consolidated in the statement? Just like the balance sheet, the consolidated income statement includes all the revenues of all consolidated businesses, even if Xerox owns less than 100% of them. Therefore, the item Minorities' Interests in Earnings of Subsidiaries is required to reflect the fact that Xerox is not the only claimant to the revenues and expenses listed in the consolidated income statement.

Finally, Exhibit 15.6 on page 292 contains the operating cash flow section of the consolidated statement of cash flows for Xerox Corporation for the 2001 fiscal year.

We can see the line item Minorities' Interests in Earnings of Subsidiaries in the amount of $42 million. It is added back to net income in order to get cash flow from operations because it was subtracted in the computation of net income but did not require a cash outflow. The consolidated statement of cash flows lists 100% of the operational

Exhibit 15.5

Xerox

Income Statement

The revenues and expenses relate to the parent and all consolidated subsidiaries.

Xerox Corporation Consolidated Statements of Income (amounts in millions, except per share data)	
	2001
Revenues	
Sales	$ 7,443
Service, outsourcing and rentals	8,436
Finance income	1,129
Total Revenues	$17,008
Costs and Expenses	
Cost of sales	$ 5,170
Cost of service, outsourcing and rentals	4,880
Equipment financing interest	457
Research and development expenses	997
Selling, administrative and general expenses	4,728
Restructuring and asset impairment charges	715
Gain on sale of half of interest in Fuji Xerox	(773)
Gain on affiliate's sale of stock	(4)
Other expenses, net	473
Total Costs and Expenses	$16,643

Income (Loss) before Income Taxes (Benefits), Equity
    Income, Minorities' Interests, Extraordinary Gain
    and Cumulative Effect of Change in Accounting
    Principle
	$ 365

Income taxes (benefits)	485
(Loss) Income before Equity Income, Minorities' Interests, Extraordinary Gain and Cumulative Effect of Change in Accounting Principle	$ (120)
Equity in net income of unconsolidated affiliates	53
Minorities' interests in earnings of subsidiaries	(42)
(Loss) Income before Extraordinary Gain and Cumulative Effect of Change in Accounting Principle	$ (109)
Extraordinary gain on extinguishment of debt, net of taxes of $26	40
Cumulative effect of change in accounting principle	(2)
Net (Loss) Income	$ (71)

Equity in Net Income of Unconsolidated Affiliates is Xerox's share of the income of its active investments that are accounted for using the equity method.

Minorities' Interests in Earnings of Subsidiaries is minorities shareholders' share of the income of Xerox's consolidated subsidiaries.

cash flows of the parent and all consolidated subsidiaries, because 100% of all the cash is listed on the consolidated balance sheet, which leads to the requirement that it be added back into net income.

The $20 million item, Undistributed Equity in Income of Affiliated Companies, is subtracted in the computation of cash flows from operations because it was included in the income statement but was not received in cash from the subsidiaries. Look at the income statement in Exhibit 15.5 to see that Equity in Net Income of Unconsolidated Affiliate amounts to $53 million. Therefore, the parent Xerox Corporation, while recognizing $53 million in income from its equity method affiliates, received only $33 million ($53 − $20) in cash dividends from these affiliates.

This brief tour of Xerox's reports confirms that much of what is presented in the financial statements of major corporations is related to the accounting for their active investments. To set the stage for our discussion of GAAP for active investments, we discuss the economics of these investments in the next section.

Exhibit 15.6
Xerox
Cash Flow Statement

Xerox Corporation
Consolidated Statements of Cash Flows (operating section only)
(amounts in millions)

Cash Flows from Operating Activities	2001
Net (loss) income	$ (71)
Adjustments required to reconcile net (loss) income to cash flows from operating activities:	
Depreciation and amortization	1,332
Provisions for receivables and inventory	748
Restructuring and other charges	715
Cash payments for restructurings	(484)
Gain on early extinguishment of debt	(66)
Gains on sales of businesses and assets	(765)
Minorities' interests in earnings of subsidiaries	42
Undistributed equity in income of affiliated companies	(20)
Decrease (increase) in inventories	319
Increase in on-lease equipment	(271)
Decrease (increase) in finance receivables	162
Decrease (increase) in accounts receivable	115
(Decrease) increase in accounts payable and accrued compensation and benefits costs	(270)
Net change in current and deferred income taxes	456
(Decrease) increase in other current and non-current liabilities	(160)
Early termination of derivative contracts	(148)
Other, net	(68)
Net cash provided by operating activities	$1,566

Minorities' Interests in Earnings of Subsidiaries is added back because it reduces net income, but does not require cash.

Undistributed Equity in Income of Affiliated Companies is the excess of Xerox's share of the income of its unconsolidated active investments over the dividends Xerox received from those investments.

Economics of Active Investments

OBJECTIVE:
Learn to understand the economic motivation for engaging in active investments.

This economic analysis is applicable to the purchase of any group of assets, a division of a company, a fraction of a company, or a company itself.

The empirical corporate finance literature shows that in general most of the value from combination (7 in the example) accrues to the current shareholders of Company B. Acquirers tend to overpay for acquisitions either because they misestimate the synergies from the combination or they become irrationally caught up in a bidding war.

Suppose Company A is thinking of acquiring all of the common stock of Company B. The following simplified economic framework presents a view of the acquisition. As we indicated in Chapter 7, the stock market provides a pretty good indicator of the current total economic value of a firm. So let us suppose that the aggregate value of all of the common stock in the stock market for Company A is V_A, and for Company B is V_B. Let V_{A+B} denote the value of the resultant company formed by the combination of Company A and Company B. Then, in order for the combination to make sense it must be true that

$$V_{A+B} > V_A + V_B$$

Perceived operating efficiency, increased market power, or other **synergies** related to the combination of the companies must increase the combined value or the combination should not be attempted.

Let's pick some simple numbers for sake of illustration. Suppose $V_A = 20$, $V_B = 10$, and $V_{A+B} = 37$. Then the maximum that Company A would be willing to pay for Company B, call it P_B, is 17 (the 10 in current value for Company B plus the 7 incremental value that is estimated to be added if the two companies are combined). Of course they would hope to acquire Company B for less; they would have a zero expected return on their investment if they paid 17.

So, the process of negotiating to acquire Company B is guided by the knowledge that the purchase price must be

$$V_{A+B} - V_A > P_B > V_B$$

or in terms of the simple example,

$$37 - 20 > P_B > 10$$

Now, if P_B is say, 14, and if all goes as expected, Company A will expect to have a combined company worth 37, and they will have made 3 on the transaction ($17 - 14$, or $37 - 34$).

The accounting problem is how to record P_B in the financial statements of the parent (investor) company.

GAAP for Active Investments

GAAP for investments are governed largely by the percentage ownership of the investee company. The presumption built into GAAP is that the holder of any stake of at least 20% has significant influence over the operations of the company. Therefore, any investment of at least 20% is assumed to be an active investment.

Equity Method

A company that owns at least 20% and less than 50% of another company's common stock usually uses the equity method to account for its investment. The **equity method** requires the investor corporation to carry its investment on the balance sheet at its historical cost, adjusted for the investor's pro rata share of the investee corporation's retained earnings. The investor also recognizes its pro rata share of the investee's net income in its own net income in the accounting period in which the investee earns the net income.

This brief description contains a great deal of information, so let's do an example to illustrate. Suppose that on January 1, 2004, ABC Corporation purchases 40% (20,000 shares) of SUB Corporation's common stock for $400,000. The entry in ABC Corporation's books to record the purchase is

Investment in Unconsolidated Affiliate 400,000
    Cash 400,000

SUB Corporation's net income for the year ended December 31, 2004, is $50,000. The entry[3] on ABC Corporation's books to accrue its 40% share of the net income is

Investment in Unconsolidated Affiliate 20,000
    Equity in Net Earnings of Unconsolidated Affiliate 20,000

On January 31, 2005, SUB Corporation declares a dividend of $20,000. ABC makes the following entry:

Dividend Receivable 8,000
    Investment in Unconsolidated Affiliate 8,000

The ABC Corporation reduces its investment account because the dividend represents a return of a portion of its investment.

On March 10, 2005, the dividend is paid.

Cash 8,000
    Dividend Receivable 8,000

---

[3]This entry assumes that SUB's book value was $1,000,000 (40% of $1,000,000 = $400,000) on the date ABC purchased the 20,000 shares of common stock. If the investor's purchase price is greater than the investee's book value, the difference attributable to the values of identifiable assets is depreciated and/or amortized and charged to equity in net earnings of unconsolidated affiliate. The equity method also requires an adjustment to current year's earnings and the investment account for any intercompany transactions between ABC and SUB. This note will make more sense after we discuss consolidations.

OBJECTIVE:
Learn to become familiar with GAAP for active investments in corporations.

20% ownership only establishes a presumption, which may be overcome by the facts of a particular case. If significant influence exists with less than 20% ownership, the investor should use the equity method. If the investor can prove that it does not have significant influence over the investee, even though it owns more than 20%, it should account for it as a passive investment.

The equity method journal entries, which are based on the investor corporation having significant influence on the investee's financial policies, are in accordance with the accrual method of accounting. They record the income on the investor corporation's books in the accounting period in which the income is earned by the investee corporation.

The T-accounts in ABC's books for its 40% investment in SUB would appear as follows:

Other entries may be made to the cash account during this time period. We have shown only those related to the investment in SUB.

Investment in Unconsolidated Affiliates			Equity in Net Earnings of Unconsolidated Affiliates	
Dr.	Cr.		Dr.	Cr.
400,000	8,000			20,000
20,000				

Cash			Dividend Receivable	
Dr.	Cr.		Dr.	Cr.
8,000	400,000		8,000	8,000

Equity in net earnings of unconsolidated affiliates is often classified on the income statement as other income.

As a reader of financial statements, you should understand that although the equity in net earnings of unconsolidated affiliates increases net earnings, it does not increase working capital or cash flow from operations. The investor company's cash flow is increased only by the amount of cash dividends it is paid by the investee corporation. An add-back, for the amount by which the equity in net earnings of unconsolidated affiliates exceeds the cash dividends received from the unconsolidated affiliate, is made to net income in arriving at cash flow from operations in the indirect method cash flow statement.

Investment in Unconsolidated Affiliates is classified as a noncurrent asset on the balance sheet of the investor. (Sometimes, it is included in Other Assets.) The account reflects the cost of the investment plus (minus if a deficit) the investor corporation's pro rata share of the investee corporation's retained earnings since the date of acquisition. Two additional subtleties are noteworthy. First, a company cannot make a profit by dealing with itself. Therefore, any profits recorded by the investee on transactions with the investor must be eliminated. Second, as we discuss later when we address the accounting at the time an active investment is made, the investor may have to write up the assets of the investee in Investment in Unconsolidated Affiliates at the time of the investment. This approach will cause amortization or depreciation in the investor's accounting to be in excess of the depreciation or amortization taken by the investee.

Consolidation Method

If a corporation owns more than 50% of the common stock of any other corporation(s) it must present consolidated financial statements. This set of financial statements combines the corporation's financial statements with those of its majority-owned investments.

The basic idea behind consolidated financial statements is to present one set of financial statements for the entire group of companies controlled by the parent company. Several issues must be dealt with when such statements are constructed. How much of the assets and liabilities of the subsidiary companies are presented in the consolidated statements if the parent does not own 100% of the stock of the subsidiary? Should the consolidated statements list all of the net assets of the subsidiary or just the fraction of them that the parent owns? If all of the net assets are listed in the consolidated statements, then how will the statements signal the readers that the parent does not actually

Unlike under the equity method, where the purchase price of the shares of the subsidiary show up in an investment (asset) account, individual assets and liabilities of the subsidiary will be combined with those of the parent's in the consolidated financial statement.

own all of them? At what values should the assets and liabilities of the acquired company be listed in the consolidated statement?

Minority Interest

The question of how much of the net assets to list in the consolidated statement for majority owned companies is always answered as follows: Because the parent *controls* (but may not own) all of the net assets of the subsidiary, the consolidated statement should list all of the net assets of the subsidiary. The consolidated balance sheet will contain an account, often entitled Minority Interest, which will measure the dollar value of the minority owners' claims against the net assets of the subsidiary. This account usually will appear between the liabilities and the shareholders' equity sections of the consolidated balance sheet.

The consolidated income statement will also list all of the revenues and expenses (income) of the subsidiary. It will contain a line item often entitled Minority Interest, which represents the minority owners' share of the net income of the subsidiary for that accounting period. Minority Interest is subtracted from revenues minus expenses in order to arrive at net income, which reflects the parent's income plus the parent's claim to the percentage of the income of the subsidiary that they own.

*So the term **minority interest** is often used to mean two different things—one in the income statement and one in the balance sheet. Be aware of the context in which it is being used to know which one it is!*

Valuation

The consolidated balance sheet is created by combining the parent's net assets with the net assets of the subsidiary valued *at the price the parent had to pay* for the net assets. This requirement is consistent with the general notion that when an entity acquires net assets they are valued at their acquisition cost.

It may help to think in some detail about how a consolidated balance sheet is constructed. For simplicity, let's assume the consolidated balance sheet is being constructed at the time of acquisition of the subsidiary by the parent.

How to create a consolidated balance sheet at the time of acquisition

- All identifiable assets and liabilities of the subsidiary are valued at their fair market values before combining them with the parent's assets and liabilities.
- If the parent paid more than the fair value of all of the identifiable net assets, then the excess of the purchase price over the fair market value of the identifiable net assets acquired is called **goodwill.** Goodwill will be listed on the consolidated balance sheet.
- If the parent bought less than 100% of the subsidiary, then a minority interest account will appear on the consolidated balance sheet, because even though all the assets and liabilities of the subsidiary appear in the consolidated balance sheet, the parent does not own 100% of them.

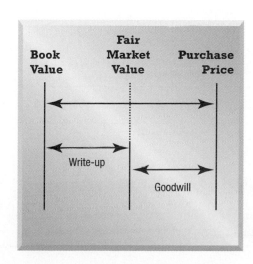

We should also note the following about the consolidated income statement:

- No income from the acquisition is recognized until the subsidiary earns income after the acquisition date.
- All of the revenues and expenses of the subsidiary are listed in the consolidated income statement. If the parent does not own 100% of the subsidiary, then a minority interest representing the minority's percentage claim to the net income of the subsidiary is shown on the income statement. It is similar to an expense in the sense that it decreases consolidated net income.
- Depreciation and amortization expense in the consolidated income statement will usually be larger than the sum of the depreciation and amortization expenses of the parent and subsidiary before acquisition. Remember, the assets of the subsidiary are written up to their fair market values; thus, depreciation and amortization are higher than they would have been if they were not written up.

How to create a consolidated income statement at the time of acquisition

See Appendix 15.1 for a worksheet to construct a consolidated balance sheet at the time of acquisition.

• All intercompany transactions must be eliminated. The consolidated entity cannot make a profit by selling to itself. (This requirement can also affect the balance sheet if, for example, the parent makes loans to the subsidiary. The consolidated entity cannot owe itself money.)

In sum, the consolidation process consists of combining the accounts of the parent and all the consolidated subsidiaries, eliminating intercompany accounts and transactions, recording the difference between the purchase price paid for a subsidiary and its book value at date of purchase, indicating the minority (less than 50%) interest of the stockholders in the subsidiary corporations, and making all other necessary adjustments in order to prepare a consolidated balance sheet, consolidated income statement, and consolidated statement of changes in financial position.

Review Questions

1. What two methods are used to show one corporation's active investment in the common stock of another, and when is each used?

2. Give the entry to record the declaration of a dividend by a subsidiary that is accounted for using the equity method.

3. How does a *minority interest* account arise, and where is it shown on the balance sheet?

4. What are intercompany transactions, and why must they be eliminated in forming consolidated financial statements?

5. What is the investing company's share of the earnings of a subsidiary accounted for with the equity method recognized by the investing company?

Do GAAP Capture the Economics?

OBJECTIVE:
Learn to compare the accounting for active investments in corporations with the underlying economics.

At the time of the acquisition of an active investment, GAAP capture the economics of the transaction. The theory is simple—when assets are acquired they should enter the balance sheet of the acquiring company at the cost to acquire them.

Subsequent to acquisition, whether GAAP capture the economics depends on whether the values of the acquired assets, including goodwill, go up or down. If their values go up, GAAP will only capture the increase if the asset is a marketable security that is marked-to-market. If the values go down, the application and execution of the impairment tests determine how well GAAP capture values. Applying impairment tests to goodwill seems like a particularly difficult task, and we expect that important differences between book and market values of assets will remain, even when impairments have been recognized.

Acquisition Accounting

Percent Ownership	Accounting Rules
own < 20%	Available-for-sale
20% < own < 50%	Equity method
own > 50%	Consolidation

Ratio Analysis of Consolidated Statements

OBJECTIVE:
Learn to understand how GAAP for active investments affect financial ratios.

When consolidated statements account for groups of businesses and operations in many different fields, it becomes difficult to make comparisons across companies. Footnotes in annual reports that show accounting numbers for major segments of the consolidated en-

Every company is required to report the results of operations for the major segments of their business. This information appears as a footnote in the annual report.

tity's operations are often useful. Some companies even partition their income statements and balance sheets so that the reader can see what the numbers look like for major segments of their operations. For example, Ford Motor Company has two-part income statements and balance sheets that show numbers for their general manufacturing business operations and their financing activities separately.

Conclusion

This completes the last financial reporting topic we present in this book. Our coverage has been aimed at hitting important topics—topics that are representative of GAAP for other items and topics you are likely to encounter. We have not, however, covered every financial reporting topic you will come upon in your career, nor have we laid out every nuance of GAAP for the items covered. It is not possible to cover every topic and every detail of every topic. Even if it were possible, it would not be wise to do so. A working knowledge of accounting is not a photographic memorization of all its rules and conventions. A working knowledge of accounting is an understanding of how accounting functions at its most basic levels, of what its aims are and the limitations it encounters in trying to achieve those aims. This kind of working knowledge is what truly helps a decision maker understand what information he or she *wants* and what information he or she *has*. Using the information you have to get the information you want is the true art of financial statement analysis. The next and final chapter of this book discusses financial statement analysis.

Key Terms

active investment *287*

consolidated subsidiaries *286*

consolidation *287*

equity method *293*

goodwill *295*

intercompany accounts *289*

intercompany transactions *289*

minority interest *287*

parent *286*

passive investment *287*

subsidiaries *286*

synergies *292*

Appendix 15.1: Constructing a Consolidated Balance Sheet on the Date of Acquisition

We will present a worksheet for preparing a consolidated balance sheet at the time of acquisition. The consolidation elimination and adjusting entries are recorded only on the worksheets used to prepare consolidated financial statements. They are not recorded on the books and records of the affiliated companies, which are separate accounting and legal entities.

Consolidated Balance Sheet

Assume that Parent Corporation purchased all of the common stock of Sub Corporation on December 31, 2005, by paying cash exactly in the amount of Sub Corporation's book value of $200. The entry on Parent Corporation's books at the time of this purchase is

Investment in Sub Corporation 200
  Cash 200

Exhibit A15.1.1 shows how to prepare a consolidated balance sheet on December 31, 2005.

Exhibit A15.1.1 Consolidated Balance Sheet Worksheet—Acquisition at Book Value

Parent Corporation
Worksheet to Produce a Consolidated Balance Sheet as of December 31, 2005
Acquisition at Book Value

Account	Individual Company Statements Parent	Sub	Combined Balance Sheet	Eliminations Debit		Credit		Consolidated Balance Sheet
Cash	$ 200	$ 40	$ 240					$ 240
Accounts Receivable	108	70	178			(2a)	20	158
Notes Receivable	80	—	80			(2b)	80	—
Inventory	200	170	370					370
Investment in Sub Corporation	200	—	200			(3)	200	—
Fixed Assets (net of accumulated depreciation)	1,012	180	1,192					1,192
	$1,800	$460	$2,260					$1,960
Accounts Payable	$ 100	$ 90	$ 190	(2a)	20			$ 170
Notes Payable	—	80	80	(2b)	80			—
Other Current Liabilities	80	20	100					100
Long-Term Liabilities	220	70	290					290
Common Stock	600	140	740	(3)	140			600
Retained Earnings	800	60	860	(3)	60			800
	$1,800	$460	$2,260		$300		$300	$1,960

1. List the balance sheet accounts of each company on a worksheet and combine them.
2. Find and eliminate intercompany accounts and transactions.
   a. Suppose that on December 31, 2005, Sub Corporation owes Parent Corporation $20 for merchandise it purchased on credit. Parent Corporation sold Sub Corporation the merchandise at Parent's cost. Accounts Receivable and Accounts Payable of $20 must be eliminated:

   Accounts Payable 20
     Accounts Receivable 20

   This elimination reduces the combined Accounts Receivable to $158, the amount customers owe the consolidated entity. The consolidated Accounts Payable are reduced to $170, the amount owed to outside creditors.
   b. Parent's Notes Receivable and Sub's Notes Payable represent a loan by Parent Corporation to Sub Corporation. These accounts should be eliminated:

   Notes Payable 80
     Notes Receivable 80

In Parent Corporation's books (not the consolidated books) the investment in Sub Corporation will be carried under the equity method.

The consolidated balance sheet will not reflect this note because it is an intercompany item. The consolidated entity has neither a note receivable nor a note payable with any outside entity.

Suppose these are all the intercompany accounts and transactions. We proceed to the next step.

3. Eliminate Parent Corporation's Investment in Sub Corporation and Sub Corporation's shareholders' equity accounts.

Common Stock	140	
Retained Earnings	60	
Investment in Sub Corporation		200

Note that this entry balances because Parent Corporation acquired Sub Corporation at its book value on the balance sheet date.

4. Add across the rows to get the consolidated balance sheet in the last column.

The consolidated balance sheet is now complete. This case is especially easy because Parent Corporation bought 100% of Sub Corporation at its book value on the balance sheet date. We next suppose Parent paid more than the book value of Sub Corporation for 100% of Sub Corporation's equity, and then examine what happens when Parent Corporation buys less than 100% Sub's equity.

If Parent Corporation paid less than book value for Sub, the identifiable net assets must be reduced to the amount actually paid for them. Any remaining amount is negative goodwill, usually called Excess of Fair Value of Net Assets over Purchase Price, and it must be recognized immediately as a gain.

Example with Acquisition at More Than Book Value

Let's assume all the same facts of the previous section, except we suppose Parent Corporation paid $250 instead of $200 for Sub Corporation's common stock. This purchase price is $50 more than Sub's net assets or book value of $200 (assets of $460 minus liabilities of $260) on December 31, 2005. (Also, Parent Corporation will have $50 less in cash than it did when we assumed it only paid $200 for Sub.)

The entry on Parent Corporation's books on December 31, 2005, is

Investment in Sub Corporation	250	
Cash		250

Preparation of the consolidation worksheet will force the issue of what to do with the $50 excess of Parent's investment over Sub's book value when we try to eliminate the $250 Investment in Sub Corporation. GAAP require that Parent Corporation first allocate any excess of the amount paid over book value to the identifiable assets of Sub Corporation. Any remainder is assigned to Goodwill, sometimes more descriptively called Excess of Purchase Price over Fair Value of Identifiable Net Assets.

Assume that an appraisal indicates that the fixed assets of Sub Corporation have a fair value of $210 ($30 more than their book value of $180) and the market value of Sub's other assets and liabilities are approximately equal to their book value. When we eliminate the Investment in Sub Corporation, we write up the fixed assets by $30. We then have $20 left to record as Goodwill. The elimination entry, (3), in the consolidation worksheet is

Common Stock	140	
Retained Earnings	60	
Fixed Assets	30	
Goodwill	20	
Investment in Sub Corporation		250

Any time we have more fixed assets, depreciation calculations must reflect this increased book value. The depreciation expense relating to the $30 increase in fixed assets will appear on the consolidated income statement.

The worksheet for the assumptions in this case appears in Exhibit A15.1.2 on page 300. Note that the $30 increase in fixed assets appears only on the consolidated balance sheet and not on the balance sheets of either Parent Corporation or Sub Corporation. The $20 excess of purchase price over the fair value of net assets appears on the consolidated balance sheet as Goodwill.

The final case we consider arises when Parent Corporation does not purchase 100% of the equity of Sub Corporation. In this case, a remaining minority interest in Sub Corporation must be reflected in the consolidated balance sheet.

Exhibit A15.1.2 Consolidated Balance Sheet Worksheet—Acquisition at Greater than Book Value

Parent Corporation
Worksheet to Produce a Consolidated Balance Sheet as of December 31, 2005
Acquisition at Greater than Book Value

Account	Individual Company Statements Parent	Sub	Combined Balance Sheet	Eliminations Debit	Credit	Consolidated Balance Sheet
Cash	$ 150	$ 40	$ 190			$ 190
Accounts Receivable	108	70	178		(2a) $ 20	158
Notes Receivable	80	—	80		(2b) 80	—
Inventory	200	170	370			370
Investment in Sub Corporation	250	—	250		(3) 250	—
Fixed Assets (net of accumulated depreciation)	1,012	180	1,192	(3) $ 30		1,222
Goodwill	—	—	—	(3) 20		20
	$1,800	$460	$2,260			$1,960
Accounts Payable	$ 100	$ 90	$ 190	(2a) 20		$ 170
Notes Payable	—	80	80	(2b) 80		—
Other Current Liabilities	80	20	100			100
Long-Term Liabilities	220	70	290			290
Common Stock	600	140	740	(3) 140		600
Retained Earnings	800	60	860	(3) 60		800
	$1,800	$460	$2,260	$350	$350	$1,960

Example with Minority Interest

Assume all the same facts as before, except that Parent Corporation's $250 investment buys only 80% of the outstanding common stock of Sub Corporation. The entry on Parent Corporation's books on December 31, 2005, is

This example with minority interest does not result in an accurate reflection of the economic information in Parent's acquisition of Sub. Parent's payment of $250 for 80% of Sub implies that Sub's total value is $312.50.

Investment in Sub Corporation   250
     Cash   250

This price of $250 is $90 more than 80% of Sub's net assets of $200 on December 31, 2005. Preparation of the consolidation worksheet will force the issue of what to do with this $90 excess when we try to eliminate the $250 Investment in Sub Corporation. Again, we first look to write up Sub's identifiable assets, then record goodwill. However, we also must recognize that Parent bought only 80% of Sub, and that a minority interest in Sub of 20% remains.

Because Parent's investment represents an 80% stake of Sub, when we eliminate the Investment in Sub Corporation, we should eliminate only 80% of Sub's Common Stock and 80% of its Retained Earnings. Eighty percent of Sub's Common Stock is $112 (0.8 × $140), and 80% of Sub's Retained Earnings is $48 (0.8 × $60). Again, suppose an appraisal finds that Sub's assets are worth $30 more than their book value. Common practice is to write up Sub's assets for only the 80% Parent acquired, so we increase Fixed Assets by $24 (0.8 × $30). The elimination entry for Parent's 80% investment in Sub would be:

Considering the identifiable assets are worth $30 more than their book value leaves the economic value of goodwill at $82.50. Because we took the Minority Interest at book value, this elimination records only Parent's share of the $30 increase in the value of the identifiable assets and of the $82.50 goodwill. A less-often used, but allowable, approach is to write up the Minority Interest to allow the recording of Sub's implied total value.

After the date of the acquisition, Parent's Retained Earnings will increase by its share of Sub's undistributed earnings subsequent to acquisition. Minority Interest will change to reflect the minority's share of these undistributed earnings.

Common Stock	....	112
Retained Earnings	....	48
Fixed Assets	....	24
Goodwill	....	66
Investment in Sub Corporation	....	250

Note how the plug to Goodwill is now $66. Also note that some of Sub's common stock and retained earnings remain. We reclassify this portion into Minority Interest with the following entry:

Common Stock	....	28
Retained Earnings	....	12
Minority Interest	....	40

The effect of this entry is to show that minority stockholders have a claim of $40 against the consolidated entity. This amount is the book value (in Sub's books) of the minority's 20% at the date of its acquisition by Parent.

Disagreements often arise as to whether Minority Interest is a liability or equity account; it is usually listed between the liability and equity sections on the consolidated balance sheet.

The consolidated worksheet and consolidated balance sheet for Parent Corporation on December 31, 2005, assuming it acquired 80% of the common stock of Sub Corporation for $250 on December 31, 2005, are shown in Exhibits A15.1.3 and A15.1.4. [The entry to eliminate Parent's Investment in Sub Corporation is labeled (3a), and the entry to set up Minority Interest is labeled (3b).]

Exhibit A15.1.3 Consolidated Balance Sheet Worksheet with Minority Interest

Parent Corporation
Worksheet to Produce a Consolidated Balance Sheet as of December 31, 2005
Acquisition of an 80% Share at Greater than Book Value

Account	Individual Company Statements		Combined Balance Sheet	Eliminations		Consolidated Balance Sheet
	Parent	Sub		Debit	Credit	
Cash	$ 150	$ 40	$ 190			$ 190
Accounts Receivable	108	70	178		(2a) $ 20	158
Notes Receivable	80	—	80		(2b) 80	—
Inventory	200	170	370			370
Investment in Sub Corporation	250	—	250		(3a) 250	—
Fixed Assets (net of accumulated depreciation)	1,012	180	1,192	(3a) $ 24		1,216
Goodwill	—	—	—	(3a) 66		66
	$1,800	$460	$2,260			$2,000
Accounts Payable	$ 100	$ 90	$ 190	(2a) 20		$ 170
Notes Payable	—	80	80	(2b) 80		—
Other Current Liabilities	80	20	100			100
Long-Term Liabilities	220	70	290			290
Minority Interest	—	—	—		(3b) 40	40
Common Stock	600	140	740	(3a) 112		600
				(3b) 28		
Retained Earnings	800	60	860	(3a) 48		800
				(3b) 12		
	$1,800	$460	$2,260	$390	$390	$2,000

Exhibit A15.1.4

Parent Corporation Consolidated
Balance Sheet

Parent Corporation
Consolidated Balance Sheet
December 31, 2005

Assets

Current assets:	
Cash	$ 190
Accounts receivable	158
Inventory	370
Total currents	$ 718
Fixed assets (net of accumulated depreciation)	1,216
Other assets:	
Goodwill	66
Total assets	$2,000

Liabilities and Stockholders' Equity

Current liabilities:	
Accounts payable	$ 170
Other current liabilities	100
Total current liabilities	$ 270
Long-term liabilities	290
Total liabilities	$ 560
Minority interest	$ 40
Stockholder's equity:	
Common stock	$ 600
Retained earnings	800
Total stockholders' equity	$1,400
Total liabilities and stockholders' equity	$2,000

Appendix 15.2: Acquisitions, Divestitures, and the Articulation of Consolidated Financial Statements

In Chapter 8, we learned that the recognition of bad debts expense and write-offs of bad debts don't get in the way of the basic relationship between sales, accounts receivable, and collections from customers, provided that we work with Accounts Receivable, net.

Beginning early in this book, we stressed the articulation of financial statements. Indirect cash flow statements have been particularly useful for us, because they reconcile cash flows from operations with GAAP net income, and they illustrate how balance sheets and income statements work together in the accrual process. We explained this process in Chapter 4 where, for example, we showed that collections from customers is equal to Sales adjusted for the change in Accounts Receivable, provided there are no increases in Accounts Receivable other than Sales, and no decreases other than collections from customers.

When a business acquires another, increases may occur in some accounts because of the acquisition. When a business sells part of itself to another business, decreases in some accounts may be caused by the divestiture. Acquisitions and divestitures are investing activities, not operations. Most corporations of any size are frequently acquiring and divesting themselves of parts of businesses. As a result, in most financial statements you will encounter, the changes in the balance sheet accounts are not equal to the adjustments required to reconcile net income to cash flows from operations.

Consider the Xerox balance sheets given in Exhibit 15.1 and the cash flow statement given in Exhibit 15.6. The change in Accounts Receivable, net from December 31, 2000, to December 31, 2001, is

Balance at December 31, 2000	$2,269
Balance at December 31, 2001	1,896
Decrease in accounts receivable	$ 373

But the decrease in Accounts Receivable in 2001 shown as the adjustment in the operations section of the cash flow statement is $115.

Similarly, the change in the inventories on the balance sheets is

Balance at December 31, 2000	$1,983
Balance at December 31, 2001	1,364
Decrease in inventories	$ 619

But the decrease in inventories in 2001 shown as the adjustment in the operations section of the cash flow statement is $319.

Because the increases shown as adjustments in the statement of cash flows exceed the difference in the balance sheet accounts, we can deduce that Xerox must have divested itself of parts of some of its businesses.

Xerox is too big and its disclosures are too complex for us to be able to make much more headway using its financial statements. So let's study an easier case. Consider the financial statements of Aristotle Corporation. Its 10K describes it as "a holding company which, through one operating subsidiary, currently conducts business in one segment, the health and medical education products market." Its balance sheet is given in Exhibit A15.2.1 on page 304.

Note that Accounts Receivable, net on the balance sheets increased $299, from $0 to $299. Inventories increased from $0 to $989.

Exhibit A15.2.2 on page 305 shows Aristotle's cash flow statement for 1999. You can see that the adjustment for accounts receivable is only $92, and the adjustment for inventories is $203. Both are consistent with a *decrease* in the current asset account.

You can also see from the investing section of the cash flow statement that Aristotle purchased a business, Simulaids, during fiscal 1999. Aristotle makes some detailed disclosures of this purchase, which are contained in Exhibit A15.2.3 on page 306.

Using Aristotle's disclosures in Exhibit A15.2.3, we can derive the adjustments for Accounts Receivable, net and Inventories on the cash flow statement. Consider first Accounts Receivable, net. It began at zero, and Aristotle purchased $391 thousand of accounts receivable when it bought Simulaids. It ended the year with $299, so the adjustment in the cash flow statement is $92:

Beginning balance	$ 0
Purchased in Simulaids acquisition	391
Less ending balance	(299)
Excess of collections from customers over sales	
subsequent to acquisition	$ 92

Now consider Inventories. It, too, began at zero. Aristotle purchased $1,192 in the Simulaids acquisition, and the ending balance was $989. The adjustment to help reconcile Cost of Goods Sold to payments to suppliers must then be $203:

Beginning balance	$ 0
Purchased in Simulaids acquisition	1,192
Less ending balance	(989)
Excess of amounts of inventory used over	
purchases subsequent to acquisition	$ 203

Exhibit A15.2.1

Aristotle Corporation
Consolidated Balance Sheets

The Aristotle Corporation and Subsidiaries
Consolidated Balance Sheets
As of June 30
(amounts in thousands)

Assets	1999	1998
Current assets:		
Cash and cash equivalents	$ 5,849	$ 12,271
Marketable securities	702	202
Marketable securities and cash equivalents held in escrow, at market value	157	600
Accounts receivable	299	—
Current maturities of notes receivable	102	208
Inventories	989	—
Tax receivable	1,150	—
Other current assets	85	360
Total current assets	$ 9,333	$ 13,641
Property and equipment, net	$ 1,478	$ 4
Other assets:		
Marketable securities, at market value	$ 1,386	$ 867
Marketable securities held in escrow, at market value	552	—
Goodwill, net of amortization of $39 in 1999	5,685	—
Other noncurrent assets	51	70
	$ 7,674	$ 937
	$ 18,485	$ 14,582

Accounts Receivable, net increased $299

Inventories increased $989

Liabilities and Stockholders' Equity	1999	1998
Current liabilities:		
Short-term borrowings	$ 5,000	—
Current maturities of capital lease obligations	25	—
Current maturities of Series F, G and H Preferred Stock	799	$ 805
Accounts payable	143	—
Accrued expenses	829	648
Accrued transaction costs	0	1,704
Accrued tax reserves	720	720
Total current liabilities	$ 7,516	$ 3,877
Capital lease obligations, net of current maturities	$ 111	$ —
Series E Redeemable Preferred Stock	$ 2,250	$ 2,250

Stockholders' Equity:

	1999	1998
Common stock, $0.01 par value, 3,000,000 shares authorized, 1,240,727 and 1,209,027 shares issued in 1999 and 1998	$ 13	$ 11
Additional paid-in capital	160,403	160,248
Retained earnings (deficit)	(151,600)	(151,770)
Treasury stock, at cost, 7,609 shares and 7,287 shares in 1999 and 1998, respectively	(47)	(30)
Net unrealized investment losses	(161)	(4)
Total stockholders' equity	$ 8,608	$ 8,455
	$ 18,485	$ 14,582

Exhibit A15.2.2

Aristotle Corporation
Consolidated Statement of
Cash Flows

The Aristotle Corporation and Subsidiaries
Consolidated Statement of Cash Flows
For the Year Ended June 30, 1999
(amounts in thousands)

Cash Flows from Operating Activities:

Net income	$ 403
Adjustments to reconcile net income to net cash provided by (used in) operating activities:	
Gain from sale of discontinued operations	(911)
Depreciation and amortization	59
Loss on disposal of property and equipment	9
Changes in assets and liabilities, net of business acquired:	
Accounts receivable	92
Inventories	203
Tax receivable	(1,150)
Other assets	476
Accounts payable	64
Accrued expenses	(12)
Net cash provided by (used in) operating activities	$ (767)

Adjustment for Accounts Receivable is $92, and for Inventories it is $203. Both are adjusting income up to get cash flows.

Cash Flows from Investing Activities:

Purchase of marketable securities	$ (1,285)
Proceeds from disposal of discontinued operations	911
Accrued transaction costs	(1,704)
Purchase of property and equipment	(17)
Purchase of Simulaids, net of $237 of cash acquired	(8,463)
Net cash provided by (used in) investing activities	$(10,558)

Aristotle purchased a business, Simulaids.

Cash Flows from Financing Activities:

Proceeds from short-term borrowings	$ 5,000
Repayment of capital lease obligations	(4)
Purchase of treasury stock	(17)
Proceeds from exercise of stock options	157
Payment of dividends on preferred stock	(233)
Net cash provided by (used in) financing activities	$ 4,903
Increase (Decrease) in Cash and Cash Equivalents	$ (6,422)
Cash and Cash Equivalents, beginning of period	12,271
Cash and Cash Equivalents, end of period	$ 5,849

The amount spent for acquisition of receivables, inventories, and Simulaids' other assets (and liabilities) is included in the investing section of the cash flow statement.

So we see that the adjustments in an indirect method cash flow statement are the portions of the changes in the balance sheet accounts required to reconcile net income to cash flows from operations. When corporations divest businesses or acquire others, these adjustments are not the same as the change in the balance sheet accounts.

Exhibit A15.2.3

Aristotle Corporation Excerpts from Notes to Financial Statements

---

Excerpts from Aristotle's Notes

Acquisition of Simulaids, Inc. -

Effective April 30, 1999, pursuant to a Stock Purchase Agreement dated as of April 30, 1999, Aristotle acquired all of the outstanding stock (the Acquisition) of Simulaids, Inc. (Simulaids), a privately held New York corporation. As a result, the Company's 1999 consolidated statement of operations includes the results of operations of Simulaids since the date of the Acquisition.

. . .

The Acquisition purchase price of approximately $8,700, which includes $300 of transaction and tax obligations resulting from the Acquisition, was paid utilizing approximately $3,700 of cash and $5,000 of bank financing. The fair value of assets acquired and liabilities assumed amounted to $3,388 and $412, respectively. The excess cost over the fair value of net assets acquired amounted to $5,724 and is reflected as goodwill in the accompanying financial statements, net of amortization based on a straight-line basis over 25 years.

The Acquisition has been accounted for using the purchase method of accounting and, accordingly, the purchase price has been allocated to the assets and liabilities acquired based on their fair market values at the date of the Acquisition. The following summarizes the allocation of the purchase price of Simulaids:

Cash	$ 237
Accounts receivable	391
Inventories	1,192
Property, plant and equipment	1,486
Other assets	82
Goodwill	5,724
Accounts payable and accrued expenses	(156)
Other liabilities	(256)
	$8,700

Appendix 15.3: Pooling of Interests

Sometimes majority-owned subsidiaries have been accounted for using the **pooling of interests** method. Pooling is not allowed now, but many companies' financial statements will contain the effects of the past use of pooling for many years. Pooling could only be used in situations where one corporation acquired at least 90% of the stock of another corporation in a single transaction. Furthermore, the parent must have given up only stock to effect the purchase. A pooling of interests was the uniting of the ownership interests of two companies by an exchange of common stock. A number of other restrictions affected pooling. Unlike the purchase method, pooling failed to capture the economic information in the prices of acquired assets and liabilities at the time of acquisition.

Under pooling of interests, consolidated statements were constructed as follows.

How consolidated statements at the time of acquisition were created under pooling

- For the balance sheet, the *book values* of the parent and subsidiary were added together. No adjustment was made for the fact that the parent company may have paid substantially more than book value for the net assets of the subsidiary.
- The income statement simply added the two income statements together. Even if the acquisition was made late in the fiscal year, the consolidated income statement for the year would show the sum of both the parent's and subsidiary's entire income for the year.
- Because no write-up of assets was made upon acquisition, no increased depreciation or amortization of goodwill was included in the consolidated pooling-of-interests income statement.

The differences between purchase and pooling of interests accounting for majority-owned acquisitions is summarized in the following tables.

Consolidated Balance Sheet

	Pooling	Purchase Compared to Pooling
Assets	No write-up of assets to fair market values; therefore no goodwill	Higher asset values because of goodwill and asset write-ups to fair market values
Retained earnings	Parent and subsidiary retained earnings added together	Lower, at acquisition consolidated retained earnings equal to just the parent's retained earnings

Consolidated Income Statement

	Pooling	Purchase Compared to Pooling
Revenue and expenses	Added together for entire year no matter when acquisition occurred in the year	Income reflects only earnings of the subsidiary since the date of acquisition
Goodwill amortization	None	Amortized goodwill prior to 2002; impairment loss thereafter
Depreciation and amortization expense	Based on book values of parent and subsidiary	Based on book value of parent and fair market value of the subsidiary at date of acquisition

chapter 16

Financial Statement Analysis and the Valuation of Common Stock

In this chapter you will learn:

1 To use your knowledge of accounting in analyzing financial reports

2 To use accounting numbers to compare a company with itself over time

3 To use accounting numbers to compare a company with others in the same industry

4 To use accounting fundamentals to forecast future cash flows

5 To use projections of future cash flows to estimate the value of a company

In late December of 2000, one of the guests on the Jerry Springer Show was explaining why her boyfriend was going to leave his wife for her. The basis of her argument was, and we quote:

"He give me everything, Jerry, everything. He love me. He give me ev-re-thang."

The girlfriend didn't fare too well. Her boyfriend chose to stay with his wife, and she received a decidedly hostile reaction during the audience participation part of the show. One young lady, offering a small slip of paper, said:

"You said he gives you everything, honey, but that's not right. He didn't give you my number. Here's my number so you can call and make an appointment so I can FIX YOUR HAIR!"

No one person, or accounting book, can offer everything. We have covered the structure of accounting (Part 1), the economic concepts behind it (Part 2), and a lot of the details of accounting conventions (Part 3). Much more remains to be learned about these topics, but we will leave that task to other courses. For now, we want to revisit one last topic before ending this book: how accounting is used in making decisions.

An extremely careful reader (with a photographic memory) might detect that we have played a little fast and loose with the connection between accounting and economic decisions. In Chapter 1, we stressed that accounting is the writing of a financial history of an entity. We argued that accounting's history is useful because it helps decision makers make better economic decisions, such as whether to grant credit to a loan applicant, how much to pay for a share of stock, and how to compensate corporate executives. In Chapters 6 through 15, we stressed the connections between accounting values and economic values, taking for granted that understanding these connections

would be helpful in making better economic decisions. But we have not been explicit about the link between accounting knowledge and better economic decisions. The purpose of this chapter is to examine the use of accounting in making one specific economic decision: how much to pay for a share of common stock.

It is not the only decision we could have chosen, but it is one of the best for our purposes. Because common stock is a residual, assessing how much to pay for it is a comprehensive exercise that involves understanding every aspect of how a corporation creates and captures value. Accounting reports are extremely useful in obtaining this understanding.

Like our exploration of AOL's financial reporting in Chapter 5, we focus on a specific company at a specific time strictly for the purpose of illustration. Our approach and the techniques we use are generally applicable. The target of our valuation is Coldwater Creek, Inc., a small catalog sales company. We will use its financial reports and other data to estimate the value of its common stock at February 26, 2000. Our approach is to project the future cash flows that Coldwater Creek might be expected to produce, and then discount them to obtain a present value as of February 26, 2000. The approach relies heavily on accounting data and accounting techniques.

This chapter has the following goals:

1. To illustrate the use of accounting reports and disclosures in making one type of economic decision

2. To introduce the time-series analysis of accounting data

3. To introduce the cross-sectional analysis of accounting data

Background: Valuation of a Company Using Discounted Cash Flow Analysis

A widely accepted method of estimating the value of a company is based on the *expected present value* analysis that was introduced in Chapter 6. Two inputs are required for expected present value analysis: estimates of the future cash flows that will be generated by the company and estimates of appropriate interest rates. Up to this point, we assumed these estimates are given, but in practice they must be developed. Estimating interest rates is the province of finance. Accounting information is most useful in estimating future cash flows.

The process of estimating future cash flows is shown in Figures 16.1, 16.2, and 16.3 (see page 312). At a basic level, the approach is to estimate cash flows from operations and cash flows required for investing. (It is not necessary to be concerned with financing at this point.)

Figure 16.1

Projection of Cash Flows

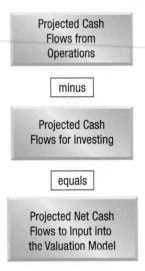

The projected income statements by themselves are not enough to project cash flows from operations. Think about the indirect method for constructing cash flow statements: It starts with net income, but then adjusts for changes in the current asset and current liability accounts to get cash flow from operations.

Estimates of future operating cash flows are constructed by first estimating future income. This process begins with estimates of sales. The past performance of the company is analyzed to gain an understanding of how expenses are related to sales. The balances in current asset and liability accounts that are required for the level of sales are estimated, and the results are combined into projected cash flow from operations.

Next, an estimate is made of the incremental investment in long-lived assets required to support the projected levels of sales. These projected cash flows for investing are subtracted from the projected cash flows from operations to give a projection of

Figure 16.2

How Projected Sales, Expenses, and Working Capital Lead to a Projection of Cash Flows

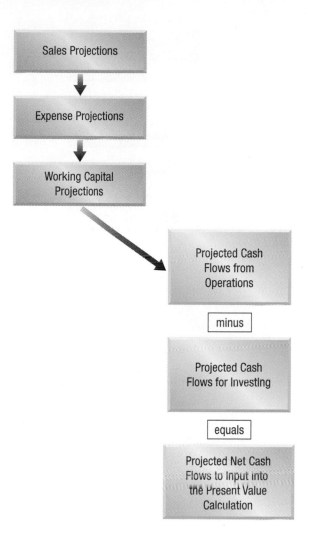

Understanding the company's operations, competitive situation, resources, and obligations is vital.

the net cash flows that will be generated by the company. This method is applied to project the net cash flows of the company in each of the following several years, say five. Finally, a terminal value of the company is estimated (the value of the company at the end of the fifth year). The present value of these cash flows is computed using an estimate of the cost of capital to the investor. This present value is the current estimate of the value of the company.

The process of making all of these estimates begins with a thorough understanding of the operations, the competitive situation, the resources, and the obligations of the company being evaluated. The financial statements are the primary source of information about the company's operations and financial status. We begin our analysis of Coldwater Creek with an examination of its financial statements.

Review Questions

1. Chapter 6 covered expected present values. What is a present value?

2. What is usually the first thing projected when projecting future cash flow?

3. Why must changes in the current asset and current liability accounts be included in estimating future cash flows?

Figure 16.3

Types of Analysis Required for a Projection of Cash Flows

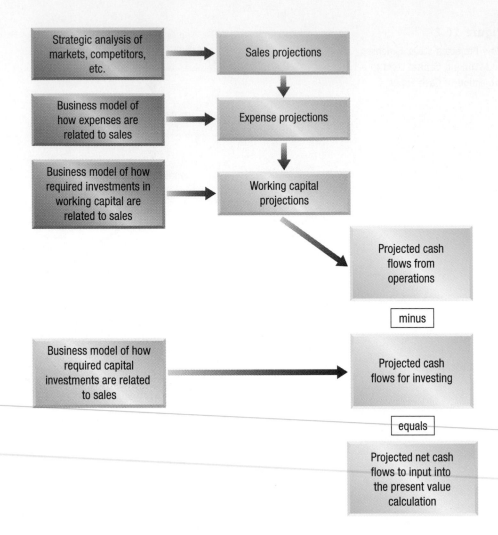

Coldwater Creek[1]

OBJECTIVE:
Learn to use your knowledge of accounting in analyzing financial reports.

Coldwater Creek, Inc., "is a retailer of women's apparel, jewelry, gifts, and soft home accessories, primarily marketing its merchandise through targeted catalog mailings, an interactive e-commerce Web site (http://www.coldwatercreek.com) and full-line retail stores."[2] Its target customers are women between 35 and 55 years of age with household incomes in excess of $50,000. According to its management:

*Coldwater Creek
10K excerpt*

> *The fiscal year ended February 26, 2000 ("fiscal 1999") was a milestone year in the sixteen-year history of Coldwater . . . as we embarked on a major program of evolution and expansion. First and foremost, we successfully transitioned the Company from its historical roots as a single-channel catalog retailer into a more dynamic retailer with two channels, being Direct and Retail. Our Direct Channel is comprised of catalog and e-commerce whereas our Retail Channel is comprised of full-line retail stores. We believe that our new multi-channel structure will position us well for targeting increased growth and market share in the future.*

[1]The analysis that follows is meant for *educational and illustrative purposes only*. We do not intend for anyone to rely on this particular analysis in deciding anything about the actual value of Coldwater Creek, the effectiveness of its management, or likely future results that might be produced by Coldwater Creek. This analysis is designed to demonstrate a style of analysis, not to produce reliable results. In no way do we intend this analysis to constitute any investment advice, and the reader is strongly cautioned not to take it as such.

[2]Coldwater Creek Inc., Form 10K for the fiscal year ended February 26, 2000.

Before we actually look at the content of Coldwater's financial statements, we should read the auditor's report to determine whether the financial statements are at all reliable. Coldwater used Arthur Andersen as its auditor. Andersen's report is dated April 4, 2000, and it states, in part:

Coldwater Creek
Excerpt from auditor's
opinion

> *In our opinion, the financial statements . . . present fairly, in all material respects, the financial position of Coldwater Creek Inc. and subsidiary as of February 26, 2000, and February 27, 1999, and the results of their operations and their cash flows for each of the three years in the period ended February 26, 2000, in conformity with accounting principles generally accepted in the United States.*

With this assurance as to the basis on which the financial statements were prepared, we can take the second step toward paying attention to their content, which is to think about what we expect to see given the description of Coldwater's operations. Coldwater is a retail company. Think through the asset side of the balance sheet, step-by-step. Take the current assets first. A retailer might or might not have a large amount of accounts receivable, depending on its credit policies. We would not expect to see large financial current assets, like security holdings. We should expect almost every retailer to stock inventories of merchandise. Likely, there will be some prepaid expenses.

Now think about the current liabilities. Some accounts payable are likely due to the suppliers of its merchandise inventories. Perhaps Coldwater will have some short-term loans that provide current financing and liquidity, but we do not expect a large amount of such financial liabilities. Most every business will have some accrued liabilities, such as wages payable.

What about the long-lived assets? Surely some fixed assets will be necessary for office space and warehousing. Some assets may be associated with the retail stores and the e-commerce initiative. But Coldwater is not a manufacturer, so we would not expect large amounts of property, plant, and equipment.

The long-term liabilities and equities reflect Coldwater's financing decisions, which are not necessarily tied to the nature of its operations. Therefore, we should have an open mind about these items.

What would we expect from Coldwater's income statements? Because it is a retailer, we might expect the income statement to be fairly simple. By far the largest revenue should be from sales to customers. Cost of goods sold should be the largest expense. We should expect to see some large expenses for selling and marketing.

We now turn to an examination of Coldwater's financial statements, beginning with its balance sheets.

Coldwater's Balance Sheets

Coldwater's recent balance sheets are given in Exhibit 16.1 on page 314. Given the expectations that we just developed, do we see any unusual items? Coldwater has about $123 million in total assets, almost half of which is inventory (about $60 million). About $39 million of the total assets is property and equipment.

Two kinds of assets appear that might be surprising. First, current and long-term assets show labels that contain the phrase "catalog costs." Because Coldwater operates a large catalog business, this phrasing shouldn't surprise us too much, although we will want to look at the nature of these accounts. In other words, we want to understand what costs are reflected in these accounts, and we want to understand why they are assets.

The second item that might catch our eyes is the executive loans. Even though they are a small part of Coldwater's total assets, we want to look carefully at them because of the special position executives enjoy that allows them to decide on the use of Coldwater's assets.

Virtually all of Coldwater's liabilities are accounts payable and accrued liabilities (roughly $44 million out of $46 million in total liabilities). Coldwater has no long-term liabilities listed on its balance sheet. We will want to look at the footnotes to see

Exhibit 16.1

Coldwater Creek
Balance Sheets

Coldwater Creek, Inc.
Balance Sheets
For the Years Ended
(amounts in thousands, except share data)

Assets	02/26/00	02/27/99
Current Assets:		
Cash and cash equivalents	$ 7,533	$ 149
Receivables	5,741	2,683
Inventories	60,203	56,474
Prepaid expenses	1,319	1,234
Prepaid catalog costs	3,994	4,274
Deferred income taxes	915	—
TOTAL CURRENT ASSETS	$ 79,705	$ 64,814
Deferred catalog costs	2,817	3,195
Property and equipment, net	38,895	31,236
Executive loans	1,453	1,376
TOTAL ASSETS	$122,870	$100,621

Catalog costs

Executive loans

Liabilities and Stockholders' Equity

	02/26/00	02/27/99
Current Liabilities:		
Revolving line of credit	—	$ 9,938
Accounts payable	$ 30,098	17,086
Accrued liabilities	13,549	7,668
Income taxes payable	2,140	4,445
Deferred income taxes	—	1,080
Total Current Liabilities	$ 45,787	$ 40,217
Deferred income taxes	513	298
Total Liabilities	$ 46,300	$ 40,515
Commitments and contingencies		

Stockholders' Equity

	02/26/00	02/27/99
Preferred stock, $0.01 par value, 1,000,000 shares authorized, none issued and outstanding	—	—
Common stock, $0.01 par value, 15,000,000 shares authorized, 10,319,345 and 10,183,117 issued and outstanding, respectively	$ 103	$ 102
Additional paid-in capital	41,579	39,287
Retained earnings	34,888	20,717
Total Stockholders' Equity	$ 76,570	$ 60,106
Total Liabilities and Stockholders' Equity	$122,870	$100,621

Common shares outstanding: 10.3 million shares

whether Coldwater has obligations under operating leases, since many retailers lease store space.

Now let's get into more detail. Recall that working capital is the difference between current assets and current liabilities. Working capital is an assessment of the amount of excess current resources available to meet current obligations. For a retailer like Coldwater, working capital management is typically a crucial factor in determining profitability. Too little working capital could lead to a situation in which not enough resources are readily available to meet obligations. Too much working capital ties up funds unnecessarily.

Working capital (millions):	
Current assets	$ 80
Current liabilities	(46)
Working capital	$ 34

Coldwater has working capital of about $34 million at February 26, 2000. By itself, this amount tells us very little. At least the working capital is positive, which is virtually necessary in Coldwater's business. But later we will develop some more precise indications as to whether this amount of working capital is sufficient or excessive.

At this stage of our analysis, we are more concerned with obtaining a basic understanding of Coldwater's balance sheet. Therefore, we will go more deeply into the two areas we identified as a bit mysterious: catalog costs and executive loans.

Catalog Costs

We need to go to the footnotes to get information about catalog costs. The notes read, in part:

Coldwater Creek
10K excerpt

> Catalog costs include all direct costs associated with the production and mailing of the Company's direct mail catalogs and are classified as prepaid catalog costs until the catalogs are mailed.
>
> When the Company's catalogs are mailed, these costs are reclassified as deferred catalog costs and amortized over the periods in which the related revenues are expected to be realized. Substantially all revenues are generated within the first three months after a catalog is mailed. Catalog expenses were $84.1 million in fiscal 1999, $95.7 million in fiscal 1998, and $66.6 million in fiscal 1997.

Not surprisingly, Coldwater incurs costs in the production and mailing of catalogs. These costs are expected to generate future benefits, so they are assets. The note tells us that these costs are accumulated in the current asset account, Prepaid Catalog Costs, until the catalogs are mailed. Upon mailing, the costs are reclassified from Prepaid Catalog Costs into the noncurrent asset account, Deferred Catalog Costs. These deferred catalog costs are matched against revenues by a process of amortization.

Executive Loans

The note about the executive loans reads, in part:

Coldwater Creek
10K excerpt

> Effective June 30, 1997, the Company established an Executive Loan Program under which the Company may make, at its sole discretion and with prior approvals from the Chief Executive Officer and the Board of Directors' Compensation Committee, secured long-term loans to key executives other than Dennis and Ann Pence. Each loan is secured by the executive's personal net assets, inclusive of all vested stock options in the Company, bears interest at three percent per annum, and becomes due and payable on the earlier of (i)the date ten days before the date on which the vested stock options serving as partial security expire or (ii) ninety days from the date on which the executive's employment with the Company terminates for any reason.

These amounts are secured by personal assets and must be approved by the CEO and the Compensation Committee. One may question whether the interest rate on the loan is high enough, but given that Coldwater has total assets of about $123 million, a few percentage points of interest on loans of about $1.5 million is a minor matter. We have no reason at this point to question these loans further.

Review Questions

1. What business is Coldwater Creek in?

2. Do any unusual items appear on Coldwater Creek's recent balance sheets? If so, what are they?

3. Why begin an examination of financial statements by reading the auditor's opinion?

Time-Series Benchmarks

OBJECTIVE:

Learn to use accounting numbers to compare a company with itself over time.

This type of "eye-balling" of Coldwater's balance sheet gives us a preliminary look at its assets, liabilities, and equities, but we need to be more formal if we are going to generate the best forecasts of its future cash flows. Exhibit 16.2 takes the first step in achieving this formality. It shows condensed versions of Coldwater's balance sheets in which all the values are expressed as a percentage of total assets.

Exhibit 16.2

Coldwater Creek
Percentage Balance Sheets

Coldwater Creek, Inc.
Condensed Balance Sheets
In Percentage of Total Assets
For the Years Ended

Assets	02/26/00	02/27/99
Current Assets:		
Cash and cash equivalents	6.1%	0.1%
Accounts receivable	4.7	2.7
Inventories	49.0	56.1
Other	5.1	5.5
Total Current Assets	64.9%	64.4%
Total noncurrent assets	35.1	35.6
Total Assets	100.0%	100.0%
Liabilities and Stockholders' Equity		
Current Liabilities		
Accounts payable	24.5%	17.0%
Accrued liabilities	11.0	7.6
Other liabilities	2.2	15.7
Total Liabilities	37.7%	40.3%
Stockholders' Equity		
Common stock and additional paid-in capital	33.9%	39.1%
Retained earnings	28.4	20.6
Total Stockholders' Equity	62.3%	59.7%
Total Liabilities and Stockholders' Equity	100.0%	100.0%

Benchmarks are comparison points against which an item is judged.

Time-series benchmarks are used to compare a company with itself through time.

Just converting the balance sheet to percentage terms helps us make assessments about Coldwater's mix of assets, but we could make the exercise a lot more informative if we establish some quantitative **benchmarks** against which to judge Coldwater's situation. You probably automatically used one benchmark in examining Exhibit 16.2 by simply comparing the percentages in the February 26, 2000, balance sheet against those for February 27, 1999, in the adjacent column.

Comparing a company against itself in earlier periods is an example of **time-series benchmark** analysis. We can see that Coldwater's balance sheet in percentage terms looks pretty much the same at February 26, 2000, as it did at February 27, 1999. That assessment gives us some assurance that the February 26, 2000, numbers are not too unusual for Coldwater, at least relative to those at February 27, 1999. But maybe both sets of numbers are odd. Why not look at, say, five years' worth of percentage balance sheets to get a better feel for how typical Coldwater's February 26, 2000, numbers are? Exhibit 16.3 gives five years of balance sheet data for Coldwater.

Coldwater Creek, Inc.
Condensed Balance Sheets
In Percentage of Total Assets (rounded)
For the Years Ended

Assets	02/26/00	02/27/99	02/28/98	03/01/97	03/02/96
Current Assets:					
Cash	6.1%	0.1%	0.3%	14.7%	1.8%
Accounts receivable	4.7	2.7	4.1	3.8	6.7
Inventories	49.0	56.1	54.0	40.8	35.2
Other	5.1	5.5	5.6	3.0	3.2
Total Current Assets	64.9%	64.4%	64.1%	62.2%	46.9%
Total noncurrent assets	35.1	35.6	35.9	37.8	53.1
Total Assets	100.0%	100.0%	100.0%	100.0%	100.0%
Liabilities and Stockholders' Equity					
Liabilities:					
Accounts payable	24.5%	17.0%	27.8%	29.1%	26.2%
Accrued liabilities	11.0	7.6	10.7	9.6	10.7
Other liabilities (virtually all current)	2.1	15.7	11.8	1.2	1.1
Total Liabilities	37.7%	40.3%	50.2%	40.0%	38.1%
Stockholders' Equity					
Common stock and additional paid-in capital	33.9%	39.1%	39.6%	62.7%	0.3%
Retained earnings	28.4	20.6	10.2	(2.7)	61.6
Total Stockholders' Equity	62.3%	59.7%	49.8%	60.0%	61.9%
Total Liabilities and Stockholders' Equity	100.0%	100.0%	100.0%	100.0%	100.0%

Exhibit 16.3

Coldwater Creek
Percentage Balance Sheets for
Five Years

Review Questions

1. What is a benchmark?

2. What is a time-series benchmark?

Current Ratio

We have encountered more financial statistics that are relevant than just Coldwater's assets as a percent of total assets. The current ratio is current assets divided by current liabilities. It captures some of the same liquidity issues as working capital, but the current ratio does it in the form of a fraction. Exhibit 16.4 on page 318 shows the current ratio and other important balance sheet ratios.

Quick Ratio

The quick ratio is a more conservative look at liquidity. The quick ratio is equal to current assets that are most liquid, such as cash, receivables, and marketable securities, divided by current liabilities. Cash and receivables are Coldwater's only ultra-liquid assets, and its quick ratio is just cash and receivables divided by current liabilities.

Coldwater Creek, Inc.
Important Balance Sheet Ratios
For the Years Ended

	02/26/00	02/27/99	02/28/98	03/01/97	03/02/96
Current ratio	1.72	1.60	1.28	1.56	1.23
Quick ratio	0.29	0.07	0.09	0.40	0.22
Debt-to-equity (total liabilities divided by equity)	0.60	0.67	1.01	0.67	0.61
Long-term debt to equity	0.0	0.0	0.0	0.0	0.0

Exhibit 16.4

Coldwater Creek
Important Balance Sheet Ratios

Debt-to-Equity

The debt-to-equity ratio provides a first look at capital structure. People compute debt-to-equity ratios in a variety of ways, but we will start simply by dividing total liabilities by total shareholders' equity.

Long-Term Debt-to-Equity

Long-term debt-to-equity provides an indication of the relative sources of long-term capital. Coldwater has no long-term debt, so its long-term debt-to-equity ratio is zero.

Coldwater's latest balance sheet looks fairly typical, as assessed by comparing its balance sheets over time.

These data offer us some assurance that Coldwater's latest balance sheet is typical, at least for Coldwater. Current assets hovers at about 64% of total assets, except at March 2, 1996, which is easily the most unusual year of the five. Coldwater is a fairly new and rapidly growing company, and we would be surprised to find all the percentages totally stable from year to year. For example, Coldwater's total assets almost tripled in the year from March 2, 1996, to March 1, 1997, going from about $23 million to $62 million. It took from March 1, 1997, to February 26, 2000, for Coldwater's assets to double again, going from about $62 million to about $123 million. It ought not surprise us too much that some differences appear in Coldwater's percentage balance sheets at the start and end of this five-year period.

Cross-Sectional Benchmarks

OBJECTIVE:
Learn to use accounting numbers to compare a company with others in the same industry.

Cross-sectional benchmarks are used to compare a company with similar companies.

In statistical terms, we are concerned with whether Coldwater's financial statistics exhibit *stationarity*. The problem is that Coldwater or its environment might have changed so much between March 2, 1996, and February 26, 2000, that comparing the two sets of balance sheet numbers at those dates might be a pretty meaningless exercise. In addition to the time-series analysis, we would like to assess Coldwater's financial statistics at February 26, 2000, against a set of numbers that represent conditions on or near that date. We could make this assessment by comparing Coldwater's numbers to those of *comparable companies* at dates close to February 26, 2000. Comparing different companies at the same point in time is called **cross-sectional benchmark** analysis.

The first problem we face in doing cross-sectional analysis is to pick companies similar enough to Coldwater that a comparison is meaningful. The starting point in this exercise is usually the Standard Industrial Classification (SIC) Code of the company of interest. SIC Codes put firms in groups using criteria relating to the businesses in which the firms operate. Coldwater's SIC Code is 5961, which is the code for catalog/mail order houses.

Unfortunately, the SIC Codes don't give a very precise grouping of firms. For example, Amazon.com, PC Connection Inc., 800 JR Cigar Inc. (whatever that is!), Hello Direct Inc. (sells telecommunications equipment), and SkyMall Inc. (sells merchandise through catalogs placed on airplanes) are all in the same SIC Code grouping as Coldwater. To choose comparable companies, we often start from the SIC Code list, then narrow it through knowledge of the industry and the application of criteria such as the similarity of the amounts of total assets of the firms.

Included in the catalog/mail order houses group are Spiegel Inc., Lands' End Inc., Lillian Vernon Corp., and J. Jill Group Inc. They all sell merchandise similar to Coldwater. They vary quite a bit in size, however. At the end of their 1999 fiscal years, Spiegel had total assets in excess of $2.2 billion, whereas J. Jill had total assets of about $101 million. Clearly, trying to compare the balance sheets of these companies without first scaling them, for example, by stating everything as a percentage of total assets, would be a fruitless exercise. Who could make sense of comparing Lands' End's inventory of $162 million with Coldwater's $60 million?

Exhibit 16.5 shows the percentage balance sheet for the 1999 fiscal years of Coldwater, Spiegel, Lands' End, Lillian Vernon, and J. Jill. Coldwater is in the middle in terms of cash and receivables, and on the high end in terms of inventory. Coldwater's investment in noncurrent assets looks to be in the middle of the group.

Exhibit 16.5   Coldwater Creek and Competitors Percentage Balance Sheets, Asset Side Only

Asset Side of Condensed Balance Sheets of Coldwater Creek and Competitors For the Ends of the 1999 Fiscal Years

Assets	Coldwater	J. Jill	Lands' End	Lands' End (adjusted TO FIFO)	Lillian Vernon	Spiegel
Current Assets:						
Cash	6.1%	5.9%	16.8%	16.0%	25.0%	2.1%
Accounts receivable	4.7	0.0	3.9	3.7	15.8	43.5
Inventories	49.0	21.4	35.6	38.4	24.0	22.3
Other	5.1	22.0	7.1	6.9	4.0	6.4
Total Current Assets	64.9%	49.3%	63.4%	65.0%	68.8%	74.3%
Total noncurrent assets	35.1	50.7	36.6	35.0	31.2	25.7
Total Assets	100.0%	100.0%	100.0%	100.0%	100.0%	100.0%
Fiscal year-end	02/26/00	12/25/99	01/28/00	01/28/00	02/26/00	12/25/99
Inventory method	FIFO	FIFO	LIFO	FIFO	Ave. Cost	FIFO

Exhibit 16.5 contains two more lines that we should consider when comparing balance sheets of retailers such as Coldwater. First is the fiscal year-end. Retail is often a highly seasonal business, with a lot of activity around the end of the calendar year. Inventories typically rise in the late fall and drop after the holiday season. A balance sheet for a retailer as of November 15, therefore, might be a lot different from one as of February 28. Exhibit 16.5 shows that all five firms have fiscal year-ends just after the holidays. Please note that we follow Coldwater's convention of calling the twelve months ended February 26, 2000, as the 1999 fiscal year.

The second thing we should consider with retailers is the inventory accounting method. Only Lands' End is on LIFO, and we have restated its percentage balance sheets to a FIFO basis, using the methods presented in Chapter 9.

What conclusions might we draw from our analysis thus far? Coldwater's balance sheets appear to be fairly stable over the last three or four years. In comparison to its competitors, Coldwater might have an opportunity to cut its investment in inventories.

Review Questions

1. What is a cross-sectional benchmark?

2. What does cross-sectional analysis add to time-series analysis?

Coldwater's Income Statements

The same techniques we used to analyze Coldwater's balance sheets can be used to gain insight into its income statements. Before we look at the statements, recall what we expect to see. We expect a fairly simple income statement, with the largest revenue from sales to customers. Cost of goods sold should be the largest expense, and we should expect to see some large expenses for selling and marketing.

Exhibit 16.6 shows three years of Coldwater's income statements. Consistent with what we should expect, we see a fairly simple statement. Sales, Cost of Goods Sold, Selling, General, and Administrative Expenses, and the Provision for Income Taxes are the only large numbers. Net income of about $14 million was produced from sales of roughly $328 million. Cost of Sales and Selling, General, and Administrative Expenses were roughly $156 million and $150 million, respectively.

Exhibit 16.6

Coldwater Creek
Income Statements

Coldwater Creek, Inc.
Income Statements
For the Years Ended
(amounts in thousands)

	2/26/00	02/26/99	02/27/98
Net sales	$328,267	$325,231	$246,697
Cost of sales	156,186	156,198	120,126
GROSS PROFIT	$172,081	$169,033	$126,571
Selling, general, and administrative expenses	150,349	150,655	107,083
INCOME FROM OPERATIONS	$ 21,732	$ 18,378	$ 19,488
Interest, net, and other	864	(697)	57
Gain on sale of Milepost Four assets	826	—	—
INCOME BEFORE PROVISION FOR INCOME TAXES	$ 23,422	$ 17,681	$ 19,545
Provision for income taxes	9,251	6,990	7,857
NET INCOME	$ 14,171	$ 10,691	$ 11,688
NET INCOME PER SHARE—BASIC	$1.38	$1.05	$1.15
NET INCOME PER SHARE—DILUTED	$1.34	$1.02	$1.10

Exhibit 16.7 shows Coldwater's percentage income statements in which all the numbers are expressed as a percent of sales. We can see that Cost of Sales has been hovering at about 48%, whereas Selling, General, and Administrative Expenses have been about 45% to 46%. Net income is in the neighborhood of 4% of sales.

Coldwater's gross margin percentage is the highest of the five.

Just as with our analysis of the balance sheet, we would like to know how Coldwater's income statement numbers compare with other firms in its industry. Exhibit 16.8 shows selected income statement percentages for Coldwater and four competitors. Note that Coldwater's cost of goods sold as a percent of sales is the lowest of the five firms.

Also, Coldwater's net income as a percent of sales is the highest of the five firms. For a retail firm like Coldwater, these comparisons are good indications that it is a well-managed operation.

Exhibit 16.7

Coldwater Creek
Percentage Income Statements

Coldwater Creek, Inc.
Percentage Income Statements
For the Years Ended

	2/26/00	02/26/99	02/27/98
Net sales	100.0%	100.0%	100.0%
Cost of sales	47.6	48.0	48.7
GROSS PROFIT	52.4%	52.0%	51.3%
Selling, general, and administrative expenses	45.8	46.3	43.4
INCOME FROM OPERATIONS	6.6%	5.7%	7.9%
Interest, net, and other	0.2	(0.3)	0.0
Gain on sale of Milepost Four assets	0.3	0.0	0.0
INCOME BEFORE PROVISION FOR INCOME TAXES	7.1%	5.4%	7.9%
Provision for income taxes	2.8	2.1	3.2
NET INCOME	4.3%	3.3%	4.7%

Selected Income Statement Percentages of Coldwater Creek and Competitors
For the Ends of the 1999 Fiscal Years

	Coldwater	J. Jill	Lands' End	Lands' End (adjusted to FIFO)	Lillian Vernon	Spiegel
Sales	100.0%	100.0%	100.0%	100.0%	100.0%	100.0%
Cost of goods sold	47.6	66.7	53.5	54.0	46.8	54.9
Gross margin	52.4%	33.3%	46.5%	46.0%	53.2%	45.1%
Net income	4.3%	(0.3)%	3.6%	2.6%	2.7%	3.5%
Special items	0.2	(1.5)	0.1	0.3	0.0	0.1
Extraordinary items	0.0	0.0	0.0	0.0	0.0	0.0
Net income before special and extraordinary items	4.1%	1.2%	3.5%	2.3%	2.7%	3.4%
Inventory method	FIFO	FIFO	LIFO	FIFO	Ave. Cost	FIFO

Exhibit 16.8

Coldwater Creek and
Competitors
Percentage Income Statements

Key Step: Articulation

After looking briefly at Coldwater's income statements and balance sheets, we now need to see how they fit together. We want to project the cash flow that Coldwater could deliver to an investor. Cash flow depends on both the resources generated by Coldwater's earnings process and on the investments in current and noncurrent assets that are required to keep the earnings process going. So we need to understand how Coldwater's earnings process reflected in its income statements is linked to the net investment (i.e., assets and liabilities) shown on its balance sheets.

Turnover ratios link income
statement flows to balance
sheet stocks.

The most natural way to make this link for some balance sheet items is to use **turnover ratios.** For example, consider Coldwater's inventory turnover. Inventory turnover was defined in Chapter 9 as cost of sales divided by average inventory. This ratio links an income statement number, cost of sales, with an average inventory number from the balance sheets. Therefore, it can form the basis of a set of projections that encompass the links between these two statements.

For fiscal 1999, Coldwater's inventory turnover was 2.7:

Cost of sales	$156 million
Beginning inventory	$56 million
Ending inventory	$60 million
Average inventory	$58 million
Inventory turnover ($156/$58)	2.7 times

Now suppose we project Coldwater's sales in 2000 to increase 12.5% over its sales in 1999. This projection translates into projected 2000 sales of $369 million. Suppose we expect cost of sales to be about 47% of sales. We would then project cost of sales to be about $173 million:

Projected sales ($328 × 1.125)	$369 million
CGS%	47%
Projected CGS ($369 × 0.47)	$173 million

Suppose we project Coldwater's inventory turnover to remain at 2.7 times. Coldwater's beginning inventory for 2000 is its $60 million ending inventory for fiscal 1999. The combination of the turnover prediction and the beginning inventory yields a projected ending inventory of $68 million:

$$2.7 = \text{CGS/Average inventory}$$

$$2.7 = \text{CGS}/[1/2(\$60 \text{ million} + x)]$$

$$2.7 = \$173 \text{ million}/[1/2(\$60 \text{ million} + x)]$$

$$2.7 \times [1/2(\$60 \text{ million} + x)] = \$173 \text{ million}$$

$$x = [\$173 \text{ million}/(2.7 \times 1/2)] - \$60 \text{ million}$$

$$x = \$68 \text{ million}$$

This method essentially ties projected inventory to sales. To see this relationship, substitute for cost of sales in the second equation earlier:

$$2.7 = \text{CGS}/[1/2(\$60 \text{ million} + x)]$$

$$2.7 = (0.47 \times \text{Sales})/[1/2(\$60 \text{ million} + x)]$$

Solving this equation for the ending inventory, x, as a function of sales gives

$$x = [(0.47 \times \text{Sales})/(2.7 \times 1/2)] - \$60 \text{ million}$$

or

$$x = (0.348 \times \text{Sales}) - \$60 \text{ million}$$

Using the turnover method projects inventory as 34.8% of sales minus $60 million.

Percentages of sales is a simpler way to link income statement and balance sheet projections.

A mechanically simpler way to tie income statement and balance sheet projections together is to project all balance sheet amounts as a simple percent of sales. Our projected $68 million in inventory is about 18.4% of projected sales:

$$\text{Projected inventory/Projected sales} = \$68 \text{ million}/\$369 \text{ million}$$

$$= 0.184$$

The percent-of-sales method is commonly used. It is not quite the same as the turnover approach. Figure 16.4 shows that the two methods generate close results when sales are in the neighborhood of $369 million, but they disagree more as sales gets further away from $369 million. The turnover method projects lower inventory levels for sales over $369 million and higher inventory levels for sales less than $369 million.

We would like to choose the best method of making projections. The more time and effort we devote to understanding Coldwater's operations and plans, the better chance we have of adopting a more accurate projection method. Our purpose in this chapter is to illustrate the role of accounting in the valuation process, so we will not go into depth about

Figure 16.4

Projected Inventory Levels Using Percent of Sales and Turnover Methods

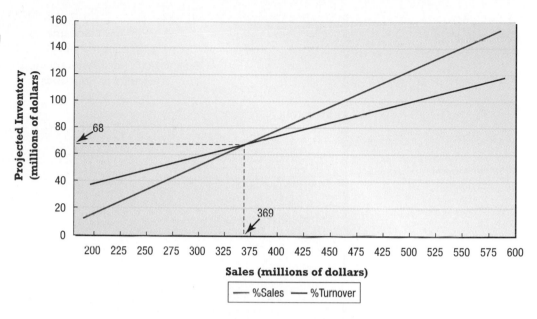

various ways of making projections. We will adopt the expedient approach of projecting balance sheet amounts as percents of sales. However, you should not forget that the ultimate quality of an analysis is vitally dependent on the accuracy of the projections we make.

OBJECTIVE:

Learn to use accounting fundamentals to forecast future cash flows.

Projections

The first step in projecting Coldwater's future cash flows is to forecast sales. Until 1999, Coldwater's sales grew at a phenomenal rate. Exhibit 16.9 gives Coldwater's sales for the last five years and calculates sales growth in each year.

Exhibit 16.9

Coldwater Creek Sales Growth

Coldwater Creek Sales and Sales Growth For Fiscal Years					
Year	1995	1996	1997	1998	1999
Sales (millions)	$76	$143	$247	$325	$328
Growth rate		88%	72%	32%	1%

Cash flow projections begin with projecting sales.

The extremely high growth rates in 1996 and 1997 are typical for a small company, and future growth is unlikely to be so high. On the other hand, the small growth rate achieved in 1999 likely is not indicative of Coldwater's future growth, either. Without digging into it too deeply, we will project that Coldwater's sales will grow 12.5% per year over the next five years. After five years, we predict Coldwater's sales will be stable.

We base the predictions of other income statement items on the sales predictions. Aside from sales, the other main items on Coldwater's income statements are cost of sales, selling, general, and administrative expenses, and the provision for income taxes (i.e., income tax expenses). These categories are a bit too aggregated for our needs, because depreciation and amortization expenses are not identified. We need to estimate them if we are going to project correctly the capital expenditures required to support Coldwater's earnings process.

Examination of Coldwater's cash flow statement in Exhibit 16.10 on page 324 shows that depreciation and amortization in 1999 was about $7.2 million. That amount is a

Exhibit 16.10
Coldwater Creek
Cash Flow Statement

Coldwater Creek, Inc.
Cash Flow Statement
For the Year Ended February 26, 2000
(amounts in thousands)

Operating Activities:

Net income	$ 14,171
Noncash items:	
Depreciation and amortization	7,242
Deferred income tax (benefit) provision	(1,780)
Gain on sale of Milepost Four assets	(826)
Other, net	(30)
Net change in current assets and liabilities:	
Receivables	(1,881)
Inventories	(4,449)
Prepaid expenses	(85)
Prepaid catalog costs	280
Accounts payable	13,012
Accrued liabilities	5,881
Income taxes payable	(1,421)
Decrease (increase) in deferred catalog costs	378
NET CASH PROVIDED BY (USED IN) OPERATING ACTIVITIES	$ 30,492

Depreciation and amortization → (points to "Depreciation and amortization" line)

Investing Activities:

Purchase of property and equipment	$(16,647)
(Loans to) repayments of loans to executives	(77)
Proceeds from sale of Milepost Four assets	1,546
Purchase of marketable securities	(2,280)
Proceeds from sale of marketable securities	2,239
Proceeds from sale of land	639
NET CASH USED IN INVESTING ACTIVITIES	$(14,580)

Financing Activities:

Net (repayments of) advances under revolving line of credit	$ (9,938)
Net proceeds from exercises of stock options	1,410
Distributions to stockholders	—
NET CASH (USED IN) PROVIDED BY FINANCING ACTIVITIES	$ (8,528)
NET INCREASE (DECREASE) IN CASH AND CASH EQUIVALENTS	$ 7,384
Cash and cash equivalents, beginning	149
CASH AND CASH EQUIVALENTS, ENDING	$ 7,533

Supplemental Cash Flow Data:

Cash paid for interest	$47
Cash paid for income taxes	$12,656
Tax benefit realized from exercises of stock options	$883

Cost of goods sold, depreciation and amortization, and selling, general, and administrative expenses are projected as a percentage of sales.

Income tax expense is projected as a percentage of net income.

little more than 20% of Coldwater's beginning total noncurrent assets, and it is about 2.5% of Coldwater's sales.

Our earlier analysis suggests that cost of sales is about 47% of sales. Selling, general, and administrative expenses were about 46% of sales. However, depreciation and amortization expenses are included in the cost of sales and the selling, general, and administrative expenses. For simplicity, we assume that all depreciation and amortization falls in selling, general, and administrative expenses. Selling, general, and administrative expenses, exclusive of depreciation and amortization, is thus 43.5% of sales. Although Coldwater had a small amount of interest expense in 1999, it has no long-term debt and we will ignore interest expense in our projections. Income tax expenses are assumed to be 38% of net income before tax. Exhibit 16.11 gathers these assumptions about the income statement.

Exhibit 16.11

Coldwater Creek
Assumptions for Projecting Income Statements

Coldwater Creek Assumptions for Projecting Income Statements	
Sales Growth	12.5% per year for 5 years 0 thereafter
Cost of sales as a percent of sales	47.0%
Selling, general, and administrative expenses as a percent of sales	43.5
Depreciation expense as a percent of sales	2.5
Income tax expenses as a percent of net income before tax	38.0

Exhibit 16.12 contains the application of these assumptions to produce projected income statements for Coldwater Creek for fiscal 2000 through 2004 and beyond. We project that Coldwater's net income will rise from the $14.0 million it earned in fiscal 1999 to $25.7 million in fiscal 2004.

Exhibit 16.12

Coldwater Creek
1999 Income Statement and Projected Income Statements Thereafter

Coldwater Creek Income Statement and Forecasted Income Statements for Fiscal Years (amounts in millions)							
	1999	2000	2001	2002	2003	2004	Beyond
Sales	$328.0	$369.0	$415.1	$467.0	$525.4	$591.1	$591.1
CGS	156.0	173.4	195.1	219.5	246.9	277.8	277.8
Gross Profit	$172.0	$195.6	$220.0	$247.5	$278.5	$313.3	$313.3
SG&A	143.0	160.5	180.6	203.2	228.6	257.1	257.1
Op Inc bef depr	$ 29.0	$ 35.1	$ 39.4	$ 44.4	$ 49.9	$ 56.2	$ 56.2
Depr & Amort	7.0	9.3	10.3	11.7	13.1	14.8	14.8
Op Profit	$ 22.0	$ 25.8	$ 29.1	$ 32.7	$ 36.8	$ 41.4	$ 41.4
Interest Exp	1.0	0.0	0.0	0.0	0.0	0.0	0.0
NIBT	$ 23.0	$ 25.8	$ 29.1	$ 32.7	$ 36.8	$ 41.4	$ 41.4
Income Tax	9.0	9.8	11.0	12.4	14.0	15.7	15.7
Net Income	$ 14.0	$ 16.0	$ 18.0	$ 20.3	$ 22.8	$ 25.7	$ 25.7

Recall that Coldwater's fiscal year x ends in February of year x + 1.

At this point, it would be helpful if you have a really, really good memory. Do you recall the Total Toy Store example in Chapter 4? The Total Toy Store was earning a profit, but it was not generating enough cash to cover its required investment in accounts receivable and inventories. The president of Total Toy was mystified by this situation, which needed to be addressed by borrowing funds to tide the business over until it generated sufficient cash flow.

An investor is not directly concerned with whether Coldwater Creek needs to borrow to finance its growth, but an investor is definitely interested in the cash flow generated by the company. Eventually, the investor will have to receive some return on the investment, which at some point has to be a distribution of cash from the company in the form of a dividend. We want to project the cash generated by Coldwater that could be distributed to its shareholders without harming Coldwater's earnings process that generates the income we have projected. As we argued earlier, to derive this cash flow, sometimes called **free cash flow** by financial experts, we need to project Coldwater's balance sheets.

Free cash flow is the cash flow that could be distributed to investors without harming the earnings process.

We don't need to project Coldwater's balance sheets in as much detail as the company's annual report presents them. Because free cash flow is an ultimate target of our projections, we want to project cash separately. We have seen that inventory is a substantial portion of Coldwater's current assets, so it makes sense to project it separately. Examining Coldwater's balance sheets shows they have few other current assets, even including receivables. Therefore, let's project the other current assets as one amount.

Coldwater's noncurrent assets consist almost entirely of net property, plant, and equipment, so let's just project noncurrent assets as one amount.

Coldwater's purchase of inventories gives rise to an accounts payable account, which we will separate from its other current liabilities. Coldwater has no long-term debt, so we will project it to remain at zero.

We need to project Coldwater's shareholders' equity, but we need to be careful. The projections of all the assets and liabilities imply a value for shareholders' equity. So we don't have free rein to plop in any old projection of shareholders' equity. We have also projected income, which feeds into shareholders' equity. The retained earnings account must be consistent with the rest of the balance sheet predictions and the income and dividend predictions.

To make sure we don't project income statements, free cash flows, and balance sheets that are inconsistent, we plug in the shareholders' equity from the balance sheet equation. Then we will analyze the retained earnings account for the amount of dividends. This process, if executed correctly, will project the dividends equal to the free cash flows that Coldwater could pay to its shareholders without harming its earnings process. To help make things clearer, we will project retained earnings separately from common stock and additional paid-in capital.

Exhibit 16.13 gives the assumptions we use to project balance sheets. As we stated earlier, we will use the percent-of-sales approach, which projects balance sheet items as a simple function of projected sales.

Exhibit 16.13

Coldwater Creek Assumptions for Projecting Balance Sheets

Coldwater Creek Assumptions for Projecting Balance Sheets	
Cash as a percent of sales	2.5%
Inventory as a percent of sales	18.4
Other current assets as a percent of sales	3.0
Noncurrent assets as a percent of sales	13.0
Accounts payable as a percent of sales	10.0
Other current liabilities as a percent of sales	6.0

Exhibit 16.14 contains the application of these assumptions to produce a set of projected balance sheets for Coldwater as of the end of fiscal years 2000 to 2004 and beyond. Notice how the projection of total assets climbs to $218 million in fiscal 2004, after which it is projected to remain stable.

Coldwater Creek
Balance Sheet and Forecasted Balance Sheets as of the End of Fiscal Years
(amounts in millions)

	1999	2000	2001	2002	2003	2004	Beyond
Cash	$ 7.5	$ 9.2	$ 10.4	$ 11.7	$ 13.1	$ 14.8	$ 14.8
Inventory	60.2	67.9	76.4	85.9	96.7	108.8	108.8
Other current assets	11.9	11.1	12.4	14.0	15.8	17.7	17.7
Total current assets	$ 79.6	$ 88.2	$ 99.2	$111.6	$125.6	$141.3	$141.3
Net noncurrent assets	43.2	48.0	54.0	60.7	68.3	76.8	76.8
Total assets	$122.8	$136.2	$153.2	$172.3	$193.9	$218.1	$218.1
Accounts payable	$ 30.1	$ 36.9	$ 41.5	$ 46.7	$ 52.5	$ 59.1	$ 59.1
Other current liabilities	16.1	22.2	24.9	28.0	31.6	35.5	35.5
Common stock and additional paid-in capital	41.7	41.7	41.7	41.7	41.7	41.7	41.7
Retained earnings	34.9	35.4	45.1	55.9	68.1	81.8	81.8
Total liabilities and shareholders' equity	$122.8	$136.2	$153.2	$172.3	$193.8	$218.1	$218.1

Exhibit 16.14

Coldwater Creek
Forecasted Balance Sheets

We can now project free cash flows in a number of ways, which all ought to give the same results. As stated earlier, one way is to analyze the retained earnings account for the implied dividends. For example, we project retained earnings to increase to $35.4 million at the end of fiscal 2000 from its beginning amount of $34.9 million. Earnings in fiscal 2000 are projected to be $16.0 million. These figures imply projected dividends (free cash flow) of $15.5 million:

Retained Earnings

	Dr.	Cr.	
		34.9	Balance at end of fiscal 1999
Projected dividends (free cash flow)	15.5		
		16.0	Net income for fiscal 2000
		35.4	Balance at the end of fiscal 2000

Another way to see what's going on is to use the indirect method cash flow worksheet we introduced in Chapter 4. This worksheet is contained in Exhibit 16.15 on page 328. Exhibit 16.16 also on page 328 contains projected indirect method cash flow statements for fiscal 2000 to 2004 and beyond.

Review Questions

1. Why is assessing sales growth important in projecting future cash flows?

2. Where did we find Coldwater's depreciation and amortization expense? Why did we need it?

3. What role can the indirect method for cash flow statements play in making projections of future cash flows?

Exhibit 16.15   Coldwater Creek   Cash Flow Statement Worksheet

Coldwater Creek
Indirect Method Cash Flow Worksheet Using Projections for Fiscal 2000
(amounts in millions rounded)

	Balance Sheet 2/26/00			Adjustments			Balance Sheet 2/26/01	
	Dr	Cr		Dr	Cr		Dr	Cr
Inventory	60.2		Increase in inventories	7.7			67.9	
Other current assets	11.9				0.8	Decrease in other current assets	11.1	
Noncurrent assets	43.2		Capital expenditures	9.8	5.0	Depreciation and amortization	48.0	
Accounts payable		30.1			6.8	Increase in accounts payable		36.9
Other current liabilities		16.1			6.0	Increase in other current liabilities		22.1
Common stock and APIC		41.7						41.7
Retained earnings		34.9	Dividends	15.5	16.0	Net income		35.4
Cash	7.5						9.2	
	122.8	122.8					136.2	136.2
			Net income	16.0	15.5	Dividends		
			Depreciation and amortization	5.0	7.7	Increase in inventory		
			Increase in accounts payable	6.8				
			Increase in other current liabilities	6.0				
			Decrease in other current assets	0.8				
					9.8	Capital expenditures		
				67.6	67.6			

Exhibit 16.16   Coldwater Creek   Projections of Free Cash Flows

Coldwater Creek
Projected Free Cash Flows Using Indirect Method for Fiscal Years Ended in February
(amounts in millions rounded)

	2000	2001	2002	2003	2004	Beyond
Net income	$16.0	$18.0	$20.3	$22.8	$25.7	$25.7
Depreciation and amortization	9.2	10.4	11.7	13.1	14.8	14.8
Increase in inventory	(7.7)	(8.5)	(9.5)	(10.7)	(12.1)	0.0
Change in other current assets	0.8	(1.4)	(1.6)	(1.8)	(2.0)	0.0
Increase in accounts payable	6.8	4.6	5.2	5.8	6.6	0.0
Increase in other current liabilities	6.0	2.8	3.1	3.5	3.9	0.0
Cash flow from operations	$31.2	$25.9	$29.1	$32.7	$36.9	$40.4
Cash flow for investing	(14.0)	(16.4)	(18.4)	(20.7)	(23.3)	(14.8)
Required increase in cash	(1.7)	(1.2)	(1.3)	(1.5)	(1.6)	0.0
Free cash flow	$15.5	$ 8.4	$ 9.4	$10.6	$11.9	$25.7

Valuation

OBJECTIVE:
Learn to use projections of future cash flows to estimate the value of a company.

A **perpetuity** is a level stream of cash flows received forever. The present value of a perpetuity is the amount received divided by the interest rate.

Given a discount rate, we can now estimate the value of Coldwater Creek by discounting the projected cash flows contained in Exhibit 16.16. For simplicity, we assume all cash flows occur at the end of the fiscal year, and we suppose the applicable discount rate is 10 percent. There are two steps to the discounting. First, we must discount the projected free cash flows received in February 2001 to 2005 (the **forecast horizon**). Second, we must discount the projected cash flows from beyond 2005.

Calculations discussed in Chapter 6 and contained in Exhibit 16.17 show the present value of the projected cash flows for years ending February 2001 through 2005 is $42.7 million. To calculate the present value of the projected cash flows received beyond 2005, first note that a constant amount is being projected for every year: $25.7 million. Standard finance texts demonstrate that the present value of such a stream as of its beginning is the amount of the periodic receipts divided by the interest rate. In our case, that works out to $257 million. But that is the present value at February 2005. Discounting the $257 million back to February 2000 yields a present value of $159.6 million. These calculations are shown in Exhibit 16.18 on page 330.

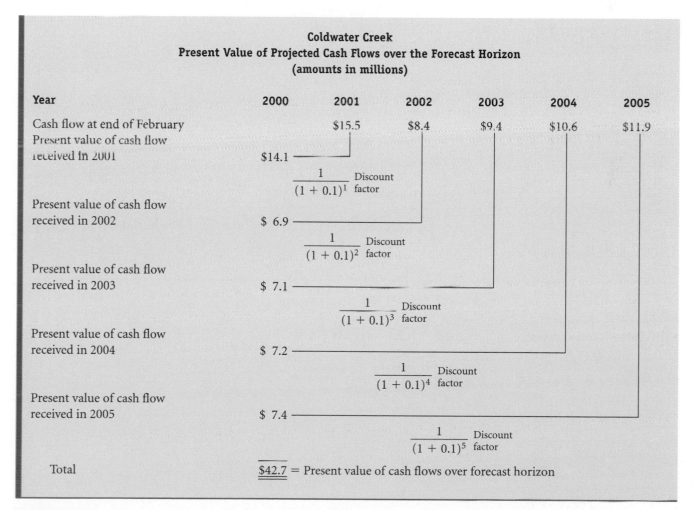

Coldwater Creek
Present Value of Projected Cash Flows over the Forecast Horizon
(amounts in millions)

Year	2000	2001	2002	2003	2004	2005
Cash flow at end of February		$15.5	$8.4	$9.4	$10.6	$11.9
Present value of cash flow received in 2001	$14.1					
		$\frac{1}{(1 + 0.1)^1}$ Discount factor				
Present value of cash flow received in 2002	$ 6.9					
		$\frac{1}{(1 + 0.1)^2}$ Discount factor				
Present value of cash flow received in 2003	$ 7.1					
		$\frac{1}{(1 + 0.1)^3}$ Discount factor				
Present value of cash flow received in 2004	$ 7.2					
		$\frac{1}{(1 + 0.1)^4}$ Discount factor				
Present value of cash flow received in 2005	$ 7.4					
		$\frac{1}{(1 + 0.1)^5}$ Discount factor				
Total	$42.7 = Present value of cash flows over forecast horizon					

Exhibit 16.17
Coldwater Creek
Present Value of Projected Cash Flows over the Forecast Horizon

Adding the value of the projected cash flows from beyond 2005 to the present value of the projected cash flows over the forecast horizon window yields a total estimated present value of $202.3 million (see Exhibit 16.19 on page 330).

Exhibit 16.18 Coldwater Creek Present Value of Projected Cash Flows after the Forecast Horizon

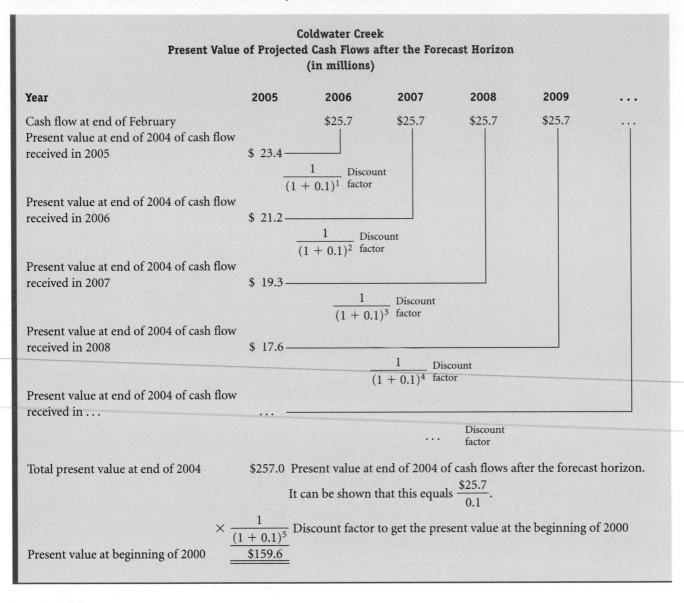

Coldwater Creek
Present Value of Projected Cash Flows after the Forecast Horizon
(in millions)

Year	2005	2006	2007	2008	2009	...
Cash flow at end of February		$25.7	$25.7	$25.7	$25.7	...
Present value at end of 2004 of cash flow received in 2005	$ 23.4					

$\dfrac{1}{(1 + 0.1)^1}$ Discount factor

Present value at end of 2004 of cash flow received in 2006 $ 21.2

$\dfrac{1}{(1 + 0.1)^2}$ Discount factor

Present value at end of 2004 of cash flow received in 2007 $ 19.3

$\dfrac{1}{(1 + 0.1)^3}$ Discount factor

Present value at end of 2004 of cash flow received in 2008 $ 17.6

$\dfrac{1}{(1 + 0.1)^4}$ Discount factor

Present value at end of 2004 of cash flow received in ...   ...

Discount factor

Total present value at end of 2004 $257.0 Present value at end of 2004 of cash flows after the forecast horizon.

It can be shown that this equals $\dfrac{\$25.7}{0.1}$.

$\times \dfrac{1}{(1 + 0.1)^5}$ Discount factor to get the present value at the beginning of 2000

Present value at beginning of 2000 $159.6

Exhibit 16.19 Coldwater Creek Present Value of Projected Cash Flows

Coldwater Creek
Present Value of Projected Cash Flows
(amounts in millions)

Present value of projected cash flows over the forecast horizon	$ 42.7
Present value of projected cash flows after the forecast horizon	159.6
Estimated total value	$202.3

The balance sheet in Exhibit 16.1 shows that Coldwater has about 10.3 million shares outstanding. Our estimated value per share is

$$\$202.3 \text{ million}/10.3 \text{ million shares} = \$19.64 \text{ per share}$$

The actual closing price of Coldwater Creek common stock on February 26, 2000, was $18.125, very close to our estimation considering the rough quality of the estimates and projections we used.

Review Questions

1. What is the forecast horizon we used in our analysis of Coldwater Creek?

2. What contributes more to our estimate of Coldwater's value: projected cash flows over the forecast horizon or projected cash flows beyond the forecast horizon? Why?

Conclusion

Financial statement analysis is the subject of a great many books, as well as being the foundation of a lot of Wall Street careers. We merely scratched the surface here, but we hope our treatment illustrated the importance of the accounting knowledge you have acquired. Real knowledge of income statements, balance sheets, and cash flow statements is extremely important in the process of developing cash flow projections. This knowledge can be valuable in many other places. For example, the managers of Coldwater Creek likely employ analyses similar to what we did for valuation in order to plan future capital expenditures, to create cash budgets, and to know whether the company is on target to deliver appropriate value to shareholders.

Key Terms

benchmarks *316*	free cash flow *326*	time-series benchmarks *316*
cross-sectional benchmarks *318*	perpetuity *329*	turnover ratios *321*
forecast horizon *329*		

Final Thoughts

We hope that this book has helped you acquire a knowledge of accounting to help you address the problems you will face in your careers. But being professors, we also hope the book stimulated your interest in accounting and encouraged you to study it further. Such efforts hold the potential to be rewarding, both in terms of personal development and in acquiring useful knowledge and skills.

Glossary

A

Abnormal Accounting Earnings Accounting earnings in excess of a specified interest rate times beginning book value. For example, if accounting earnings is $10, the specified interest rate is 8%, and the beginning book value of the firm is $90, abnormal accounting earnings are: $10 − (0.08 × $90) = $10 − $7.2 = $2.8.

Abnormal Economic Earnings Economic earnings in excess of the appropriate interest rate times beginning investment value. For example, if economic earnings is $10, the appropriate interest rate is 8%, and the beginning investment value of the firm is $90, abnormal economic earnings are: $10 − (0.08 × $90) = $10 − $7.2 = $2.8. The appropriate interest rate is determined by the financial markets' evaluation of the company's risk.

Accelerated Depreciation Any accounting depreciation method that records a decreasing pattern of depreciation expense over an asset's life.

Account A record of a specific category of asset, liability, equity, revenue, or expense.

Accounting The gathering and reporting of a financial history of an organization.

Accounting Conventions The rules and customs of accounting for applying economic concepts to practical situations.

Accounting Return on Equity Accounting earnings divided by the book value of equity. Often, the average book value of equity over the year is used in the denominator.

Accounting Valuation The act of assigning an item a monetary value to be reported in the balance sheet.

Accounts Payable Money owed to suppliers for items purchased from them.

Accounts Receivable The amounts due from customers in payment for goods delivered or services performed by the entity.

Accrual Accounting Any method of accounting that separates the measurement of revenues and expenses from the receipt and expenditure of cash.

Accrued Liabilities Money owed to providers of goods and services.

Active Investment An investment whose purpose is to obtain influence over another corporation in order to affect its operations.

Additional Paid-In Capital (APIC) The excess of the amount raised by an issuance of stock and the total par value of the shares issued.

Adjunct Account An account that is added to the value of another account to show book value. For example, Premium on Bonds is an adjunct account because it is added to Bonds Payable to show the book value of bonds.

Adjusting The process of updating the amounts in the accounts in the absence of a specific transaction.

Aging Method of Estimating Allowance for Doubtful Accounts Aging is a method used in the process of adjusting the Allowance for Doubtful Accounts and Bad Debts Expense. Aging determines the ending balance in the Allowance for Doubtful Accounts by stratifying the individual accounts receivable by the ages (i.e., the time since the receivable was generated) of the accounts. An estimated uncollectible percentage is applied to each stratum. An adjusting entry is made to bring the total ending balance in the Allowance for Doubtful Accounts up to the sum of the estimated uncollectibles in all the strata.

Allocation Process Any procedure that assigns costs in a mechanical way.

Allowance for Bad Debts, Allowance for Doubtful Accounts, Allowance for Uncollectibles These are different names for a contra-asset account to Accounts Receivable. The contra-asset reflects uncertainty about collections.

Amortization A process of systematically writing off an account over time. Conceptually identical to depreciation for tangible assets, amortization is the name of the process applied to intangible assets.

Amortized Cost Acquisition cost adjusted for applicable amounts such as accrued interest on a zero-coupon bond held as a marketable security.

Articulation The fitting together of the financial statements.

Asset A "probable future economic benefit obtained or controlled by an entity as a result of a past transaction."

Asset Impairment Adjustment An adjustment to the book value of an asset to remove an excess of the asset's book value over its economic value. Asset impairment adjustments are required when management obtains knowledge that book value is in excess of economic value, and when the sum of the asset's future cash flows is less than its book value.

Available-for-Sale Security A debt or equity instrument held as an investment that is not a trading security or a held-to-maturity security.

Average Cost Method A process of finding the cost of goods sold and ending inventory by assigning the weighted average cost of units available for use in the period to each unit sold or in ending inventory.

B

Balance Sheet A list of resources available, resources committed, and the difference between the two.

Balance Sheet Approach Name for framing the problem of making accounting adjustments by focusing on the amounts shown on the balance sheet.

Basic Earnings Per Share (Basic EPS) Net income divided by the weighted average number of shares outstanding.

Benchmarks Comparison points against which an item is judged.

Board of Directors A group elected by the shareholders that has ultimate responsibility for governing the corporation.

Bonds Financial instruments an entity uses to raise money; they promise payment of cash in the future from the issuer.

Book Value The value assigned to an item by an accountant.

C

Callable Bonds Bonds that contain a provision that allows the issuer to repurchase them from the holder for specified terms.

Capital Gain The increase in the economic value of an asset.

Capital Lease A lease that is essentially a financed purchase.

Capitalization of an Amount Recording an expenditure as an asset, versus an expense.

Cash Readily transferable value.

Cash Equivalents Items like bank accounts, Treasury bills, and money market funds that can readily be turned into cash.

Cash Flow Statement A statement which describes the flows of cash into and out of an organization over a period of time.

Cash Flows Increases or decreases in cash.

Closing an Account The act of bringing an account's balance to zero.

Collateral Assets of a borrower that a lender may claim if the borrower defaults.

Common Stock Units of ownership in a public corporation.

Compound Interest Interest calculations that take account of unpaid interest earned or owed when calculating future interest.

Compounding The process of calculating compound interest.

Comprehensive Income A U.S. GAAP amount that adjusts net income for several items that have been recorded directly to equity, such as gains or losses on securities available-for-sale.

Consolidation The amounts in each account represent the total amounts applicable to a corporation and all its consolidated subsidiaries.

Contingent Liability An obligation that will arise only if some specified event, or contingency, arises.

Contra-Asset Account An account that is used to reduce the book value of an asset account relative to the amount in the primary account. For example, Accumulated Depreciation is a contra-asset account to Property, Plant, and Equipment, and it is deducted in computing the net book value of the Property, Plant, and Equipment.

Contra-Equity Account An account that is used to reduce the book value of equity relative to the amount in the primary equity accounts. For example, Treasury Stock is a contra-equity account that is deducted in computing the net book value of shareholders' equity.

Contra-Liability Account An account that is used to reduce the book value of a liability relative to the amount in the primary account. For example, Discount on Bonds Payable is a contra-liability account to Bonds Payable, and it is deducted from the face value in computing the net book value of the Bonds Payable.

Contributed Capital The amount invested by stockholders.

Control Account An account that is the aggregate of detailed accounts. For example, Accounts Receivable is a control account because it is the sum of detailed, customer-specific accounts.

Convertible Bonds Bonds that allow the holder to convert the bond into some other type of financial instrument.

Convertible Financial Instrument A financial instrument such as a preferred stock or bond that can be exchanged for another instrument, usually common stock.

Copyrights Give holders the rights to publish original works of artistic or literary expression.

Corporate Charter The primary legal document specifying the governance of the corporation.

Cost of Sales The resources (wages to workers and cost of materials) that went out of a company in order to generate sales.

Coupon Rate A rate on a bond that, when applied to the face value, determines periodic payments made to the holders.

Covenants Restrictions on a borrower's actions (negative covenants) or requirements that must be fulfilled by the borrower (positive covenants).

Credit Financing Raising funds by incurring debt.

Credits (right-side entries) Bonds, bank loans, mortgages, accounts receivables, and other debts.

Cross-Sectional Analysis The comparison of two companies at the same point in time.

Cross-Sectional Benchmarks Benchmarks used to compare a company with similar companies.

Cumulative Preferred Stock Preferred stock whose total unpaid dividends must be paid before dividends can be paid to common shareholders.

Current Assets An asset that is expected to be converted into cash or used within the next operating cycle, which is almost always defined as one year.

Current Liabilities Liabilities whose expected sacrifice will occur within one year.

Current Maturities of Long-Term Debt The amount of long-term debt that will come due within one year of the balance sheet date.

Current Ratio Current Assets/Current Liabilities = Current Ratio A measure of a company's solvency because this ratio determines if a company has sufficient assets to pay its current liabilities.

D

Date of Issuance The date on which a financial instrument, such as a stock or bond, is formally exchanged between the issuer and purchaser.

Debits Entries on the left side of a T-account. Used to help prevent sign errors in keeping accounts.

Debt Securities Contacts specifying amounts owed and time of payments. Examples are bonds, notes, and mortgages.

Debt-to-Equity Ratio Total Liabilities/ Total Equities = Debt-to-Equity Ratio A measure of debt divided by shareholders' equity. Analysts use different debt measures, e.g., total debt or long-term debt.

Declining Balance Depreciation A method that takes a multiple of the straight-line depreciation applied to the remaining book value of the asset as depreciation expense in any period.

Deduction The name for an expense in TAP.

Default Violation of the terms of a debt agreement, either by failing to make required payments or by violating a covenant. Violation of a positive covenant is sometimes called technical default.

Deferred Income Taxes An asset or a liability account that arises from GAAP's attempt to do accrual accounting on income taxes and the temporary differences between GAAP and TAP.

Deferred Tax Asset An asset account that arises from GAAP's attempt to do accrual accounting on income taxes and the temporary differences between GAAP and TAP.

Deferred Tax Liability A liability account that arises from GAAP's attempt to do accrual accounting on income taxes and the temporary differences between GAAP and TAP.

Depreciable Cost The amount to be depreciated for an asset, which is most often its acquisition cost less estimated salvage value.

Depreciation The systematic allocation of the cost of an asset to the periods that it benefits.

Depreciation and Amortization Expense The allocation of part of the cost of property and equipment to the period.

Depreciation Tax Shield The dollar amount of taxes saved by the depreciation adjustment.

Diluted Earnings Per Share (Diluted EPS) Net income divided by the weighted average number of shares including shares outstanding and those that could become outstanding upon the exercise or conversion of existing convertible financial instruments.

Direct Method A method of presenting cash flow from operations in terms of their uses and sources.

Disclosure The act of providing information about the organization and the construction of its accounting reports.

Discount Factor A number that is used to obtain a present value by multiplying it by the amount of the cash flow. The discount factor when the interest rate is i and the cash flow is to be received at the end of n periods is:

$$\frac{1}{(1+i)^n}.$$

Discount on Bonds The difference between the face value of bonds and their net book value. At issuance, the discount is the difference between the face value and the amount raised by their issuance.

Discounted Value The present value of a cash flow to be received in the future.

Dividends Payments that corporations make to their shareholders.

Dividends Payable The amount owed by the corporation to shareholders when dividends declared by the board of directors have not yet been paid.

E

Earnings-Per-Share (EPS) Net income divided by a number of shares. See Basic EPS and Diluted EPS.

EBIT Earnings before interest and taxes.

EBITDA Earnings before interest, taxes, depreciation, and amortization.

Economic Concepts The ideas that guide the construction of accounting reports.

Economic Depreciation The change in economic value from the beginning to the end of a period.

Economic Income An organization's change in wealth, excluding capital transactions with its owners, over a period of time.

Economic Return on Equity Economic earnings divided by the economic value of the investment at the beginning of the period. For common stock, often defined as ending stock price plus dividends minus beginning price, all divided by the beginning stock price.

Employee Benefit Plan Liabilities A pension plan corporations offer to their employees which provides for cash payments during retirement.

Entity The person or organization about which accounting's financial history is written.

Equity Holders (shareholders, stakeholders, stockholders, residual owners, residual claimants) The holders of the common stock of a corporation.

Equity Method A method that requires the investor corporation to carry its investment lance sheet at its historical cost, adjusted for the investor's pro rata share of the investee's retained earnings.

Equity Securities Financial instruments with a combination of decision rights, lack of seniority, and no entitlements to or maxima for payments that sufficiently differentiate them from debt securities.

Executory Instrument A financial instrument or contract that calls for action from both parties.

Exercise Price The amount that the holder of an option or warrant must pay to receive a share of common stock.

Expected Present Value The discounted value of the expected cash flow from an uncertain cash flow stream.

Expected Value A weighted average of the amounts of cash to be received times the probabilities of receiving those amounts.

Expenses Gross decreases in net assets resulting from operations over a period of time.

Expiration Date The last date on which the holder of the right to buy a share of common stock for the exercise price can exercise that right.

Extraordinary Items Gains and losses that arise from events that are both unusual and infrequent. These must be separately disclosed in the calculation of net income.

F

Face Value A nominal amount of a bond that, along with the coupon rate, determines the periodic payments given to the holder of the bond and which is given to the holder of the bond on its maturity date.

Financial Accounting Standards Board (FASB) A private, not-for-profit organization that is the primary arbiter of GAAP in the United States.

Financial Activities Actions aimed at acquiring and repaying funds to be used over a long period of time. Represent receipts from or payments to suppliers of money to the firm. Typically these suppliers are investors in a company's common stock or entities which have loaned it money (debt holders).

Financial Instruments Contracts that determine payments among the parties to them.

Financial Value The amount of money an item will bring in if sold.

Finished Goods Inventories Inventories of completed goods that are awaiting sale.

First-in, First-out (FIFO) An inventory/cost of goods sold accounting method that makes the cost flow assumption that the first items that were purchased in a period were the first ones that were sold that period.

Fiscal Year The twelve-month period that an entity takes as a year for the purpose of presenting financial statements.

Floating Rates Interest rates on loans or notes that vary according to formulas.

Flow The increase or decrease in a stock over time.

Food and Beverage Expense The cost of all the food and beverage items recorded as sold under Revenues.

Free Cash Flow The cash flow that could be distributed to investors without harming the earnings process.

Future Value The amount that a cash flow stream will accumulate to at a given interest rate by a given time in the future.

G

General Administrative Expense The resources consumed on general administrative functions during the period.

General Ledger A master file in which individual accounts are kept.

Generally Accepted Accounting Principles (GAAP) Commonly understood and accepted conventions for gathering, organizing, and reporting accounting's financial history of an organization.

Goodwill The difference between the acquisition cost of a company and the net economic value of its identifiable assets and liabilities.

Gross Profit Percentage Sales less cost of goods sold expressed as a percentage of sales.

H

Half-Year Convention The custom of treating, for accounting purposes, any asset purchased in a period as being purchased at the midpoint of that period.

Held-to-Maturity Securities Marketable debt securities that the holder intends to keep until they mature.

Holding Gain/Loss The increase or decrease in the value of an asset or liability over a period in which it is held by the entity.

I

Implicit Interest Rate For a financial instrument or transaction that does not state an interest rate, the interest rate implied by the other terms of that instrument.

Income (in TAP) In TAP, income without modifiers means revenues.

Income (Loss) The increase (decrease) in net assets resulting from operations over a period of time.

Income Statement A statement that lists the resources aquired and consumed through an organization's operations over a period of time.

Income Tax A tax that is calculated as a percentage of a net income calculation, called taxable income.

Income Tax Expense The resources which must be given to the government based on income a company generated during the year.

Indirect Method A method which shows how net income must be adjusted to get back to cash flows.

Institutional Context The environment that shapes the consequences of adopting specific accounting conventions.

Intangible Assets Assets that have no physical existence.

Interest The charge for the ability to transfer cash across time periods.

Inventory Raw material, supplies, work-in-process, and finished goods.

Inventory Turnover Cost of goods sold dividend by average inventory.

Investing Activities Actions taken to acquire or dispose of productive assets of the company.

Issued Shares Shares of stock that have been issued by a corporation, whether currently outstanding or not.

J

Journal A book in which original transactions are first recorded.

L

Last-in, First-out (LIFO) An inventory/cost of goods sold accounting method that makes the cost flow assumption that the last items that were purchased in a period were the first ones that were sold that period.

Leases A financial instrument that gives the lessee the right to use property of the lessor in exchange for payments by the lessee.

Liability A "probable future sacrifice of economic benefits arising from present obligations of an entity to transfer assets or provide services as a result of a past transaction or event."

Licenses Legal rights to market products, service specified territories, or use patented products or processes, copyrighted material, or trademarked names or symbols.

LIFO Conformity Rule The TAP requirement that any U.S. taxpayer who uses LIFO for tax purposes must also use LIFO for GAAP purposes.

LIFO Reserve The difference between the FIFO value of inventories and the LIFO value of inventories.

Liquidating Dividend A distribution to shareholders of the remaining assets of a business when that business ceases operations.

Liquidation The selling of all of an entity's assets and distributing them to debtors and residual claimants.

Liquidity The ease with which an asset can be converted into cash.

Liquid Assets Assets that can easily be converted into cash.

London Interbank Offer Rate (LIBOR) The interest rate that most international banks charge one another for overnight loans, typically denominated in Eurodollars.

Long-Lived Assets Assets whose useful lives are more than one year.

Long-Term Debt Debt whose maturity date is beyond one year.

Long-Term Liabilities Financial instruments that usually specify a schedule of payments, restrictions on the actions of the borrower, and creditor and debtor rights in both normal times and if the borrower defaults.

Loss The unfortunate situation in which expenses exceed revenues.

Loss Carryback TAP rule that allows tax losses to be used to recover previously paid taxes.

Loss Carryforward TAP rule that allows tax losses to be used to offset future taxes.

Lower-of-Cost-or-Market (LOCM) GAAP requirement that the book values of inventories on balance sheets be no greater than their market values on the balance sheet date.

M

Market Capitalization The total value of a company's outstanding shares of stock.

Market-to-Book Ratio The market value of a firm's common stock divided by the book value of its shareholders' equity.

Market Valuation Methods The ways markets assign values.

Market Value The value assigned to an item by a market.

Marketable Securities Investments in financial assets, such as shares of stocks and bonds.

Matching The process of making sure all the costs incurred in generating the revenues recognized in a period are taken as expenses in that period.

Maturity Date The date at which the maker of a bond or note must pay its holder the face value.

Merchandise Inventories Inventories held by a retailer for resale.

Minority Interest An ownership interest in the common stock of a corporation that is less than or equal to 50% of the total stock outstanding.

Modified Accelerated Cost Recovery System (MACRS) The TAP system of depreciation.

N

Negative Covenants Restrictions on a borrower's actions.

Net Assets The excess of the entity's economic resources (assets) over its obligations (liabilities).

Net Income Revenues minus expenses.

Net Income Available to Common Shareholders Net income minus preferred dividends.

Net Realizable Value The sales price of an asset less the costs that must be incurred to bring it to saleable condition and to execute the sale.

Noncurrent Assets Assets that have benefits that are expected to be realized over periods beyond one year from the balance sheet date.

Noncurrent or Long-Term Liabilities Liabilities whose expected sacrifice will occur after one year.

Normal Accounting Earnings A specified interest rate times beginning book value. For example, if the specified interest rate is 8% and the beginning book value of the firm is $90, normal accounting earnings are: $0.08 \times \$90 = \$7.2$.

Normal Economic Earnings The appropriate interest rate times beginning investment value. For example, if the appropriate interest rate is 8% and the beginning investment value of the firm is $90, normal economic earnings are: $0.08 \times \$90 = \$7.2$. The appropriate interest rate is determined by the financial markets' evaluation of the company's risk.

O

Off-Balance-Sheet Financing Any method of raising funds for a transaction that does not result in a liability being recognized under GAAP.

Operating Activities Actions that are neither investing nor financing activities, yet are intended to generate net income for a company.

Operating Expenses   The dollar value of the costs incurred in running a business.

Operating Lease   A lease that is treated as a rental agreement under GAAP.

Option (Stock)   The right to buy a share of stock at a specified price (the exercise price) on or before a specified date (the expiration date).

Outstanding Shares   Shares issued by a corporation that are being held by shareholders.

P

Parent   A corporation that controls other corporations.

Par Value   A nominal amount of a common or preferred stock. For a preferred stock, it may determine a dividend by being multiplied times an interest rate.

Passive Investment   An investment in which the objective is to earn a return on cash not immediately needed for current operations, without getting involved in the running of the investee.

Patents   Give holders the rights to exclude others from using the patented products or processes.

Percent-of-Sales Method for Estimating Bad Debt Expense   Percent-of-sales is a method used in the process of adjusting the Allowance for Doubtful Accounts and Bad Debts Expense. Percent-of-sales determines the Bad Debts Expense for the period by applying a percentage to the sales of the period.

Period   In compound interest calculations, the longest amount of time over which interest is not compounded.

Period Expenses   Expenses that are assumed to be properly matched to the sales of the period in which the expense is incurred.

Periodic Inventory Method   A system of accounting for inventories that only occasionally generates a calculation of the book value of the inventory account.

Permanent Differences   Differences between GAAP and TAP amounts that will never go to zero.

Perpetual Inventory System   A system of accounting for inventories that continually generates a calculation of the book value of the inventory account.

Perpetuity   A series of level cash payments that is scheduled to last forever.

Pooling of Interests   The uniting of the ownership interests of two companies by an exchange of common stock.

Positive Covenants   Requirements that must be fulfilled by a borrower.

Preferred Stock   A class of stock without ordinary voting rights but an earlier chance than common stockholders at receiving dividends.

Premium on Bonds   The excess of the book value of bonds over their face value. At the date of issuance, the premium in the amount raised from the issue less the total face value.

Prepaid Expenses   Amounts already paid for goods and services to be delivered in the future.

Present Value   The worth of an investment as it stands.

Product Development Expense   The resources consumed doing research and development during the period.

Pro Forma Statements   Financial statements prepared as if some set of assumptions are met or hypothetical events occur.

Property, Plant, and Equipment   The land, buildings, manufacturing machines, delivery vehicles, etc., that entities hold for use in the businesses over several periods.

Purchased Asset   An asset that is bought from another entity.

Q

Quick Ratio   Cash plus marketable securities plus accounts receivable, all divided by current liabilities.

R

Receivables   Money owed for goods sold or services provided.

Receivables Turnover   Equals sales on account divided by the average accounts receivable.

Recognition   The act of recording an item in the accounting records.

Recourse   The right of the purchaser of an account receivable to look to the seller of the account receivable for payment.

Redeemable   A property of preferred stock that allows the holder to exchange it for cash.

Replacement Cost   The cost of replacing an item.

Restrictive Recognition   The failure to reflect all relevant economic information in a set of accounts. All sets of accounting conventions currently known, including GAAP, TAP, and International Accounting Standards, display restrictive recognition.

Retained Earnings   Past earnings not distributed to stockholders.

Revenues   Gross increases in net assets resulting from operations over a period of time.

S

Sales and Marketing Expenses   The amount a sales force was compensated for generating the revenues.

Sales Revenue   The dollar value of all the products a company sold during the period (the inflow of resources from sales).

Securities and Exchange Commission (SEC)   A U.S. government agency that regulates the trading of public companies.

Self-Constructed Assets   Assets that are made by the entity that will use them.

Senior Debt   Debt that is first in line for repayment should the entity go bankrupt.

Seniority   Determines the place in line for repayment of a financial instrument should the issuer go bankrupt.

Shareholder Equity   The total of the book values of all the shareholders' equity accounts: Common Stock, Additional Paid-In Capital, Retained Earnings,

Treasury Stock, and Other Comprehensive Income.

Shareholder Resolutions Proposals made by shareholders to require or permit specified actions by a corporation.

Short-Term Borrowings Monetary amounts due for repayment of bank loans, notes payable, and other commercial paper that must be paid within one year.

Simple Interest Interest that is not compounded. Therefore, in a simple interest calculation, the interest rate is applied only to the initial amount of the debt, not the initial amount plus unpaid interest. Simple interest calculations are sometimes required in legal damage calculations.

Solvent, Solvency The state of having enough financial resources to meet all obligations.

Stock Ownership rights to business entities.

Stock Dividend The recalibration of shareholders' claims by giving to current shareholders a fairly small number of new shares for each share held.

Stock Split The recalibration of shareholders' claims by giving to current shareholders a fairly large number of new shares for each share held.

Straight-Line Depreciation A method of allocating the cost of an asset less salvage value to the periods of its useful life by assigning equal amounts to each period.

Subordinated Debt A debt security that is behind another debt security in the line for repayment, should the issuer go bankrupt.

Subsidiaries Many separate entities combined under one corporate umbrella.

Sum-of-Years'-Digits Depreciation An accelerated method of depreciation that applies a fraction equal to the years remaining in an asset's life divided by the sum of the digits in the years of its life to the depreciable cost of the asset.

Supplies Inventories Inventories of miscellaneous items.

T

T-Account Graphic representation of an account in the form of a large T, where the account title is written across the top, debits are recorded in the area under the top and to the left of the middle line, and credits are recorded in the area under the top and to the right of the middle line.

Tangible Assets Assets that have a physical existence.

Tax Accounting Principles (TAP) The accounting conventions and rules that govern the reporting of taxable income.

Tax Bases The TAP book values of assets and liabilities.

Taxable Income The amount to which the tax rate is applied to determine an income tax. In TAP terms, it is income minus deductions.

Technical Default Violation of one or more positive covenants.

Temporary Accounts Accounts that are always closed before the preparation of a balance sheet.

Temporary (Timing) Differences Differences between TAP and GAAP amounts that will reverse over time. For example, the tax basis on an asset depreciated using MACRS may differ for a time from its book value under a GAAP method, but eventually both methods will reduce the book value of the asset to the same amount.

Time-Series Benchmarks Benchmarks used to compare a company with itself through several years.

Times-Interest-Earned Net income before interest and taxes divided by interest expense.

Total Equity The difference between total assets and total liabilities.

Trademarks Legal rights to names or symbols.

Trading Security A debt or equity security purchased as part of a conscious management decision to try to generate profits through buying and selling securities.

Transaction An exchange between two or more parties.

Treasury Stock Method Accounting for the repurchase and reissuance of its own stock by an entity that uses a contra-equity account, Treasury Stock, instead of formally retiring and reissuing the shares.

Trial Balance A listing of accounts on an entity by debit and credit balance that helps catch errors in making accounting entries.

Turnover Ratios Ratios that link income statement flows to balance sheet stocks.

U

Unbilled Services Inventories Amounts worked by a service firm that have not yet been billed to clients. Typically, part of the work-in-process for a service firm.

Unearned Revenues The monetary amounts received by an entity that accepts up-front payments of cash in exchange for future delivery of its products.

Units-of-Production Depreciation A depreciation method tied to the physical use of an asset.

Unrealized Holding Gains Represent the difference in the current market price of the security from the acquisition cost of the security; these securities have not been sold, however.

Unsecured Notes Debt that only depends on the general creditworthiness of the issuer for repayment.

Useful Life The time frame over which an asset is capable of providing benefits to its owner.

V

Valuation An assignment of a monetary amount.

Valuation Allowance for a Deferred Tax Asset A contra-asset account that is used to reflect uncertainty in the realization of the tax benefits recorded as in the deferred tax asset account.

W

Warrant Another name for an option; i.e., the right to buy a share of stock on or before a specified date at a specified price.

Warranties Rights given to the purchasers of a product or service that provide benefits should the product or service be defective.

Wealth The difference between the total economic value of all an entity's assets and the total economic value of all its liabilities.

Working Capital Current assets minus current liabilities.

Work-in-Process Inventories (WIP) Inventories of units on which production has begun but is not completed.

Z

Zero-Coupon Bond A bond that makes no coupon payments. The only promised payment is the face value at the maturity date.

Answers to Review Questions

Chapter 1

Page 8

1.

Cash	A
Buildings	A
Salaries of the sales force	E
$5 owed	L
Mortgage due to bank	L
Sales	R

2.

Wages paid	O
Cash from mortgage	F
Cash dividends paid	F
Cash paid to supplier of inventory	O
Cash paid to purchase a machine	I

Page 12

1. Examples include:

   - Whether to grant a loan.
   - How much to pay for a share of common stock.
   - Whether to grant a rate increase to an electric utility.
   - How much in damages the loser of a lawsuit must pay.
   - How much of a bonus to pay a plant manager.
   - Whether to enter a new market.

2. Financial statements have footnotes because financial disclosure is a complex business. The notes tell us some of the specifics about the company's environment, what accounting methods the company has used, what the accounting numbers might be if alternative methods had been used, and some of the major contingencies that are not formally included in the statements proper.

Page 19

1. The FASB, a private, not-for-profit organization, sets GAAP in the United States. It publicly declares an agenda, promulgates "Exposure Drafts" of proposed standards, holds open meetings, and invites input from interested parties. The FASB has been delegated this authority by the SEC, a government agency with legal authority to determine GAAP.

2. There are other examples, but here is one that is different. A taxpayer has incentives to bias reported income downward in order to minimize income tax payments.

However, it is important to understand that *tax accounting rules are different from GAAP, and this book is about GAAP.* Chapter 14 covers GAAP for taxes in more detail.

Other examples include:

- An entrepreneur seeking a loan from a bank or funding from a venture capitalist might have incentives to bias accounting numbers to look favorable.
- A firm that is subject to scrutiny for earning excess profits (e.g., an oil company) might have incentives to bias accounting numbers to look less favorable.
- A utility subject to rate regulation might have an incentive to bias accounting numbers to look less favorable in order to gain more generous increases in its rates. (Recently, a rather severe controversy arose about whether electric utilities in California were genuinely in financial difficulty and should have been allowed to continue to impose large rate increases.)

Chapter 2

Page 36

1. An **asset** is a probable future economic benefit obtained or controlled by an entity as a result of a past transaction. Cash, marketable securities, accounts receivable, inventories, prepaid expenses, patents, copyrights, trademarks, and property, plant, and equipment are all examples of assets. A **liability** is a probable future sacrifice of economic benefits arising from present obligations of an entity to transfer assets or provide services as a result of a past transaction or event. Accounts payable, accrued liabilities, unearned revenues, warranties, and bonds payable are all examples of liabilities. **Equity** is the difference between assets and liabilities. Accounting valuation of assets uses several different methods, including market value, expected realizable value, lower of cost or market, present value of future cash flows, and historical cost. Accounting valuation of liabilities is the expected amount that will be paid, perhaps adjusted for the time value of money.

2. The **entity** is the person or organization about which accounting's financial history is being written.

3. The rights conveyed by the contract may be an asset from an economic point of view, but they are not an asset under GAAP. The contract would not appear on the balance sheet as an asset, because GAAP do not record *executory contracts*, which are contracts that require future performance from both parties. That is, GAAP view the contract as determining what services will be provided in the future and what will be paid for those services, but until the services have been provided, no asset is recognized under GAAP. (Neither is a liability for payment recognized until services have been performed.)

4. The land is on the balance sheet at its historical cost of $300,000. The carrying value of the land is unaffected by the appraisal.

Page 40

1. A **debit** is an entry on the left side of a T-account. A **credit** is an entry on the right side of a T-account. We would expect to find a debit balance in Inventory and credit balances in **Bonds Payable** and **Common Stock.** The reason is the convention that increases in assets are debits and increases in liabilities and equities are credits.

2. False. A balanced trial balance means that the trial balance is *consistent*, not necessarily *correct*. For example, if an arbitrary entry is made that debits **Cash** and credits **Common Stock** for an equal amount, the trial balance will balance but it will be

wrong. An accounting can reflect the receipt of cash and the issuance of common stock, but it alone cannot *make* cash or additional common shares.

3. Websell would debit **Cash** and credit a liability, **Rent Received in Advance**, for the prepayment.

Chapter 3
Page 53

1. **Revenues** are increases in net assets resulting from operations over a period of time. **Expenses** are decreases in net assets resulting from operations over a period of time. Revenue is recognized when the earnings process is substantially complete, a transaction has taken place, and collection is reasonably assured. **Matching** is the process of making sure all costs incurred in generating the revenues recognized in a period are taken as expenses in that period.

2. There are many allowable responses. An example is a patent that is purchased and paid for in one year and used in the next.

3. An example is a house painting contractor who receives payment for one-third of the contract price before beginning the painting.

4. An asset is a future benefit, and there is an opportunity cost associated with not selling it for cash or exchanging it to settle liabilities. An expense is the usage of an item, which by definition is the expiration of its future benefits.

Chapter 6
Page 114

1. The following table lists the adjustments and has an X in the column indicating the approach:

Adjustment	Estimate expense, plug ending balance	Estimate ending balance, plug expense
b	X	
c	X	
d	X	
e		X
f	X	
g	X	
h	X	
i	X	
j	X	
k		X
m	X	

2. We first take adjustment b for Prepaid Insurance and Insurance Expense. It would be easy to think of this adjustment as focusing on how much of the insurance coverage remained, as opposed to how much was used. In fact, the same type of logic could be used—computing a monthly rate for the coverage and applying that to the months remaining, instead of the months used.

   Now take adjustment h for Depreciation Expense and Accumulated Depreciation. Estimating the value of the equipment at year-end might be easy, for example, if there is a market for used equipment, or very difficult, for example, if the equipment was specially designed for Websell. Once a value estimate for the equipment at year-end is obtained, depreciation expense would be the change in value over the year.

Page 117

1. $5,000 \times (1 + 0.06)^{10} = \$5,000 \times 1.79085 = \$8,954.24.$

2. $\$5,000 \times \left(1 + \dfrac{0.06}{2}\right)^{10 \times 2} = \$5,000 \times (1 + 0.03)^{20} = \$5,000 \times 1.80611 = \$9,030.56.$

3. $\$1,000 \times (1.05)^3 + \$1,000 \times (1.05)^2 + \$1,000 \times (1.05)^1 = \$3,310.13$

4. $\$1,000 \times \left(1 + \dfrac{0.05}{5}\right)^{15} + \$1,000 \times \left(1 + \dfrac{0.05}{5}\right)^{10} + \$1,000 \times \left(1 + \dfrac{0.05}{5}\right)^{5}$

   $= [\$1,000 \times (1.01)^{15}] + [\$1,000 \times (1.01)^{10}] + [\$1,000 \times (1.01)^{5}]$

   $= \$1,160.97 + \$1,104.62 + \$1,051.01$

   $= \$3,316.60$

Page 118

1. $x \times (1.07)^3 = \$3,000$

   $x = \dfrac{\$3,000}{(1.07)^3} = \$2,448.89$

2. Calculate the present value at 10% of $1,300 received two years from now. If that is greater than $1,000, you are better off with the $1,300 to be received in two years. If its present value is less than $1,000, you are better off with $1,000 now.

$$\frac{\$1,300}{(1.10)^2} = \$1,074.38$$

Therefore, you are better off receiving $1,300 two years from now.

Another way to do this problem is to take the future value at 10% of $1,000. At the end of two years, the $1,000 would compound up to:

$$\$1,000 \times (1.10)^2 = \$1,210,$$

which is less than you would have at that point if you took the $1,300.

3. The most I would be willing to pay is the present value at 8% of the stream of $1,000 payments:

$$\frac{\$1,000}{(1.08)^1} + \frac{\$1,000}{(1.08)^2} + \frac{\$1,000}{(1.08)^3} = \$925.926 + \$857.339 + \$793.832 = \$2,577.10 \text{ (rounded)}.$$

Page 124

1. Normal earnings are equal to the interest rate times the beginning investment: $0.06 \times \$1,175.47 = \$70.53$.

2. Exhibit 6.4 on page 123 shows that the expected cash flow on December 31, 2006, is $1,150. To get the present value of this cash flow on December 31, 2006, we must discount it for two periods: $\$1,150/(1.06)^2 = \$1,023.50$. The value at December 31, 2005, is shown in Figure 6.8 to be $1,175.47. Therefore, the total change value during 2006 is a decrease of $151.97 ($1,175.47 − $1,023.50). Normal earnings for 2006 are $70.53, as shown in 1 above. Abnormal earnings are, therefore, negative $222.50 (−$151.97 − $70.53).

Chapter 7

Page 135

1. BvA$_1$ examples include cash, accounts receivable, and marketable securities.
   BvA$_2$ examples include some inventories and automobiles.
   BvA$_3$ examples include specially constructed machinery.
   BvL$_1$ examples include accounts payable and short-term loans.
   BvL$_2$ examples include some types of long-term debt.
   BvL$_3$ examples include warranty liabilities.

2. We can't provide a blanket answer, since it depends on what company you selected. But the answer is less important at this stage than your engaging in the active learning process involved in making a good-faith attempt to carry out the exercise.

Page 149

1. There would be $75,000 − $39,380 = $35,620$ million more to explain. Therefore, there would be a total of $290,574 + $35,620 = $326,194$ million to explain.

2. Analyzing Microsoft is far more difficult. Fewer of its assets can be separately identified and valued by examining the market prices for the same or similar assets. Most of Microsoft's value stems from expectations of the cash flows it will generate, which are very difficult to estimate given the nature of its business. Harrodsburg, on the other hand, has mostly financial assets and liabilities that can be separately identified and whose market values are easier to assess.

3. It depends on what we mean by correct. Stock market values change a lot, but there is scientific evidence that the changes are unpredictable. Anyone who can predict stock values better than the market will very likely make a lot of money. However, with many people trying to do this, stock market prices do pretty well.

   All this is contingent on the information available to the stock market and to the person assessing whether the market has "correctly" valued the stock. For example, if we are the only ones who know that an oil company has just struck the largest, cheapest-to-extract oil deposit in history, we will view the market value as being incorrectly low. But given an equal footing of information between the market and an individual investor, the safest working hypothesis is that the market values things pretty well.

   We would expect the stock market to be very accurate in valuing stocks of companies in stable, well-known businesses that rely mainly on assets for which there are good markets. We would expect the market to be less accurate for companies with only a little track record that rely on speculative technology to supply innovative goods and services. These types of companies often use a lot of intellectual property, including human capital, in their operations, and human capital is notoriously difficult to value.

Chapter 8

Page 163

1. Aging takes the balance in **Accounts Receivable** at the end of the year and sorts it by how long ago the transaction occurred that gave rise to that receivable. Experience has shown that "older" accounts have less likelihood of ever being collected. Percentages of likely uncollectibles for each age category are applied to the totals in that category and the results added to obtain an estimate of the **Allowance for Uncollectibles** required to value properly the estimated amount that will be collected

from the **Accounts Receivable.** The Bad Debts Expense then falls out as a "plug" in the **Allowance for Uncollectibles.**

The percentage-of-sales method just estimates bad debt expense as a percent of sales and plugs the balance in the allowance account.

2. Cash 118
        Accounts Receivable 118

    12/31/2006 (To recognize collection of cash from companies owing Service Co. from 2005 sales.)

    Allowance for Doubtful Accounts 7
        Accounts Receivable 7

    12/31/2006 (To write off accounts we know will not be collected.)

    Accounts Receivable 125
        Sales Revenue 125

    12/31/2006 (To recognize revenue and to anticipate collection of the receivable.)

    If we focus on recording the bad debts expense that is associated with billings for 2006, we would record 0.06 × $125,000 = $7,500 in Bad Debts Expense.

    Bad Debts Expense 7.5
        Allowance for Doubtful Accounts 7.5

    12/31/2006 (To record bad debt expense in anticipation of not collecting 100% of receivables.)

    METHOD ONE: Focus on the percentage of sales expected not to be collected.

Allowance for Doubtful Accounts			
		10	12/31/05
12/31/06	7	7.5	12/31/06
			Ending balance
		10.5	at 12/31/06

(10.5 is the "plug", i.e., the number that drops out)

Now we move to 2007, where events now proceed as expected. Collections are $117.5 thousand.

    Cash 117.5
        Accounts Receivable 117.5

    12/31/2007 (To recognize collection of cash from companies owing Service Co. from 2006 sales.)

    Allowance for Doubtful Accounts 7.5
        Accounts Receivable 7.5

    12/31/2007 (To write off accounts we know will not be collected.)

    Accounts Receivable 125
        Sales Revenue 125

    12/31/2007 (To recognize revenue and to anticipate collection of the receivable.)

    If we focus on recording the bad debts expense that is associated with billings for 2007, we would record 0.06 × $125,000 = $7,500 in Bad Debts Expense.

    Bad Debts Expense 7.5
        Allowance for Doubtful Accounts 7.5

    12/31/2007 (To record bad debt expense in anticipation of not collecting 100% of receivables.)

The Allowance for Doubtful Accounts using the percentage-of-sales method looks like this:

METHOD ONE: Focus on the percentage of sales expected not to be collected.

Allowance for Doubtful Accounts			
		10	12/31/05
12/31/06	7	7.5	12/31/06 Expense
		10.5	12/31/06 Balance
Write-off 12/31/07	7.5	7.5	12/31/07 Expense
			Balance at
		10.5	12/31/07

Only the entries recording bad debt expense are different using the aging method. Instead of the above entries recording bad debt expense, we would have the following analysis.

Each year, we would adjust the balance in the Allowance for Doubtful Accounts so that the net receivable ends up at $117,500. That is, we would solve $125,000 − X = $117,500 and find that the ending balance in the Allowance for Doubtful Accounts must be $7,500.

Analyzing the account, we would determine that at December 31, 2006, we must add $4,500 to the Allowance for Doubtful Accounts:

Bad Debts Expense 4.5
    Allowance for Doubtful Accounts 4.5

12/31/2006 (To record bad debt expense in anticipation of not collecting 100% of receivables.)

At December 31, 2007, we must add $7,500 to the Allowance for Doubtful Accounts:

Bad Debts Expense 7.5
    Allowance for Doubtful Accounts 7.5

12/31/2007 (To record bad debt expense in anticipation of not collecting 100% of receivables.)

Using aging, the Allowance for Doubtful Accounts T-account looks like this:

METHOD TWO: Focus on the ending balance in the Allowance for Doubtful Accounts.

Allowance for Doubtful Accounts			
		10	12/31/05
12/31/06	7	4.5	12/31/06 Expense
		7.5	12/31/06 Balance
Write-off 12/31/07	7.5	7.5	12/31/07 Expense
			Balance at
		7.5	12/31/07

Chapter 9

Page 179

1. **LIFO** is last-in, first-out. It means that in computing ending inventory and cost of goods sold, the cost of items *sold* is assigned in reverse chronological order of their *purchase*, beginning from the most recent items purchased in a period. **FIFO** is first-in, first-out. It means that in computing ending inventory and cost of goods sold, the cost of items sold is assigned in chronological order of their purchase, beginning from the goods on hand at the beginning of the period. **Average cost** means that in

computing ending inventory and cost of goods sold, the average unit cost of the beginning inventory and items purchased in a period is used to determine the cost of goods sold and remaining inventory.

2. Yes, it is still a positive net present value project. In fact, its net present value is higher than when the purchase was made at $1.05 per unit, since the cash outflow is reduced but the cash inflow remains the same. The cash outflow on December 31, 2003, when purchases are at $0.95 per unit is $114. This means the net cash flow at December 31, 2003, is ($4) instead of ($16), and the NPV for Widget Company is:

$$\text{NPV} = -100 - \frac{\$4}{1.1} + \frac{\$10}{1.1^2} + \frac{\$144}{1.1^3} = \$12.82.$$

First, we redo the case of FIFO. The Inventory T-account is:

Widget Co. Inventory Account under FIFO Flow Assumption

Inventory (FIFO)

1/1/03	Beginning balance	0		
1/1/03	Purchase (100 @ $1)	100		
12/31/03	Purchase (120 @ $0.95)	114	100	Transfer to CGS (100 @ $1)
1/1/04	Balance (120 @ $0.95)	114		
12/31/04	Purchase (100 @ $1.10)	110	95	Transfer to CGS (100 @ $0.95)
1/1/05	Balance (20 @ $0.95 +			Transfer to CGS (20 @ $0.95 +
	100 @ $1.10)	129	129	100 @ $1.10)
1/1/06	Balance	0		

Ending inventory values can be read from the above T-account. Net incomes are:

Widget Co. Net Incomes Using FIFO

	2003	2004	2005
Revenues	$ 110	$120	$ 144
Cost of goods sold	(100)	(95)	(129)
Net income (pretax)	$ 10	$ 25	$ 15

Now we redo the LIFO case. First, the Inventory T-account is:

Widget Co. Inventory Account under LIFO Flow Assumption

Inventory (LIFO)

1/1/03	Beginning balance	0		
1/1/03	Purchase (100 @ $1)	100		
12/31/03	Purchase (120 @ $0.95)	114	95	Transfer to CGS (100 @ $0.95)
1/1/04	Balance (20 @ $0.95 +			
	100 @ $1)	119		
12/31/04	Purchase (100 @ $1.10)	110	110	Transfer to CGS (100 @ $1.10)
1/1/05	Balance (20 @ $0.95 +			Transfer to CGS (20 @ $0.95 + 100
	100 @ $1)	119	119	@ $1)
1/1/06	Balance	0		

Ending inventory values can be read from the above T-account. Net incomes are:

Widget Co. Net Incomes Using LIFO

	2003	2004	2005
Revenues	$110	$120	$144
Cost of goods sold	95	110	119
Net income (pretax)	$ 15	$ 10	$ 25

Page 181

1. To calculate the market-to-book ratios and accounting returns on equity:

Market-to-Book Ratios under Average Cost

	2003	2004
Market value of inventory	$126.00	$132.00
Book value of inventory	$123.27	$127.24
Market value/Book value	1.022	1.037

Accounting Rates of Return under Average Cost

	2003	2004	2005
Beginning book value of inventory	$100.00	$123.27	$127.24
Net income	$7.27	$13.97	$16.76
Net income/Beginning book value	0.0727	0.1133	0.1317

Collecting the results for LIFO and FIFO from the chapter and these results for average cost, we have:

Market-to-Book Ratios under Various Cost Flow Assumptions

	2003	2004
FIFO	1.04	1.09
Average cost	1.022	1.037
LIFO	1.0	1.008

Accounting Rates of Return under Various Cost Flow Assumptions

	2003	2004	2005
LIFO	0.05	0.083	0.19
Average cost	0.0727	0.1133	0.1317
FIFO	0.10	0.119	0.099

As is apparent, the market-to-book ratios and accounting rates of return for average cost are between those for LIFO and FIFO.

2. Because it has more recent costs on the balance sheet in the inventory account, FIFO has market-to-book ratios closer to 1, regardless of whether prices rise or fall.

Chapter 10

Page 190

1. The total profit on the transaction is the sales price of $880.00 less the original cost of $735.03:

Sales price of securities	$880.00
Less original cost	(735.03)
Profit on transactions	$144.97

The cash flows were $735.03 out on January 1, 2003, and $880.00 in on January 3, 2006.
There were profits in 2004, 2005, and 2006. In 2004, there was a profit of $58.80. In 2005, there was a profit of $81.17. In 2006, there was a profit of $5.00.

2. The unadjusted book value of the security on December 31, 2005, was $793.83. (See the T-account in Exhibit 10.6.) If the market value of the security on that date was $790.00, an adjustment reducing its carrying value by $3.83 is required to write it down to its market value:

Unrealized Loss on Marketable Securities—Trading 3.83
    Marketable Securities—Trading 3.83

12/31/2005 (To mark to market the Marketable Securities—Trading.)

If the security were sold for $810.00 on January 3, 2006, the entry would be:

Cash 810.00
    Marketable Securities—Trading 790.00
    Gain on Marketable Securities—Trading 20.00

1/03/2006 (To record the sale of the Marketable Securities—Trading.)

Page 192

1. When a security is classified as a trading security, profits or losses show up on the income statement in every period from when the security is purchased until when it is sold. When a security is classified as available-for-sale, profits or losses only show up on the income statement in the period in which the security is sold.

2. The unadjusted book value of the security on December 31, 2005, was $793.83. (See the T-account in Exhibit 10.7.) If the market value of the security on that date was $790.00, an adjustment reducing its carrying value by $3.83 is required to write it down to its market value. However, unlike the trading security case, the unrealized loss is an equity account, not a temporary account:

Unrealized Loss on Marketable Securities—Available-for-Sale   3.83
    Marketable Securities—Trading 3.83

12/31/2005 (To mark to market the Marketable Securities—Available-for-Sale.)

To record the sale of the security for $810.00 on January 3, 2006:

Cash 810.00
Unrealized Gain on Marketable Securities—
Available-for-Sale (58.80 − 3.83) 54.97
    Marketable Securities—Trading 790.00
    Realized Gain on Marketable Securities—Available-for-Sale 74.97

12/31/2005 (To mark to market the Marketable Securities—Available-for-Sale.)

Page 194

1.

	Held-to-Maturity	Available-for-Sale	Trading
Debt security	Interest revenue is accrued using the interest rate implicit in the purchase price of the debt security. The balance sheet reflects the historical cost of the security, adjusted for the effects of accrued interest. That is, the balance sheet reflects the amortized cost of the security, not its market value.	The balance sheet reflects the market value of the security at the balance sheet date. The balance sheet also has an equity account that reflects the cumulative difference between the historical cost and the current market value of the security. The income statement is only affected in the period the security is sold, at which time the security's book value and unrealized gains or losses (equity account) must be adjusted to zero.	The balance sheet reflects the market value of the security at the balance sheet date. The other side of the entry to adjust the security to market value is an unrealized gain or loss, which is reflected in the income statement. Like any other item that hits the income statement, it is reflected in retained earnings through the process of closing the temporary accounts.
Equity security	This case is not possible. An equity security cannot be held to maturity.	Same as above	Same as above

Chapter 11

Page 207

1. a. Under straight-line depreciation, the depreciation expense each year is:

$$\frac{\$600 - \$100}{5 \text{ years}} = \$100 \text{ per year}$$

b. Under double-declining balance depreciation, the depreciation expense each year is given in the following table:

Double-Declining Balance Depreciation

Year	Remaining Book Value	Declining Balance Rate	Declining Balance Depreciation	Straight-Line on Remaining Depreciable Balance	Depreciation Expense
1	$600	2 × 20% = 40%	$240	$\frac{\$500}{5} = \$100$	$240.0
2	360	40%	144	$\frac{\$260}{4} = \$65$	144.0
3	216	40%	86.4	$\frac{\$116}{3} = \$38.67$	86.4
4	129.6	40% or amount to get book value to salvage value of $100	29.6	$\frac{\$29.6}{2} = \$14.8$	29.6
5	100.0		0		0
Sum					$500.0

c. Under sum-of-years'-digits depreciation, the depreciation expense each year is given in the following table:

Sum-of-Years'-Digits Depreciation

Year	Digit	Depreciation Rate	Depreciable Cost	Depreciation Expense
1	1	5/15	$600 − $100 = $500	$166.67
2	2	4/15	500	133.33
3	3	3/15	500	100.00
4	4	2/15	500	66.67
5	5	1/15	500	33.33
Sum	15	1		$500.00

2. Intangible assets are most often shown in one line that is cost net of accumulated amortization. Tangible assets are sometimes shown in three lines: cost, accumulated depreciation, and net.

3. Economic depreciation is the change in the economic value of the asset. Economic depreciation can be appreciation when the asset increases in value. We have seen this already with marketable debt securities, which sometimes increase in value because of unpaid interest.

4. It is easy and fulfills the requirement of GAAP to provide depreciation using a systematic and rational method. No GAAP depreciation method likely correctly reflects economic depreciation anyway, so a simple expedient may be good enough.

Page 212

1. Straight-line depreciation is $100 per year ($300/3 years). Double-declining balance depreciation is given in the following table:

Double-Declining Balance Depreciation

Year	Remaining Book Value	Declining Balance Rate	Declining Balance Depreciation	Straight-Line on Remaining Balance	Depreciation Expense
1	300	2 × 33.33% = 66.67%	$200	$\frac{\$300}{3} = \$100$	$200.0
2	100	66.67%	66.67	$\frac{\$100}{2} = \$50$	66.67
3	33.33	66.67%	22.23	$\frac{\$33.33}{1} = \$33.33$	33.33
Sum					$300.0

2. For straight-line depreciation, the entry is the same each year:

Depreciation Expense 100
    Accumulated Depreciation 100

For double-declining balance depreciation, the entries are:

Year 1

Depreciation Expense 200
    Accumulated Depreciation 200

Year 2

Depreciation Expense 66.67
    Accumulated Depreciation 66.67

Year 3

Depreciation Expense 33.33
    Accumulated Depreciation 33.33

3. In year 1, net income under straight-line will be $100 higher than under double-declining balance because depreciation expense under straight-line is only $100, while under double-declining balance depreciation expense is $200.

4. If the company buys one asset every year and each asset lasts three years, then in year 4 it will have three assets. Under straight-line depreciation, each of those assets generates a depreciation expense of $100; therefore, total depreciation expense would be 3 × $100, or $300.

    Under double-declining balance depreciation, total depreciation expense depends on the age of each asset. The company would have one asset in its first year of life, one in its second year of life, and one in its third year. Therefore, total depreciation expense would be: $200 + $66.67 + $33.33 = $300, the same as under straight-line.

    Both depreciation methods give the same total depreciation because:

    a. Both methods fully depreciate the assets over their lives.
    b. The cost of the assets has remained constant.
    c. The company is in a steady state in which the number of new assets purchased in a period equals the number of old assets being retired in that period.

Chapter 12

Page 228

1. Cash 95
    Discount on Bonds Payable 5
        Bonds Payable 100

2. Cash 105
      Bonds Payable 100
      Premium on Bonds Payable 5

3. The coupon payment would be $100 × (0.08/2) = $4. Interest expense would be $105 × (0.06/2) = $3.15. Therefore, the premium amortization must be $4.00 − $3.15 = $0.85. The entry would be:

Interest Expense 3.15
Premium on Bonds Payable 0.85
      Cash 4.00

4. Because the substance of the transaction is a financed purchase.

5. The two types of leases are operating leases and capital, or financing, leases. A lease must be treated as a capital lease if any one of the following conditions is met:
  a. The life of the lease is greater than or equal to 75% of the life of the asset.
  b. The present value of the lease payments is greater than or equal to 90% of the fair market value of the asset.
  c. There is a bargain purchase option any time during the life of the lease.

6. A gain or loss on the retirement of a bond arises when the amount the company pays to repurchase the bond from its holder differs from the bond's book value.

Chapter 13

Page 257

1. Cash 75
      Common Stock 50
      Additional Paid-In Capital 25

2. Yes, it is like the retirement of common stock. The company transfers assets (or creates an obligation) to a shareholder in exchange for the company's stock.

3. Treasury Stock is a contra-equity account that appears in the equity section of the balance sheet.

4. No. Purchases and sales of the company's own stock are capital transactions with its shareholders, not transactions that give rise to profit or loss. These transactions can result in net distributions to or additional contributions from shareholders, but these additional contributions from shareholders are not profit and distributions to shareholders are not losses. (If you have trouble with this question, review Chapter 3.)

5. Declaration:

Retained Earnings 75
      Dividends Payable 75

Payment:

Dividends Payable 75
      Cash 75

6. Liabilities would go down, and equity would go up by the same amount.

7. It would not affect the financial statements, except that the par value per share and the number of shares would have to reflect the recalibration of stockholders' equity into 50% more shares.

Chapter 14

Page 274

1. Yes, TAP is a set of accounting principles and it produces an income statement and a balance sheet.

2. Yes, debit and credit techniques work for any set of accounting principles, including TAP.

3. TAP depreciation is governed by the Modified Accelerated Cost Recovery System (MACRS). It typically involves shorter depreciable lives than are allowable under GAAP depreciation. MACRS depreciation is typically 150%-declining balance depreciation with a half-year convention.

4. If a company has a loss when it computes its taxable income under TAP, it can use that loss as the basis to recover taxes it has paid in the past. This is a tax loss carryback.

5. If a company has a loss when it computes its taxable income under TAP, it can use that loss as the basis to reduce taxes it would otherwise have to pay in the future. This is a tax loss carryforward. Taxpayers use tax loss carryforwards because the use of tax loss carrybacks is limited to the recovery of taxes paid in the previous three years.

6. The LIFO conformity rule states that *if* a taxpayer uses LIFO for tax purposes, the taxpayer *must* use LIFO for financial reporting purposes. That is, if LIFO is among the TAP rules a company uses, then LIFO must be used for GAAP purposes as well.

7. No, leases are not treated the same way. There are slightly different rules for what constitutes a capital lease under TAP and GAAP.

Page 282

1. Temporary differences between GAAP and TAP are differences that will eventually go away. The item appears in both GAAP and TAP statements, but in different years.

2. Permanent differences between GAAP and TAP are differences that will never go away. The item appears in only one of the statements.

3. Deferred tax assets arise because GAAP attempt to do accrual accounting for income taxes. If GAAP record an asset at a lower amount or a liability at a higher amount than TAP, and if that difference is a temporary one, then when the asset is depreciated or the obligation is discharged for TAP purposes, a tax deduction in excess of the expense recognized for GAAP will be generated. The amount of the saved tax is a deferred tax asset.

4. Deferred tax liabilities arise because GAAP attempt to do accrual accounting for income taxes. If GAAP record an asset at a higher amount or a liability at a lower amount than TAP, and if that difference is a temporary one, then when the asset is depreciated or the obligation is discharged for TAP purposes, a tax deduction less than the expense recognized for GAAP will be generated. The amount of the extra tax is a deferred tax liability.

Chapter 15

Page 296

1. The equity method is used when the parent owns between 20% and 50% of the subsidiary. The consolidation method is used when the parent owns more than 50% of

the subsidiary. (*Note:* The percentages used here really establish presumptions about the amount of influence that the parent has over the operations of the subsidiary. The amount of influence is actually supposed to determine the accounting method used.)

2. Dividends Receivable   xxx
        Investment in Subsidiary   xxx

3. Minority interest arises when the company owns less than 100% of a subsidiary. It is usually shown between liabilities and shareholders' equity.

4. An intercompany transaction is a transaction that occurs among parties, all of which are within the same consolidated group of companies. Such transactions must be eliminated in producing the financial statements of the company as a whole because they are not transactions with outsiders.

5. The investing company's share of the subsidiary's earnings is recognized when the earnings are recognized as earned by the subsidiary.

Chapter 16

Page 311

1. The present value of a cash flow stream is the starting amount that would generate the cash flow stream at a given interest rate.

2. Sales.

3. These changes represent investments that must be made, or that can be recovered, in generating the income that is projected. Net income is not cash, and as we saw in Chapter 4, changes in these accounts must be factored in to translate income to cash flows.

Page 315

1. From its own 10K, Coldwater Creek "is a retailer of women's apparel, jewelry, gifts and soft home accessories, primarily marketing its merchandise through targeted catalog mailings, an interactive e-commerce web site . . . and full-line retail stores."

2. Yes, catalog costs and executive loans may be considered unusual.

3. If the auditor's opinion states that the financial statements are not reliable, it could be a waste of time analyzing them.

Page 317

1. A benchmark is a point of comparison.

2. A time-series benchmark is a point of comparison for different periods of time.

Page 320

1. A cross-sectional benchmark is a point of comparison from the same period of time, but from a different entity.

2. It helps address the issue of nonstationarity in a time series. That is, the past may no longer be relevant in determining proper benchmarks because things may have changed too much. Cross-sectional analysis uses benchmarks from the same time period, so it controls somewhat for the effects of changes through time.

Page 327

1. Many projections of future cash flows are derived from projections of earnings, and projecting future sales is usually the most important part of projecting future earnings.

2. It is an add-back in the statement of cash flows. We need it because some of Coldwater's expenses include depreciation and amortization, and we are going to project future capital expenditures in a later step.

3. One can use the indirect method to deduce cash flow projections from projections of income statements and balance sheets.

Page 331

1. We used a forecast horizon of five years.

2. The projected cash flows beyond the forecast horizon contribute more. A major reason for this is that we are projecting growth for Coldwater over the forecast horizon, which means Coldwater will have to make capital investments and investments in working capital. After the forecast horizon, we have assumed that Coldwater is not in such a rapid growth phase and therefore it produces higher cash flows after the horizon.

General Index